The Longman Anthology of Contemporary American Poetry

J. Claire

Second Edition

This anthology spans forty years of unparalleled vigor and achievement in American poetry. Its fifty-six poets, remarkable for their variety in age, geography, temperament, and formal practices, present a composite portrait of current American poetry that is striking in its beauty, energy, and imagination. This is a book whose contents promise to enrich the lives of its readers with delight and reflection for years to come. Included are:

D0077442

THE LONGMAN ANTHOLOGY OF
CONTEMPORARY
AMERICAN POETRY

SECOND EDITION

Stuart Friebert

Oberlin College

David Young

Oberlin College

Longman

New York & London

**The Longman Anthology of Contemporary American Poetry:
1950 to the Present**

Second Edition

Longman Inc., 95 Church Street, White Plains, N.Y. 10601

Associated companies:
Longman Group Ltd., London
Longman Cheshire Pty., Melbourne
Longman Paul Pty., Auckland
Copp Clark Pitman, Toronto
Pitman Publishing Inc., New York

Executive editor: Gordon T. R. Anderson
Production editor: Louise M. Kahan
Text design: Lynn M. Luchetti
Cover design: Jill Francis Wood
Cover photograph: Lawrence A. Wood
Production supervisor: Eduardo Castillo

LIBRARY OF CONGRESS
Library of Congress Cataloging-in-Publication Data
The Longman anthology of contemporary American poetry : 1950 to the
   present / [edited by] Stuart Friebert, David Young.—2nd ed.
      p.   cm.
   ISBN 0-8013-0046-0
      1. American poetry—20th century.   I. Friebert, Stuart, 1931-
II. Young, David, 1936-
PS613.L6 1988
811'.54'08—dc19

ISBN 0-8013-0046-0

                                                                88-557
89   90   91   92   93   94   9   8   7   6   5   4   3   2   1   CIP

Acknowledgments

Citations follow the order in which the poets appear in the book.

"Puella Parvula," copyright 1949 by Wallace Stevens; "Large Red Man Reading," "This Solitude of Cataracts," "Metaphor as Degeneration," and "Angel Surrounded by Paysans," copyright 1950 by Wallace Stevens; "Final Soliloquy of the Interior Paramour," copyright 1951 by Wallace Stevens; "Vacancy in the Park," "The World as Meditation," and "The Poem That Took the Place of a Mountain," copyright 1952 by Wallace Stevens; "Not Ideas About the Thing but the Thing Itself," copyright 1954 by Wallace Stevens; reprinted from *The Collected Poems of Wallace Stevens*, by permission of Alfred A. Knopf, Inc., and Faber and Faber Ltd.

"Self Portrait," "Landscape with the Fall of Icarus," "The Hunters in the Snow," "The Parable of the Blind," "Iris," "To a Dog Injured in the Street," "The Artist," and "The Sparrow," by William Carlos Williams; reprinted from *Pictures from Brueghel and Other Poems*. Copyright © 1954, 1955, 1962 by William Carlos Williams. "The Artist" was first published in *The New Yorker*. Reprinted by permission of New Directions Publishing Co.

Dream Songs #9, #12, #23, #76, #107, and #366 from *The Dream Songs* by John Berryman. Copyright © 1959, 1962, 1963, 1964, 1965, 1966, 1968, 1969 by John Berryman. "American Lights, Seen from Off Abroad" from *Short Poems* by John Berryman. Copyright © 1958 by John Berryman. "Certainty Before Lunch," "Gislebertus' Eve," and "Washington in Love," from *Delusions, Etc.* by John Berryman. Copyright © 1969, 1971 by John Berryman. Reprinted by permission of Farrar, Straus and Giroux, Inc., and Faber and Faber Ltd.

"Over 2000 Illustrations and a Complete Concordance," "At the Fishhouses," "The Prodigal," "Sestina," "First Death in Nova Scotia," and "In the Waiting Room" from *The Complete Poems 1927–1979* by Elizabeth Bishop. Copyright © 1947, 1948, 1951, 1956, 1962, 1969 by Elizabeth Bishop. Reprinted by permission of Farrar, Straus and Giroux, Inc.

"Notes from the Childhood and the Girlhood," "The Bean Eaters," "The Last Quatrain of the Ballad of Emmett Till," "A Sunset of the City," and "The Lovers of the Poor" by Gwendolyn Brooks. Reprinted by permission of the author.

"Sheep," "Blue Winter," "Hogwash," "Like Ghosts of Eagles," "Silent Poem," "December," and "Yes, What?" by Robert Francis; reprinted from *Robert Francis: Collected Poems, 1936–1976* (Amherst: University of Massachusetts Press, 1976), copyright © 1938, 1965, 1966, 1970, 1973, 1976 by Robert Francis.
   "Apple Peeler," "Cold," "Boy Riding Forward Backward," "Waxwings," "Bluejay," and

"Cypresses" by Robert Francis; reprinted from *The Orb Weaver*, copyright © 1953, 1954, 1956, 1959 by Robert Francis, by permission of Wesleyan University Press. "Boy Riding Forward Backward" first appeared in *The Saturday Review* and *New Poems by American Poets II.* "Apple Peeler" first appeared in *New Poems by American Poets I.* "Bluejay" first appeared in *Amherst Poets.* "Cold" first appeared in *Poetry.* "Cypresses" first appeared in *The Transatlantic Review.*

"Runagate Runagate," "Those Winter Sundays," "Night, Death, Mississippi," "Homage to the Empress of the Blues," "Aunt Jemima of the Ocean Waves," and " 'Mystery Boy' Looks for Kin in Nashville," by Robert Hayden; reprinted from *Angle of Ascent, New and Selected Poems,* copyright © 1975, 1972, 1970, 1966 by Robert Hayden, by permission of Liveright Publishing Corporation.

"A Hunt in the Black Forest," "The House in the Wood," and "Field and Forest," reprinted by permission of Macmillan Publishing Co. from *The Lost World* by Randall Jarrell. Copyright © 1948, 1962, 1964, 1965 by Randall Jarrell; renewed 1976 by Mary Jarrell. "A Hunt in the Black Forest" originally appeared in *Poetry.*
    "Losses," "The Death of the Ball Turret Gunner," "Protocols," and "Seele im Raum" from *The Complete Poems* by Randall Jarrell. Copyright © 1944, 1945, 1950, 1955 by Mrs. Randall Jarrell. Copyright © renewed 1971, 1973, 1977 by Mrs. Randall Jarrell. Reprinted by permission of Farrar, Straus and Giroux, Inc., and Faber and Faber Ltd.
    "Cinderella" from *The Woman at the Washington Zoo* by Randall Jarrell, copyright © 1960 by Randall Jarrell. Reprinted by permission of Atheneum Publishers, an imprint of Macmillan Publishing Co., and Faber and Faber Ltd.

"Beyond the Alps" and "Skunk Hour" from *Life Studies* by Robert Lowell. Copyright © 1956, 1959 by Robert Lowell. "Water," "Those Before Us," "July in Washington," "For the Union Dead," and "The Lesson" from *For the Union Dead* by Robert Lowell. Copyright © 1956, 1960, 1961, 1962, 1963, 1964 by Robert Lowell. Reprinted by permission of Farrar, Straus and Giroux, Inc., and Faber and Faber Ltd.

"Child on Top of a Greenhouse" copyright © 1946 by Editorial Publications, Inc.; "My Papa's Waltz" copyright © 1942 by Hearst Magazines, Inc.; "Cuttings" and "Cuttings (later)" copyright © 1948 by Theodore Roethke; "The Shape of the Fire" copyright © 1947 by Theodore Roethke; "First Meditation" copyright © 1955 by Theodore Roethke; "Journey to the Interior" copyright © 1964 by Beatrice Roethke as Administratrix of the Estate of Theodore Roethke. All poems from *The Collected Poems of Theodore Roethke.* Reprinted by permission of Doubleday Publishing, a division of Bantam, Doubleday, Dell Publishing Group, Inc.; and Faber and Faber Ltd.

From "Eighth Elegy. Children's Elegy" from *Beast in View,* copyright © 1944 by Muriel Rukeyser, Copyright renewed; "Children, the Sandbar, That Summer" from *Body of Waking,* copyright © 1958 by Muriel Rukeyser, Copyright renewed; "The Speed of Darkness" from *The Speed of Darkness,* copyright © 1968 by Muriel Rukeyser; "Waiting for Icarus" from *Breaking Open,* copyright © 1973 by Muriel Rukeyser; "Then" and "Resurrection of the Right Side" from *The Gates,* copyright © 1976 by Muriel Rukeyser. All reprinted by permission of International Creative Management, Inc.

"Ceremony," "Traveling Through the Dark," "The Rescued Year," "Observation Car and Cigar," "In a Museum in the Capital," and "Accountability" from *Stories That Could Be True* by William Stafford, copyright © 1960, 1964, 1965, 1971, 1976 by William Stafford; "The Epitaph Ending in And" and "Bring the North" from *The Rescued Year* by William Stafford, copyright © 1965, 1969 by William Stafford; "School Days" from *A Glass Face in the Rain* by William Stafford, copyright © 1979 by William Stafford; "Serving with Gideon" from *An Oregon Message* by William Stafford, copyright 1987 by William Stafford. All reprinted by permission of Harper & Row, Publishers, Inc.
    "Notice What This Poem Is Not Doing" copyright © 1980 by William Stafford. Reprinted from *Things That Happen Where There Aren't Any People* by permission of BOA Editions, Ltd.

"Three Easters," "Making Old Bones," "Drift," and "In Love with Wholes" by Alberta Turner from *A Belfry of Knees.* "Water Eased of Its Cliffs by Falling," "Fourth Wish," and "On the Nature of Food" by Alberta Turner. All reprinted by permission of the author.

(Continued on page 624)

Contents

Contents

PART THREE TWENTY POETS BORN BETWEEN 1920 AND 1930 / 159

Introduction

This anthology presents the work of fifty-six American poets over a period of more than forty years, from the end of World War II to the present. The poets are grouped in five sections, by their birth dates, and each poet is represented by about 200 lines of poetry. The present version is both a revision and an updating of an anthology, produced six years ago, which contained forty-eight poets and had a cutoff date of 1980. It was generally successful in what it set out to accomplish; this improved version, however, carries through to the end of the 1980s and is more representative of the wide spectrum of American poetry in the postwar period. As a result of suggestions from fellow editors and poets, from those who used the anthology in their classrooms and those who refused to, and from literary critics and general readers, we added twelve names to the table of contents; in order to make room for those new names, we reluctantly had to drop four previous poets and to reduce the representation of some of the others. This version, however, is a far more just and representative look at American poetry through the past four decades. Inevitably, there are still omissions that will distress advocates of this or that style, school, or individual poet, but our firm commitment to the idea that each poet should be represented by a sizable selection of more or less equal length has simply made it impossible to include every poet who might reasonably have a claim to inclusion. What can be said is that we have done our best according to our own judgment and in light of the views of others, and that every poet included is represented by enough poetry to give readers an adequate notion of that poet's scope and range of achievement. Generous representation has also allowed us to include longer poems, such as Robert Penn Warren's "A Tale of Time," James Merrill's "Lost in Translation," James Dickey's "Falling," Denise Levertov's "Olga Poems," and Larry Levis's "Linnets." Most anthologies cannot manage such inclusions, but without them we would not be able to indicate how longer poems have become, especially in recent years, a new feature and a source of strength in our native poetry.

Two common structures for anthologies are the alphabetical, which makes it easy to find your way around, and the chronological, which attempts to do justice to the fact of literary history. Our book is something of a hybrid of these possibilities. Within the five groupings, which are basically the decades in which they were born, the poets are presented alphabetically. The groupings range in size from two to twenty poets and constitute, in one sense, a collection of five anthologies. A word about each group would seem to be in order here.

We might have titled the first group "Two Old Masters." Wallace Stevens and William Carlos Williams were the two poets from the first generation of great modernists who were still producing first-quality work in the postwar period. For that reason, along with the whole scope of their respective accomplishments, they were extremely important to the poets who followed them. Pound, Frost, Moore, and Eliot were still living in this period, but we do not see them as having the same importance to the postwar decades. The other writer we considered adding to this section was W. H. Auden. His presence in this country since 1939 had an incalculable effect on contemporary American poetry, but on close inspection we decided that his work is still very much that of a British poet; his presence in this collection would have been misleading. He also belongs, by virtue of birth date, to the second group of poets. Nevertheless, students who wish to understand American postwar poetry fully will sooner or later want to familiarize themselves with Auden's work.

The second group of poets were born between 1900 and 1920, with the majority clustered around 1914. Most of these—all except Gwendolyn Brooks, William Stafford, Alberta Turner, and Robert Penn Warren—are no longer living. The group as a whole reflects a melancholy pattern of early death, suicide, alcoholism, and mental illness. Just why such difficult, unhappy lives should characterize so many poets of this generation is not easy to explain. Most of them came of age as poets in the 1940s, and it is interesting to consider the different ways in which they confronted, in their lives and in their art, the looming presence of World War II. Many of the poetic canons in this group are now complete. The achievement and variety of this generation, especially as seen in figures like Jarrell, Bishop, and Roethke, is becoming impressively clear.

The next group of poets, born in the 1920s, is by far the largest—twenty in number—and perhaps for that reason the most difficult to generalize about. Nevertheless, certain patterns show up in the lives and work of many of these poets. They tended to begin as formalists, writing poetry based in the traditional techniques of rhyme and meter and using traditional forms like the sonnet, rhymed couplet, ballad, or villanelle. Many of them rebelled against these early influences and underwent dramatic stylistic changes. In place of the English tradition they had emulated, they sought foreign influences, such as French and Spanish surrealism, and native precedents for "open forms" such as Whitman and Williams. The same rebellion led many of them away from impersonal poems and toward various forms of the subjective, as well as into areas previously considered unfruitful for the poet:

political activism (e.g., Bly, Kinnell, and Levertov), feminism (most notably in the work of Adrienne Rich), and explorations in personal mythology (in writers as various as Ginsberg, Merwin, O'Hara, and Sexton). Even those who remained more loyal to their formalist beginnings (e.g., Justice, Merrill, and Wilbur) reflect the cross-currents that have kept this generation of poets lively, controversial, and at odds with themselves and each other in a kind of productive tension.

The next group of poets, who were born in the 1930s, happens to be our own generation. Does that mean we can see them more clearly, or less so? Time will tell. Meanwhile, we note a remarkable variety of interests and technical means in this group, marking a sense that they share in a kind of cultural salvage operation. They are much interested in the continuities of the human imagination and its means of helping us survive. And they are less anxious, perhaps, about matters of form and style than the generation preceding them, less inclined to turn against their own work and influences in search of new definitions of self and new aesthetics. Their tolerance of one another's ways is notable, and their dislike of schools and dogmas concomitantly high. These poets, with the exception of the late Sylvia Plath, are still writing vigorously. The book on their respective careers is still very much open, and it would be premature to try to characterize them too fully.

The fifth and last group, ten poets born in the 1940s and early 1950s, is our most speculative and, in some ways, our most varied. It contains poets as established as Sandra McPherson and James Tate and as new as Rita Dove and Franz Wright. We noted in our earlier edition that the poets of this group seem able to enter the lives of others effectively, with a concomitant increased interest in narrative poetry and dramatic monologue. We also remarked on their interest in having poetry communicate with the other arts and with other forms of knowledge—biography, history, science, psychology. These tentative generalizations still seem useful.

While generations are always interesting to contemplate, our primary emphasis is on each of these fifty-six poets as individual artists. For that reason, each poet's section is introduced with an essay that explores formal and thematic tendencies in the poet's work and, where relevant, some consideration of development. These brief critical discussions are intended to provoke thought and precipitate discussion rather than to be definitive accounts of their subjects. They try to provide an avenue into consideration of the poet's work that will help readers form insights and opinions of their own.

The question of how and whether to annotate the selections was perhaps the most troubling one we faced. With a good poem, one could conceivably annotate every line. Safer, perhaps, to offer no annotation. We compromised by providing occasional annotations suggesting how background information may bear on a poem. A full and complete annotation of this anthology must finally be the work of individual readers.

In addition to the introductions and occasional annotations, we have included a selective bibliography for poets whose work has attracted critical attention.

The number of people who deserve acknowledgment for their part in this anthology is very substantial. Our own students have helped us see more clearly the book's strengths and weaknesses. Almost all of the living poets included have been generous in making suggestions about their own work and that of others, as well as in the crucial area of helping negotiate reasonable permissions fees. As with the first version, we owe much to the advice and reactions of Gordon Anderson, Diane Vreuls, and David Walker. We are also indebted to Dolorus Nevels for her generous help with correspondence and clerical matters.

Stuart Friebert
David Young

Two Poets Born in the Nineteenth Century

Wallace Stevens (1879–1955)

© Rollie McKenna, 1962

Theta he starting date of this anthology is 1950; when that year began, Wallace Stevens, an insurance company executive in Hartford, Connecticut, had just turned seventy. He was to live only five more years, but old age and declining health neither forced him into retirement nor affected his artistic vigor. He continued to go to work each day and to compose his poems while walking to and from the office and on weekends. The later poems are richly inventive, making Stevens's career an interesting counterexample to the familiar story of the poet who dies young or experiences a drying up of talent. On the surface, Stevens's life was remarkably uneventful, but as a poet who continued to experiment and develop into his seventies he is a figure of considerable interest.

Stevens's later poetry has a reputation for being excessively abstract or philosophical, a misconception that the playfulness and imaginative daring of the poems presented here should help dispel. There are, of course, ideas in the air, but not for purposes of solemn demonstration or tedious argument. Stevens is like a juggler who can miraculously add abstract concepts to a swirl of plates, cups, balls, and fruit. All his life he deliberately counterpointed the human desire to propound and generalize with the intrusions of an unruly reality. In his later poems, the magisterial moments of summary, the large perspectives on life and death that exhilarate us (as in "The Poem That Took the Place of a Mountain"), are matched by a skeptical mocking of any pretense to final statements and definitive beliefs. Stevens felt that the world was so shifting and changeable, so illusory and unknowable, that even our best intuitions about it must be momentary and glancing. Poetry, he accordingly thought, might well replace religion as the best way of approaching matters of solace and belief, since dogmas tend to be static and resist change, while metaphor, the mode of the poet, tends to reflect and even celebrate it.

The characters in Stevens's poems are caught between their human need for order and meaning and the shifting, unknowable reality that surrounds them. Their efforts to systematize and fix experience are treated with both tenderness and ridicule. Thus, the man in "This Solitude of Cataracts" cannot enjoy the river he walks beside because he wants "a permanent realization," while the dead who have left the world behind and entered a changeless realm in "Large Red Man Reading" want only to return to this world and "would have wept to step barefoot into reality." Stevens would like us to walk through this world and value it for what it is. "Death is the mother of beauty," as an early poem, "Sunday Morning," baldly puts it: the impermanence of things gives them their meaning and value. What will aid us most on any walk "barefoot into reality" is the imagination. It knows how to relish the forms, colors, and textures of reality without claiming to own or classify them. Better still, it knows that the stories it invents to make sense or order of experience are just that: stories and inventions. The imagination is the true hero of a Stevens poem, and the varied forms it takes in the selection presented here—a large red man, an angel, Penelope, a candle—suggest some of his delight in celebrating it.

Readers encountering Stevens for the first time through this selection will find that it takes a while to enter the holiday revelry of language and meaning. The simultaneous affirmation and deprecation take time to adjust to, and the nimble shifts of diction and tone may seem to shut us out before they finally invite us in. But to understand one poem thoroughly is to find that the others are suddenly much easier, and before we know it we are hooked. Those whom Stevens's music enchants will want to trace it back through his earlier work to his initial collection, *Harmonium* (1923), and then forward through his middle books, *Ideas of Order* (1935), *The Man with the Blue Guitar* (1937), *Parts of a World* (1942), and *Transport to Summer* (1947). In that context, the poems presented here from *The Auroras of Autumn* (1950) and *The Rock* (the final section of *The Collected Poems* of 1954) will mean even more. There is a large body of commentary on Stevens, not all of it helpful; the critics have been rather solemn and misguided about him. In addition to the poetry, his essays, collected in *The Necessary Angel,* and his letters (*Selected Letters of Wallace Stevens,* edited by his daughter, Holly Stevens) are the best way to extend an acquaintance with him.

What Stevens will finally mean to American poetry is still being determined, but along with William Carlos Williams, he begins to loom as large as Walt Whitman or Emily Dickinson. The stylistic innovations of Stevens, his elegance of manner and consistency of vision, and his confident expansion of the horizons of modern poetry are among the features that have made him attractive to poets who have come after him. His influence on the poets of the last thirty years—on Wilbur, Justice, and Ashbery, among others—has been so thorough and so various that it seems especially appropriate to have his work begin this volume.

DY

Large Red Man Reading

There were ghosts that returned to earth to hear his phrases,
As he sat there reading, aloud, the great blue tabulae.
They were those from the wilderness of stars that had expected more.

There were those that returned to hear him read from the poem of life,
Of the pans above the stove, the pots on the table, the tulips among
    them,
They were those that would have wept to step barefoot into reality,

That would have wept and been happy, have shivered in the frost
And cried out to feel it again, have run fingers over leaves
And against the most coiled thorn, have seized on what was ugly

And laughed, as he sat there reading, from out of the purple tabulae,
The outlines of being and its expressing, the syllables of its law:
Poesis, poesis, the literal characters, the vatic lines,

Which in those ears and in those thin, those spended hearts,
Took on color, took on shape and the size of things as they are
And spoke the feeling for them, which was what they had lacked.

This Solitude of Cataracts

He never felt twice the same about the flecked river,
Which kept flowing and never the same way twice, flowing

Through many places, as if it stood still in one,
Fixed like a lake on which the wild ducks fluttered,

Ruffling its common reflections, thought-like Monadnocks.
There seemed to be an apostrophe that was not spoken.

There was so much that was real that was not real at all.
He wanted to feel the same way over and over.

He wanted the river to go on flowing the same way,
To keep on flowing. He wanted to walk beside it,

Under the buttonwoods, beneath a moon nailed fast.
He wanted his heart to stop beating and his mind to rest

In a permanent realization, without any wild ducks
Or mountains that were not mountains, just to know how it would be,

Just to know how it would feel, released from destruction,
To be a bronze man breathing under archaic lapis,

Without the oscillations of planetary pass-pass,
Breathing his bronzen breath at the azury centre of time.

Metaphor as Degeneration

If there is a man white as marble
Sits in a wood, in the greenest part,
Brooding sounds of the images of death,

So there is a man in black space
Sits in nothing that we know,
Brooding sounds of river noises;

And these images, these reverberations,
And others, make certain how being
Includes death and the imagination.

The marble man remains himself in space,
The man in the black woods descends unchanged.
It is certain that the river

Is not Swatara. The swarthy water
That flows round the earth and through the skies,
Twisting among the universal spaces,

Is not Swatara. It is being.
That is the flock-flecked river, the water,
The blown sheen—or is it air?

How, then, is metaphor degeneration,
When Swatara becomes this undulant river
And the river becomes the landless, waterless ocean?

Here the black violets grow down to its banks
And the memorial mosses hang their green
Upon it, as it flows ahead.

Puella Parvula

Every thread of summer is at last unwoven.
By one caterpillar is great Africa devoured
And Gibraltar is dissolved like spit in the wind.

But over the wind, over the legends of its roaring,
The elephant on the roof and its elephantine blaring,
The bloody lion in the yard at night or ready to spring

From the clouds in the midst of trembling trees
Making a great gnashing, over the water wallows
Of a vacant sea declaiming with wide throat,

Over all these the mighty imagination triumphs
Like a trumpet and says, in this season of memory,
When the leaves fall like things mournful of the past,

Keep quiet in the heart, O wild bitch. O mind
Gone wild, be what he tells you to be: *Puella.*
Write *pax* across the window pane. And then

Be still. The *summarium in excelsis* begins . . .
Flame, sound, fury composed . . . Hear what he says,
The dauntless master, as he starts the human tale.

Angel Surrounded by Paysans

One of the countrymen:

                                       There is
    A welcome at the door to which no one comes?

The angel:
    I am the angel of reality,
    Seen for the moment standing in the door.

    I have neither ashen wing nor wear of ore
    And live without a tepid aureole,

    Or stars that follow me, not to attend,
    But, of my being and its knowing, part.

    I am one of you and being one of you
    Is being and knowing what I am and know.

    Yet I am the necessary angel of earth,
    Since, in my sight, you see the earth again,

    Cleared of its stiff and stubborn, man-locked set,
    And, in my hearing, you hear its tragic drone

    Rise liquidly in liquid lingerings
    Like watery words awash; like meanings said

By repetitions of half-meanings. Am I not,
Myself, only half of a figure of a sort,

A figure half seen, or seen for a moment, a man
Of the mind, an apparition apparelled in

Apparels of such lightest look that a turn
Of my shoulder and quickly, too quickly, I am gone?

Vacancy in the Park

March . . . Someone has walked across the snow,
Someone looking for he knows not what.

It is like a boat that has pulled away
From a shore at night and disappeared.

It is like a guitar left on a table
By a woman, who has forgotten it.

It is like the feeling of a man
Come back to see a certain house.

The four winds blow through the rustic arbor,
Under its mattresses of vines.

The Poem That Took
the Place of a Mountain

There it was, word for word,
The poem that took the place of a mountain.

He breathed its oxygen,
Even when the book lay turned in the dust of his table.

It reminded him how he had needed
A place to go to in his own direction,

How he had recomposed the pines,
Shifted the rocks and picked his way among clouds,

For the outlook that would be right,
Where he would be complete in an unexplained completion:

The exact rock where his inexactnesses
Would discover, at last, the view toward which they had edged,

Where he could lie and, gazing down at the sea,
Recognize his unique and solitary home.

The World as Meditation

> *J'ai passé trop de temps à travailler mon*
> *violon, à voyager. Mais l'exercise essentiel*
> *du compositeur—la méditation—rien ne l'a*
> *jamais suspendu en moi . . . Je vis un rêve*
> *permanent, qui ne s'arrête ni nuit ni jour.*
>
> GEORGES ENESCO

Is it Ulysses that approaches from the east,
The interminable adventurer? The trees are mended.
That winter is washed away. Someone is moving

On the horizon and lifting himself up above it.
A form of fire approaches the cretonnes of Penelope,
Whose mere savage presence awakens the world in which she dwells.

She has composed, so long, a self with which to welcome him,
Companion to his self for her, which she imagined,
Two in a deep-founded sheltering, friend and dear friend.

The trees had been mended, as an essential exercise
In an inhuman meditation, larger than her own.
No winds like dogs watched over her at night.

She wanted nothing he could not bring her by coming alone.
She wanted no fetchings. His arms would be her necklace
And her belt, the final fortune of their desire.

But was it Ulysses? Or was it only the warmth of the sun
On her pillow? The thought kept beating in her like her heart.
The two kept beating together. It was only day.

It was Ulysses and it was not. Yet they had met,
Friend and dear friend and a planet's encouragement.
The barbarous strength within her would never fail.

She would talk a little to herself as she combed her hair,
Repeating his name with its patient syllables,
Never forgetting him that kept coming constantly so near.

Final Soliloquy of the Interior Paramour

Light the first light of evening, as in a room
In which we rest and, for small reason, think
The world imagined is the ultimate good.

This is, therefore, the intensest rendezvous.
It is in that thought that we collect ourselves,
Out of all the indifferences, into one thing:

Within a single thing, a single shawl
Wrapped tightly round us, since we are poor, a warmth,
A light, a power, the miraculous influence.

Here, now, we forget each other and ourselves.
We feel the obscurity of an order, a whole,
A knowledge, that which arranged the rendezvous.

Within its vital boundary, in the mind.
We say God and the imagination are one . . .
How high that highest candle lights the dark.

Out of this same light, out of the central mind,
We make a dwelling in the evening air,
In which being there together is enough.

Not Ideas About the Thing but the Thing Itself

At the earliest ending of winter,
In March, a scrawny cry from outside
Seemed like a sound in his mind.

He knew that he heard it,
A bird's cry, at daylight or before,
In the early March wind.

The sun was rising at six,
No longer a battered panache above snow . . .
It would have been outside.

It was not from the vast ventriloquism
Of sleep's faded papier-mâché . . .
The sun was coming from outside.

That scrawny cry—it was
A chorister whose c preceded the choir.
It was part of the colossal sun,

Surrounded by its choral rings,
Still far away. It was like
A new knowledge of reality.

NOTES

Large Red Man Reading. Stevens sometimes uses color as broadly and emphatically as an Expressionist painter. The hero of this poem is not an American Indian but a figure like someone in a painting by Chagall or Klee.

This Solitude of Cataracts. The pre-Socratic philosopher Heraclitus is said to have characterized time and incessant change by the maxim "You can't step in the same river twice." This poem begins with a deliberate variation on that idea.

Metaphor as Degeneration. Swatara, a mythical river of darkness and nullity, is mentioned in another poem, "The Countryman," and seems to be Stevens's own invention, inspired by the word "swarthy."

Puella Parvula. The title means "poor little girl."

The World as Meditation. The epigraph translates as follows: "I have spent too much time in practicing my violin, in traveling. But the essential exercise of the composer—meditation—has never been interrupted in me. I live in a permanent dream, which does not stop, either by day or by night."

WALLACE STEVENS

Books

The Necessary Angel (essays), 1951

Collected Poems, 1954

Opus Posthumous, 1957

Letters, ed. Holly Stevens, 1966

The Palm at the End of the Mind: Selected Poems and a Play, ed. Holly Stevens, 1972

Criticism

Frank Kermode, *Wallace Stevens,* 1960; Marie Borroff, ed., *Wallace Stevens: A Collection of Critical Essays,* 1963; Joseph N. Riddel, *The Clairvoyant Eye,* 1965; Helen Vendler, *On Extended Wings,* 1969; Harold Bloom, *Wallace Stevens: The Poems of Our Climate,* 1977; "Wallace Stevens: A Birthday Celebration," FIELD, No. 21 (Fall 1979); Peter Brazeau, *Parts of a World: Wallace Stevens Remembered: An Oral Biography,* 1983; David Walker, *The Transparent Lyric: Reading and Meaning in the Poetry of Stevens and Williams,* 1984.

William
Carlos
Williams
(1883–1963)

John D. Schiff

illiam Carlos Williams managed to combine a lifelong dedication to poetry with a medical practice in New Jersey. He did this by writing emphatically about the life around him—the ordinary, and even drab, people, events, and landscapes that made up his routine. His poetry combined vigorous formal experimentation, often in the direction of abandoning traditional forms and mastering the possibilities of free verse, of which he remains the most influential practitioner, with a plainness and directness of manner entirely suited to his native subjects and settings: city streets, vacant lots, workers and their tools, a retarded servant girl, a wheelbarrow, scraps of conversation, a sheet of paper rolling along in the wind. Nature is a vigorous presence in his poems, and it is celebrated without ever being idealized; it is puddles rather than lakes, sparrows rather than nightingales, weeds rather than roses. Everything is presented tautly, with a minimum of comment or judgment, in the simplest language and according to a lifelong preference for the concrete as expressed in the famous motto "No ideas but in things."

The music of Williams's poems seems at first to be a deliberate absence of music, and it takes some time to perceive the finely controlled dance that the hesitations and abruptnesses of the free verse line accomplish; reading aloud should include experimentation with the pauses to be found on the page, listening for the plain, emerging music. Our recognition of this unlikely lyricism involves the same kind of delighted surprise that we experience from the poet's ways of finding beauty in unexpected places; subject and style have the same aims, and an aesthetic of discovery through reduction and directness lies behind everything Williams did. To put it in terms of the visual analogies that very much interested him, his poems combine the freshness and daring of cubist painting with the candor and unmediated confrontation of photography.

Williams's career, like Stevens's, was long and productive. Early in the century he began writing romantic, Keatsian poems; he responded to the innovations of modernism in all the arts during the first two decades of the century, briefly sampled the expatriate life that his friend Ezra Pound had chosen, then settled down in New Jersey to his medical practice and his highly distinctive poems. By 1950 he was in the midst of his major long poem, *Paterson,* and the shorter pieces represented here. He had by then developed a poetic device peculiarly suited both to American speech and to his artistic needs, the "variable foot." This was a unit of varying length—one word or several—which was supposed to have the same weight and duration in the poem. Grouped in threes to make up a triadic line, these variable feet led Williams to some of his finest writing, and his excitement about his "new measure" seems in retrospect to have been justified. In a poem like "The Sparrow," we see how the triadic line combines the staccato and fragmentary nature of American speech with a dreamy fluency that is both haunting and hypnotic.

Like Stevens, Williams was an enormous influence on the poets who followed, both the more direct imitators who carried on the free verse style (in this collection, most notably, Robert Creeley, Denise Levertov, and Dennis Schmitz) and those who borrowed parts of his aesthetic without trying to approximate his style: Ginsberg, O'Hara, Jarrell, Lowell, and others. His personal generosity and availability made him an important figure to younger writers; in the declining years of the late 1950s and early 1960s, after he was crippled by a series of strokes, his home was a place of pilgrimage for many American poets.

No poet since Whitman has been so successful in merging an artistic program with a distinctive sense of what it means to be American. As Williams wrote his later poems, American poetry was entering its most vigorous period, and the fact that he could finally take for his subjects the paintings of a Dutch master without diluting the distinctively native quality of his poetry is one indication of the way in which his art was thoroughly infused with the language, manners, experience, and attitudes of his own country. For that, for his vision of the world's beauty and energy manifesting themselves in unlikely ways and places, and for his technical finesse with a new verse form, all subsequent poets are greatly in his debt.

_DY_

Pictures from Brueghel

I Self-Portrait

In a red winter hat blue
eyes smiling
just the head and shoulders

crowded on the canvas
arms folded one
big ear the right showing

the face slightly tilted
a heavy wool coat
with broad buttons

gathered at the neck reveals
a bulbous nose
but the eyes red-rimmed

from over-use he must have
driven them hard
but the delicate wrists

show him to have been a
man unused to
manual labor unshaved his

blond beard half trimmed
no time for any-
thing but his painting

II Landscape with
the Fall of Icarus

According to Brueghel
when Icarus fell
it was spring

a farmer was ploughing
his field
the whole pageantry

of the year was
awake tingling
near

the edge of the sea
concerned
with itself

sweating in the sun
that melted
the wings' wax

unsignificantly
off the coast
there was

a splash quite unnoticed
this was
Icarus drowning

III The Hunters in the Snow

The over-all picture is winter
icy mountains
in the background the return

from the hunt it is toward evening
from the left
sturdy hunters lead in

their pack the inn-sign
hanging from a
broken hinge is a stag a crucifix

between his antlers the cold
inn yard is
deserted but for a huge bonfire

that flares wind-driven tended by
women who cluster
about it to the right beyond

the hill is a pattern of skaters
Brueghel the painter
concerned with it all has chosen

a winter-struck bush for his
foreground to
complete the picture . . .

IX The Parable of the Blind

This horrible but superb painting
the parable of the blind
without a red

in the composition shows a group
of beggars leading
each other diagonally downward

across the canvas
from one side
to stumble finally into a bog

where the picture
and the composition ends back
of which no seeing man

is represented the unshaven
features of the des-
titute with their few

pitiful possessions a basin
to wash in a peasant
cottage is seen and a church spire

the faces are raised
as toward the light
there is no detail extraneous

to the composition one
follows the others stick in
hand triumphant to disaster

Iris

a burst of iris so that
come down for
breakfast

we searched through the
rooms for
that

sweetest odor and at
first could not
find its

source then a blue as
of the sea
struck

startling us from among
those trumpeting
petals

To a Dog Injured in the Street

It is myself,
            not the poor beast lying there
                        yelping with pain
that brings me to myself with a start—
            as at the explosion
                        of a bomb, a bomb that has laid
all the world waste.
            I can do nothing
                        but sing about it
and so I am assuaged
            from my pain.
A drowsy numbness drowns my sense
            as if of hemlock
                        I had drunk. I think
of the poetry
            of René Char
                        and all he must have seen
and suffered
            that has brought him
                        to speak only of
sedgy rivers,
            of daffodils and tulips
                        whose roots they water,
even to the free-flowing river
            that laves the rootlets
                        of those sweet-scented flowers
that people the
            milky
                        way
I remember Norma
            our English setter of my childhood
                        her silky ears
and expressive eyes.
            She had a litter
                        of pups one night
in our pantry and I kicked
            one of them
                        thinking, in my alarm,
that they
            were biting her breasts
                        to destroy her.

I remember also
     a dead rabbit
          lying harmlessly
on the outspread palm
     of a hunter's hand.
          As I stood by
watching
     he took a hunting knife
          and with a laugh
thrust it
     up into the animal's private parts.
          I almost fainted.
Why should I think of that now?
     The cries of a dying dog
          are to be blotted out
as best I can.
     René Char
          you are a poet who believes
in the power of beauty
     to right all wrongs.
          I believe it also.
With invention and courage
     we shall surpass
          the pitiful dumb beasts,
let all men believe it,
     as you have taught me also
          to believe it.

The Artist

Mr. T.
     bareheaded
          in a soiled undershirt
his hair standing out
     on all sides
          stood on his toes
heels together
     arms gracefully
          for the moment
curled above his head.
     Then he whirled about
          bounded
into the air
     and with an *entrechat*
          perfectly achieved

completed the figure.
    My mother
        taken by surprise
where she sat
    in her invalid's chair
        was left speechless.
Bravo! she cried at last
    and clapped her hands.
        The man's wife
came from the kitchen:
    What goes on here? she said.
        But the show was over.

The Sparrow

(To My Father)

This sparrow
    who comes to sit at my window
        is a poetic truth
more than a natural one.
    His voice,
        his movements,
his habits—
    how he loves to
        flutter his wings
in the dust—
    all attest it;
        granted, he does it
to rid himself of lice
    but the relief he feels
        makes him
cry out lustily—
    which is a trait
        more related to music
than otherwise.
    Wherever he finds himself
        in early spring,
on back streets
    or beside palaces,
        he carries on
unaffectedly
    his amours.
        It begins in the egg,
his sex genders it:
    What is more pretentiously
        useless

or about which
             we more pride ourselves?
                          It leads as often as not
to our undoing.
             The cockerel, the crow
                          with their challenging voices
cannot surpass
             the insistence
                          of his cheep!
Once
             at El Paso
                          toward evening,
I saw—and heard!—
             ten thousand sparrows
                          who had come in from
the desert
             to roost. They filled the trees
                          of a small park. Men fled
(with ears ringing!)
             from their droppings,
                          leaving the premises
to the alligators
             who inhabit
                          the fountain. His image
is familiar
             as that of the aristocratic
                          unicorn, a pity
there are not more oats eaten
             nowadays
                          to make living easier
for him.
             At that,
                          his small size,
keen eyes,
             serviceable beak
                          and general truculence
assure his survival—
             to say nothing
                          of his innumerable
brood.
             Even the Japanese
                          know him
and have painted him
             sympathetically,
                          with profound insight

into his minor
   characteristics.
      Nothing even remotely
subtle
   about his lovemaking.
      He crouches
before the female,
   drags his wings,
      waltzing,
throws back his head
   and simply—
      yells! The din
is terrific.
   The way he swipes his bill
      across a plank
to clean it,
   is decisive.
      So with everything
he does. His coppery
   eyebrows
      give him the air
of being always
   a winner—and yet
      I saw once,
the female of his species
   clinging determinedly
      to the edge of
a water pipe,
   catch him
      by his crown-feathers
to hold him
   silent,
      subdued,
hanging above the city streets
   until
      she was through with him.
What was the use
   of that?
      She hung there
herself,
   puzzled at her success.
      I laughed heartily.
Practical to the end,
   it is the poem
      of his existence

that triumphed
      finally;
            a wisp of feathers
flattened to the pavement,
        wings spread symmetrically
           as if in flight,
the head gone,
        the black escutcheon of the breast
           undecipherable,
an effigy of a sparrow,
        a dried wafer only,
           left to say
and it says it
        without offense,
           beautifully;
This was I,
      a sparrow.
        I did my best;
farewell.

NOTES

Pictures from Brueghel. Williams's admiration for the naturalism, vigor, and scope of Brueghel's art makes them kindred spirits. It is interesting to compare Williams's handling of the Icarus painting with W. H. Auden's very different treatment of the same subject in the poem "Musées de Beaux Arts."

To a Dog Injured in the Street. The fifth triad paraphrases the opening lines of Keats's "Ode to a Nightingale." René Char is a French poet who was active in the French Resistance movement during World War II.

WILLIAM CARLOS WILLIAMS

Books

Collected Earlier Poems, 1938, 1951

Collected Later Poems, 1944, 1948, 1950, 1963

Paterson, 1958

The Autobiography of William Carlos Williams, 1951

Selected Essays, 1954

Selected Letters, 1957

Pictures from Brueghel, 1962

Selected Poems, 1963, 1985

The Collected Poems, Vol. 1, 1986; Vol. 2, 1988

Criticism, Interviews

J. Hillis Miller, ed., *William Carlos Williams: A Collection of Critical Essays,* 1966; Thomas Whitaker, *William Carlos Williams,* 1968; Emily Mitchell Wallace, *A Bibliography of William Carlos Williams,* 1968; James Breslin, *William Carlos Williams, An American Artist,* 1970; Jerome Mazzaro, *William Carlos Williams, The Later Poems,* 1973; "William Carlos Williams: A FIELD Symposium," *FIELD,* No. 29 (Fall 1981); Paul Mariani, *William Carlos Williams: A New World Naked,* 1982; David Walker, *The Transparent Lyric: Reading and Meaning in the Poetry of Stevens and Williams,* 1984.

Twelve Poets Born Between 1900 and 1920

John
Berryman
(1914–1972)

© Rollie McKenna, 1969

A professor at the University of Minnesota at the time of his death, John Berryman, who had also taught at Brown, Princeton, and Harvard, made ample use of his considerable learning in his poems. They are characterized by a cutting wit that at times turns on both poet and subject alike, but underneath are wellsprings of affection and concern for our human lot. While at times he brooded his life away trying to come to terms with his father's suicide, insulating himself with writing and teaching until drink and sickness led him finally to take his own life, Berryman fought to remain vital in his work and wanted to be remembered as a man who worked hard. To the end he was at work on lives of Shakespeare and Christ, and on a novel called *Recovery*. He was one of those who lived, and lived by, his poetry, spending literally years on matters of style and form, paying constant tribute to his literary sources and influences. He remained the scholar-poet, and much of what he wrote was a response to reading around in his favorites, Yeats, Apollinaire, Auden, Pound, Stevens, Rilke, Coleridge, Poe, and Kafka, "a wide cast of characters," as he noted elsewhere about the many figures in *The Dream Songs*.

Many critics have called attention to the complex mix of self-pity, delusions of grandeur, and childlike innocence that form the main strings of his cat's cradle; when the poems fail, it is because he pulls one string at the expense of the others. More important, he was trying, as he noted in a remark on his "three epics" (*Homage to Mistress Bradstreet, The Dream Songs*, and the unfinished *Proemio*), to "include instructions to them [his children] on every subject I feel sufficiently strongly about and either know inside-out or am wholly perplext by."

Robert Lowell called *The Dream Songs*, which stand at the center of Berryman's work, "one of the glories of the age, the most heroic work in English poetry since the war" (cited in Cooper's *The Autobiographical Myth of Robert Lowell*). Dense with learning, aflow with cryptic references and dream meanings, sounding a little like a xylophone played by a master musician, *The Dream Songs* are nonetheless, in their strict forms, "provocative, practically an innovation" (Louis Simpson, *A Revolution in Taste*), coming as they did at a time when free verse had gained the upper hand. Introducing *The Dream Songs* in 1966, Berryman said they were about "a white American who sometimes appears in blackface and who has suffered an irreversible loss." They are more personal than he liked to admit; they are also about all of us, and lest we grow too gloomy at the prospect, Berryman added that he and Saul Bellow almost killed themselves laughing at them. One is reminded of Kafka: his work made others feel awful, but he and his friends would read it out loud and laugh themselves silly. So it is up to the reader to watch for the humor and see the poke in the ribs for what it is: the way to start disentangling guilt and innocence.

The poems presented here underline the great sense of fun Berryman had singing the song of his poems. If we're reminded of "The Bells of St. Clements" while reading "American Lights, Seen from Off Abroad," so much the better; we can sing along, making up two-liners about our hometown lights. Berryman's wit in these ditties is tempered by great affection, and his sense of timing is a fine comic's. In "Washington in Love" the poem's fragmentary character establishes a paradigmatic way of looking at our history that Berryman sought in all subjects. The critic John Haffenden says he came across sixteen pages of notes for an "Ur-Washington in

Love" in Berryman's attic. All has been reduced to seven lines in our version, seven little chapter headlines behind which history crackles and flashes. Berryman the teacher is at work here; the reader has to enter history, flesh out the possible versions. "Gislebertus' Eve" gives Berryman another opportunity to romp through the history of great ideas. As in *The Dream Songs,* he invests the speaker (his father? himself as an old-time director of history, à la John Ford, the filmmaker?) with a dramatic presence that identifies "the passion for secrets the passion worst of all"—the word *passion* fairly bristling to escape. Of all the props Berryman used, the sassy cabaret-style monologue allowed him a measure of religious identity in the face of bitter disillusionment and emptiness. From this no-man's-land, this sweep across the history of foolish propositions, or ideas, he could be saved only by parodying the parody: "I too find it delicious."

Whether rubbing our noses in what we have been up to militarily and politically, or confronting us with our personal limitations, *The Dream Songs* lament terrible things that *have* happened between nation and people, leader and follower, father and son. But they play their little anthems out so engagingly that we are caught up in the music, and the image of our going "out," or off the stage, is realized in taut structures under such pressure as to convey a feeling of animated strength.

During the course of his career, Berryman was much recognized. He was awarded Guggenheim and Rockefeller fellowships, a grant from the National Arts Council, and the National Book Award as well as the Pulitzer Prize.

SF

American Lights, Seen from Off Abroad

Blue go up & blue go down
to light the lights of Dollartown

Nebuchadnezzar had it so good?
wink the lights of Hollywood

I never think, I have so many things,
flash the lights of Palm Springs

I worry like a madwoman over all the world,
affirm the lights, all night, at State

I have no plans, I mean well,
swear the lights of Georgetown

I have the blind staggers
call the lights of Niagara

We shall die in a palace
shout the black lights of Dallas

I couldn't dare less, my favorite son,
fritter the lights of Washington

(I have a brave old So-and-So,
chuckle the lights of Independence, Mo.)

I cast a shadow, what I mean,
blurt the lights of Abilene

Both his sides are all the same
glows his grin with all but shame

He can do nothing night & day
wonder his lovers. So they say.

"Basketball in outer space"
sneers the White New Hampshire House

I'll have a smaller one, later, Mac,
hope the strange lights of Cal Tech

I love you one & all, hate shock,
bleat the lights of Little Rock

I cannot quite focus
cry the lights of Las Vegas

I am a maid of shots & pills,
swivel the lights of Beverly Hills

Proud & odd, you give me vertigo,
fly the lights of San Francisco

I am all satisfied love & chalk,
mutter the great lights of New York

I have lost your way
say the white lights of Boston

Here comes a scandal to blight you to bed.
Here comes a cropper. That's what I said.

Lévanto, 7 October 1957

Certainty Before Lunch

Ninety percent of the mass of the Universe
(90%!) may be gone in collapsars,
pulseless, lightless, forever, if they exist.
My friends the probability man & I

& his wife the lawyer are taking a country walk
in the flowerless April snow in exactly two hours
and maybe won't be back. Finite & unbounded
the massive spirals absolutely fly

distinctly apart, by math *and* observation,
current math, this morning's telescopes
& inference. My wife is six months gone
so won't be coming. That mass must be somewhere!

or not? just barely possibly *may not*
BE anywhere? My Lord, I'm glad we don't
on x or y depend for Your being there.
I know You are there. The sweat is, I am here.

Washington in Love

I

Rectitude, and the terrible upstanding member

II

The music of our musketry is: *beautiful*

III

Intolerable Sally, loved in vain

IV

Mr Adams of Massachusetts . . . I accept, gentlemen.

V

Aloes. Adders. Roman gratitude.

VI

My porch elevation from the Potomac is 174', 7½".

VII

Bring the wounded, Martha! *Bring the wounded, men.*

Gislebertus' Eve

> *Most men are not wicked . . . They*
> *are sleep-walkers, not evildoers.*
>
> KAFKA TO G JANOUCH

Eve & her envy roving slammed me down
prone in discrepancy: I can't get things right:
the passion for secrets the passion worst of all,
the ultimate human, from Leonardo & Darwin

to the austere Viennese with the cigar
and Bohr a-musing: 'The opposite of a true
statement is a false statement. But the opposite
of a profound truth may be another profound truth.'

So now we see where we are, which is all-over
we're nowhere, son, and suffering we know it,
rapt in delusion, where weird particles
frantic & Ditheletic orbit our

revolutionary natures. She snaked out a soft
small willing hand, curved her ivory fingers on
a new taste sensation, in reverie over
something other,
sank her teeth in, and offered him a bite.

I too find it delicious.

from The Dream Songs
9

Deprived of his enemy, shrugged to a standstill
horrible Henry, foaming. Fan their way
toward him who will

in the high wood: the officers, their rest,
with p.a. echoing: his girl comes, say,
conned in to test

if he's still human, see: she love him, see,
therefore she get on the Sheriff's mike & howl
'Come down, come down'.
Therefore he un-budge, furious. He'd flee
but only Heaven hangs over him foul.
At the crossways, downtown,

he dreams the folks are buying parsnips & suds
and paying rent to foes. He slipt & fell.
It's golden here in the snow.
A mild crack: a far rifle. Bogart's duds
truck back to Wardrobe. Fancy the brain from hell
held out so long. Let go.

12

Sabbath

There is an eye, there was a slit.
Nights walk, and confer on him fear.
The strangler tree, the dancing mouse
confound his vision; then they loosen it.
Henry widens. How did Henry House
himself ever come here?

Nights run. Tes yeux bizarres me suivent
when loth at landfall soft I leave.
The soldiers, Coleridge Rilke Poe,
shout commands I never heard.
They march about, dying & absurd.
Toddlers are taking over. O

ver! Sabbath belling. Snoods converge
on a weary-daring man.
What now can be cleared up? from the Yard the visitors urge.
Belle thro' the graves in a blast of sun
to the kirk moves the youngest witch.
Watch.

23
The Lay of Ike

> This is the lay of Ike.
> Here's to the glory of the Great White—awk—
> who has been running—er—er—things in recent—ech—
> in the United—If your screen is black,
> ladies & gentlemen, we—I like—
> at the Point he was already terrific—sick
>
> to a second term, having done no wrong—
> no right—no right—having let the Army—bang—
> defend itself from Joe, let venom' Strauss
> bile Oppenheimer out of use—use Robb,
> who'll later fend for Goldfine—Breaking no laws,
> he lay in the White House—sob!!—
>
> who never understood his own strategy—whee—
> so Monty's memoirs—nor any strategy,
> wanting the ball bulled thro' all parts of the line
> at once—proving, by his refusal to take Berlin,
> he misread even Clauswitz—wide empty grin
> that never lost a vote (O Adlai mine).

76
Henry's Confession

> Nothin very bad happen to me lately.
> How you explain that?—I explain that, Mr Bones,
> terms o' your bafflin odd sobriety.
> Sober as man can get, no girls, no telephones,
> what could happen bad to Mr Bones?
> —*If* life is a handkerchief sandwich,
>
> in a modesty of death I join my father
> who dared so long agone leave me.
> A bullet on a concrete stoop
> close by a smothering southern sea
> spreadeagled on an island, by my knee.
> —You is from hunger, Mr Bones,
>
> I offers you this handkerchief, now set
> your left foot by my right foot,
> shoulder to shoulder, all that jazz,
> arm in arm, by the beautiful sea,
> hum a little, Mr Bones.
> —I saw nobody coming, so I went instead.

107

Three 'coons come at his garbage. He be cross,
I figuring porcupine & took Sir poker
unbarring Mr door,

& then screen door. Ah, but the little 'coon,
hardly a foot (not counting tail) got in with
two more at the porch-edge

and they swirled, before some two swerve off
this side of crab tree, and my dear friend held
with the torch in his tiny eyes
two feet off, banded, but then he gave &
shot away too. They were all the same size,
maybe they were brothers,

it seems, and is, clear to me we are brothers.
I wish the rabbit & the 'coons could be friends,
I'm sorry about the poker
but I'm too busy now for nipping or quills
I've given up literature & taken down pills,
and that rabbit doesn't trust me

366

Chilled in this Irish pub I wish my loves
well, well to strangers, well to all his friends,
seven or so in number,
I forgive my enemies, especially two,
races his heart, at so much magnanimity,
can it at all be true?

—Mr Bones, you on a trip outside yourself.
Has you seen a medicine man? You sound will-like,
a testament & such.
Is you going?—Oh, I suffer from a strike
& a strike & three balls: I stand up for much,
Wordsworth & that sort of thing.

The pitcher dreamed. He threw a hazy curve,
I took it in my stride & out I struck,
lonesome Henry.
These Songs are not meant to be understood, you understand.
They are only meant to terrify & comfort.
Lilac was found in his hand.

NOTES

American Lights, Seen from Off Abroad. "A brave old So-and-So" refers to former President Harry S. Truman. "Abilene" should conjure up former President Dwight D. Eisenhower, who was born there.

Gislebertus' Eve. Gislebertus was a twelfth-century French sculptor. His "Eve" is on the stone panels of St. Lazare at Autun. The "austere Viennese with the cigar" is Sigmund Freud. "Bohr" was Niels Bohr, Danish physicist, who developed a theory of atomic structure. "Ditheletic" means believing in the existence of two antagonistic principles, one good and one evil.

Dream Song 9. The film *High Sierra*, directed by John Ford and starring Humphrey Bogart and Ida Lupino, is the subject of the poem.

Dream Song 12: Sabbath. "Tes yeux bizarres me suivent" means "Your bizarre eyes follow me" which may (if not made up!) be a line from Apollinaire, according to a French scholar consulted.

Dream Song 23: The Lay of Ike. "Ike" is former President Dwight D. Eisenhower. The "Point" is West Point. "Joe" is Senator Joseph McCarthy, who "went after" communists in the military and government. "Strauss" is a commissioner of the Atomic Energy Commission during the Eisenhower administration. "Robb" refers again to Strauss, whose first name was Robert. "Goldfine" is Bernard Goldfine, a businessman involved in shady deals during the Eisenhower administration. "Oppenheimer" is J. Robert Oppenheimer, U.S. nuclear physicist who worked on atomic bombs and was suspected of communist connections. "Monty": Sir Bernard Law Montgomery, British field marshal who became famous during World War II. "Clauswitz" (*sic*) refers to Karl von Clausewitz (1780–1831), German military officer and author of books on military strategy. "Adlai": Adlai E. Stevenson, former governor of Illinois and twice an unsuccessful candidate against Eisenhower for the presidency.

Dream Song 76: Henry's Confession. "Mr Bones" is a kind of alter ego for Henry, who, Berryman once said, could be thought of as "Death" come to fetch Henry at the end.

JOHN BERRYMAN

Books

Poems, 1942

The Dispossessed, 1948

Homage to Mistress Bradstreet, 1956

His Thoughts Made Pockets & The Plane Buckt, 1958

Stephen Crane (biography), 1962

77 Dream Songs, 1964

Short Poems, 1967

His Toy, His Dream, His Rest, 1968

The Dream Songs, 1969

Love & Fame, 1972

Delusions, Etc., 1972

Henry's Fate & Other Poems, 1967, 1972

Recovery (novel), 1973

The Freedom of the Poet (essays and stories), 1976

We Dream of Honour: John Berryman's Letters to His Mother (edited by Richard J. Kelly), 1988

Criticism

William J. Martz, *John Berryman*, 1969; Ernest C. Stefanik, Jr., *John Berryman: A Descriptive Bibliography*, 1972; J. M. Linebarger, *John Berryman*, 1974; John Haffenden, *John Berryman: A Critical Commentary*, 1980; John Haffenden, *The Life of John Berryman*, 1982; Eileen Simpson, *Poets in Their Youth*, 1982; Bruce Bawer, *The Middle Generation: The Lives and Poetry of Delmore Schwartz, Randall Jarrell, John Berryman, and Robert Lowell*, 1986; Harry Thomas, ed., *Berryman's Understanding*, 1988.

Elizabeth
Bishop
(1911–1979)

William Stafford

A pungent sense of wonder inhabits everything that Elizabeth Bishop wrote, and her powerful capacity for pursuing and capturing the marvelous and the mysterious in her dense, meticulous poems is her leading attribute as an artist. Her poems can be solemn and rather childlike in their approach to the world, and they can glitter with wit and sophistication, but these varieties of tone share a purposeful, even relentless, air of pursuit, a boring in on a subject so as to make it reveal, through penetrating observation, its hidden and magical characteristics. In this she goes farther than her friend and mentor, Marianne Moore. Take, for example, the imaginative intensity with which Bishop invades and inhabits the experience of the Prodigal Son in "The Prodigal." At first she seems to be searching out the negative qualities of his exile, but gradually the delight starts to mix in with the miseries to form a truer portrait of the runaway's ambivalence. When the deliberately flat ending (off-rhymed after a series of full rhymes) tells us that "it took him a long time/finally to make his mind up to go home," it doesn't surprise us, given the disquieting beauty of the barn and barnyard, a curious analogue to the Nativity setting that closes "Over 2000 Illustrations and a Complete Concordance."

To speak of a sense of wonder is not to dismiss emotions like dismay and terror. The world's richness is a strangeness too, about which the poet is both candid and precise: "In Mexico the dead man lay/in a blue arcade; the dead volcanoes/glistened like Easter lilies." Two kinds of death, one disquieting and the other comforting, framed by an odd beauty and a strange comparison that allow comfort and disquiet to mix together. What frightens the speaker of this poem ("Over 2000 Illustrations") most turns out to be a "holy grave" that seems empty and meaningless, suggesting that the search for natural wonders and exotic beauty is really a search for divinity and the meaning it would give the world. The speaker must finally imagine the epiphany—in this case the "old Nativity"—that would justify the appetite behind the travels and catalogues of this poem. The poet John Ashbery has called the last line of this poem among the most memorable and mysterious in contemporary poetry. Its sense of glory also suggests a simultaneous innocence and a yielding to extinction.

A small private income, a love of travel, and a taste for the exotic allowed Elizabeth Bishop to explore and live in unusual settings. The geographical extremes of her first book, *North and South* (1946), seemed to be New England and Key West, but in her later poems these stretch out to Nova Scotia on the one hand and Brazil on the other. While her years of residence in Brazil produced many fine poems, we found ourselves preferring her "northern" poems, and the present selection reflects that preference. The relative strength of poems like "At the Fishhouses" and "First Death in Nova Scotia," as well as examples not included here, like the fine later poem "The Moose" and the unforgettable story "In the Village" (which was included in her collection of poems, *Questions of Travel*), may have to do with their roots in her childhood. She was born in Worcester, Massachusetts, but because her father died when she was an infant and her mother was committed to a mental institution when she was four, she was raised by her maternal grandparents in Nova Scotia. Poems like "Sestina" and "In the Waiting Room" have a strong autobiographical basis.

It is not surprising that such a poet would be drawn to the formal and obsessive qualities of the sestina, and Elizabeth Bishop has left us two of the best examples in the language, "A Miracle for Breakfast" and the less well-known but possibly superior example represented here. It is also not surprising that Bishop is a superb portrayer of childhood. Children are variously presented in this selection, most notably perhaps in "Sestina," "First Death in Nova Scotia," and "In the Waiting Room." This last poem, from her late collection *Geography III* (1976), shows the simplified style of precisely monitored, crisp reportage that especially characterizes her later work. Elizabeth Bishop's poetic canon is one of the smallest among the poets of her generation, but its importance and integrity continue to impress new readers, who discover in her poems a balanced exactness and unsentimental sense of the sublime that are far too rare in poetry.

DY

Over 2000 Illustrations and a Complete Concordance

Thus should have been our travels:
serious, engravable.
The Seven Wonders of the World are tired
and a touch familiar, but the other scenes,
innumerable, though equally sad and still,
are foreign. Often the squatting Arab,
or group of Arabs, plotting, probably,
against our Christian Empire,
while one apart, with outstretched arm and hand
points to the Tomb, the Pit, the Sepulcher.
The branches of the date-palms look like files.
The cobbled courtyard, where the Well is dry,
is like a diagram, the brickwork conduits
are vast and obvious, the human figure
far gone in history or theology,
gone with its camel or its faithful horse.
Always the silence, the gesture, the specks of birds
suspended on invisible threads above the Site,
or the smoke rising solemnly, pulled by threads.
Granted a page alone or a page made up
of several scenes arranged in cattycornered rectangles
or circles set on stippled gray,
granted a grim lunette,
caught in the toils of an initial letter,
when dwelt upon, they all resolve themselves.
The eye drops, weighted, through the lines
the burin made, the lines that move apart
like ripples above sand,
dispersing storms, God's spreading fingerprint,
and painfully, finally, that ignite
in watery prismatic white-and-blue.
Entering the Narrows at St. Johns
the touching bleat of goats reached to the ship.
We glimpsed them, reddish, leaping up the cliffs
among the fog-soaked weeds and butter-and-eggs.
And at St. Peter's the wind blew and the sun shone madly.
Rapidly, purposefully, the Collegians marched in lines,
crisscrossing the great square with black, like ants.
In Mexico the dead man lay
in a blue arcade, the dead volcanoes
glistened like Easter lilies.

The jukebox went on playing "Ay, Jalisco!"
And at Volubilis there were beautiful poppies
splitting the mosaics: the fat old guide made eyes.
In Dingle harbor a golden length of evening
the rotting hulks held up their dripping plush.
The Englishwoman poured tea, informing us
that the Duchess was going to have a baby.
And in the brothels of Marrakesh
the little pockmarked prostitutes
balanced their tea-trays on their heads
and did their belly-dances; flung themselves
naked and giggling against our knees,
asking for cigarettes. It was somewhere near there
I saw what frightened me most of all:
A holy grave, not looking particularly holy,
one of a group under a keyhole-arched stone baldaquin
open to every wind from the pink desert.
An open, gritty, marble trough, carved solid
with exhortation, yellowed
as scattered cattle-teeth;
half-filled with dust, not even the dust
of the poor prophet paynim who once lay there.
In a smart burnoose Khadour looked on amused.

Everything only connected by "and" and "and."
Open the book. (The gilt rubs off the edges
of the pages and pollinates the fingertips.)
Open the heavy book. Why couldn't we have seen
this old Nativity while we were at it?
—the dark ajar, the rocks breaking with light,
an undisturbed, unbreathing flame,
colorless, sparkless, freely fed on straw,
and, lulled within, a family with pets,
—and looked and looked our infant sight away.

At the Fishhouses

Although it is a cold evening,
down by one of the fishhouses
an old man sits netting,
his net, in the gloaming almost invisible
a dark purple-brown,
and his shuttle worn and polished.

The air smells so strong of codfish
it makes one's nose run and one's eyes water.
The five fishhouses have steeply peaked roofs
and narrow, cleated gangplanks slant up
to storerooms in the gables
for the wheelbarrows to be pushed up and down on.
All is silver: the heavy surface of the sea,
swelling slowly as if considering spilling over,
is opaque, but the silver of the benches,
the lobster pots, and masts, scattered
among the wild jagged rocks,
is of an apparent translucence
like the small old buildings with an emerald moss
growing on their shoreward walls.
The big fish tubs are completely lined
with layers of beautiful herring scales
and the wheelbarrows are similarly plastered
with creamy iridescent coats of mail,
with small iridescent flies crawling on them.
Up on the little slope behind the houses,
set in the sparse bright sprinkle of grass,
is an ancient wooden capstan,
cracked, with two long bleached handles
and some melancholy stains, like dried blood,
where the ironwork has rusted.
The old man accepts a Lucky Strike.
He was a friend of my grandfather.
We talk of the decline in the population
and of codfish and herring
while he waits for a herring boat to come in.
There are sequins on his vest and on his thumb.
He has scraped the scales, the principal beauty,
from unnumbered fish with that black old knife,
the blade of which is almost worn away.

Down at the water's edge, at the place
where they haul up the boats, up the long ramp
descending into the water, thin silver
tree trunks are laid horizontally
across the gray stones, down and down
at intervals of four or five feet.

Cold dark deep and absolutely clear,
element bearable to no mortal,
to fish and to seals . . . One seal particularly
I have seen here evening after evening.

He was curious about me. He was interested in music;
like me a believer in total immersion,
so I used to sing him Baptist hymns.
I also sang "A Mighty Fortress Is Our God."
He stood up in the water and regarded me
steadily, moving his head a little.
Then he would disappear, then suddenly emerge
almost in the same spot, with a sort of shrug
as if it were against his better judgment.
Cold dark deep and absolutely clear,
the clear gray icy water . . . Back, behind us,
the dignified tall firs begin.
Bluish, associating with their shadows,
a million Christmas trees stand
waiting for Christmas. The water seems suspended
above the rounded gray and blue-gray stones.
I have seen it over and over, the same sea, the same,
slightly, indifferently swinging above the stones,
icily free above the stones,
above the stones and then the world.
If you should dip your hand in,
your wrist would ache immediately,
your bones would begin to ache and your hand would burn
as if the water were a transmutation of fire
that feeds on stones and burns with a dark gray flame.
If you tasted it, it would first taste bitter,
then briny, then surely burn your tongue.
It is like what we imagine knowledge to be:
dark, salt, clear, moving, utterly free,
drawn from the cold hard mouth
of the world, derived from the rocky breasts
forever, flowing and drawn, and since
our knowledge is historical, flowing, and flown.

The Prodigal

The brown enormous odor he lived by
was too close, with its breathing and thick hair,
for him to judge. The floor was rotten; the sty
was plastered halfway up with glass-smooth dung.
Light-lashed, self-righteous, above moving snouts,
the pigs' eyes followed him, a cheerful stare—
even to the sow that always ate her young—
till, sickening, he leaned to scratch her head.

But sometimes mornings after drinking bouts
(he hid the pints behind a two-by-four),
the sunrise glazed the barnyard mud with red;
the burning puddles seemed to reassure.
And then he thought he almost might endure
his exile yet another year or more.

But evenings the first star came to warn.
The farmer whom he worked for came at dark
to shut the cows and horses in the barn
beneath their overhanging clouds of hay,
with pitchforks, faint forked lightnings, catching light,
safe and companionable as in the Ark.
The pigs stuck out their little feet and snored.
The lantern—like the sun, going away—
laid on the mud a pacing aureole.
Carrying a bucket along a slimy board,
he felt the bats' uncertain staggering flight,
his shuddering insights, beyond his control,
touching him. But it took him a long time
finally to make his mind up to go home.

Sestina

September rain falls on the house.
In the failing light, the old grandmother
sits in the kitchen with the child
beside the Little Marvel Stove,
reading the jokes from the almanac,
laughing and talking to hide her tears.

She thinks that her equinoctial tears
and the rain that beats on the roof of the house
were both foretold by the almanac,
but only known to a grandmother.
The iron kettle sings on the stove.
She cuts some bread and says to the child,

It's time for tea now; but the child
is watching the teakettle's small hard tears
dance like mad on the hot black stove,
the way the rain must dance on the house.
Tidying up, the old grandmother
hangs up the clever almanac

on its string. Birdlike, the almanac
hovers half open above the child,
hovers above the old grandmother
and her teacup full of dark brown tears.
She shivers and says she thinks the house
feels chilly, and puts more wood in the stove.
It was to be, says the Marvel Stove.
I know what I know, says the almanac.
With crayons the child draws a rigid house
and a winding pathway. Then the child
puts in a man with buttons like tears
and shows it proudly to the grandmother.

But secretly, while the grandmother
busies herself about the stove,
the little moons fall down like tears
from between the pages of the almanac
into the flower bed the child
has carefully placed in the front of the house.

Time to plant tears, says the almanac.
The grandmother sings to the marvellous stove
and the child draws another inscrutable house.

First Death in Nova Scotia

In the cold, cold parlor
my mother laid out Arthur
beneath the chromographs:
Edward, Prince of Wales,
with Princess Alexandra,
and King George with Queen Mary.
Below them on the table
stood a stuffed loon
shot and stuffed by Uncle
Arthur, Arthur's father.

Since Uncle Arthur fired
a bullet into him,
he hadn't said a word.
He kept his own counsel
on his white, frozen lake,
the marble-topped table.
His breast was deep and white,
cold and caressable;
his eyes were red glass,
much to be desired.

"Come," said my mother,
"Come and say good-bye
to your little cousin Arthur."
I was lifted up and given
one lily of the valley
to put in Arthur's hand.
Arthur's coffin was
a little frosted cake,
and the red-eyed loon eyed it
from his white, frozen lake.

Arthur was very small.
He was all white, like a doll
that hadn't been painted yet.
Jack Frost had started to paint him
the way he always painted
the Maple Leaf (Forever).
He had just begun on his hair,
a few red strokes, and then
Jack Frost had dropped the brush
and left him white, forever.

The gracious royal couples
were warm in red and ermine;
their feet were well wrapped up
in the ladies' ermine trains.
They invited Arthur to be
the smallest page at court.
But how could Arthur go,
clutching his tiny lily,
with his eyes shut up so tight
and the roads deep in snow?

In the Waiting Room

In Worcester, Massachusetts,
I went with Aunt Consuelo
to keep her dentist's appointment
and sat and waited for her
in the dentist's waiting room.
It was winter. It got dark
early. The waiting room
was full of grown-up people,
arctics and overcoats,
lamps and magazines.

My aunt was inside
what seemed like a long time
and while I waited I read
the *National Geographic*
(I could read) and carefully
studied the photographs:
the inside of a volcano,
black, and full of ashes;
then it was spilling over
in rivulets of fire.
Osa and Martin Johnson
dressed in riding breeches,
laced boots, and pith helmets.
A dead man slung on a pole
—"Long Pig," the caption said.
Babies with pointed heads
wound round and round with string;
black, naked women with necks
wound round and round with wire
like the necks of light bulbs.
Their breasts were horrifying.
I read it right straight through.
I was too shy to stop.
And then I looked at the cover;
the yellow margins, the date.

Suddenly, from inside,
came an *oh!* of pain
—Aunt Consuelo's voice—
not very loud or long.
I wasn't at all surprised;
even then I knew she was
a foolish, timid woman.
I might have been embarrassed,
but wasn't. What took me
completely by surprise
was that it was *me*:
my voice, in my mouth.
Without thinking at all
I was my foolish aunt,
I—we—were falling, falling,
our eyes glued to the cover
of the *National Geographic*,
February, 1918.

I said to myself: three days
and you'll be seven years old.
I was saying it to stop
the sensation of falling off
the round, turning world
into cold, blue-black space.
But I felt: you are an *I*,
you are an *Elizabeth,*
you are one of *them.*
Why should you be one, too?
I scarcely dared to look
to see what it was I was.
I gave a sidelong glance
—I couldn't look any higher—
at shadowy gray knees,
trousers and skirts and boots
and different pairs of hands
lying under the lamps.
I knew that nothing stranger
had ever happened, that nothing
stranger could ever happen.
Why should I be my aunt,
or me, or anyone?
What similarities—
boots, hands, the family voice
I felt in my throat, or even
the *National Geographic*
and those awful hanging breasts—
held us all together
or made us all just one?
How—I didn't know any
word for it—how "unlikely" . . .
How had I come to be here,
like them, and overhear
a cry of pain that could have
got loud and worse but hadn't?

The waiting room was bright
and too hot. It was sliding
beneath a big black wave,
another, and another.
Then I was back in it.
The War was on. Outside,
in Worcester, Massachusetts,

were night and slush and cold,
and it was still the fifth
of February, 1918.

NOTES

Over 2000 Illustrations and a Complete Concordance. Experience of the world
presented first in terms of the encyclopedia illustrations the child pores over,
then as real travel. A "burin" (line 27) is the tool used by the engraver to etch
the plate.

ELIZABETH BISHOP

Books

North & South, 1946

*Poems: North & South—A Cold
Spring,* 1955

The Diary of Helena Morley
(translator), 1957

· *Questions of Travel,* 1965

The Complete Poems, 1969

*Anthology of Contemporary
Brazilian Poetry* (editor,
translator), 1972

Geography III, 1976

Criticism, Interviews

Ann Stevenson, *Elizabeth Bishop,* 1966; "An Interview with Elizabeth
Bishop," *Shenandoah* 17 (Winter 1966): 3–19; David Kalstone, *Five
Temperaments,* 1977; *World Literature Today,* special Elizabeth Bishop
issue (Winter 1977); "The Work! A Conversation with Elizabeth Bishop,"
Ploughshares 3 (1977); "Elizabeth Bishop: A Symposium," *FIELD,* No. 31
(Fall 1984); Harold Bloom, ed., *Elizabeth Bishop* (Modern Critical Views
Series), 1986.

Gwendolyn
Brooks
(b. 1917)

Raised on the Harvard Classics, and regularly exposed to the spoken word of poetry by a father who would recite to his family, Gwendolyn Brooks took up writing poetry and sending her poems out while still in her teens. Like Anne Sexton, she attended only junior college, and went about the serious business of reading and writing by way of joining occasional workshops and developing relationships with other writers informally. Her first collection, published by Harper's in 1945, won her considerable acclaim, and her second, *Annie Allen* (1949), brought her the first Pulitzer Prize awarded to a black poet. It is not hard to understand her rapid ascent, for her poems were (and have largely remained) readily accessible by way of their rhythms, rhymes, and large subjects—"I write about people and about circumstances that have been influenced by horrible happenings in our society," she has said. While focusing on black people's stories and struggles, she has always managed to keep her eye on all of humanity without sacrificing specificity, local detail, and diction.

Her short piece on Emmett Till shows her ability to move in swiftly on a huge story, Till's wretched murder, one of the most powerful *causes célèbres* of the Civil Rights movement of our time, and to select a fresh approach that bypasses any clichés. Not only is the text cut down from what might have been a long, narrative treatment (see its very title, "The Last Quatrain of the Ballad of Emmett Till"), but the focus is essentially on Till's mother—any mother?—who is boldly sketched in with a few, dissonant color strokes. The larger turbulence is etched in at the end, phrased in a sort of post-Dickinsonian manner ("Chaos in windy grays / through a red prairie"). Brooks has cited her admiration for Dickinson, as well as her indebtedness to other masters of rhyme and slant rhyme, notably Langston Hughes and Robert Frost. It is not hard to hear echoes of Emerson and Whitman as well.

From the beginning of her career, Gwendolyn Brooks has found ways to play with rhyme and structure in her own fashion, and not stray far from solid working habits. As Paul Berman has noted, "Both her work and her basic attitude to life and letters have remained remarkably constant." Stanza after stanza, poem after poem present her unique mix, with end rhymes relieved, in the most successful moments, by hard stops and starts, newly minted compounds, surprising reversals, and words repeated in as many combinations as possible, all the while preserving standard punctuation to protect the reader. In this combination of experiment and tradition, she is perhaps most like Robert Francis and Theodore Roethke of her own generation, but she shares solutions with the more modern masters of composed forms as well, like Charles Wright and Nancy Willard, who also do not eschew snapping off powerful rhymes as they keep strict beats going against surprising themes.

Known to be fundamentally optimistic and to be interested in both the "funny and serious" in equal measure, Brooks, in poems as widely separated as "A Sunset of the City" and "The Lovers of the Poor," can be as understanding and forgiving of others' shortcomings (of, say, "The Ladies from the Ladies' Betterment League") as she is of her own. This ability to see something of others in herself lets us trust her vision for us all, one which is firmly based on "kindness. That is my religion" (from an interview).

In one of her best-known poems, "The Bean Eaters," which seems so effortless and artless, one can perhaps most readily see how she transforms traditional form and catches us up in a much larger story, which the prose moment at the end establishes even as it returns to a light rhyme ("twinges"—"fringes"). It does so because it rushes us with the end of the couple's life together. Beans may be all they have to eat, and the room is not only rented, it's a "back room," *but* they have their mementos from the past that will keep some joy alive for them. A home has been lost, we surmise, but this old couple is not to be pitied. They will "keep putting on their clothes / And putting things away." The very list of items surrounding them as they eat—beads, receipts, dolls, cloths, tobacco crumbs, vases and fringes—is enough to sustain their memories, and enough to trace human habit when it comes to determination. The breaking away from "poetry" to prose suggests that both are necessary to preserve our lives.

Having served as poetry consultant to the Library of Congress (an opportunity she used to invite many hitherto unheralded poets to read in the nation's capital), as Poet Laureate of her own state of Illinois, where she has lived most of her life, and as visiting writer and speaker at many institutions, Gwendolyn Brooks has long been in the front rank of those artists who have made it possible for others to succeed.

SF

Notes from the Childhood and the Girlhood

the parents: people like our marriage
Maxie and Andrew

Clogged and soft and sloppy eyes
Have lost the light that bites or terrifies.

There are no swans and swallows any more.
The people settled for chicken and shut the door.

But one by one
They got things done:
Watch for porches as you pass
And prim low fencing pinching in the grass.

Pleasant custards sit behind
The white Venetian blind.

Sunday chicken

Chicken, she chided early, should not wait
Under the cranberries in after-sermon state.
Who had been beaking about the yard of late.

Elite among the speckle-gray, wild white
On blundering mosaic in the night.
Or lovely baffle-brown. It was not right.

You could not hate the cannibal they wrote
Of, with the nostril bone-thrust, who could dote
On boiled or roasted fellow thigh and throat.

Nor hate the handsome tiger, call him devil
To man-feast, manifesting Sunday evil.

old relative

After the baths and bowel-work, he was dead.
Pillows no longer mattered, and getting fed
And anything that anybody said.

Whatever was his he never more strictly had,
Lying in long hesitation. Good or bad,
Hypothesis, traditional and fad.

She went in there to muse on being rid
Of relative beneath the coffin lid.
No one was by. She stuck her tongue out; slid.

Since for a week she must not play "Charmaine"
Or "Honey Bunch," or "Singing in the Rain."

the ballad of late Annie

Late Annie in her bower lay,
Though sun was up and spinning.

The blush-brown shoulder was so bare,
Blush-brown lip was winning.

Out then shrieked the mother-dear,
"Be I to fetch and carry?
Get a broom to whish the doors
Or get a man to marry."

"Men there were and men there be
But never men so many
Chief enough to marry me,"
Thought the proud late Annie.

"Whom I raise my shades before
Must be gist and lacquer.
With melted opals for my milk,
Pearl-leaf for my cracker."

throwing out the flowers

The duck fats rot in the roasting pan,
And it's over and over and all,
The fine fraught smiles, and spites that began
Before it was over and all.

The Thanksgiving praying's away with the silk.
It's over and over and all.
The broccoli, yams and the bead-buttermilk
Are dead with the hail in the hall,
    All
Are dead with the hail in the hall.

The three yellow 'mums and the one white 'mum
Bear to such brusque burial
With pity for little encomium
Since it's over and over and all.

Forgotten and stinking they stick in the can.
And the vase breath's better and all, and all.
And so for the end of our life to a man,
Just over, just over and all.

"do not be afraid of no"

"Do not be afraid of no,
Who has so far so very far to go":

New caution to occur
To one whose inner scream set her to cede, for softer lapping and
     smooth fur!

Whose esoteric need
Was merely to avoid the nettle, to not-bleed.

Stupid, like a street
That beats into a dead end and dies there, with nothing left to
     reprimand or meet.

And like a candle fixed
Against dismay and countershine of mixed

Wild moon and sun. And like
A flying furniture, or bird with lattice wing; or gaunt thing, a-stammer
     down a nightmare neon peopled with condor, hawk and shrike.

To say yes is to die
A lot or a little. The dead wear capably their wry

Enameled emblems. They smell.
But that and that they do not altogether yell is all that we know well.

It is brave to be involved,
To be not fearful to be unresolved.

Her new wish was to smile
When answers took no airships, walked a while.

        "pygmies are pygmies still, though percht on Alps"
                                         —Edward Young

But can see better there, and laughing there
Pity the giants wallowing on the plain.
Giants who bleat and chafe in their small grass,
Seldom to spread the palm; to spit; come clean.

Pygmies expand in cold impossible air,
Cry fie on giantshine, poor glory which
Pounds breast-bone punily, screeches, and has
Reached no Alps: or, knows no Alps to reach.

The Bean Eaters

They eat beans mostly, this old yellow pair.
Dinner is a casual affair.
Plain chipware on a plain and creaking wood,
Tin flatware.

Two who are Mostly Good.
Two who have lived their day,
But keep on putting on their clothes
And putting things away.

And remembering . . .
Remembering, with twinklings and twinges,
As they lean over the beans in their rented back room that
  is full of beads and receipts and dolls and cloths,
  tobacco crumbs, vases and fringes.

The Last Quatrain of the Ballad of Emmett Till

after the murder,
after the burial

Emmett's mother is a pretty-faced thing;
  the tint of pulled taffy.
She sits in a red room,
  drinking black coffee.
She kisses her killed boy.
  And she is sorry.
Chaos in windy grays
  through a red prairie.

A Sunset of the City

Kathleen Eileen

Already I am no longer looked at with lechery or love.
My daughters and sons have put me away with marbles and dolls,
Are gone from the house.
My husband and lovers are pleasant or somewhat polite
And night is night.

It is a real chill out,
The genuine thing.
I am not deceived, I do not think it is still summer
Because sun stays and birds continue to sing.

It is summer-gone that I see, it is summer-gone.
The sweet flowers indrying and dying down,
The grasses forgetting their blaze and consenting to brown.

It is a real chill out. The fall crisp comes.
I am aware there is winter to heed.
There is no warm house
That is fitted with my need.

I am cold in this cold house this house
Whose washed echoes are tremulous down lost halls.
I am a woman, and dusty, standing among new affairs.
I am a woman who hurries through her prayers.

Tin intimations of a quiet core to be my
Desert and my dear relief
Come: there shall be such islanding from grief,
And small communion with the master shore.
Twang they. And I incline this ear to tin,
Consult a dual dilemma. Whether to dry
In humming pallor or to leap and die.

Somebody muffed it? Somebody wanted to joke.

The Lovers of the Poor

         arrive. The Ladies from the Ladies' Betterment
            League
Arrive in the afternoon, the late light slanting
In diluted gold bars across the boulevard brag
Of proud, seamed faces with mercy and murder hinting
Here, there, interrupting, all deep and debonair,
The pink paint on the innocence of fear;
Walk in a gingerly manner up the hall.
Cutting with knives served by their softest care,
Served by their love, so barbarously fair.
Whose mothers taught: You'd better not be cruel!
You had better not throw stones upon the wrens!
Herein they kiss and coddle and assault
Anew and dearly in the innocence
With which they baffle nature. Who are full,
Sleek, tender-clad, fit, fiftyish, a-glow, all
Sweetly abortive, hinting at fat fruit,
Judge it high time that fiftyish fingers felt
Beneath the lovelier planes of enterprise.
To resurrect. To moisten with milky chill.
To be a random hitching-post or plush.
To be, for wet eyes, random and handy hem.

          Their guild is giving money to the poor.
The worthy poor. The very very worthy
And beautiful poor. Perhaps just not too swarthy?
Perhaps just not too dirty nor too dim
Nor—passionate. In truth, what they could wish
Is—something less than derelict or dull.
Not staunch enough to stab, though, gaze for gaze!
God shield them sharply from the beggar-bold!
The noxious needy ones whose battle's bald
Nonetheless for being voiceless, hits one down.
          But it's all so bad! and entirely too much for
             them.
The stench; the urine, cabbage, and dead beans,
Dead porridges of assorted dusty grains,
The old smoke, *heavy* diapers, and, they're told,
Something called chitterlings. The darkness. Drawn
Darkness, or dirty light. The soil that stirs.
The soil that looks the soil of centuries.
And for that matter the *general* oldness. Old
Wood. Old marble. Old tile. Old old old.
Not homekind Oldness! Not Lake Forest, Glencoe.
Nothing is sturdy, nothing is majestic,
There is no quiet drama, no rubbed glaze, no
Unkillable infirmity of such
A tasteful turn as lately they have left,
Glencoe, Lake Forest, and to which their cars
Must presently restore them. When they're done
With dullards and distortions of this fistic
Patience of the poor and put-upon.
          They've never seen such a make-do-ness as
Newspaper rugs before! In this, this "flat,"
Their hostess is gathering up the oozed, the rich
Rugs of the morning (tattered! the bespattered. . . .)
Readies to spread clean rugs for afternoon.
Here is a scene for you. The Ladies look,
In horror, behind a substantial citizeness
Whose trains clank out across her swollen heart.
Who, arms akimbo, almost fills a door.
All tumbling children, quilts dragged to the floor
And tortured thereover, potato peelings, soft-
Eyed kitten, hunched-up, haggard, to-be-hurt.
          Their League is allotting largesse to the Lost.
But to put their clean, their pretty money, to put
Their money collected from delicate rose-fingers
Tipped with their hundred flawless rose-nails seems . . .

        They own Spode, Lowestoft, candelabra,
Mantels, and hostess gowns, and sunburst clocks,
Turtle soup, Chippendale, red satin "hangings,"
Aubussons and Hattie Carnegie. They Winter
In Palm Beach; cross the Water in June; attend,
When suitable, the nice Art Institute;
Buy the right books in the best bindings; saunter
On Michigan, Easter mornings, in sun or wind.
Oh Squalor! This sick four-story hulk, this fibre
With fissures everywhere! Why, what are bringings
Of loathe-love largesse? What shall peril hungers
So old old, what shall flatter the desolate?
Tin can, blocked fire escape and chitterling
And swaggering seeking youth and the puzzled wreckage
Of the middle passage, and urine and stale shames
And, again, the porridges of the underslung
And children children children. Heavens! That
Was a rat, surely, off there, in the shadows? Long
And long-tailed? Gray? The Ladies from the Ladies'
Betterment League agree it will be better
To achieve the outer air that rights and steadies,
To hie to a house that does not holler, to ring
Bells elsetime, better presently to cater
To no more Possibilities, to get
Away. Perhaps the money can be posted.
Perhaps they two may choose another Slum!
Some serious sooty half-unhappy home!—
Where loathe-love likelier may be invested.
        Keeping their scented bodies in the center
Of the hall as they walk down the hysterical hall,
They allow their lovely skirts to graze no wall,
Are off at what they manage of a canter,
And, resuming all the clues of what they were,
Try to avoid inhaling the laden air.

GWENDOLYN BROOKS

Books

A Street in Bronzeville, 1945

Annie Allen, 1949

Maud Martha, 1953

Bronzeville Boys and Girls, 1956

The Bean Eaters, 1960

Selected Poems, 1963

In the Mecca: Poems, 1968

Riot, 1969

Family Pictures, 1970

Aloneness, 1971

The World of Gwendolyn Brooks, 1971

Report From Part One, 1972

The Tiger Who Wore White Gloves, 1974

Beckonings, 1975

Criticism, Interviews

Arthur P. Davis, "Gwendolyn Brooks: Poet of the Unheroic," *College Language Association Journal* (July 1963); George Stavos, "An Interview with Gwendolyn Brooks," *Contemporary Literature* (November 1970); Charles Israel, "Gwendolyn Brooks," *Dictionary of Literary Biography* (1980); Eugene Kraft, "An Interview with Gweldolyn Brooks," *Cottonwood Review* 38–39 (1986); D. H. Melhem, *Gwendolyn Brooks: Poetry and the Heroic Voice,* 1987.

Robert Francis (1901–1987)

Stephen Friebert

It is a troublesome fact that Robert Francis, one of our best poets, is still so little known. His modest and retiring life near Amherst, Massachusetts, may partly explain his obscurity, along with a relatively slow development—his best poems were written after he turned fifty—and a number of years spent in the shadow of his friend and mentor, Robert Frost. Then, too, it must be noted that Francis's poems are modest in scale and scope, and that in a time when it has been fashionable for poets to stress angst and anguish, their own and that of others, Francis has made a serious exploration of pleasure and delight. He was, as he said in his autobiography, *The Trouble with Francis* (1971), a deeply pessimistic man, but his poems, while they occasionally reflect that outlook, mostly search out the properties of the natural world and of language that can act to offset or qualify the pessimism.

The short, precise, exquisitely balanced poems that Francis wrote find the same properties to celebrate in nature and language: effects of doubling, rhyming, compounding, punning, and echoing. The flow of experience reveals curious and chancy links between objects and among words, and the poet catches them on the wing. Francis does not so much create metaphors and forge likenesses as he does find them, discover them, in natural things—toads, cypresses, waxwings, weather—and in words that rhyme, pun, wed in compounds, or reveal sudden family resemblances based on etymology, consonance, or similarity of meaning. For years cypresses have been "teaching birds / In little schools, by little skills, / How to be shadows." The shading of "schools" into "skills" is partly an effect of rhyming and punning, partly an observation of the world. Similarly, the two riders in "Boy Riding Forward Backward" are like "Swallows that weave and wave and sweep / And skim and swoop and skitter until / The last trees take them." This is a celebration both of the way swallows behave and of the language's capacity for verbs. When good likenesses appear between the words themselves and the things they name or imitate, a special pleasure is created from simultaneous matching in nature and language, the two realities of world and word. "Bluejay" provides a fine example when the bird and the beloved father's unlikely affection for it allow the off-rhyme of "feather" and "father" to bring the poem to its perfect close. Other poems may revel directly in the delights of language—"Hogwash" and "Yes, What?"—or in the felicities of the natural world—"Cold" and "Blue Winter"—but the combination of language as pleasure and nature as beauty, and their delicate interaction, is usually at the heart of a Francis poem. "Silent Poem," a daring series of compound nouns, is a distillation of these interests, a one-of-a-kind poem that only a poet as devoted to language and nature as Francis could possibly have written.

The twin subjects of language and nature both have their human dimension, of course, and Francis can marvel at human virtuosity, as in "Boy Riding Forward Backward" and "Apple Peeler," and delineate human folly, as he does quite variously in "Like Ghosts of Eagles" and "December." Nevertheless, his strongest affirmations of human skill are those implicit in the craft and economy of his poems. Whether their order is of a traditional sort, an apparently effortless use of rhyme and meter, or innovative, Francis's poems are always distinguished by formal excellence, an unusual grace, and shapeliness. One senses that they are the products of a great patience and perfectionism, a willingness to work and wait until things come just right. The result is a poem that holds its interest longer than most.

Robert Francis's life, as described in the disarming autobiography cited above, reflected the patience and economy of the poems. He lived in near-solitude most of his life, on a minuscule income, learning how to make do with little and live off the land, transferring the lessons of simplicity and independence into adroit, tough-minded lyric poems and into lucid prose (besides *The Trouble with Francis,* there is a book of prose "potshots," *The Satirical Rogue on Poetry,* and a memoir, *Frost: A Time to Talk*). The grace and uncanny precision of his poems suggests comparisons with other poets—Herrick, Hardy, Emily Dickinson—but what is finally most notable about Robert Francis is his uniqueness, the distinctive mind and temper that inform each poem.

DY

Sheep

From where I stand the sheep stand still
As stones against the stony hill.

The stones are gray
And so are they.

And both are weatherworn and round,
Leading the eye back to the ground.

Two mingled flocks—
The sheep, the rocks.

And still no sheep stirs from its place
Or lifts its Babylonian face.

Blue Winter

Winter uses all the blues there are.
One shade of blue for water, one for ice,
Another blue for shadows over snow.
The clear or cloudy sky uses blue twice—
Both different blues. And hills row after row
Are colored blue according to how far.
You know the bluejay's double-blue device
Shows best when there are no green leaves to show.
And Sirius is a winterbluegreen star.

Boy Riding Forward Backward

Presto, pronto! Two boys, two horses.
But the boy on backward riding forward
Is the boy to watch.

He rides the forward horse and laughs
In the face of the forward boy on the backward
Horse, and *he* laughs

Back and the horses laugh. They gallop.
The trick is the cool barefaced pretense
There is no trick.

They might be flying, face to face,
On a fast train. They might be whitecaps
Hot-cool-headed,

One curling backward, one curving forward,
Racing a rivalry of waves.
They might, they might—

Across a blue of lake, through trees,
And half a mile away I caught them:
Two boys, two horses.

Through trees and through binoculars
Sweeping for birds. Oh, they were birds
All right, all right,

Swallows that weave and wave and sweep
And skim and swoop and skitter until
The last trees take them.

Waxwings

Four Tao philosophers as cedar waxwings
chat on a February berrybush
in sun, and I am one.

Such merriment and such sobriety—
the small wild fruit on the tall stalk—
was this not always my true style?

Above an elegance of snow, beneath
a silk-blue sky a brotherhood of four
birds. Can you mistake us?

To sun, to feast, and to converse
and all together—for this I have abandoned
all my other lives.

Apple Peeler

Why the unbroken spiral, Virtuoso,
Like a trick sonnet in one long, versatile sentence?

Is it a pastime merely, this perfection,
For an old man, sharp knife, long night, long winter?

Or do your careful fingers move at the stir
Of unadmitted immemorial magic?

Solitaire. The ticking clock. The apple
Turning, turning as the round earth turns.

Bluejay

So bandit-eyed, so undovelike a bird
to be my pastoral father's favorite—
skulker and blusterer
whose every arrival is a raid.

Love made the bird no gentler
nor him who loved less gentle.
Still, still the wild blue feather
brings my mild father.

Cold

Cold and the colors of cold: mineral, shell,
And burning blue. The sky is on fire with blue
And wind keeps ringing, ringing the fire bell.

I am caught up into a chill as high
As creaking glaciers and powder-plumed peaks
And the absolutes of interstellar sky.

Abstract, impersonal, metaphysical, pure,
This dazzling art derides me. How should warm breath
Dare to exist—exist, exult, endure?

Hums in my ear the old Ur-father of freeze
And burn, that pre-post-Christian Fellow before
And after all myths and demonologies.

Under the glaring and sardonic sun,
Behind the icicles and double glass
I huddle, hoard, hold out, hold on, hold on.

Cypresses

At noon they talk of evening and at evening
Of night, but what they say at night
Is a dark secret.

Somebody long ago called them the Trees
Of Death and they have never forgotten.
The name enchants them.

Always an attitude of solitude
To point the paradox of standing
Alone together.

How many years they have been teaching birds
In little schools, by little skills,
How to be shadows.

Hogwash

The tongue that mothered such a metaphor
Only the purest purist could despair of.

Nobody ever called swill sweet but isn't
Hogwash a daisy in a field of daisies?

What beside sports and flowers could you find
To praise better than the American language?

Bruised by American foreign policy
What shall I soothe me, what defend me with

But a handful of clean unmistakable words—
Daisies, daisies, in a field of daisies?

Like Ghosts of Eagles

The Indians have mostly gone
but not before they named the rivers
the rivers flow on
and the names of the rivers flow with them
    Susquehanna   Shenandoah

The rivers are now polluted plundered
but not the names of the rivers
cool and inviolate as ever
pure as on the morning of creation
    Tennessee   Tombigbee

If the rivers themselves should ever perish
I think the names will somehow somewhere hover
like ghosts of eagles
those mighty whisperers
    Missouri   Mississippi.

Silent Poem

backroad   leafmold   stonewall   chipmunk
underbrush   grapevine   woodchuck   shadblow

woodsmoke   cowbarn   honeysuckle   woodpile
sawhorse   bucksaw   outhouse   wellsweep

backdoor   flagstone   bulkhead   buttermilk
candlestick   ragrug   firedog   brownbread

hilltop   outcrop   cowbell   buttercup
whetstone   thunderstorm   pitchfork   steeplebush

gristmill   millstone   cornmeal   waterwheel
watercress   buckwheat   firefly   jewelweed

gravestone   groundpine   windbreak   bedrock
weathercock   snowfall   starlight   cockcrow

December

Dim afternoon December afternoon
Just before dark, their caps
A Christmas or un-Christmas red
The hunters.

Oh, I tell myself that death
In the woods is far far better
Than doom in the slaughterhouse.
Still, the hunters haunt me.

Does a deer die now or does a hunter
Dim afternoon December afternoon
By cold intent or accident but always
My death?

Yes, What?

What would earth do without her blessed boobs
her blooming bumpkins garden variety
her oafs   her louts   her yodeling yokels
and all her Breughel characters
under the fat-faced moon?

Her nitwits   numskulls   universal
nincompoops   jawohl   jawohl   with all
their yawps   burps   beers   guffaws
her goofs   her goons   her big galoots
under the red-face moon?

ROBERT FRANCIS

Books

Stand With Me Here, 1936
Valhalla and Other Poems, 1938
The Sound I Listened For, 1944
We Fly Away (novel), 1948
The Face Against the Glass, 1950
The Orb Weaver, 1960
Come Out Into the Sun, 1965
The Satirical Rogue on Poetry
   (criticism), 1968

The Trouble with Francis
   (autobiography), 1971
Frost: A Time to Talk (memoir),
   1972
Like Ghosts of Eagles, 1974
Collected Poems, 1936–1976, 1976
Pot Shots at Poetry (prose), 1980

Criticism

John Holmes, "Constants Carried Forward," *Massachusetts Review* (Summer 1961); David Young, "Out of the Shadow," *New Republic* (7 August 1971); Donald Hall, "Two Poets Named Robert," *Ohio Review* (Fall 1977); Symposium in Honor of Robert Francis's 80th Birthday, *FIELD*, No. 25 (Fall 1981).

Robert
Hayden
(1913–1980)

© 1981 by Jill Krementz

U ntil 1966, when the *Selected Poems* appeared, Robert Hayden was little known. That seems surprising as we look back at his life's work, which started taking shape in the 1930s. Even the earliest full collection, *Heart-Shape in the Dust* (1940), is much more than an imitation of Auden, or apprenticeship poetry, as some have called it. In the long period that followed until his second volume was published in 1955, Hayden kept working away quietly while teaching at Fisk, until the critics and the public began to pay some attention to him. He has suffered the usual put-down of being considered merely a spokesman for black issues and causes, with a condescending glance at his artistic merits: "the surest poetic talent of any Negro poet in America," as one magazine put it. While there has been little criticism to date that takes the poetry seriously as poetry, he is no longer emerging, and it is clear that his reputation will continue to grow.

Hayden's poems deal with many compelling historical struggles—the Baha'i faith, slavery, Malcolm X, Kennedy, and King—and seem to be seeking a *Dauer im Wechsel,* or permanence in change, as Goethe put it. Many readers will be attracted to the "romantic realist" spirit that Hayden himself felt infused the poems. Ultimately, however, Hayden's stature and power as a poet flow mainly from his uncanny ways of telling stories, both real and imagined. He is as accomplished a modern balladeer of our cities and streets as Philip Levine, with whom Hayden shares Detroit as home ground. It is this fascination with stories, which Hayden tells with rough-cut abandon, that we rise to. And how his characters talk! We don't mind if people don't really talk like that; we want them to from now on. Aunt Jemima—one of his great women characters—leaps off the pancake box (or better, in Hayden's vision, out of the freak show *he* finds her in) and onto the sand beside us, suggesting, cajoling, whispering a smarter way to live. Hayden's mystery people emerge in their true landscapes where we meet them and are startled out of our clichés.

Michael Harper tells of Hayden's calling him up again and again, worried about just the right word or phrasing, still fiddling with poems that had long since been published and honored. Such revising impulses let us sense the tremendous pressure the poems have been under, as he "molded and resolved with confidence and precision," in Gwendolyn Brooks's words (*Negro Digest*). Another important aspect of the care and skill he brought to each word, rethinking many poems till the day he died, is the exhaustive research he invested in his subjects. "Night, Death, Mississippi," "Runagate Runagate," and the gutsy tribute to Bessie Smith, "Homage to the Empress of the Blues," are not only contemporary ballads that range the imagination and the memory as they track the human experience of slavery and subjugation, they are historical documents as well, laying bare the facts of those survival stories. It is no wonder that Hayden won the prestigious World Festival of the Arts Prize and the Russell Loines Award and was *twice* named consultant to the Library of Congress. He was a *recording* artist of the facts and fantasies he felt we must not lose sight of, and drove himself to keep us fixed on our rights as well as our responsibilities. But what is especially moving is how he could restrain all the learning, all the political and religious fervor he unleashed on most subjects, to preserve the most delicate touch for the hardest of stories to tell: "Those Winter

Sundays" takes us to the heart of the love struggle with our parents, and ultimately ourselves. The first stanza is paid out carefully, as if counting out bills on a counter, the alliterative rhythms that would otherwise jump out discordantly smacking into place. The second stanza, reaching back in a nineteenth-century reverie for the memory of the sleeping child waking to see his father up early even on Sunday, making a fire, tightens in the last line on the unexpected adjective: "fearing the chronic angers of that house." Then the marvelous move in the final stanza to an exalted, almost self-consciously poetic turn that casts the real spell: the child-adult lolling at first, "What did I know, what did I know," as if dreaming of guilt and innocence, before seeing ahead to "love's austere and lonely offices." "Offices," with its brace of adjectives, carries us sadly away.

SF

" 'Mystery Boy' Looks for Kin in Nashville"

Puzzle faces in the dying elms
promise him treats if he will stay.
Sometimes they hiss and spit at him
like varmints caught
in a thicket of butterflies.

A black doll,
one disremembered time,
came floating down to him
through mimosa's fancywork leaves and blooms
to be his hidden bride.

From the road beyond the creepered walls
they call to him now and then,
and he'll take off in spite of the angry trees,
hearing like the loudening of his heart
the name he never can he never can repeat.

And when he gets to where the voices were—
Don't cry, his dollbaby wife implores;
I know where they are, don't cry.
We'll go and find them, we'll go
and ask them for your name again.

Aunt Jemima of the Ocean Waves

I

Enacting someone's notion of themselves
(and me), The One And Only Aunt Jemima
and Kokimo The Dixie Dancing Fool
do a bally for the freak show.

I watch a moment, then move on,
pondering the logic that makes of them
(and me) confederates
of The Spider Girl, The Snake-skinned Man . . .

Poor devils have to live somehow.

I cross the boardwalk to the beach,
lie in the sand and gaze beyond
the clutter at the sea.

II

Trouble you for a light?
I turn as Aunt Jemima settles down
beside me, her blue-rinsed hair
without the red bandanna now.

I hold the lighter to her cigarette.
Much obliged. Unmindful (perhaps)
of my embarrassment, she looks
at me and smiles. You sure

do favor a friend I used to have.
Guess that's why I bothered you
for a light. So much like him that I—
She pauses, watching white horses rush

to the shore. Way them big old waves
come slamming whopping in,
sometimes it's like they mean to smash
this no-good world to hell.

Well it could happen. A book I read—
Crossed that very ocean years ago.
London, Paris, Rome,
Constantinople too—I've seen them all.

Back when they billed me everywhere
as the Sepia High Stepper,
Crowned heads applauded me.
Years before your time. Years and years.

I wore me plenty diamonds then,
and counts or dukes or whatever they were
would fill my dressing room
with the costliest flowers. But of course

there was this one you resemble so.
Get me? The sweetest gentleman.
Dead before his time. Killed in the war
to save the world for another war.

High-stepping days for me
were over after that. Still I'm not one
to let grief idle me for long.
I went out with a mental act—

mind-reading—Mysteria From
The Mystic East—veils and beads
and telling suckers how to get
stolen rings and sweethearts back.

One night he was standing by my bed,
seen him plain as I see you,
and warned me without a single word:
Baby, quit playing with spiritual stuff.

So here I am, so here I am,
fake mammy to God's mistakes.
And that's the beauty part,
I mean, ain't that the beauty part.

She laughs, but I do not, knowing what
her laughter shields. And mocks.
I light another cigarette for her.
She smokes, not saying any more.

Scream of children in the surf,
adagios of sun and flashing foam,
the sexual glitter, oppressive fun. . . .
An antique etching comes to mind:

"The Sable Venus" naked on
a baroque Cellini shell—voluptuous
imago floating in the wake
of slave-ships on fantastic seas.

Jemima sighs, Reckon I'd best
be getting back. I help her up.
Don't you take no wooden nickels, hear?
Tin dimes neither. So long, pal.

Night, Death, Mississippi

I

A quavering cry. Screech-owl?
Or one of them?
The old man in his reek
and gauntness laughs—

One of them, I bet—
and turns out the kitchen lamp,
limping to the porch to listen
in the windowless night.

Be there with Boy and the rest
if I was well again.
Time was. Time was.
White robes like moonlight

In the sweetgum dark.
Unbucked that one then
and him squealing bloody Jesus
as we cut it off.

Time was. A cry?
A cry all right.
He hawks and spits,
fevered as by groinfire.

Have us a bottle,
Boy and me—
he's earned him a bottle—
when he gets home.

       II

Then we beat them, he said,
beat them till our arms was tired
and the big old chains
messy and red.

O Jesus burning on the lily cross

Christ, it was better
than hunting bear
which don't know why
you want him dead.

O night, rawhead and bloodybones night

You kids fetch Paw
some water now so's he
can wash that blood
off him, she said.

O night betrayed by darkness not its own

Homage to the Empress of the Blues

Because there was a man somewhere in a candystripe silk shirt,
gracile and dangerous as a jaguar and because a woman moaned
for him in sixty-watt gloom and mourned him Faithless Love
Twotiming Love Oh Love Oh Careless Aggravating Love,

    She came out on the stage in yards of pearls, emerging like
    a favorite scenic view, flashed her golden smile and sang.

Because grey laths began somewhere to show from underneath
torn hurdygurdy lithographs of dollfaced heaven;
and because there were those who feared alarming fists of snow
on the door and those who feared the riot-squad of statistics,

> She came out on the stage in ostrich feathers, beaded satin,
> and shone that smile on us and sang.

Those Winter Sundays

Sundays too my father got up early
and put his clothes on in the blueblack cold,
then with cracked hands that ached
from labor in the weekday weather made
banked fires blaze. No one ever thanked him.

I'd wake and hear the cold splintering, breaking.
When the rooms were warm, he'd call,
and slowly I would rise and dress,
fearing the chronic angers of that house,

Speaking indifferently to him,
who had driven out the cold
and polished my good shoes as well.
What did I know, what did I know
of love's austere and lonely offices?

Runagate Runagate

I

Runs falls rises stumbles on from darkness into darkness
and the darkness thicketed with shapes of terror
and the hunters pursuing and the hounds pursuing
and the night cold and the night long and the river
to cross and the jack-muh-lanterns beckoning beckoning
and blackness ahead and when shall I reach that somewhere
morning and keep on going and never turn back and keep on going

> Runagate
> > Runagate
> > > Runagate

Many thousands rise and go
many thousands crossing over

> > > O mythic North
> > > O star-shaped yonder Bible city

Some go weeping and some rejoicing
some in coffins and some in carriages
some in silks and some in shackles

       Rise and go or fare you well

No more auction block for me
no more driver's lash for me

     If you see my Pompey, 30 yrs of age,
     new breeches, plain stockings, negro shoes;
     if you see my Anna, likely young mulatto
     branded E on the right cheek, R on the left,
     catch them if you can and notify subscriber.
     Catch them if you can, but it won't be easy.
     They'll dart underground when you try to catch them,
     plunge into quicksand, whirlpools, mazes,
     turn into scorpions when you try to catch them.

And before I'll be a slave
I'll be buried in my grave

     North star and bonanza gold
     I'm bound for the freedom, freedom-bound
     and oh Susyanna don't you cry for me

          Runagate

          Runagate

    II

Rises from their anguish and their power,

          Harriet Tubman.

     woman of earth, whipscarred,
     a summoning, a shining

     Mean to be free

And this was the way of it, brethren brethren,
way we journeyed from Can't to Can.
Moon so bright and no place to hide,
the cry up and the patterollers riding,
hound dogs belling in bladed air,
And fear starts a-murbling, Never make it,
we'll never make it. *Hush that now,*
and she's turned upon us, levelled pistol
glinting in the moonlight:
Dead folks can't jaybird-talk, she says;
you keep on going now or die, she says.

Wanted   Harriet Tubman   alias The General
alias Moses   Stealer of Slaves

In league with Garrison   Alcott   Emerson
Garrett   Douglass   Thoreau   John Brown

Armed and known to be Dangerous

Wanted   Reward   Dead or Alive

      Tell me, Ezekiel, oh tell me do you see
      mailed Jehovah coming to deliver me?

Hoot-owl calling in the ghosted air,
five times calling to the hants in the air.
Shadow of a face in the scary leaves,
shadow of a voice in the talking leaves:

      Come ride-a my train

      Oh that train, ghost-story train
      through swamp and savanna movering movering,
      over trestles of dew, through caves of the wish,
      Midnight Special on a sabre track movering movering,
      first stop Mercy and the last Hallelujah.

      Come ride-a my train

        Mean mean mean to be free.

NOTES

" '*Mystery Boy' Looks for Kin in Nashville.*" It's said that the poem is based on an account Hayden came across in a newspaper of a young girl (!) who escaped from a sanitarium.

Aunt Jemima of the Ocean Waves. Aunt Jemima is the person who appears on the packages of the Aunt Jemima pancake products.

Homage to the Empress of the Blues. This poem celebrates the great blues singer Bessie Smith.

Runagate Runagate. A runagate is an archaic word for a fugitive or runaway (slave). Harriet Tubman, herself an escaped slave, returned from freedom to help many blacks escape. Garrison was a leader of the abolition movement. Alcott was a U.S. transcendentalist philosopher and reformer. Douglass was the U.S. black leader and orator who fought against slavery.

ROBERT HAYDEN

Books

Heart-Shape in the Dust, 1940

Figure of Time, 1955

Selected Poems, 1966

Words in the Mourning Time, 1970

Angle of Ascent, 1975

American Journal, 1982

Collected Poems (edited by Frederick Glaysher), 1985

Interviews, Criticism

How I Write / 1, 1972; J. O'Brien, ed., *Interviews with Black Writers*, 1973; R. Layman, ed., *Conversations with Black Writers*, 1, 1977; Robert Stepto, "After Modernism, After Hibernation," in *Chant of Saints*, 1979; Fred M. Fertow, *Robert Hayden*, 1984; Pontheolla T. Williams, *Robert Hayden: A Critical Analysis of His Poetry*, 1987; Harold Bloom, ed., *American Poetry: 1946–1965*, 1987.

Randall Jarrell
(1914–1965)

Greensboro Daily News

R andall Jarrell, a poet of great force and originality, stands apart in many ways from the rest of his generation. Technical brilliance and allusive density did not tempt him as they did others. From poets who had explored the power of plainness and directness—Whitman, Frost, Rilke, Williams—he drew the inspiration for his own relatively unadorned style, a powerful instrument that speaks candidly to issues at the center of everyday lives. How ordinary people live and how they cope with their terror, need, and ignorance are things Jarrell writes about in a way that few poets have equaled.

A southerner by birth (Nashville, Tennessee), Jarrell spent some childhood years in Hollywood (as lovingly recorded in the "Lost World" poems of his last book), majored in psychology at Vanderbilt, taught briefly at Kenyon (where John Crowe Ransom was a senior teacher and Robert Lowell an undergraduate), served in the Air Force during World War II, and taught for many years at a small women's college (Greensboro) in North Carolina. He was, by all reports, a gifted teacher.

As a writer, Jarrell was something of a double personality. The reviewer and critic was notorious for wit, sophistication, and self-confidence. The poet, in contrast, could seem self-effacing, almost clumsy. In fact, the way in which Jarrell banished his brilliant and urbane side from his poems protected him from clever modishness, allowing him to explore the world with a sense of freshness and wonder. His willingness to be childlike, even to center his poetry on the experiences of childhood, gives him interesting links with Elizabeth Bishop and Theodore Roethke and helps explain his additional success as a writer of children's books.

Hindsight shows us that Jarrell was the poet of his generation who came most fully to terms with the Second World War. Most of the poetry that war produced is no longer read or studied, but Jarrell's war poems continue to exert their power. One secret of their success may lie in the poet's willingness to let the speechless war dead—the soldiers and the concentration camp victims—speak through him. This creates a rhetorical advantage, since it keeps the poems understated and does not put the poet in the position of claiming that he understands the war or can comment on it from a position of easy self-righteousness. The power of poems like "Losses," "The Death of the Ball Turret Gunner" and "Protocols" seems to stem partly from that fact and partly from the poet's uncanny ability—what Keats, in praising Shakespeare, called "negative capability"—to put himself into the lives and imaginations of others, an ability Jarrell also reveals in such later masterpieces as "Seele im Raum."

After the war, almost as though his negative capability had made him want to know the enemy that others would hate and dismiss, Jarrell developed a passionate interest in German culture and civilization; the world of his poems is peopled with culture heroes like Freud, the brothers Grimm, Rilke, Dürer, Richard Strauss, and Goethe. This interest, which contributed so much to his best poetry, is centered on the rich imaginative world of the German fairy tales. As metaphors for the human condition, as vehicles of psychological insight—both Freud and Jung are immensely relevant here—these tales became the foundation for a number of Jarrell's most searching and mysterious poems, as exemplified in the present selection by "Cinderella," "A Hunt in the Black Forest," and "The House in the Wood."

Not long after the publication of his finest volume (*The Lost World*, 1965), Randall Jarrell was struck by a car while walking at night. Some have called the death a suicide, others an accident. In any case, it was an untimely loss of a poet who had accomplished much and was still growing.

Jarrell's *Complete Poems* is available in paperback. Also of note are his novel, *Pictures from an Institution* (1954), and his three books of essays: *Poetry and the Age* (1954, reprinted 1980), *A Sad Heart at the Supermarket* (1962), and *The Third Book of Criticism* (1969). His children's books include *The Bat Poet* and *The Animal Family*. Jarrell can be doctrinaire in his Freudianism and repetitive in his deliberate plainness, but his best poems are challenging in their range and unforgettable in their compassionate humanity, and his honesty and imaginative depth continue to win him new readers.

DY

Losses

It was not dying: everybody died.
It was not dying: we had died before
In the routine crashes—and our fields
Called up the papers, wrote home to our folks,
And the rates rose, all because of us.
We died on the wrong page of the almanac,
Scattered on mountains fifty miles away;
Diving on haystacks, fighting with a friend,
We blazed up on the lines we never saw.
We died like aunts or pets or foreigners.
(When we left high school nothing else had died
For us to figure we had died like.)

In our new planes, with our new crews, we bombed
The ranges by the desert or the shore,
Fired at towed targets, waited for our scores—
And turned into replacements and woke up
One morning, over England, operational.
It wasn't different: but if we died
It was not an accident but a mistake
(But an easy one for anyone to make).
We read our mail and counted up our missions—
In bombers named for girls, we burned
The cities we had learned about in school—
Till our lives wore out; our bodies lay among
The people we had killed and never seen.
When we lasted long enough they gave us medals;
When we died they said, "Our casualties were low."

They said, "Here are the maps"; we burned the cities.

It was not dying—no, not ever dying;
But the night I died I dreamed that I was dead,
And the cities said to me: "Why are you dying?
We are satisfied, if you are; but why did I die?"

The Death of the Ball Turret Gunner

From my mother's sleep I fell into the State,
And I hunched in its belly till my wet fur froze,
Six miles from earth, loosed from its dream of life,
I woke to black flak and the nightmare fighters.
When I died they washed me out of the turret with a hose.

Protocols

(Birkenau, Odessa; the children speak alternately.)

We went there on the train. *They had big barges that they towed.*
We stood up, there were so many I was squashed.
There was a smoke-stack, then they made me wash.
It was a factory, I think. *My mother held me up*
And I could see the ship that made the smoke.

When I was tired my mother carried me.
She said, "Don't be afraid." But I was only tired.
Where we went there is no more Odessa.
They had water in a pipe—like rain, but hot;
The water there is deeper than the world

And I was tired and fell in in my sleep
And the water drank me. That is what I think.
And I said to my mother, "Now I'm washed and dried,"
My mother hugged me, and it smelled like hay
And that is how you die. And that is how you die.

Seele im Raum

It sat between my husband and my children.
A place was set for it—a plate of greens.
It had been there: I had seen it
But not somehow—but this was like a dream—
Not seen it so that I knew I saw it.
It was as if I could not know I saw it
Because I had never once in all my life
Not seen it. It was an eland.
An eland! *That* is why the children
Would ask my husband, for a joke, at Christmas:
"Father, is it Donner?" He would say, "No, Blitzen."
It had been there always. Now we put silver
At its place at meals, fed it the same food
We ourselves ate, and said nothing. Many times
When it breathed heavily (when it had tried
A long useless time to speak) and reached to me
So that I touched it—of a different size
And order of being, like the live hard side
Of a horse's neck when you pat the horse—
And looked with its great melting tearless eyes

Fringed with a few coarse wire-like lashes
Into my eyes, and whispered to me
So that my eyes turned backward in their sockets
And they said nothing—
                              many times
I have known, when they said nothing,
That it did not exist. If they had heard
They _could_ not have been silent. And yet they heard;
Heard many times what I have spoken
When it could no longer speak, but only breathe—
When I could no longer speak, but only breathe.

And, after some years, the others came
And took it from me—it was ill, they told me—
And cured it, they wrote me: my whole city
Sent me cards like lilac-branches, mourning
As I had mourned—
                      and I was standing
By a grave in flowers, by dyed rolls of turf,
And a canvas marquee the last brown of earth.

It is over.
It is over so long that I begin to think
That it did not exist, that I have never—
And my son says, one morning, from the paper:
"An eland. Look, an eland!"
                              —It was so.

Today, in a German dictionary. I saw _elend_
And the heart in my breast turned over, it was—

It was a word one translates _wretched_.

It is as if someone remembered saying:
"This is an antimacassar that I grew from seed,"
And this were true.
                      And, truly,
One could not wish for anything more strange—
For anything more. And yet it wasn't _interesting_ . . .
—It was worse than impossible, it was a joke.

And yet when it was, I _was_—
Even to think that I once thought
That I could see it is to feel the sweat
Like needles at my hair-roots, I am blind

—It was not even a joke, not even a joke.

Yet how can I believe it? Or believe that I
Owned it, a husband, children? Is my voice the voice
Of that skin of being—of what owns, is owned

In honor or dishonor, that is borne and bears—
Or of that raw thing, the being inside it
That has neither a wife, a husband, nor a child
But goes at last as naked from this world
As it was born into it—

And the eland comes and grazes on its grave.

                  This is senseless?
Shall I make sense or shall I tell the truth?
Choose either—I cannot do both.

I tell myself that. And yet it is not so,
And what I say afterwards will not be so:
To be at all is to be wrong.
                  Being is being old
And saying, almost comfortably, across a table
From—
         from what I don't know—
                   in a voice
Rich with a kind of longing satisfaction:
"To own an eland! That's what I call life!"

Cinderella

Her imaginary playmate was a grown-up
In sea-coal satin. The flame-blue glances,
The wings gauzy as the membrane that the ashes
Draw over an old ember—as the mother
In a jug of cider—were a comfort to her.
They sat by the fire and told each other stories.

"What men want. . . ." said the godmother softly—
How she went on it is hard for a man to say.
Their eyes, on their Father, were monumental marble.
Then they smiled like two old women, bussed each other,
Said, "Gossip, gossip"; and, lapped in each other's looks,
Mirror for mirror, drank a cup of tea.

Of cambric tea. But there is a reality
Under the good silk of the good sisters'
Good ball gowns. *She* knew. . . . Hard-breasted, naked-eyed,
She pushed her silk feet into glass, and rose within
A gown of imaginary gauze. The shy prince drank
A toast to her in champagne from her slipper

And breathed, "Bewitching!" Breathed, "I am bewitched!"
—She said to her godmother, "Men!"
And, later, looking down to see her flesh
Look back up from under lace, the ashy gauze
And pulsing marble of a bridal veil,
She wished it all a widow's coal-black weeds.

A sullen wife and a reluctant mother,
She sat all day in silence by the fire.
Better, later, to stare past her sons' sons,
Her daughters' daughters, and tell stories to the fire.
But best, dead, damned, to rock forever
Beside Hell's fireside—to see within the flames

The Heaven to whose gold-gauzed door there comes
A little dark old woman, the God's Mother,
And cries, "Come in, come in! My son's out now,
Out now, will be back soon, may be back never,
Who knows, eh? We know what they are—men, men!
But come, come in till then! Come in till then!"

A Hunt in the Black Forest

After the door shuts and the footsteps die,
He calls out: "Mother?"
The wind roars in the leaves: his cold hands, curled
Within his curled, cold body, his blurred head
Are warmed and tremble; and the red leaves flow
Like cells across the spectral, veined,
Whorled darkness of his vision.
                              The red dwarf
Whispers, "The leaves are turning"; and he reads
The dull, whorled notes, that tremble like a wish
Over the branched staves of the wood.

The stag is grazing in the wood.

A horn calls, over and over, its three notes.
The flat, gasped answer sounds and dies—
The geese call from a hidden sky.
The rain's sound grows into the roar
Of the flood below the falls; the rider calls

To the shape within the shades, a dwarf
Runs back into the brush. But smoke
Drifts to the gelding's nostrils, and he neighs.
From the wet starlight of the glade
A hut sends out its chink of fire.

The rider laughs out: in the branches, birds
Are troubled, stir.

He opens the door. A man looks up
And then slowly, with a kind of smile,
Acts out his own astonishment.
He points to his open mouth: the tongue
Is cut out. Bares shoulder, points
To the crown branded there, and smiles. The hunter frowns.
The pot bubbles from the embers in the laugh
The mute laughs. With harsh habitual
Impatience, the hunter questions him.
The man nods vacantly—
Shaken, he makes his gobbling sound
Over and over. The hunter ladles from the pot
Into a wooden bowl, the shining stew.
He eats silently. The mute
Counts spoonfuls on his fingers. Come to ten,
The last finger, he laughs out in joy
And scuttles like a mouse across the floor
To the door and the door's darkness. The king breathes hard,
Rises—and something catches at his heart,
Some patient senseless thing
Begins to squeeze his heart out in its hands.
His jerking body, bent into a bow,
Falls out of the hands onto the table,
Bends, bends further, till at last it breaks.
But, broken, it still breathes—a few whistling breaths
That slow, are intermittent, cease.

Now only the fire thinks, like a heart
Cut from its breast. Light leaps, the shadows fall
In the old alternation of the world . . .

Two sparks, at the dark horn of the window,
Look, as stars look, into the shadowy hut,
Turn slowly, searching:
Then a bubbled, gobbling sound begins,
The sound of the pot laughing on the fire.
—The pot, overturned among the ashes,
Is cold as death.

Something is scratching, panting. A little voice
Says, "Let *me*! Let *me*!" The mute
Puts his arms around the dwarf and raises him.

The pane is clouded with their soft slow breaths,
The mute's arms tire; but they gaze on and on,
Like children watching something wrong.
Their blurred faces, caught up in one wish,
Are blurred into one face: a child's set face.

The House in the Wood

At the back of the houses there is the wood.
While there is a leaf of summer left, the wood

Makes sounds I can put somewhere in my song,
Has paths I can walk, when I wake, to good

Or evil: to the cage, to the oxen, to the House
In the Wood. It is a part of life, or of the story

We make of life. But after the last leaf,
The last light—for each year is leafless,

Each day lightless, at the last—the wood begins
Its serious existence; it has no path,

No house, no story; it resists comparison . . .
One clear, repeated, lapping gurgle, like a spoon

Or a glass breathing, is the brook,
The wood's fouled midnight water. If I walk into the wood

As far as I can walk, I come to my own door,
The door of the House in the Wood. It opens silently:

On the bed is something covered, something humped
Asleep there, awake there—but what? I do not know.

I look, I lie there, and yet I do not know.
How far out my great echoing clumsy limbs

Stretch, surrounded only by space! For time has struck,
All the clocks are stuck now, for how many lives,

On the same second. Numbed, wooden, motionless,
We are far under the surface of the night.

Nothing comes down so deep but sound: a car, freight cars,
A high soft droning, drawn out like a wire

Forever and ever—is this the sound that Bunyan heard
So that he thought his bowels would burst within him?—

Drift on, on, into nothing. Then someone screams
A scream like an old knife sharpened into nothing.

It is only a nightmare. No one wakes up, nothing happens,
Except there is gooseflesh over my whole body—

And that too, after a little while, is gone.
I lie here like a cut-off limb, the stump the limb has left . . .

Here at the bottom of the world, what was before the world
And will be after, holds me to its black

Breasts and rocks me: the oven is cold, the cage is empty,
In the House in the Wood, the witch and her child sleep.

Field and Forest

When you look down from the airplane you see lines,
Roads, ruts, braided into a net or web—
Where people go, what people do: the ways of life.

Heaven says to the farmer: "What's your field?"
And he answers: "Farming," with a field,
Or: "Dairy-farming," with a herd of cows.
They seem a boy's toy cows, seen from this high.

Seen from this high,
The fields have a terrible monotony.

But between the lighter patches there are dark ones.
A farmer is separated from a farmer
By what farmers have in common: forests,
Those dark things—what the fields were to begin with.
At night a fox comes out of the forest, eats his chickens.
At night the deer come out of the forest, eat his crops.

If he could he'd make farm out of the forest,
But it isn't worth it: some of it's marsh, some rocks,
There are things there you couldn't get rid of
With a bulldozer, even—not with dynamite.
Besides, he likes it. He had a cave there, as a boy;

He hunts there now. It's a waste of land,
But it would be a waste of time, a waste of money,
To make it into anything but what it is.

At night, from the airplane, all you see is lights,
A few lights, the lights of houses, headlights,
And darkness. Somewhere below, beside a light,
The farmer, naked, takes out his false teeth:
He doesn't eat now. Takes off his spectacles:
He doesn't see now. Shuts his eyes.
If he were able to he'd shut his ears,
And as it is, he doesn't hear with them.
Plainly, he's taken out his tongue: he doesn't talk.
His arms and legs: at least, he doesn't move them.
They are knotted together, curled up, like a child's.
And after he has taken off the thoughts
It has taken him his life to learn,
He takes off, last of all, the world.

When you take off everything what's left? A wish,
A blind wish; and yet the wish isn't blind,
What the wish wants to see, it sees.

There in the middle of the forest is the cave
And there, curled up inside it, is the fox.

He stands looking at it.
Around him the fields are sleeping: the fields dream.
At night there are no more farmers, no more farms.
At night the fields dream, the fields *are* the forest.
The boy stands looking at the fox
As if, if he looked long enough—
                                he looks at it.
Or is it the fox that's looking at the boy?
The trees can't tell the two of them apart.

NOTES

Losses. Spoken collectively by dead young bomber crews who bombed Germany
in World War II. The first stanza deals with their deaths during the training
period, the second with their deaths in combat over "The cities we had
learned about in school."

The Death of the Ball Turret Gunner. Jarrell's note: "A ball turret was a plexiglass
sphere set into the belly of a B-17 or B-24, and inhabited by two .50 caliber
machine-guns and one man, a short small man. When this gunner tracked

with his machine-guns a fighter attacking his bomber from below, he revolved
with the turret; hunched upside-down in his little sphere, he looked like the
foetus in the womb. The fighters which attacked him were armed with cannon
firing explosive shells. The hose was a steam hose."

Protocols. Two experiences of mass extermination, told in tandem by victims who
did not understand what was happening to them. The gas used in the
"showers" into which the victims were herded is said to have smelled like
clover or hay.

Seele im Raum. Jarrell: " 'Seele im Raum' is the title of one of Rilke's poems: 'Soul
in Space' sounded so glib that I couldn't use it instead. An eland is the largest
sort of African antelope—the males are as big as a horse, and you often see
people gazing at them, at the zoo, in uneasy wonder." One way to read this
poem is to consider it as spoken by a housewife who has been cured of
schizophrenia; she remembers her illness with wonder, uneasiness, and a
kind of nostalgia. She may have been a mental patient; she was also a
visionary.

Cinderella. The poem makes us reconsider the fairy tale's relation to wish
fulfillment. Cinderella's wish seems not to have been for her prince after all.

A Hunt in the Black Forest. A child goes to sleep (compare Rilke's Third Duino
Elegy) and dreams a dream that is both a German fairy tale and an Oedipal
wish fulfillment.

Field and Forest. A more playful version, in an American setting, of the dream
journeys enacted in the preceding poems.

RANDALL JARRELL

Books

Five Young American Poets (with
others), 1940

Blood for a Stranger, 1942

Little Friend, Little Friend, 1945

Losses, 1948

The Seven-League Crutches, 1951

Poetry and the Age (criticism), 1953

Pictures from an Institution (novel),
1954

Selected Poems, 1955

The Woman at the Washington Zoo,
1960

A Sad Heart at the Supermarket
(essays), 1962

Selected Poems, 1964

The Lost World, 1965

The Third Book of Criticism (essays),
1969

The Complete Poems, 1969

Goethe's Faust: Part One
(translation), 1974

Randall Jarrell's Letters, 1984

Criticism

Charles M. Adams, *Randall Jarrell: A Bibliography*, 1958; Robert Lowell,
Peter Taylor, Robert Penn Warren, eds., *Randall Jarrell 1914–1965*, 1967;
Suzanne Ferguson, *The Poetry of Randall Jarrell*, 1971; Bernetta Quinn,
Randall Jarrell, 1981; "Randall Jarrell: A Symposium," *FIELD*, No. 35
(Fall 1986).

Robert Lowell
(1917–1978)

© Rollie McKenna, 1968

In the best poems of Robert Lowell historical issues are mixed with dilemmas of the self in an explosive tension that illuminates both. Lowell was deeply critical of Americans for their neglect and dislike of their own history, and he associates individual isolation and anguish (which he knew firsthand from periodic mental illness) with America's inability to connect past and present in the form of viable traditions. No doubt this attitude was partly formed by his early apprenticeship to two southern poets, Allen Tate and John Crowe Ransom, who practiced variations on T. S. Eliot's religious conservatism and cultural nostalgia (Lowell was at this time a Roman Catholic convert) in specifically American settings. It can also be traced to his membership in an illustrious New England family whose past was a good deal more distinguished than its present.

Lowell's precocity and technical brilliance caused him to be singled out early as a major poet, a burden that probably made an uneven career more problematic. Certainly there are elements of self-regard in almost everything he wrote, and a writer less convinced of the magnitude of his talent would probably have been more cautious about what he chose to consider publishable work. Lowell continues to be obscured by an inflated reputation that may have to be discredited before we can discover the true nature of his contribution to American letters.

Throughout the 1950s Lowell was a traditional poet—heroic couplets, pastoral elegies, and the like—of formidable dimensions. His dramatic change of manner at the end of the decade was much remarked upon and very influential. Under the influence of a new mentor, William Carlos Williams, he put aside the dense, allusive, ornate manner of the poems he had written in *Lord Weary's Castle* (1946) and *The Mills of the Kavanaughs* (1951) and turned to more open forms and a more personal subject matter that eventually gave rise to the term "confessional poetry." The early style is represented in this collection by "Beyond the Alps," which also inaugurates Lowell's new style. The poem opens *Life Studies* (1959) and commemorates Lowell's decision to abandon his Roman Catholicism. A change of style coincides with a change of faith, and we watch both occurring in the literal and metaphoric journey this poem teasingly and mournfully describes.

Life Studies is also represented here by "Skunk Hour" and "For the Union Dead," which appears as the last poem in some editions under the title "Colonel Shaw and the Massachusetts 54th." The latter poem migrated to his next volume as the title poem, and that collection is also represented here by "July in Washington," "Those Before Us," "Water," and "The Lesson." *Life Studies* and *For the Union Dead* represent Lowell at his best, in midcareer when the personal-historical tension was most finely balanced in his work. As the historical had perhaps been too dominant in his earlier work, so the personal took over in subsequent volumes.

Lowell also produced an interesting volume of plays, *The Old Glory,* in which his preoccupation with American history leads to some effective adaptations of short stories by Hawthorne and Melville. *Imitations,* a volume of translations/adaptations in which a number of poets are "Lowellized," made to sound like their translator, would seem to be misnamed: it is not that Lowell imitates Baudelaire, Montale, and others, but that he makes them imitate him. *Appropriations* might be a better title.

The volume does contain some dazzling passages, reflections as much of Lowell's considerable skills as of his sources.

If Lowell's poetic manner changed drastically with *Life Studies,* certain features of his style remained constant throughout his work. He was fond of strong verbs as a means of charging—and sometimes overcharging—a poem with energy. He used slang effectively, and he could sometimes pile up three adjectives around a noun, a trick few poets can duplicate. When the poems have little substance or vision, this coarse-grained and energized style rings hollow, but when it connects firmly with Lowell's fierce and anguished vision of the demented self in an impoverished landscape against a background of historical crisis, it has an authenticity and weight that are unforgettable.

DY

Beyond the Alps

(On the train from Rome to Paris. 1950, the year Pius
XII defined the dogma of Mary's bodily assumption.)

Reading how even the Swiss had thrown the sponge
in once again and Everest was still
unscaled, I watched our Paris pullman lunge
mooning across the fallow Alpine snow.
O bella Roma! I saw our stewards go
forward on tiptoe banging on their gongs.
Life changed to landscape. Much against my will
I left the City of God where it belongs.
There the skirt-mad Mussolini unfurled
the eagle of Caesar. He was one of us
only, pure prose. I envy the conspicuous
waste of our grandparents on their grand tours—
long-haired Victorian sages accepted the universe,
while breezing on their trust funds through the world.

When the Vatican made Mary's Assumption dogma,
the crowds at San Pietro screamed *Papa.*
The Holy Father dropped his shaving glass,
and listened. His electric razor purred,
his pet canary chirped on his left hand.
The lights of science couldn't hold a candle
to Mary risen—at one miraculous stroke,
angel-wing'd, gorgeous as a jungle bird!
But who believed this? Who could understand?
Pilgrims still kissed Saint Peter's brazen sandal.
The Duce's lynched, bare, booted skull still spoke.
God herded his people to the *coup de grâce*—
the costumed Switzers sloped their pikes to push,
O Pius, through the monstrous human crush. . . .

Our mountain-climbing train had come to earth.
Tired of the querulous hush-hush of the wheels,
the blear-eyed ego kicking in my berth
lay still, and saw Apollo plant his heels
on terra firma through the morning's thigh . . .
each backward, wasted Alp, a Parthenon,
fire-branded socket of the Cyclops' eye.
There were no tickets for that altitude
once held by Hellas, when the Goddess stood,

prince, pope, philosopher and golden bough,
pure mind and murder at the scything prow—
Minerva, the miscarriage of the brain.

Now Paris, our black classic, breaking up
like killer kings on an Etruscan cup.

Skunk Hour

For Elizabeth Bishop

Nautilus Island's hermit
heiress still lives through winter in her Spartan cottage;
her sheep still graze above the sea.
Her son's a bishop. Her farmer
is first selectman in our village;
she's in her dotage.

Thirsting for
the hierarchic privacy
of Queen Victoria's century,
she buys up all
the eyesores facing her shore,
and lets them fall.

The season's ill—
we've lost our summer millionaire,
who seemed to leap from an L. L. Bean
catalogue. His nine-knot yawl
was auctioned off to lobstermen.
A red fox stain covers Blue Hill.

And now our fairy
decorator brightens his shop for fall;
his fishnet's filled with orange cork,
orange, his cobbler's bench and awl;
there is no money in his work,
he'd rather marry.

One dark night,
my Tudor Ford climbed the hill's skull;
I watched for love-cars. Lights turned down,
they lay together, hull to hull,
where the graveyard shelves on the town. . . .
My mind's not right.

A car radio bleats,
"Love, O careless Love. . . ." I hear
my ill-spirit sob in each blood cell,
as if my hand were at its throat. . . .
I myself am hell;
nobody's here—

only skunks, that search
in the moonlight for a bite to eat.
They march on their soles up Main Street:
white stripes, moonstruck eyes' red fire
under the chalk-dry and spar spire
of the Trinitarian Church.

I stand on top
of our back steps and breathe the rich air—
a mother skunk with her column of kittens swills the garbage pail.
She jabs her wedge-head in a cup
of sour cream, drops her ostrich tail,
and will not scare.

For the Union Dead

"Relinquunt Omnia Servare Rem Publicam."

The old South Boston Aquarium stands
in a Sahara of snow now. Its broken windows are boarded.
The bronze weathervane cod has lost half its scales.
The airy tanks are dry.

Once my nose crawled like a snail on the glass;
my hand tingled
to burst the bubbles
drifting from the noses of the cowed, compliant fish.

My hand draws back. I often sigh still
for the dark downward and vegetating kingdom
of the fish and reptile. One morning last March,
I pressed against the new barbed and galvanized

fence on the Boston Common. Behind their cage,
yellow dinosaur steamshovels were grunting
as they cropped up tons of mush and grass
to gouge their underworld garage.

Parking spaces luxuriate like civic
sandpiles in the heart of Boston.
A girdle of orange, Puritan-pumpkin colored girders
braces the tingling Statehouse,

shaking over the excavations, as it faces Colonel Shaw
and his bell-cheeked Negro infantry
on St. Gaudens' shaking Civil War relief,
propped by a plank splint against the garage's earthquake.

Two months after marching through Boston,
half the regiment was dead;
at the dedication,
William James could almost hear the bronze Negroes breathe.

Their monument sticks like a fishbone
in the city's throat.
Its Colonel is as lean
as a compass-needle.

He has an angry wrenlike vigilance,
a greyhound's gentle tautness;
he seems to wince at pleasure,
and suffocate for privacy.

He is out of bounds now. He rejoices in man's lovely,
peculiar power to choose life and die—
when he leads his black soldiers to death,
he cannot bend his back.

On a thousand small town New England greens,
the old white churches hold their air
of sparse, sincere rebellion: frayed flags
quilt the graveyards of the Grand Army of the Republic.

The stone statues of the abstract Union Soldier
grow slimmer and younger each year—
wasp-wasted, they doze over muskets
and muse through their sideburns . . .

Shaw's father wanted no monument
except the ditch,
where his son's body was thrown
and lost with his "niggers."

The ditch is nearer.
There are no statues for the last war here;
on Boylston Street, a commercial photograph
shows Hiroshima boiling

over a Mosler Safe, the "Rock of Ages"
that survived the blast. Space is nearer.
When I crouch to my television set,
the drained faces of Negro school-children rise like balloons.

Colonel Shaw
is riding on his bubble,
he waits
for the blessèd break.

The Aquarium is gone. Everywhere,
giant finned cars nose forward like fish;
a savage servility
slides by on grease.

Water

It was a Maine lobster town—
each morning boatloads of hands
pushed off for granite
quarries on the islands,

and left dozens of bleak
white frame houses stuck
like oyster shells
on a hill of rock,

and below us, the sea lapped
the raw little match-stick
mazes of a weir,
where the fish for bait were trapped.

Remember? We sat on a slab of rock.
From this distance in time,
it seems the color
of iris, rotting and turning purpler,

but it was only
the usual gray rock
turning the usual green
when drenched by the sea.

The sea drenched the rock
at our feet all day,
and kept tearing away
flake after flake.

One night you dreamed
you were a mermaid clinging to a wharf-pile,
and trying to pull
off the barnacles with your hands.

We wished our two souls
might return like gulls
to the rock. In the end,
the water was too cold for us.

The Lesson

No longer to lie reading *Tess of the d'Urbervilles*,
while the high, mysterious squirrels
rain small green branches on our sleep!

All that landscape, one likes to think it died
or slept with us, that we ourselves died
or slept then in the age and second of our habitation.

The green leaf cushions the same dry footprint,
or the child's boat luffs in the same dry chop,
and we are where we were. We were!

Perhaps the trees stopped growing in summer amnesia;
their day that gave them veins is rooted down—
and the nights? They are for sleeping now as then.

Ah the light lights the window of my young night,
and you never turn off the light,
while the books lie in the library, and go on reading.

The barberry berry sticks on the small hedge,
cold slits the same crease in the finger,
the same thorn hurts. The leaf repeats the lesson.

Those Before Us

They are all outline, uniformly gray,
unregenerate arrowheads sloughed up by the path here,
or in the corners of the eye, they play
their thankless, fill-in roles. They never were.

Wormwood on the veranda! Plodding needles
still prod the coarse pink yarn into a dress.
The muskrat that took a slice of your thumb still huddles,
a mop of hair and a heart-beat on the porch—

there's the tin wastebasket where it learned to wait
for us playing dead, the slats it mashed in terror,
its spoor of cornflakes, and the packing crate
it furiously slashed to matchwood to escape.

Their chairs were *ex cathedra*, yet if you draw back the blinds,
(as full of windows as a fishnet now)
you will hear them conspiring, slapping hands
across the bent card-table, still leaf-green.

Vacations, stagnant growth. But in the silence,
some one lets out his belt to breathe, some one
roams in negligee. Bless the confidence
of their sitting unguarded there in stocking feet.

Sands drop from the hour-glass waist and swallow tail.
We follow their gunshy shadows down the trail—
those before us! Pardon them for existing.
We have stopped watching them. They have stopped watching.

July in Washington

The stiff spokes of this wheel
touch the sore spots of the earth.

On the Potomac, swan-white
power launches keep breasting the sulphurous wave.

Otters slide and dive and slick back their hair,
raccoons clean their meat in the creek.

On the circles, green statues ride like South American
liberators above the breeding vegetation—

prongs and spearheads of some equatorial
backland that will inherit the globe.

The elect, the elected . . . they come here bright as dimes,
and die dishevelled and soft.

We cannot name their names, or number their dates—
circle on circle, like rings on a tree—

but we wish the river had another shore,
some further range of delectable mountains,

distant hills powdered blue as a girl's eyelid.
It seems the least little shove would land us there,

that only the slightest repugnance of our bodies
we no longer control could drag us back.

NOTES

Skunk Hour. The setting is Maine. A Tudor Ford is simply "two-door," as typically shortened in want-ads.

For the Union Dead. The monument by the sculptor St. Gaudens to the Civil War regiment of black soldiers led by Colonel Shaw stands on the north side of Boston Common, facing the Statehouse. The epigraph translates as "They left everything behind to serve their country."

Those Before Us. "Ex cathedra," literally "from the chair," refers to pronouncements made by virtue of an important office (e.g., a bishop or pope).

July in Washington. The city of Washington, D.C., is laid out in the shape of a wheel.

ROBERT LOWELL

Books

Land of Unlikeness, 1944

Lord Weary's Castle, 1946

The Mills of the Kavanaughs, 195

Life Studies, 1959

Imitations (translations), 1961

For the Union Dead, 1964

The Old Glory (plays), 1965

Near the Ocean, 1967

The Voyage & Other Versions of Poems by Baudelaire (translations), 1968

Aeschylus, *Prometheus Bound* (translation), 1969

Notebook, 1967–68, 1969, rev. 1970

The Dolphin, 1973

For Lizzie and Harriet, 1973

History, 1973

Selected Poems, 1976

Day by Day, 1977

Aeschylus, *The Oresteia* (translation), 1979

Collected Prose, 1987

Criticism, Interviews

Jerome Mazzaro, *The Achievement of Robert Lowell, 1939–1959*, 1960; Interview, *Paris Review*, 25 (Spring 1961); Jerome Mazzaro, *The Poetic Themes of Robert Lowell*, 1965; Thomas Parkinson, ed., *Robert Lowell: A Collection of Critical Essays*, 1968; Philip Cooper, *The Autobiographical Myth of Robert Lowell*, 1970; Richard Fein, *Robert Lowell*, 1970; Michael London and Robert Boyers, eds., *Robert Lowell: A Portrait of the Artist in His Time*, 1973; Marjorie Perloff, *The Poetic Art of Robert Lowell*, 1973; Alan Williamson, *Pity the Monsters: The Political Vision of Robert Lowell*, 1974; Stephen Yenser, *Circle to Circle: The Poetry of Robert Lowell*, 1975; Stephen Gould Axelrod, *Robert Lowell: Life and Art*, 1978; Ian Hamilton, *Robert Lowell: A Biography*, 1982; Jeffrey Meyers, ed., *Robert Lowell: Interviews and Memoirs*, 1988.

Theodore Roethke (1908–1963)

Frank Murphy

Theodore Roethke grew up in Saginaw, Michigan, where his father ran a nursery and floral business. As his poetry matured, he ventured back to his childhood for subject matter, to the greenhouse and its associations with nurture and growth. The first poems in this selection, "Cuttings," "Cuttings (later)," "Child on Top of a Greenhouse," and "My Papa's Waltz," from the 1948 volume *The Lost Son and Other Poems,* represent his initial engagement with these materials and strike the note of his artistic authenticity: an eye for minute natural detail coupled with a gift for distinctive verbal music. They were followed, in *Praise to the End!* (1951), by poems violently experimental as to form and sensibility, represented here by "The Shape of the Fire." These poems re-create the child's world not from the safe perspective of the adult but through a reenactment of its terrors, wonders, mysteries, and confusions. Their deliberate childishness has confused readers and critics, but Roethke's fellow poets tended to recognize and respond immediately to the originality of these poems, and it was probably his example (along with Robert Lowell's in *Life Studies* a few years later) that led to the new era of formal experiment in American poetry.

Roethke was fundamentally a nature poet. His poetry is a study of the self in the natural world, a history of its quest for an ecstatic union with nature, a transcendence. This preoccupation links Roethke not only with romantic poets but with American transcendentalists and indeed with all mystics who strike a pantheistic note. The affinity with these traditions is clear in the extended and confident pair of poems that close this selection: the first section of "Meditations of an Old Woman" and "Journey to the Interior," the latter from the "North American Sequence" of his last collection, *The Far Field.* But the presence of this quest throughout Roethke's work should help readers who are aware of it to find their way through the difficult middle sequences in which coherence comes and goes and the sense of purpose is often precarious. It helps to see these poems as resembling the action paintings of the abstract expressionists with which they were contemporaneous. They use language for its own sake, as a medium of spontaneous and studious play rather than an instrument of steady communication. Roethke argued that "we must permit poetry to extend consciousness as far, as deeply, as particularly as it can," and spoke of writing poems "which try in their rhythms to catch the very movement of the mind itself." To this end he imitated nursery rhymes, proverbs and sayings, the infant babble that takes pleasure in speech as pure sound, rhythm, and iteration, as well as the ramblings of hysteria and mental illness. The collage of possibilities that results is often bewildering. But the poems have an aim, to "trace the spiritual history of the protagonist," and their lyrical closing sections reveal how much they were an effort to bring the self through confusion and need to an equilibrium in which oneness with nature is the source of a mystical contentment.

The nervous, blustery man who wrote these romantic lyrics was a fine teacher of poetry and creative writing, but an unhappy individual, suffering periodically from mental breakdowns and never fully at home in the world he loved so deeply. His work can be derivative—of Yeats, Eliot, and Dylan Thomas especially—and is no doubt uneven, but his best poems seem destined to last. A *Collected Poems* is available in paperback, and the letters and notebooks have been collected, edited, and published. There is also a sympathetic biography, *The Glass House,* by Allan Seager.

Cuttings

Sticks-in-a-drowse droop over sugary loam,
Their intricate stem-fur dries;
But still the delicate slips keep coaxing up water;
The small cells bulge;

One nub of growth
Nudges a sand-crumb loose,
Pokes through a musty sheath
Its pale tendrilous horn.

Cuttings

(later)

This urge, wrestle, resurrection of dry sticks,
Cut stems struggling to put down feet,
What saint strained so much,
Rose on such lopped limbs to a new life?

I can hear, underground, that sucking and sobbing,
In my veins, in my bones I feel it,—
The small waters seeping upward,
The tight grains parting at last.
When sprouts break out,
Slippery as fish,
I quail, lean to beginnings, sheath-wet.

Child on Top of a Greenhouse

The wind billowing out the seat of my britches,
My feet crackling splinters of glass and dried putty,
The half-grown chrysanthemums staring up like accusers,
Up through the streaked glass, flashing with sunlight,
A few white clouds all rushing eastward,
A line of elms plunging and tossing like horses,
And everyone, everyone pointing up and shouting!

My Papa's Waltz

The whiskey on your breath
Could make a small boy dizzy;
But I hung on like death:
Such waltzing was not easy.

We romped until the pans
Slid from the kitchen shelf;
My mother's countenance
Could not unfrown itself.

The hand that held my wrist
Was battered on one knuckle;
At every step you missed
My right ear scraped a buckle.

You beat time on my head
With a palm caked hard by dirt,
Then waltzed me off to bed
Still clinging to your shirt.

The Shape of the Fire

1

What's this? A dish for fat lips.
Who says? A nameless stranger.
Is he a bird or a tree? Not everyone can tell.

Water recedes to the crying of spiders.
An old scow bumps over black rocks.
A cracked pod calls.

Mother me out of here. What more will the bones allow?
Will the sea give the wind suck? A toad folds into a stone.
These flowers are all fangs. Comfort me, fury.
Wake me, witch, we'll do the dance of rotten sticks.

Shale loosens. Marl reaches into the field. Small birds pass over water.
Spirit, come near. This is only the edge of whiteness.
I can't laugh at a procession of dogs.

In the hour of ripeness the tree is barren.
The she-bear mopes under the hill.
Mother, mother, stir from your cave of sorrow.

A low mouth laps water. Weeds, weeds, how I love you.
The arbor is cooler. Farewell, farewell, fond worm.
The warm comes without sound.

> 2
> Where's the eye?
> The eye's in the sty.
> The ear's not here
> Beneath the hair.
> When I took off my clothes
> To find a nose,
> There was only one shoe
> For the waltz of To,
> The pinch of Where.

Time for the flat-headed man. I recognize that listener,
Him with the platitudes and rubber doughnuts,
Melting at the knees, a varicose horror.
Hello, hello. My nerves knew you, dear boy.
Have you come to unhinge my shadow?
Last night I slept in the pits of a tongue.
The silver fish ran in and out of my special bindings;
I grew tired of the ritual of names and the assistant keeper of the
    mollusks:
Up over a viaduct I came, to the snakes and sticks of another winter,
A two-legged dog hunting a new horizon of howls.
The wind sharpened itself on a rock;
A voice sang:

> Pleasure on ground
> Has no sound,
> Easily maddens
> The uneasy man.

> Who, careless, slips
> In coiling ooze
> Is trapped to the lips,
> Leaves more than shoes;

> Must pull off clothes
> To jerk like a frog
> On belly and nose
> From the sucking bog.

My meat eats me. Who waits at the gate?
Mother of quartz, your words writhe into my ear.
Renew the light, lewd whisper.

    3

The wasp waits.
      The edge cannot eat the center.
The grape glistens.
      The path tells little to the serpent.
An eye comes out of the wave.
      The journey from flesh is longest.
A rose sways least.
      The redeemer comes a dark way.

    4

Morning-fair, follow me further back
Into that minnowy world of weeds and ditches,
When the herons floated high over the white houses,
And the little crabs slipped into silvery craters.
When the sun for me glinted the sides of a sand grain,
And my intent stretched over the buds at their first trembling.

That air and shine: and the flicker's loud summer call:
The bearded boards in the stream and the all of apples;
The glad hen on the hill; and the trellis humming.
Death was not. I lived in a simple drowse:
Hands and hair moved through a dream of wakening blossoms.
Rain sweetened the cave and the dove still called;
The flowers leaned on themselves, the flowers in hollows;
And love, love sang toward.

    5
To have the whole air!—
The light, the full sun
Coming down on the flowerheads,
The tendrils turning slowly,
A slow snail-lifting, liquescent;
To be by the rose
Rising slowly out of its bed,
Still as a child in its first loneliness;
To see cyclamen veins become clearer in early sunlight,
And mist lifting out of the brown cat-tails;
To stare into the after-light, the glitter left on the lake's surface,

When the sun has fallen behind a wooded island;
To follow the drops sliding from a lifted oar,
Held up, while the rower breathes, and the small boat drifts quietly
    shoreward;
To know that light falls and fills, often without our knowing,
As an opaque vase fills to the brim from a quick pouring,
Fills and trembles at the edge yet does not flow over,
Still holding and feeding the stem of the contained flower.

from Meditations of an Old Woman

First Meditation

1

On love's worst ugly day,
The weeds hiss at the edge of the field,
The small winds make their chilly indictments.
Elsewhere, in houses, even pails can be sad;
While stones loosen on the obscure hillside,
And a tree tilts from its roots,
Toppling down an embankment.

The spirit moves, but not always upward,
While animals eat to the north,
And the shale slides an inch in the talus,
The bleak wind eats at the weak plateau,
And the sun brings joy to some.
But the rind, often, hates the life within.

How can I rest in the days of my slowness?
I've become a strange piece of flesh,
Nervous and cold, bird-furtive, whiskery,
With a cheek soft as a hound's ear.
What's left is light as a seed;
I need an old crone's knowing.

2

Often I think of myself as riding—
Alone, on a bus through western country.
I sit above the back wheels, where the jolts are hardest,
And we bounce and sway along toward the midnight,
The lights tilting up, skyward, as we come over a little rise,
Then down, as we roll like a boat from a wave-crest.

All journeys, I think, are the same:
The movement is forward, after a few wavers,
And for a while we are all alone,
Busy, obvious with ourselves,
The drunken soldier, the old lady with her peppermints;
And we ride, we ride, taking the curves
Somewhat closer, the trucks coming
Down from behind the last ranges,
Their black shapes breaking past;
And the air claps between us,
Blasting the frosted windows,
And I seem to go backward,
Backward in time:

     Two song sparrows, one within a greenhouse,
     Shuttling its throat while perched on a wind-vent,
     And another, outside, in the bright day,
     With a wind from the west and the trees all in motion.
     One sang, then the other,
     The songs tumbling over and under the glass,
     And the men beneath them wheeling in dirt to the cement
        benches,
     The laden wheelbarrows creaking and swaying,
     And the up-spring of the plank when a foot left the runway.

Journey within a journey:
The ticket mislaid or lost, the gate
Inaccessible, the boat always pulling out
From the rickety wooden dock,
The children waving;
Or two horses plunging in snow, their lines tangled,
A great wooden sleigh careening behind them,
Swerving up a steep embankment.
For a moment they stand above me,
Their black skins shuddering:
Then they lurch forward,
Lunging down a hillside.

3

As when silt drifts and sifts down through muddy pond-water,
Settling in small beads around weeds and sunken branches,
And one crab, tentative, hunches himself before moving along the
    bottom,
Grotesque, awkward, his extended eyes looking at nothing in particular,
Only a few bubbles loosening from the ill-matched tentacles,
The tail and smaller legs slipping and sliding slowly backward—
So the spirit tries for another life,
Another way and place in which to continue;
Or a salmon, tired, moving up a shallow stream,
Nudges into a back-eddy, a sandy inlet,
Bumping against sticks and bottom-stones, then swinging
Around, back into the tiny maincurrent, the rush of brownish-white
    water,
Still swimming forward—
So, I suppose, the spirit journeys.

4

I have gone into the waste lonely places
Behind the eye; the lost acres at the edge of smoky cities.
What's beyond never crumbles like an embankment,
Explodes like a rose, or thrusts wings over the Caribbean.
There are no pursuing forms, faces on walls:
Only the motes of dust in the immaculate hallways,
The darkness of falling hair, the warnings from lint and spiders,
The vines graying to a fine powder.
There is no riven tree, or lamb dropped by an eagle.

There are still times, morning and evening:
The cerulean, high in the elm,
Thin and insistent as a cicada,
And the far phoebe, singing,
The long plaintive notes floating down,
Drifting through leaves, oak and maple,
Or the whippoorwill, along the smoky ridges,
A single bird calling and calling;
A fume reminds me, drifting across wet gravel;
A cold wind comes over stones;
A flame, intense, visible,
Plays over the dry pods,
Runs fitfully along the stubble,
Moves over the field,
Without burning,
        In such times, lacking a god,
        I am still happy.

from North American Sequence
Journey to the Interior

1

In the long journey out of the self,
There are many detours, washed-out interrupted raw places
Where the shale slides dangerously
And the back wheels hang almost over the edge
At the sudden veering, the moment of turning.
Better to hug close, wary of rubble and falling stones.
The arroyo cracking the road, the wind-bitten buttes, the canyons,
Creeks swollen in midsummer from the flash-flood roaring into the
        narrow valley.
Reeds beaten flat by wind and rain,
Grey from the long winter, burnt at the base in late summer.
—Or the path narrowing,
Winding upward toward the stream with its sharp stones,
The upland of alder and birchtrees,
Through the swamp alive with quicksand,
The way blocked at last by a fallen fir-tree,
The thickets darkening,
The ravines ugly.

2

I remember how it was to drive in gravel,
Watching for dangerous down-hill places, where the wheels whined
        beyond eighty—
When you hit the deep pit at the bottom of the swale,
The trick was to throw the car sideways and charge over the hill, full of
        the throttle.
Grinding up and over the narrow road, spitting and roaring.
A chance? Perhaps. But the road was part of me, and its ditches,
And the dust lay thick on my eyelids,—Who ever wore goggles?—
Always a sharp turn to the left past a barn close to the roadside,
To a scurry of small dogs and a shriek of children,
The highway ribboning out in a straight thrust to the North,
To the sand dunes and fish flies, hanging, thicker than moths,
Dying brightly under the street lights sunk in coarse concrete,
The towns with their high pitted road-crowns and deep gutters,
Their wooden stores of silvery pine and weather-beaten red court-
        houses,
An old bridge below with a buckled iron railing, broken by some idiot
        plunger;
Underneath, the sluggish water running between weeds, broken wheels,
        tires, stones.

And all flows past—
The cemetery with two scrubby trees in the middle of the prairie,
The dead snakes and muskrats, the turtles gasping in the rubble,
The spikey purple bushes in the winding dry creek bed—
The floating hawks, the jackrabbits, the grazing cattle—
I am not moving but they are,
And the sun comes out of a blue cloud over the Tetons,
While, farther away, the heat-lightning flashes.
I rise and fall in the slow sea of a grassy plain,
The wind veering the car slightly to the right,
Whipping the line of white laundry, bending the cottonwoods apart,
The scraggly wind-break of a dusty ranch-house.
I rise and fall, and time folds
Into a long moment;
And I hear the lichen speak,
And the ivy advance with its white lizard feet—
On the shimmering road,
On the dusty detour.

3

I see the flower of all water, above and below me, the never receding,
Moving, unmoving in a parched land, white in the moonlight:
The soul at a still-stand,
At ease after rocking the flesh to sleep,
Petals and reflections of petals mixed on the surface of a glassy pool,
And the waves flattening out when the fishermen drag their nets over
    the stones.

In the moment of time when the small drop forms, but does not fall,
I have known the heart of the sun,—
In the dark and light of a dry place,
In a flicker of fire brisked by a dusty wind.
I have heard, in a drip of leaves,
A slight song,
After the midnight cries.
I rehearse myself for this:
The stand at the stretch in the face of death,
Delighting in surface change, the glitter of light on waves,
And I roam elsewhere, my body thinking,
Turning toward the other side of light,
In a tower of wind, a tree idling in air,
Beyond my own echo,
Neither forward nor backward,
Unperplexed, in a place leading nowhere.

As a blind man, lifting a curtain, knows it is morning,
I know this change:
On one side of silence there is no smile;
But when I breathe with the birds,
The spirit of wrath becomes the spirit of blessing,
And the dead begin from their dark to sing in my sleep.

NOTES

The Shape of the Fire. Poems of this kind do not require so much annotation as an
approach that is relaxed as to exact meanings and firm connections. They use
questions, interjections, commands, aphorisms, and other magical or super-
stitious forms of language to re-create a sense of spiritual crisis and emotional
need that moves toward a musical, rather than narrative, resolution in their
closing sections. They repay meditation and close attention, but more for their
ability to create a verbal world that imitates "the very movement of the mind
itself" than for their status as logical or coherent discourse.

THEODORE ROETHKE

Books

Open House, 1941

The Lost Son and Other Poems, 1948

Praise to the End, 1951

The Waking, Poems: 1933–1953,
1953

Words for the Wind, 1958

The Far Field, 1964

On the Poet and His Craft (essays),
1965

*The Collected Poems of Theodore
Roethke*, 1966

*Selected Letters of Theodore
Roethke*, ed. Mills, 1968

*Straw for the Fire: From the
Notebooks of Theodore Roethke,
1943–63*, ed. Wagoner, 1972

Criticism, Interviews

Ralph Mills, *Theodore Roethke*, 1963; Arnold Stein, ed., *Theodore
Roethke: Essays on the Poetry*, 1965; Karl Malkoff, *Theodore Roethke: An
Introduction to the Poetry*, 1966; Allan Seager, *The Glass House: The Life
of Theodore Roethke*, 1968; Gary Lane, ed., *A Concordance to the Poems
of Theodore Roethke*, 1972; Richard Allen Blessing, *Theodore Roethke's
Dynamic Vision*, 1974; Rosemary Sullivan, *Theodore Roethke, The Gar-
den Master*, 1975; Jenijoy La Belle, *The Echoing Wood of Theodore
Roethke*, 1976; Keith R. Moul, *Theodore Roethke's Career: An Annotated
Bibliography*, 1977; Jay Parrini, *Theodore Roethke: An American Romantic*, 1979; George Wolff, *Theodore Roethke*, 1981; Harold Bloom, ed.,
Theodore Roethke (Modern Critical Views Series), 1987.

Muriel
Rukeyser
(1913–1980)

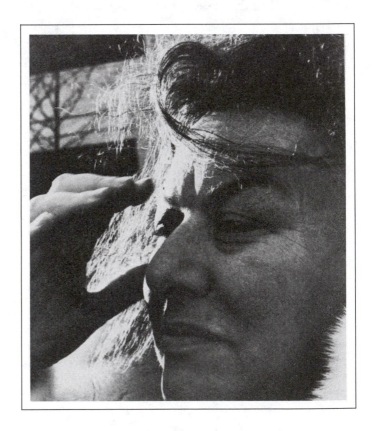

A as more and more contributions by women to all fields are being uncovered and studied, it is becoming clear that those of Muriel Rukeyser to the twin arts of poetry and translation are major and substantial. She herself could remark, in the preface to her collected poems, "It never occurred to me that my poems would be collected until after my lifetime." After early work that Jarrell reviewed harshly for its slide into rhetoric on a grand scale—allowing only that "she is sometimes so original . . ." (_Poetry & the Age_)—she continued to develop as a poet, richly exploring dream world, nightmare, and sexual fantasy in imagery and rhythms that even Jarrell sensed would come to speak for "the Common Woman of the century." She was born early enough to experience World War I and participate in the political and social developments of the 1920s and 1930s, thoughtfully intense and excited at the prospects for social change—see especially her early poems on flying and mining—and she died in 1980, having marched for causes she believed in and having continued to write poems that followed the times. She reached for two things, as she put it: "the evidence itself," as well as "the unverifiable fact, as in sex, dream, the parts of life in which we dive deep" (_The Life of Poetry_). She was especially pleased that her last publisher printed vast amounts of scientific work. "I care very much about that meeting-place, of science and poetry," she wrote.

In her work in general, and the poems presented here in particular, the speaking voice attempts to guide the reader in ways she admired in her favorite writers, Whitman, Dante, and Baudelaire: by making much of the music of speech, as well as its negative shape, or counterpoint, of silence; and by focusing on human experience, which for her meant watching people caught up in landscapes they would never leave—man/woman, husband/wife, and especially, parents/children, as protagonists and antagonists alike. "Bringing them back to life," she said she wanted mainly to animate them, to have them "speak these days." She stresses everyone's need to learn language and use it richly, "not leaving it to the unborn poets." Especially the children must confront their own predicament and not rely on adults' perceptions—"and nothing was what they said . . ." is the child's lament in one of the poems.

"Do I move toward form, do I use all my fears?" she asked. Mature writer that she was, she realized our fears not only must be faced but must be _used_ as well, and these poems approach this ideal: Past the phrases, past the pieces, they move toward their songs, singing of us in unexpected lines and structures, the prevailing voice that of an ancient sleepwalker. One can compare the later poems to those of her contemporary, Roethke, as well as to subsequent work by poets like Jean Valentine.

Elsewhere, in an essay, Rukeyser recalls Lucretius "moving the sleeping images toward the light." Reading the poems of the last books, _The Speed of Darkness_, _Breaking Open_, and _The Gates_, we look across with her "at the real/ vulnerable   involved   naked/devoted to the present" of all we care for, set down in extraordinary, natural places— the long hall, for instance—in which nothing is safe. No wonder she worries at the end of _The Gates_, "How shall we speak to the infant beginning to run?/ All those beginning to run?"

_SF_

from Eight Elegy. Children's Elegy

This is what they say, who were broken off from love:
However long we were loved, it was not long enough.

We were afraid of the broad big policeman,
of lions and tigers, the dark hall and the moon.

After our father went, nothing was ever the same,
when mother did not come back, we made up a war game.

My cat was sitting in the doorway when the planes
went over, and my cat saw mother cry;
furry tears, fire fell, wall went down;
did my cat see mother die?

Mother is gone away, my cat sits here coughing.
I cough and sit. I am nobody's nothing.

However long they loved us, it was not long enough.
For we have to be strong, to know what they did, and then
our people are saved in time, our houses built again.

You will not know, you have a sister and brother;
My doll is not my child, my doll is my mother.

However strong we are, it is not strong enough.
I want to grow up. To come back to love.

Children, the Sandbar, That Summer

Sunlight the tall women may never have seen.
Men, perhaps, going headfirst into the breakers,
But certainly the children at the sandbar.
Shallow glints in the wave suspended
We knew at the breaker line, running that shore
At low tide, when it was safe. The grasses whipped
And nothing was what they said: not safety, nor the sea.
And the sand was not what they said, but various,
Lion-grained, beard-grey. And blue. And green.
And each grain casting its shadow down before
Childhood in tide-pools where all things are food.
Behind us the shores emerged and fed on tide.
We fed on summer, the round flowers in our hands
From the snowball bush entered us, and prisoner wings,
And shells in spirals, all food.
                             All keys to unlock
Some world, glinting as strong as noon on the sandbar,
Where men and women give each other children.

The Speed of Darkness

I

Whoever despises the clitoris despises the penis
Whoever despises the penis despises the cunt
Whoever despises the cunt despises the life of the child.

Resurrection music,   silence,   and surf.

II

No longer speaking
Listening with the whole body
And with every drop of blood
Overtaken by silence

But this same silence is become speech
With the speed of darkness.

III

Stillness during war, the lake.
The unmoving spruces.
Glints over the water.
Faces, voices.   You are far away.
A tree that trembles.

I am the tree that trembles and trembles.

IV

After the lifting of the mist
after the lift of the heavy rains
the sky stands clear
and the cries of the city risen in day
I remember the buildings are space
walled, to let space be used for living
I mind this room is space
this drinking glass is space
whose boundary of glass
lets me give you drink and space to drink
your hand, my hand being space
containing skies and constellations
your face
carries the reaches of air
I know I am space
my words are air.

V

Between   between
the man : act   exact
woman : in curve   senses in their maze
frail orbits, green tries,   games of stars
shape of the body speaking its evidence

VI

I look across at the real
vulnerable   involved   naked
devoted to the present of all I care for
the world of its history leading to this moment.

VII

Life the announcer.
I assure you
there are many ways to have a child.
I bastard mother
promise you
there are many ways to be born.
They all come forth
in their own grace.

VIII

Ends of the earth join tonight
with blazing stars upon their meeting.

These sons,   these sons
fall burning into Asia.

IX

Time comes into it.
Say it.   Say it.

The universe is made of stories,
not of atoms.

X

Lying
blazing beside me
you rear beautifully and up—
your thinking face—
erotic body reaching
in all its colors and lights—

your erotic face
colored and lit—
not colored body-and-face
but now entire,
colors   lights   the world thinking and reaching.

     XI
The river flows past the city.

Water goes down to tomorrow
making its children   I hear their unborn voices
I am working out the vocabulary of my silence.

     XII
Big-boned man young and of my dream
Struggles to get the live bird out of his throat.
I am he am I?   Dreaming?
I am the bird am I?   I am the throat?

A bird with a curved beak
It could slit anything, the throat-bird.

Drawn up slowly.   The curved blades, not large.
Bird emerges   wet   being born
Begins to sing.

     XIII
My night awake
staring at the broad rough jewel
the copper roof across the way
thinking of the poet
yet unborn in this dark
who will be the throat of these hours.
No.   Of those hours.
Who will speak these days,
if not I,
if not you?

Then

When I am dead, even then,
I will still love you, I will wait in these poems,
When I am dead, even then
I am still listening to you.
I will still be making poems for you
out of silence;
silence will be falling into that silence,
it is building music.

Waiting for Icarus

He said he would be back and we'd drink wine together
He said that everything would be better than before
He said we were on the edge of a new relation
He said he would never again cringe before his father
He said that he was going to invent full-time
He said he loved me that going into me
He said was going into the world and the sky
He said all the buckles were very firm
He said the wax was the best wax
He said Wait for me here on the beach
He said Just don't cry

I remember the gulls and the waves
I remember the islands going dark on the sea
I remember the girls laughing
I remember mother saying: Inventors are like poets, a trashy lot
I remember she told me those who try out inventions are worse
I remember she added: Women who love such are the worst of all

I have been waiting all day, or perhaps longer.
I would have liked to try those wings myself.
It would have been better than this.

Resurrection of the Right Side

When the half-body dies its frightful death
forked pain, infection of snakes, lightning, pull down the voice. Waking
and I begin to climb the mountain on my mouth,
word by stammer, walk stammered, the lurching deck of earth.
Left-right with none of my own rhythms
the long-established sex and poetry.
                          I go running in sleep,
but waking stumble down corridors of self, all rhythms gone.

The broken movement of love   sex out of rhythm
one halted name   in a shattered language
ruin of French-blue lights behind the eyes
slowly the left hand extends a hundred feet
and the right hand follows follows
but still the power of sight is very weak
but I go rolling this ball of life, it rolls
and I follow it whole up the slowly-brightening slope

A whisper attempts me, I whisper without stammer
I walk the long hall to the time of a metronome
set by a child's gun-target   left-right
the power of eyesight is very slowly arriving
          in this late impossible daybreak
          all the blue flowers open

MURIEL RUKEYSER

Books

Theory of Flight, 1935

A Turning Wind, 1939

Beast in View, 1944

The Green Wave, 1948

The Life of Poetry (essays), 1949

Selected Poems, 1951

Body of Waking, 1958

Waterlily Fire: Poems 1935–1962, 1962

The Speed of Darkness, 1968

Breaking Open, 1973

The Gates, 1976

Collected Poems, 1978

Criticism

Rachel Blau DuPlessis, "The Critique of Consciousness and Myth in Levertov, Rich, and Rukeyser," in *Shakespeare's Sisters: Feminist Essays on Women Poets*, ed. Gilbert and Gubar, 1979; Louise Kertesz, *The Poetic Vision of Muriel Rukeyser*, 1979.

William Stafford
(b. 1914)

Kit Stafford

At first glance, the poems of William Stafford seem simple and direct. Their plain and relaxed manner may remind us of Robert Frost. Like Frost, however, Stafford proves on closer examination to be a very elusive poet with a distinctive private vision that slips through our grasp when we try to identify, summarize, or paraphrase it. His world is regional—he writes of the lives and landscapes of the American Midwest and West—but it is also universal, seen *sub specie aeternitatis,* in a god's-eye view that subsumes all petty issues. His speakers and narrators tend to report moments when they are taken beyond the bounds of ordinary experience, and instead of showing the terror or exhilaration most of us would feel, they tend to react with a combination of equanimity and heightened awareness. The speaker of "Ceremony" has had his hand mangled by a muskrat, but he listens entranced to the calling of an owl and experiences a vision of expanded space and time that transcends the immediacy of his pain and the disconcerting nature of his encounter. The narrator of "Traveling Through the Dark" has an unpleasant, difficult task to face—the disposal of a dead deer and her unborn but still living fawn—but his ability to enlarge his consciousness ("around our group I could hear the wilderness listen") seems to make his personal emotions of distress or guilt disappear into his sense of awe. The voice of "Accountability" matches the ultimates of cold and space against the trucks, taverns, schools, military posters, and "fragmentary explorations" of wise thinkers, to show how these large, indifferent forces surround and chasten our fragile human world.

Stafford is tender about our foolishness; his tone is neither the satirist's nor the prophet's. But his sense of the precariousness of our giving and taking of meaning from nature, all our brave certainties and frightened temporizings, can be quietly, if good-humoredly, inexorable. Poems like "The Epitaph Ending in And" are not the products of a sensibility that cultivates easy answers or comforting evasions.

What are the origins of this modest gaze and voice that turn out to have such ineffable ways of seeing and saying the world, this soft-spoken sidling into the visionary? One answer may be found in the poem "The Rescued Year," almost certainly an account of Stafford's Kansas boyhood, in which the lessons he learned from his father are shown to have stood him in good stead as a man and as a writer ever since. His father is contrasted with the preacher, whose voice booms like "empty silos" while his father's "mean attention" and "wonderfully level gaze" go far beyond the knowledge of the man in the pulpit. The father's creed is a realistic seeing of the world as it is—"to glance around and understand"—that takes the patient witness toward unsought knowledge and truth. It makes the "dull town" an Aladdin's lamp and puts the Stafford family into the company of the old man "who spent his life knowing,/unable to tell how he knew." Indeed, the memory of that year and those lessons rescues them from time itself so that the past informs the present as a long-gone train that is able to ripple miraculously backward into the station.

Stafford's religious beliefs—the Church of the Brethren—made him a conscientious objector during the Second World War. He worked in labor camps, an experience recorded in a small prose memoir, *Down in My Heart.* After the war he studied in the Writing Program at the University of Iowa, and in 1948 he moved to Oregon, where he taught at Lewis and Clark College in Portland until his retirement.

Stafford came to notice later than many of his contemporaries, but his first sizable collection, *Traveling Through the Dark* (1962), won a National Book Award. He has been a remarkably prolific poet, generous in sending work to little magazines, and much of his poetry still remains uncollected. He has described his unusual writing methods: getting up early every day and writing in an undirected, random fashion, without worrying much about purpose at that early stage, a meditative ritual of sorts. His writer's sensibility seems to wander through the world in the same way that his gaze does, curious and tolerant, taking things as they come and regarding the manifestations of the extraordinary, whether comforting or frightening, with calm good humor. The writing method that leaves the subjects and outcomes of poems such an open question has produced, inevitably, an uneven canon, and it has also tended to give us poems that are open to interpretation. "Notice What This Poem is Not Doing" is merely the most obvious example in this selection of a poem that leaves large areas of interpretation and creation to the reader. Two very different accounts of what the poem is "not doing" would be unlikely to dismay or upset Stafford; he seems ready to live with a latitude of response in the same way that he lives with the vagaries and mysteries of the natural world, sustained by an odd and private faith in the large forces that exist beyond and around our lives.

William Stafford still lives in Oregon, though he travels and reads his work widely, one of the most admired presences on the current poetry scene: handy, shrewd, generous, with a whiff of the metaphysical about him, a man like the one in "The Rescued Year" for whom the truth, once it was ready, "didn't care how it came."

DY

Ceremony

On the third finger of my left hand
under the bank of the Ninnescah
a muskrat whirled and bit to the bone.
The mangled hand made the water red.

That was something the ocean would remember:
I saw me in the current flowing through the land,
rolling, touching roots, the world incarnadined,
and the river richer by a kind of marriage.

While in the woods an owl started quavering
with drops like tears I raised my arm.
Under the bank a muskrat was trembling
with meaning my hand would wear forever.

In that river my blood flowed on.

Traveling Through the Dark

Traveling through the dark I found a deer
dead on the edge of the Wilson River road.
It is usually best to roll them into the canyon:
that road is narrow; to swerve might make more dead.

By glow of the tail-light I stumbled back of the car
and stood by the heap, a doe, a recent killing;
she had stiffened already, almost cold.
I dragged her off; she was large in the belly.

My fingers touching her side brought me the reason—
her side was warm; her fawn lay there waiting,
alive, still, never to be born.
Beside that mountain road I hesitated.

The car aimed ahead its lowered parking lights;
under the hood purred the steady engine.
I stood in the glare of the warm exhaust turning red;
around our group I could hear the wilderness listen.

I thought hard for us all—my only swerving—,
then pushed her over the edge into the river.

The Rescued Year

Take a model of the world so big
it is the world again, pass your hand,
press back that area in the west where no one lived,
the place only your mind explores. On your thumb
that smudge becomes my ignorance, a badge
the size of Colorado: toward that state by train
we crossed our state like birds and lodged—
the year my sister gracefully
grew up—against the western boundary
where my father had a job.

Time should go the way it went
that year: we weren't at war; we had
each day a treasured unimportance;
the sky existed, so did our town;
the library had books we hadn't read;
every day at school we learned and sang,
or at least hummed and walked in the hall.

In church I heard the preacher; he said
"Honor!" with a sound like empty silos
repeating the lesson. For a minute I held
Kansas Christian all along the Santa Fe.
My father's mean attention, though, was busy—this
I knew—and going home his wonderfully level gaze
would hold the state I liked, where little happened
and much was understood. I watched my father's finger
mark off huge eye-scans of what happened in the creed.

Like him, I tried. I still try,
send my sight like a million pickpockets
up rich people's drives; it is time
when I pass for every place I go to be alive.
Around any corner my sight is a river,
and I let it arrive: rich by those brooks
his thought poured for hours
into my hand. His creed: the greatest ownership
of all is to glance around and understand.

That Christmas Mother made paper
presents; we colored them with crayons
and hung up a tumbleweed for a tree.
A man from Hugoton brought my sister
a present (his farm was tilted near oil
wells; his car ignored the little

bumps along our drive: nothing
came of all this—it was just part of the year).

I walked out where a girl I knew would be;
we crossed the plank over the ditch
to her house. There was popcorn on the stove,
and her mother recalled the old days, inviting me back.
When I walked home in the cold evening,
snow that blessed the wheat had roved
along the highway seeking furrows,
and all the houses had their lights—
oh, that year did not escape me: I rubbed
the wonderful old lamp of our dull town.

That spring we crossed the state again,
my father soothing us with stories:
the river lost in Utah, underground—
"They've explored only the ones they've found!"—
and that old man who spent his life knowing,
unable to tell how he knew—
"I've been sure by smoke, persuaded
by mist, or a cloud, or a name:
once the truth was ready"—my father smiled
at this—"it didn't care how it came."

In all his ways I hold that rescued year—
comes that smoke like love into the broken
coal, that forms to chunks again and lies
in the earth again in its dim folds, and comes a sound,
then shapes to make a whistle fade,
and in the quiet I hold no need, no hurry:
any day the dust will move, maybe settle;
the train that left will roll back into our station,
the name carved on the platform unfill with rain,
and the sound that followed the couplings back
will ripple forward and hold the train.

Observation Car and Cigar

Tranquility as his breath, his eye a camera
that believes, he follows rails that only last
one trip, then vanish. (Suppose America
tried and then was the West once more, but this time
no one found it? He has felt that much
alone.) Remembering with smoke, he uses

the haze as authentic (the authentic loves not kept
for display fade authentically and become
priceless, never to be exchanged). A silver
evening light follows the train silently
over a great bridge. Like a camera that
believes, he follows an arch into faded
authentic scenes that bring something presented again
and yet all new: traveling, our loves are brought
before us and followed securely into a new evening.

The Epitaph Ending in And

In the last storm, when hawks
blast upward and a dove is
driven into the grass, its broken wings
a delicate design, the air between
wracked thin where it stretched before,
a clear spring bent close too often
(that Earth should ever have such wings
burnt on in blind color!), this will be
good as an epitaph:

Doves did not know where to fly, and

Bring the North

Mushroom, Soft Ear, Old Memory,
Root Come to Tell the Air:
bring the Forest Floor along
the valley; bring all that comes
blue into passes, long shores
around a lake, talk, talk, talk,
miles, then deep. Bring that story.

Unfold a pack by someone's door—
wrapped in leather, brought in brown,
what the miles collect.
Leave sound in an empty
house in its own room there,
a little cube hung like a birdcage
in the attic, with a swinging door.
Search out a den: try natural,
no one's, your own, a dirt
floor. Accept them all.

One way to find your place is like
the rain, a million requests
for lodging, one that wins, finds
your cheek: you find your home,
a storm that walks the waves.
You hear that cloak whip, those
chilly hands take night apart.
In split Heaven you see one sudden
eye on yours, and yours in it,
scared, falling, fallen.

Mushroom, Soft Ear, Memory,
attend what is.
Bring the North.

In a Museum in the Capital

Think of the shark's tiny brain
trapped in that senseless lust,
ripped through the tide, dismayed.

Think of The Great, helpless,
their very purposes caught
like ice that cannot be else.

And even The Wise are framed—
plans bound like a vise on the face,
and vanity roaring its claims.

The clock ticks on, every second
wandering down like a snowflake,
while an avalanche whispers our names.

Accountability

Cold nights outside the taverns in Wyoming
pickups and big semi's lounge idling, letting their
haunches twitch now and then in gusts of powder snow,
their owners inside for hours, forgetting as well
as they can the miles, the circling plains, the still town
that connects to nothing but cold and space and a few
stray ribbons of pavement, icy guides to nothing
but bigger towns and other taverns that glitter and wait:
Denver, Cheyenne.

Hibernating in the library of the school on the hill
a few pieces by Thomas Aquinas or Saint Teresa
and the fragmentary explorations of people like Alfred
North Whitehead crouch and wait amid research folders
on energy and military recruitment posters glimpsed
by the hard stars. The school bus by the door, a yellow
mound, clangs open and shut as the wind finds a loose
door and worries it all night, letting the hollow
students count off and break up and blow away
over the frozen ground.

Notice What This Poem Is Not Doing

The light along the hills in the morning
comes down slowly, naming the trees
white, then coasting the ground for stones to nominate.

Notice what this poem is not doing.

A house, a house, a barn, the old
quarry, where the river shrugs—
how much of this place is yours?

Notice what this poem is not doing.

Every person gone has taken a stone
to hold, and catch the sun. The carving
says, "Not here, but called away."

Notice what this poem is not doing.

The sun, the earth, the sky, all wait.
The crows and redbirds talk. The light
along the hills has come, has found you.

Notice what this poem has not done.

School Days

1

After the test they sent an expert
questioner to our school: "Who is this
kid Bohr?" When Bohr came in
he asked the expert, "Who are you?"
and for a long time they looked at each other,

and Bohr said, "Thanks, I thought so." Then
they talked about why the test was given.
Afterwards they shook hands, and Bohr walked
slowly away. He turned and called out, "You passed."

2

Enough sleet had pasted over the window
by three o'clock so we couldn't tell if it was dark—
and our pony would be out there in the little shed
waiting to take us home. Teacher banked the stove
with an extra log. That was the storm
of 1934. For two days we waited,
singing and praying, and I guess it worked,
even though the snow drifted over the roof.
But the pony was dead when they dug us out.

3

At a tiny desk inside my desk, a doll
bends over a book. In the book is a feather
found at the beach, from a dead gull.
While Miss Leonard reads "The Highwayman,"
I bend over my book and cry,
and fly all alone through the night
toward being the person I am.

Serving with Gideon

Now I remember: in our town the druggist
prescribed Coca-Cola mostly, in tapered
glasses to us, and to the elevator
man in a paper cup, so he could
drink it elsewhere because he was black.

And now I remember The Legion—gambling
in the back room, and no women but girls, old boys
who ran the town. They were generous,
to their sons or the sons of friends.
And of course I was almost one.

I remember winter light closing
its great blue first slowly eastward
along the street, and the dark then, deep
as war, arched over a radio show
called the thirties in the great old U.S.A.

Look down, stars—I was almost
one of the boys. My mother was folding
her handkerchief; the library seethed and sparked;
right and wrong arced; and carefully
I walked with my cup toward the elevator man.

WILLIAM STAFFORD

Books

Down in My Heart (prose), 1947

West of Your City: Poems, 1960

Traveling Through the Dark, 1962

The Rescued Year, 1966

Allegiances, 1970

Someday, Maybe, 1973

Stories That Could Be True: New and Collected Poems, 1977

Writing the Australian Crawl: Views on the Writer's Vocation (essays), 1978

Things That Happen Where There Aren't Any People, 1980

A Glass Face in the Rain, 1982

Smoke's Way, 1983

You Must Revise Your Life (essays), 1986

An Oregon Message, 1987

Criticism, Interviews

Three articles on Stafford in *Modern Poetry Studies* 6 (Spring 1975); Alberta Turner, "William Stafford and the Surprise Cliché," *South Carolina Review* 7 (April 1975); Jonathan Holden, *The Mark to Turn: A Reading of William Stafford's Poetry*, 1976; George Lensing and Ronald Moran, *Four Poets of the Emotive Imagination: Robert Bly, James Wright, Louis Simpson and William Stafford*, 1976; Peter Stitt, *The World's Hieroglyphic Beauty: Five American Poets*, 1985.

Alberta
Turner
(b. 1919)

L ike some other writers in this collection, Alberta Turner is very much a teaching poet, with considerable editing and critical work to her credit as well. Born in New York City, she graduated from Hunter and Wellesley and received a Ph.D. from Ohio State University. She has been teaching at Cleveland State University since 1964, where she also directs the Poetry Center and a lively Poetry Series. Her interests range from Milton to contemporary poetics, and she has published essays, textbooks and poems for many years. With the publication of her first book of poems, *Need* (1971), she literally put her earlier ways with poems to rest. Having written extremely formal poems that no longer satisfied her, she began doing the exercises she assigned her students, participated in informal sessions with close poet-friends, and found her way to her own voice and her own material. She has since published three other collections, books that have marked her as a highly original poet, of whom Adrienne Rich says, "A poet of dark, forceful imagism wrenched it seems from a life bristling with awareness . . . . She takes materials of domestic life and sees them through the eye of nightmare. The milk bottle, the cracked egg . . . , the parts of the body, become Boschian. . . . And the voice that is recalling all these things is measured, precise and unhysterical."

Rich goes on to stress that Turner's work must be read as a whole, and that is true because she frequently works from one fragment to the next; only when strung together (as the poems are in the books) do the fragments assume the shape of a necklace. As Turner herself has noted, "The greatest part of craftsmanship is recognizing what has happened after it has happened." First she follows the emotional thrust of the apparently inconspicuous details she selects. Then she teases them into larger wholes, where they take on surprising dimensions: from two or three coalesced images we look out on many complex, implied relationships. It is a poetry that is never rendered sterile by statements or "ideas." What goes on inside each cell, or section, within the larger wholes, is something akin to how "Proverbs, Riddles, Spells" behave (title of a poem not presented here). The mode is close to what is called hermetic, a poetry that looks to heighten the lyrical quality of each word in such a way as to congeal it, or seal it in, with little emphasis on connections, which are left to the reader to make. The result is a delicate interplay between sound and silence, and the poems ultimately depend on her finding just the right word and the right cluster of words that will "explode" in this fashion.

A large concern with death drives these poems. Alberta Turner returns to it again and again, as the necessity we must come to terms with, but there is nothing ghostly or maudlin about her attitude. She has simply watched people die around her and she deals with the declarative, visible aspects of such loss. She has herself said, "These are uncomfortable poems to write—and to read." Whether treating an animal's death, her husband's, a close friend's, or even contemplating her own, how she will act and react, there is a flintiness, a rock-ribbed humor to her responses ("Axe?/I may be sitting on it") that reminds us life has many pains, but death no pleasures.

SF

Three Easters

Walking a cliff with a lamb
in my arms   the ewe stumbling
and chattering and looking up

Climbing down
the lamb in a sling   the ewe
calling from the beach

Standing on deck
squeezing the lamb to stop our shivering
a rumor of ewe   a rumor
of shore   in mist

Making Old Bones

1

Five barrels of flour   seventy sticks
of salted butter   Is that my measure?

Two thousand and four squeezings
of wet cloths   two thousand and eight
unwrappings of warm feet?

No matter how wide I spread
my skirt   my lap won't
hold them all

2

Shame
airless like jello
a lemon-lime plug
in my nose   my mouth
too full to swallow

All it takes is a friend
pushing a basket through a window
across the street   the smell of rice
my child has burned   a small black Angus
shoving against the teat

3

Too easy just to doze
without even untying my shoes
I should grate and grunt through a tight
slit   a caul of noise   bright sting   slap
Too easy this drowse   certainly false

Yet I have starved
I ate a peach thick with ants
and a hen that pulled its feathers out
and I left my teeth on a picnic cloth

Tray under washed sand
shells on cotton under glass
coffin lined   wheels oiled—

4

There's pulse in both my feet
Her feet are numb

Hers have gangrene
but mine are warm

There's butter here if I would bake
and soap if I would carve

A young man's climbing toward me
He's my son

A young girl cries
My girl I think

She's handed me a cake
I'm squeezing it

5

You said I'd be a good girl
if I tied my shoes   if
I'd not undress my doll
in the dining room   not
turn over the stone
to bury the worm

Here's a pill   Put it
on my tongue   Here's a paper cup
and a bent straw   Drink   Don't
wet the bed   Put in my teeth

Good

Drift

Imagine bouncing   bumping   humping over a cliff
the briskets heaving   the baskets hooping   the birds inside out
Imagine settling out of the high air
loops   beaks   tiny dolls with inch-long skirts

Then imagine rain   The draggle of it
glinting mud   drying paste
one doll's skirt over its head
the feathers stuck   their quills all whichways

and wind   winds

In Love with Wholes

1

You crawl around a rim
hold grass by its flat sides
find stones with hollows for your knees
drink only on clear days when blue
falls into pools   What do you mean?

You mean   but right and wrong don't form
Just beads on string   Some are blank
Some have faces but you can't arrange them
Some are soft and won't come off
Cut the string   and someone else strings

Moles burrow blind   Wings fold frayed
You bed on old burrs with soft prongs
They find you smoothed and bury you
in an egg   What have you said?

2

In love with wholes you round the heel
toward the toe   knit two together
down to one   cut thread
hide the end
                Or you pull your skin
over your head and ease out the arms

The jar you placed in Tennessee
tilts and fills with rain   You try
a castle   it doesn't speak
A flagpole takes five men to heave it up
You stand upon that hill and turn
North beetles   East stares   South yawns

Then wings pin your arms

                         "You write death"

Not really   A moleskin
makes a doll's rug   half a day
covers a well   my aunt's black stole
shows birds where corn is sown

                   "Show birds and you starve
                               a farm"

Not really   Birds drop some

    3
Air from the north so clear
you can see a boat beach on a cloud
You follow men from that boat up a cliff
toward a fire and its cave
You breathe   lean   listen   thin   steam

But you're not gone   That's it
You're not gone

Fourth Wish

Love?
     Too dangerous.
Axe?
     I may be sitting on it.
Kill?
     And what will I sell?

Stop it. Squatting
in the center of the onion,
isn't moist silk enough
and layers of moist silk
all the way up?

No, it's not.
Plague, tied to the gate, works loose
and comes after me wagging;
a ditch crosses the road and tags along;
barbed wire lollops beside me.

When the pod of the touch-me-not is knobby,
I pinch it.
When winter has killed too many bees,
I brush pollen.
I put limp fur things
Where crows can find them.

A Deaf Mute hires me.
I hold out my hand, and He drums
a quick sum on my palm.
When I ask Him what to do,
He just stands—watching.

But you have three wishes.
        I know.
Have you wished the first?
        Yes.
Have you wished the second?
        Yes.
The third?
        That too.

On the Nature of Food

What needs to be fed?
Not the sand dollar, already spent,
not the tent, its flaps open for the couple
who've gone down to the lake and won't be back,
nor the road, its back broken in so many places
it can't leave the ground.

Not the woman revolving a grapefruit
slowly in her hands, springing her thumb,
tilting toward shine.

And not my ears, that wake paired
and poke along to the nearest tree
as far as the jay that jeers and then
to the bald top, where a crow caws them out.

We feed from, to, in, further in, all the way in,
out the other side, and down, chewing a grassblade,
down to where we think we hear water falling.
Grass grows taller as we climb down.

We feed on small surprises,
the quarter-inch more of ripe pear,
the slick swallow of watermelon seeds,
the orange that peels all the way at first pull.

And the big surprise: the roof
peeled back like a sardine tin
and God sitting down on the chair
next to us and dangling His hands
between His knees and telling us, yes,
we *have* died and to pack a small bag
with buttons and matches and a candle stub—
That surprise, that food.

Water Eased of Its Cliffs by Falling

Time to draw the left foot back and let it
take the weight, waggle the elbows, let out breath
and wait a moment before breathing in.
I need not say, "Yes, almost a relief,
Yes, I'm making do. Yes, I'm sleeping well."
Bringing me fruit has eased them. One by one
they close the door and go home.
I take my ease in the old way, in the bathroom:
house of ease, seat of ease. "The king comes
more kindly from his ease." Your tube of toothpaste
is half full. That pleases me.

              *   *   *

I didn't want to make a spectacle of myself by crying
at the funeral, so I walked across the field
and almost missed it—and bawled through it anyway.
I'll invent a formula for answering the letters.
I'll be very careful to stick the stamps on
right side up. For once a decent respect.

Mornings I brought you a mug of tea,
and you thanked me and drank a swallow before I left.
Mondays you called out, "Have you any money?"
When I said no, you always found some in your bedside
drawer. I never went without lunch.

You had enough pocket knives for all
the grandsons. Shall I keep one? You wouldn't
let me see the rabbit the cat brought home.
You said it was already half skinned. Thank you.

Did I confuse you with God and my father?
Of course no self-respecting woman
would admit that. But sometimes I goaded
you until you almost hit me—almost.
"It grieves her to think of it,
yet it eases her stomach to tell it."

*   *   *

Again, I've burned the bacon. I know you
always say cook it on low, but I'm in a rush—
"Can't you slow down and just live?"
No. Anyone can be a wife.
"Will you ever grow up?"
If only I could. It's much warmer
to be good than proud.
"Easy girl, easy girl, easy—"

ALBERTA TURNER

Books

Need, 1971

Learning to Count, 1974

Lid and Spoon, 1977

Fifty Contemporary Poets: The
  Creative Process (textbook), 1980

Poets Teaching: The Creative
  Process (textbook), 1980

To Make a Poem (textbook), 1982

A Belfry of Knees, 1983

45 Contemporary Poems: The
  Creative Process (textbook), 1985

Robert
Penn
Warren
(b. 1905)

© Jerry Bauer

R obert Penn Warren has had an active life as a writer on many fronts: as a novelist, a social commentator, and a literary critic and theorist. In his later years, however, he has turned often and fruitfully to poetry as the favored vehicle for personal rumination and the airing of his existential concerns. The longer perspectives that old age brings, especially on childhood and youth, seem to rouse his imagination to some of its finest expressions. Many poets peak in youth or middle age and then decline or even stop writing; with Warren it has been a matter of growing strength and impressive productivity.

Born in 1905 in Guthrie, Kentucky, and educated at Vanderbilt, Warren has spent his life in academic settings: at Oxford as a Rhodes Scholar, and at Vanderbilt, LSU, Minnesota, and Yale as a teacher. Associated early with the group of southern writers who called themselves The Fugitives (a group that included the poets Allen Tate and John Crowe Ransom), he found time later, while at LSU with Cleanth Brooks, to help found the enormously influential school of literary interpretation called The New Criticism. The textbook Warren wrote with Brooks, *Understanding Poetry,* can be said to have revolutionized the teaching of poetry in this country. New Criticism advocated close attention to the literary text in pursuit of the fullest appreciation of its complexity. Brooks and Warren especially emphasized the function of irony, both in modern and traditional poems, as a form of emotional counterpointing. Meanwhile, Warren's career as a novelist had achieved both critical acclaim and popular success with the publication, in 1946, of *All The King's Men,* a fictionalized account of the career of Louisiana politician Huey Long. Warren continued to produce a variety of fiction, literary criticism, and social commentary through the 1950s and 1960s, but it was also in those years that he began to write the poems and poetic sequences for which he is also known and admired today.

Warren the novelist and Warren the literary critic and historian are never very far away when Warren the poet is in the foreground. His poems have a strong narrative base, and they resonate with his knowledge of our literary traditions, especially those derived from the romantics. Warren's comfort with romantic themes and rhetoric can also be seen as part of his southern heritage. He comes from a part of the country that never made a sharp break with the nineteenth century. The Fugitives repudiated many of the values of literary modernism, aligning their aesthetic with conservative political and social values. And the southern love of grandiloquence and oratory were little affected by Imagism and comparable movements.

Warren's sense of continuity with our country's past is surely one of his strengths, but it means that his readers must be prepared to hear almost uncanny echoes, at times, of writers like Poe and Whitman. It means melodrama, and a somewhat old-fashioned handling of structure, syntax, adjective, and theme. Yet Warren can surprise us with sudden forays into modern sensibility. The point is that he is not afraid to be florid, and to raise large issues boldly. His regional heritage, along with his age and long-standing interests, privileges that boldness.

    We have elected to represent Warren by a single, longer poem, "Tale of Time" (1966). It typifies his best poetry in many ways: the strong narrative elements, the intense preoccupation with the meaning and mystery of time, the exploration of the writer's own past, and the use of sequence, a group of lyrics surrounding a crucial center, in this case the death of the poet's mother. Many of the images—the mirror, the running water, the darkness, and insomnia—are recurrent favorites in Warren's poems; the authority with which they are handled bespeaks long and brooding familiarity. It can be noted too that the momentousness of the key event, one's mother's death, helps sustain the large-scale design and the high-flown style. The range of episodes is impressive too, from the rather naturalistic visit of the father and sons to the dying black woman in the Squigg-town ghetto—an event that mirrors the mother's death for all of them—to the surrealistic dream of eating the dead. In that gruesome but compelling image, which seems to stand for the need to fully assimilate grief and to physically realize the meaning of human mortality between one's own birth and death, Warren discovers a metaphor that is southern in its gothic overtones, existentialist in its pressing of the full possibilities of figuration, and wise in its ultimate meaning. The poem's cascade of feelings—wonder, grief, amusement, terror, and a simultaneous yearning for and revulsion toward the past—add up to a powerful experience for any reader. One feels how much of himself the poet has managed to invest in it.

    Robert Penn Warren was named the first Poet Laureate at the Library of Congress, a position considered to be the equivalent of the Poet Laureate in England. He has since resigned the position because of ill health, but the designation testifies to the esteem in which he is widely held, both as a man of letters and, more especially, as a poet.

DY

Tale of Time

I What Happened

It was October. It was the Depression. Money
Was tight. Hoover was not a bad
Man, and my mother
Died, and God
Kept on, and keeps on,
Trying to tie things together, but

It doesn't always work, and we put the body
Into the ground, dark
Fell soon, but not yet, and oh,
Have you seen the last oak leaf of autumn, high,
Not yet fallen, stung
By last sun to a gold
Painful beyond the pain one can ordinarily
Get? What

Was there in the interim
To do, the time being the time
Between the clod's *chunk* and
The full realization, which commonly comes only after
Midnight? That

Is when you will go to the bathroom for a drink of water.
You wash your face in cold water.
You stare at your face in the mirror, wondering
Why now no tears come, for
You had been proud of your tears, and so
You think of copulation, of
Fluid ejected, of
Water deeper than daylight, of
The sun-dappled dark of deep woods and
Blood on green fern frond, of
The shedding of blood, and you will doubt
The significance of your own experience. Oh,
Desolation—oh, if
You were rich!
You try to think of a new position. Is this

Grief? You pray
To God that this be grief, for
You want to grieve.

This, you reflect, is no doubt the typical syndrome.

But all this will come later.
There will also be the dream of the eating of human flesh.

II The Mad Druggist

I come back to try to remember the faces she saw every day.
She saw them on the street, at school, in the stores, at church.
They are not here now, they have been withdrawn, are put away.
They are all gone now, and have left me in the lurch.

I am in the lurch because they were part of her.
Not clearly remembering them, I have therefore lost that much
Of her, and if I do remember,
I remember the lineaments only beyond the ice-blur and soot-smutch

Of boyhood contempt, for I had not thought they were real.
The real began where the last concrete walk gave out
And the smart-weed crawled in the cracks, where the last privy canted to
     spill
Over flat in the rank-nourished burdock, and would soon, no doubt,

If nobody came to prop it, which nobody would do.
The real began there: field and woods, stone and stream began
Their utterance, and the fox, in his earth, knew
Joy; and the hawk, like philosophy, hung without motion, high,
     where the sun-blaze of wind ran.

Now, far from Kentucky, planes pass in the night, I hear them and all, all
     is real.
Some men are mad, but I know that delusion may be one name for truth.
The faces I cannot remember lean at my bed-foot, and grin fit to kill,
For we now share a knowledge I did not have in my youth.

There's one I remember, the old druggist they carried away.
They put him in Hoptown, where he kept on making his list—
The same list he had on the street when he stopped my mother to say:
"Here they are, Miss Ruth, the folks that wouldn't be missed,

"Or this God-durn town would be lucky to miss,
If when I fixed a prescription I just happened to pour
Something in by way of improvement." Then leaned in that gray way of
     his:
"But you—you always say something nice when you come in my store."

In Hoptown he worked on his list, which now could have nothing to do
With the schedule of deaths continuing relentlessly,
To include, in the end, my mother, as well as that list-maker who
Had the wit to see that she was too precious to die:

A fact some in the street had not grasped—nor the attending physician,
     nor God, nor I.

III Answer Yes or No

Death is only a technical correction of the market.
Death is only the transfer of energy to a new form.
Death is only the fulfilment of a wish.

Whose wish?

IV The Interim

1

Between the clod and the midnight
The time was.
There had been the public ritual and there would be
The private realization,
And now the time was, and

In that time the heart cries out for coherence.
Between the beginning and the end, we must learn
The nature of being, in order
In the end to be, so

Our feet, in first dusk, took
Us over the railroad tracks, where
Sole-leather ground drily against cinders, as when
Tears will not come. She

Whom we now sought was old. Was
Sick. Was dying. Was
Black. Was.
Was: and was that enough? Is
Existence the adequate and only target
For the total reverence of the heart?

We would see her who,
Also, had held me in her arms.
She had held me in her arms,
And I had cried out in the wide
Day-blaze of the world. But

Now was a time of endings.

What is love?

2

Tell me what love is, for
The harvest moon, gold, heaved
Over the far woods which were,
On the black land black, and it swagged over
The hill-line. That light
Lay gold on the roofs of Squigg-town, and the niggers
Were under the roofs, and
The room smelled of urine.
A fire burned on the hearth:
Too hot, and there was no ventilation, and

You have not answered my question.

3

Propped in a chair, lying down she
Could not have breathed, dying
Erect, breath
Slow from the hole of the mouth, that black
Aperture in the blackness which
Was her face, but
How few of them are really
Black, but she
Is black, and life
Spinning out, spilling out, from
The holes of the eyes: and the eyes are
Burning mud beneath a sky of nothing.
The eyes bubble like hot mud with the expulsion of vision.

I lean, I am the
Nothingness which she
Sees.

Her hand rises in the air.
It rises like revelation.
It moves but has no motion, and
Around it the world flows like a dream of drowning.
The hand touches my cheek.
The voice says: you.

I am myself.

The hand has brought me the gift of myself.

4

I am myself, and
Her face is black like cave-blackness, and over
That blackness now hangs death, gray
Like cobweb over the blackness of a cave, but
That blackness which she is, is
Not deficiency like cave-blackness, but is
Substance.
The cobweb shakes with the motion of her breath.

My hand reaches out to part that grayness of cobweb.

My lips touch the cheek, which is black.
I do not know whether the cheek is cold or hot, but I
Know that
The temperature is shocking.
I press my lips firmly against that death,
I try to pray.

The flesh is dry, and tastes of salt.

My father has laid a twenty-dollar bill on the table.
He, too, will kiss that cheek.

5

We stand in the street of Squigg-town.
The moon is high now and the tin roofs gleam.
My brother says: *The whole place smelled of urine.*
My father says: *Twenty dollars—oh, God, what
Is twenty dollars when
The world is the world it is!*

The night freight is passing.
The couplings clank in the moonlight, the locomotive
Labors on the grade.
The freight disappears beyond the coal chute westward, and
The red caboose light disappears into the distance of the continent.
It will move all night into distance.

My sister is weeping under the sky.
The sky is enormous in the absoluteness of moonlight.

These are factors to be considered in making any final estimate.

6

There is only one solution. If
You would know how to live, here
Is the solution, and under
My window, when ice breaks, the boulder
Groans in the gorge, the foam swirls, and in
The intensity of the innermost darkness of steel
The crystal blooms like a star, and at
Dawn I have seen the delicate print of the coon-hand in silt by the riffle.

Hawk-shadow sweetly sweeps the grain.
I would compare it with that fugitive thought which I can find no word
    for.

7

Planes pass in the night. I turn
To the right side if the beating
Of my own heart disturbs me.
The sound of water flowing is
An image of Time, and therefore
Truth is all and
Must be respected, and
On the other side of the mirror into which,
At morning, you will stare, History

Gathers, condenses, crouches, breathes, waits. History
Stares forth at you through the eyes which
You think are the reflection of
Your own eyes in the mirror.
Ah, Monsieur du Miroir!

Your whole position must be reconsidered.

8

But the solution: You
Must eat the dead.
You must eat them completely, bone, blood, flesh, gristle, even
Such hair as can be forced. You
Must undertake this in the dark of the moon, but
At your plenilune of anguish.

Immortality is not impossible,
Even joy.

V What Were You Thinking, Dear Mother?

What were you thinking, a child, when you lay,
At the whippoorwill hour, lost in the long grass,
As sun, beyond the dark cedars, sank?
You went to the house. The lamps were now lit.

What did you think when the evening dove mourned,
Far off in those sober recesses of cedar?
What relevance did your heart find in that sound?
In lamplight, your father's head bent at his book.

What did you think when the last saffron
Of sunset faded beyond the dark cedars,
And on noble blue now the evening star hung?
You found it necessary to go to the house,

And found it necessary to live on,
In your bravery and in your joyous secret,
Into our present maniacal century,
In which you gave me birth, and in

Which I, in the public and private mania,
Have lived, but remember that once I,
A child, in the grass of that same spot, lay,
And the whippoorwill called, beyond the dark cedars.

VI Insomnia

1

If to that place. Place of grass.
If to hour of whippoorwill, I.
If I now, not a child. To.
If now I, not a child, should come to
That place, lie in
That place, in that hour hear
That call, would
I rise,
Go?

Yes, enter the darkness. Of.
Darkness of cedars, thinking
You there, you having entered, sly,
My back being turned, face
Averted, or
Eyes shut, for
A man cannot keep his eyes steadily open
Sixty years.

I did not see you when you went away.

Darkness of cedars, yes, entering, but what
Face, what
Bubble on dark stream of Time, white
Glimmer un-mooned? Oh,
What age has the soul, what
Face does it wear, or would
I meet that face that last I saw on the pillow, pale?
I recall each item with remarkable precision.

Would the sweat now be dried on the temples?

2

What would we talk about? The dead,
Do they know all, or nothing, and
If nothing, does
Curiosity survive the long unravelment? Tell me

What they think about love, for I
Know now at long last that the living remember the dead only
Because we cannot bear the thought that they
Might forget us. Or is
That true? Look, look at these—
But no, no light here penetrates by which
You might see these photographs I keep in my wallet. Anyway,
I shall try to tell you all that has happened to me.

Though how can I tell when I do not even know?

And as for you, and all the interesting things
That must have happened to you and that
I am just dying to hear about—

But would you confide in a balding stranger
The intimate secret of death?

3

Or does the soul have many faces, and would I,
Pacing the cold hypothesis of Time, enter
Those recesses to see, white,
Whiter than moth-wing, the child's face
Glimmer in cedar gloom, and so
Reach out that I might offer
What protection I could, saying,
"I am older than you will ever be"—for it
Is the child who once
Lay lost in the long grass, sun setting.

Reach out, saying: "Your hand—
Give it here, for it's dark and, my dear,
You should never have come in the woods when it's dark,
But I'll take you back home, they're waiting."
And to woods-edge we come, there stand.

I watch you move across the open space.
You move under the paleness of new stars.
You move toward the house, and one instant,

A door opening, I see
Your small form black against the light, and the door
Is closed, and I

Hear night crash down a million stairs.
In the ensuing silence
My breath is difficult.

Heat lightning ranges beyond the horizon.

That, also, is worth mentioning.

    4

Come,
Crack crust, striker
From darkness, and let seize—let what
Hand seize, oh!—my heart, and compress
The heart till, after pain, joy from it
Spurt like a grape, and I will grind
Teeth on flint tongue till
The flint screams. Truth
Is all. But

I must learn to speak it
Slowly, in a whisper.

Truth, in the end, can never be spoken aloud,
For the future is always unpredictable.
But so is the past, therefore

At wood's edge I stand, and,
Over the black horizon, heat lightning
Ripples the black sky. After
The lightning, as the eye
Adjusts to the new dark,
The stars are, again, born.

They are born one by one.

ROBERT PENN WARREN

Books

Thirty-six Poems, 1935

Selected Poems, 1923–1943

Brother to Dragons: A Tale in Verse and Voices, 1953

Promises: Poems 1954–1956

You, Emperors, and Others: Poems 1957–1960

Selected Poems, New and Old, 1966

Incarnations: Poems, 1966–1968

Audubon: A Vision, 1969

Or Else, Poems 1968–1975

Now and Then, Poems 1976–1978

Rumor Verified, Poems 1979–1980

New and Selected Poems, 1923–1985

Criticism

John M. Bradbury, *The Fugitives: A Critical Account*, 1958; Leonard Casper, *Robert Penn Warren: The Dark and Bloody Ground*, 1963; Louis D. Rubin Jr., *The Faraway Country*, 1963; Charles H. Bohner, *Robert Penn Warren*, 1964; John Lewis Longley, Jr., *Robert Penn Warren*, 1969; James H. Justus, *The Achievement of Robert Penn Warren*, 1981.

Twenty Poets Born Between 1920 and 1930

John
Ashbery
(b. 1927)

William Stafford

R eaders unfamiliar with this century's experimental traditions in the arts (Dada and Surrealist poetry, abstract painting, serial music, etc.) are apt to be bewildered by John Ashbery's poetry. They may begin by taking it too seriously. Then, when they have discovered its playful, parodic, and deliberately arbitrary elements, they may wrongly conclude that there is no serious intent behind it, no substance under its brilliantly manipulated surfaces. Most of all, they will be frustrated if they bring an expectation of constancy to an art obsessed with shifting and changing possibilities. You must enjoy unpredictability—of tone, subject, and style—if you are to like John Ashbery. While most poets operate at a "middle distance" of consistent attitude and set relation of work to reader, Ashbery is usually either closer or farther away than we expect, veering from an unusually candid and forthright manner at one moment to perfectly specious and impenetrable statements and combinations at the next. We must be ready for anything in reading Ashbery, because this eclectic, dazzling, inventive creator of travesties and treatises is most of all ready to include anything, go anywhere, say what is least expected, in the service of an aesthetic dedicated to liberating poetry from predictable conventions and tired traditions.

The flight from tradition becomes a tradition of its own, of course, and the attack on conventions creates new ones. Thus it is that we have learned how to "read" abstract paintings, for example, recognizing that they can "express" emotional states without representing a known visual world, and acknowledging that their emphasis on their own medium—line, color, shape, texture—is a way of making us aware of them as objects that do not so much comment on the world as join it, as separate things in their own right. It is much more difficult to achieve this effect with works of art made of language, however, since language is insistently communicative and referential. But poems by early modern masters like Wallace Stevens, insofar as they seem to be about the nature of language and the enterprise of making poetry from it, anticipate the giddy exhilaration with which Ashbery makes language into "language," skating along the borders of sense and nonsense, meaning and gibberish, rational and irrational; he is the foremost current practitioner in English of an avant-garde "tradition of the new," centered in French culture and beginning with Cubism, Dada, and Apollinaire, that has touched all writers and artists since. As one poet put it recently, whether or not we consciously subscribe to this tradition, it is now part of the very air we breathe, so that John Ashbery, different as he may seem from most working poets, represents the extreme of a tendency to which all poets respond to some degree.

All this is not to claim that Ashbery's poems are best viewed as if they were Jackson Pollock canvases or Andy Warhol soup cans. This poet's gifts are in fact stylistic and musical. His strengths are the strengths of a good writer: an inventive imagination, a sharp eye for the rich possibilities of juxtaposition, an ear that makes him a superb mimic, and an appetite for the artistic transformations to which banality can be subjected. His weaknesses are a writer's too: a certain preciousness, an apparent absence of self-criticism that makes his work uneven, a tendency to lengthiness that can induce boredom. But because so few working poets share Ashbery's full allegiance to the modern experimental tradition described above, and so many painters and not a few composers do, the value of analogies to the other arts in his case remains a useful way of helping readers approach his poems.

Our relation to any given Ashbery poem ought to be highly speculative. If we happen to know where the details were appropriated—for example, recognizing the derivation of ''Glazunoviana'' from a famous geometry problem—we may feel quite at home with the way in which they are assembled playfully with an eye toward a semiserious culminating statement. If we do not, we need to proceed with more caution. How much does ''Civilisation and Its Discontents,'' for example, have to do with Freud's book by that title? Who is the speaker? Whom is he addressing? How much should the narrative elements be seen as part of some genuine story and how much as pseudo-narrative fragments in a large collage? To rush into single-minded answers to such questions would be not only to misread the poem by limiting its possibilities but to deprive ourselves of the enjoyable uncertainties Ashbery has prepared for us. As we read the poem's touching but perfectly silly closing stanza (''I had already swallowed the poison / And could only gaze into the distance . . .''), the mixture of possibilities, from Freud to romantic novels and operas, is what should most engage us. That the poem is primarily a love poem seems clear enough, but that it may be addressed to the reader by the writer is one of many possibilities we cannot afford to overlook.

Laced into Ashbery's fun, both overt and sly, is a plangent, romantic melancholy that is perfectly serious and often quite moving, and we must be ready to respond to that as well. He writes of the limits of language and art with great feeling, as well as of the traditional poetic subjects of love and loss, old age and death, isolation and community, belief and skepticism. The present selections do not stress all these facets of Ashbery's work, nor can they adequately represent his effective work in longer poems (e.g., ''The Skaters'' and ''Self-Portrait in a Convex Mirror''). This controversial and gifted poet has been so copious and restless that readers who wish a full portrait of his poetic achievement, good and bad, will need to read him more widely. All his collections, from the brilliant first book, *Some Trees,* to the most recent as of this writing, *April Galleons,* are currently in print.

DY

Glazunoviana

The man with the red hat
And the polar bear, is he here too?
The window giving on shade,
Is that here too?
And all the little helps,
My initials in the sky,
The hay of an arctic summer night?

The bear
Drops dead in sight of the window.
Lovely tribes have just moved to the north.
In the flickering evening the martins grow denser.
Rivers of wings surround us and vast tribulation.

Civilisation and Its Discontents

A people chained to aurora
I alone disarming you

Millions of facts of distributed light

Helping myself with some big boxes
Up the steps, then turning to no neighbourhood;
The child's psalm, slightly sung
In the hall rushing into the small room.
Such fire! leading away from destruction.
Somewhere in outer ether I glimpsed you
Coming at me, the solo barrier did it this time,
Guessing us staying, true to be at the blue mark
Of the threshold. Tired of planning it again and again,
The cool boy distant, and the soaked-up
Afterthought, like so much rain, or roof.

The miracle took you in beside him.
Leaves rushed the window, there was clear water and the sound of a
    lock.
Now I never see you much any more.
The summers are much colder than they used to be
In that other time, when you and I were young.
I miss the human truth of your smile,
The halfhearted gaze of your palms,
And all things together, but there is no comic reign
Only the facts you put to me. You must not, then,
Be very surprised if I am alone: it is all for you,
The night, and the stars, and the way we used to be.

There is no longer any use in harping on
The incredible principle of daylong silence, the dark sunlight
As only the grass is beginning to know it,
The wreath of the north pole,
Festoons for the late return, the shy pensioners
Agasp on the lamplit air. What is agreeable
Is to hold your hand. The gravel
Underfoot. The time is for coming close. Useless
Verbs shooting the other words far away.

I had already swallowed the poison
And could only gaze into the distance at my life
Like a saint's with each day distinct.
No heaviness in the upland pastures. Nothing
In the forest. Only life under the huge trees
Like a coat that has grown too big, moving far away,
Cutting swamps for men like lapdogs, holding its own,
Performing once again, for you and for me.

Märchenbilder

Es war einmal. . . No, it's too heavy
To be said. Besides, you aren't paying attention any more.
How shall I put it?
"The rain thundered on the uneven red flagstones.

The steadfast tin soldier gazed beyond the drops
Remembering the hat-shaped paper boat, that soon . . ."
That's not it either.
Think about the long summer evenings of the past, the queen anne's
    lace.

Sometimes a musical phrase would perfectly sum up
The mood of a moment. One of those lovelorn sonatas
For wind instruments was riding past on a solemn white horse.
Everybody wondered who the new arrival was.

Pomp of flowers, decorations
Junked next day. Now look out of the window.
The sky is clear and bland. The wrong kind of day
For business or games, or betting on a sure thing.

The trees weep drops
Into the water at night. Slowly couples gather.
She looks into his eyes. "It would not be good
To be left alone." He: "I'll stay

As long as the night allows.'' This was one of those night rainbows
In negative color. As we advance, it retreats; we see
We are now far into a cave, must be. Yet there seem to be
Trees all around, and a wind lifts their leaves, slightly.

I want to go back, out of the bad stories.
But there's always the possibility that the next one . . .
No, it's another almond tree, or a ring-swallowing frog . . .
Yet they are beautiful as we people them

With ourselves. They are empty as cupboards.
To spend whole days drenched in them, waiting for the next whisper,
For the word in the next room. This is how the princes must have
      behaved,
Lying down in the frugality of sleep.

On Autumn Lake

Leading liot act to foriage is activity
Of Chinese philosopher here on Autumn Lake thoughtfully inserted in
Plovince of Quebec—stop it! I will not. The edge hugs
The lake with ever-more-paternalistic insistence, whose effect
Is in the blue way up ahead. The distance

By air from other places to here isn't much, but
It doesn't count, at least not the way the
Shore distance—leaf, tree, stone; optional (fern, frog, skunk);
And then stone, tree, leaf; then another optional—counts.
It's like the ''machines'' of the 19th-century Academy.
Turns out you didn't need all that training
To do art—that it was even better not to have it. Look at
The Impressionists—some of 'em had it, too, but preferred to forget it
In vast composed canvases by turns riotous
And indigent in color, from which only the notion of space is lacking.

I do not think that this
Will be my last trip to Autumn Lake
Have some friends among many severe heads
We all scholars sitting under tree
Waiting for nut to fall. Some of us studying
Persian and Aramaic, others the art of distilling
Weird fragrances out of nothing, from the ground up.
In each the potential is realized, the two wires
Are crossing.

Friends

> I like to speak in rhymes,
> because I am a rhyme myself.
>
> NIJINSKY

I saw a cottage in the sky.
I saw a balloon made of lead.
I cannot restrain my tears, and they fall
On my left hand and on my silken tie,
But I cannot and do not want to hold them back.

One day the neighbors complain about an unpleasant odor
Coming from his room. _I went for a walk_
But met no friends. Another time I go outside
Into the world. It rocks on and on.
It was rocking before I saw it
And is presumably doing so still.

The banker lays his hand on mine.
His face is as clean as a white handkerchief.
We talk nonsense as usual.
I trace little circles on the light that comes in
Through the window on saw-horse legs.
Afterwards I see that we are three.
Someone had entered the room while I was discussing my money
     problems.
I wish God would put a stop to this. I
Turn and see the new moon through glass. I am yanked away
So fast I lose my breath, a not unpleasant feeling.

I feel as though I had been carrying the message for years
On my shoulders like Atlas, never feeling it
Because of never having known anything else. In another way
I am involved with the message. I want to put it down
(In two senses of "put it down") so that you
May understand the agreeable destiny that awaits us.
You sigh. Your sighs will admit of no impatience,
Only a vast crater lake, vast as the sea,
In which the sky, smaller than that, is reflected.

I reach for my hat
And am bound to repeat with tact
The formal greeting I am charged with.
No one makes mistakes. No one runs away
Any more. I bite my lip and
Turn to you. Maybe now you understand.

The feeling is a jewel like a pearl.

What Is Poetry

The medieval town, with frieze
Of boy scouts from Nagoya? The snow

That came when we wanted it to snow?
Beautiful images? Trying to avoid

Ideas, as in this poem? But we
Go back to them as to a wife, leaving

The mistress we desire? Now they
Will have to believe it

As we believe it. In school
All the thought got combed out:

What was left was like a field.
Shut your eyes, and you can feel it for miles around.

Now open them on a thin vertical path.
It might give us—what?—some flowers soon?

My Erotic Double

He says he doesn't feel like working today.
It's just as well. Here in the shade
Behind the house, protected from street noises,
One can go over all kinds of old feeling,
Throw some away, keep others.
                                        The wordplay
Between us gets very intense when there are
Fewer feelings around to confuse things.
Another go-round? No, but the last things
You always find to say are charming, and rescue me
Before the night does. We are afloat
On our dreams as on a barge made of ice,
Shot through with questions and fissures of starlight
That keep us awake, thinking about the dreams
As they are happening. Some occurrence. You said it.

I said it but I can hide it. But I choose not to.
Thank you. You are a very pleasant person.
Thank you. You are too.

Shadow Train

Violence, how smoothly it came
And smoothly took you with it
To wanting what you nonetheless did not want.
It's all over if we don't see the truth inside that meaning.

To want is to be better than before. To desire what is
Forbidden is permitted. But to desire it
And not want it is to chew its name like a rag.
To that end the banana shakes on its stem,

But the strawberry is liquid and cool, a rounded
Note in the descending scale, a photograph
Of someone smiling at a funeral. The great plumes
Of the dynastic fly-whisk lurch daily

Above our heads, as far up as clouds. Who can say
What it means, or whether it protects? Yet it is clear
That history merely stretches today into one's private guignol.
The violence dreams. You are half-asleep at your instrument table.

But Not That One

The works, the days, uh,
And weariness of the days
Gradually getting a little longer,
Turning out to be a smile, everything

Like that. And it does make a difference,
Oh it does. Because the smile is a different not us,
Ready to rescind, cancel,
Rip out the stitches of the sky,

Then it warmed up. O a lot
Blooms, gets squashed on the tongue:
Where are you going? Who do you think you are?
Crushed leaves, berries, the stars

Continually falling, streaking the sky:
Can it be the context? No, it is old and
Sometimes the agog spectator wrenches a cry
From its own house. He thought he heard.

NOTES

Glazunoviana. Alesandr Glazunov (1865–1936) was a Russian composer. The window, the bear, and the man in the red hat come from a riddle about the North Pole.

Civilisation and its Discontents. The title is after a famous work by Freud (1930).

Märchenbilder. The title means "fairy-tale images," The opening words, "*Es war einmal,*" are the traditional "once upon a time" beginning.

Friends. Nijinsky (1890–1950) was a famous Russian ballet dancer whose career was cut short by insanity. His journal, which is quoted in the epigraph, is a moving record of his illness and isolation.

JOHN ASHBERY

Books

Some Trees, 1956

The Tennis Court Oath, 1962

Rivers and Mountains, 1966

A Nest of Ninnies (novel, with James Schuyler), 1969

The Double Dream of Spring, 1970

Three Poems, 1972

Self-Portrait in a Convex Mirror, 1975

Houseboat Days, 1977

3 Plays, 1978

As We Know, 1979

Shadow Train, 1981

A Wave, 1985

Selected Poems, 1986

April Galleons, 1987

Criticism, Interviews

David Kermani, *John Ashbery: A Comprehensive Bibliography*, 1976; David Kalstone, *Five Temperaments*, 1977; David Shapiro, *John Ashbery: An Introduction to the Poetry*, 1979; Jonathan Holden, *The Rhetoric of the Contemporary Lyric*, 1980; Harold Bloom, ed., *John Ashbery* (Modern Critical Views Series), 1985.

Robert
Bly
(b. 1926)

William Stafford

Robert Bly is rightly considered one of the dominant forces in contemporary American poetry. As a translator (he has introduced many overlooked and even unknown European, South American, and Asian writers to American readers in vigorous translations), as an editor and publisher, and as a poet, he has played a major role in shaping what we read.

Bly's friendship with other poets of his generation has meant that his ideas about literary values and concerns have been as influential in practice as in theory. James Wright provides the most notable example of this type of influence. The two poets worked closely together during the crucial years that produced Bly's *Silence in the Snowy Fields* and Wright's *The Branch Will Not Break,* and the results of their mutual influence are everywhere evident in these two books. Desperate to shake off all formal aspects that ran counter to artistic intentions, they exhorted each other to write *American* poems in plain language. Bly's friendships with other poets have also left their mark (one thinks of the young Ezra Pound in searching for an analogy). From the reading and writing Bly urged on them, two key principles emerge: poetry must arrive at a visionary sense of the world through the least rhetorical means, and must be a kind of surrealist Puritan transcendentalism in the process; or, as he put it elsewhere, poems should "try to achieve 'two presences' by adopting the line with simple syntax." To accomplish this, poems need images that burn what is seen into place.

The "line with simple syntax" is the lifeblood of Bly's poems, adopted partly for didactic reasons, the chief argument against falsely abstract language that comes from too much appreciation of earlier periods and styles; and partly because Bly needs simple syntax to carry his strong opinions on national and private matters—lying and deceit, anger and fear—to a large public. In spite of the many exclamation points that ring out the assertions of the poems, the voice speaking them can and often does drop down to be quiet, to "talk low," as one poem says of two people out in a boat. In "Listening to Bach," the fifth section of "Six Winter Privacy Poems," the ecstatic shouting is tuned down for our inner ear: "There is someone inside this music/who is not well described by the names/of Jesus, or Jehovah, or the Lord of Hosts!" Indeed, and there is someone inside the poems as well who is better described as a meditator, albeit an exhorting one—"I want to be . . . , I want to be . . . " is the way many poems seem to speak. Tomas Tranströmer, the Swedish poet Bly has translated, says of his own poems that they are "active meditations, they want to wake us up"; it is a view that applies to Bly's work as well.

Given this focus on bare-bones structure and simple diction and syntax, it is no accident that Bly has turned more and more to the prose poem. "August Rain" and "Visiting Emily Dickinson's Grave with Robert Francis" are among his finest examples in the genre. These poems look lovingly, closely, in a childlike way, at things that are part of the natural world; but as they do they make astonishing comparisons. In "August Rain," starting with a "simple" scene—it is raining—we are quickly caught up in a biblical flood of spiritual as well as physical proportions. As "The black earth turns blacker, it absorbs the rain needles without a sound"; it is as if the poem itself absorbed its words without a sound. In "Visiting Emily Dickinson's Grave" the comparison of the distance between her house and grave to the immense distance through which "Satan and his helpers rose and fell, oh vast areas, the distances between stars, between the first time love is felt in the sleeves of a dress, and the death of the person who was in that room . . . " is extremely moving for the way the poet sees eternal forces manifested in simple details, simple objects. Bly has an exciting sense of scale.

Bly was one of the organizers of "Poets Reading Against the Vietnam War"; he has always assumed the role of citizen-poet, who believes poetry is the conscience of the age. While our selections have taken little account of his pointedly political poems (with the exception of "Turning Away from Lies" and "Three Presidents"), a recent poem like "Mourning Pablo Neruda" stirs our moral senses as much as famous poems (like "The Teeth Mother Naked at Last") that moved audiences during the war. The strangely skinny shape of "Mourning Pablo Neruda" is like a vase for its elemental language. The monologue of the driver, his eye on the jar of water beside him in the car like some animal he is about to release, resists abstraction and rhetoric as it accounts for Neruda's death: "For the dead remain inside/us, as water/remains/inside granite—/hardly at all—" We'd perhaps been expecting the word "forever," the exclaiming word most poets cannot seem to avoid, where we read "hardly at all." But this is a poem of releasing, of letting go, and saying the right good-bye. Of not pretending to understand what cannot be understood. In a famous Bashō poem that Bly has translated, the morning glory, though we must learn to regard it, is one more thing that cannot be our friend. Bly's poetry is about establishing the limits of what we can see, hear, and sense, of looking at "the other," as Rilke insisted we must, without confusing worlds.

SF

Driving Toward the Lac Qui Parle River

I

I am driving; it is dusk; Minnesota.
The stubble field catches the last growth of sun.
The soybeans are breathing on all sides.
Old men are sitting before their houses on carseats
In the small towns. I am happy,
The moon rising above the turkey sheds.

II

The small world of the car
Plunges through the deep fields of the night,
On the road from Willmar to Milan.
This solitude covered with iron
Moves through the fields of night
Penetrated by the noise of crickets.

III

Nearly to Milan, suddenly a small bridge,
And water kneeling in the moonlight.
In small towns the houses are built right on the ground;
The lamplight falls on all fours in the grass.
When I reach the river, the full moon covers it;
A few people are talking low in a boat.

Three Presidents

Andrew Jackson

I want to be a white horse!
I want to be a white horse on the green mountains!
A horse that runs over wooden bridges, and sleeps
In abandoned barns . . .

Theodore Roosevelt

When I was President, I crushed snails with my bare teeth.
I slept in my underwear in the White House.
I ate the Cubans with a straw, and Lenin dreamt of *me* every night.
I wore down a forest of willow trees. I ground the snow,
And sold it.

The mountains of Texas shall heal our cornfields,
Overrun by the yellow race.
As for me, I want to be a stone. Yes!
I want to be a stone laid down thousands of years ago,
A stone with almost invisible cracks!
I want to be a stone that holds up the edge of the lake house,
A stone that suddenly gets up and runs around at night,
And lets the marriage bed fall; a stone that leaps into the water,
Carrying the robber down with him.

John F. Kennedy

I want to be a stream of water falling—
Water falling from high in the mountains, water
That dissolves everything,
And is never drunk, falling from ledge to ledge, from glass to
    glass.
I want the air around me to be invisible, resilient,
Able to flow past rocks.
I will carry the boulders with me to the valley.
Then ascending I will fall through space again:
Glittering in the sun, like the crystal in sideboards,
Goblets of the old life, before it was ruined by the Church.
And when I ascend the third time, I will fall forever,
Missing the earth entirely.

Turning Away from Lies

1

If we are truly free, and live in a free country,
When shall I be without this heaviness of mind?
When shall I have peace? Peace this way and peace that way?
I have already looked beneath the street
And there I saw the bitter waters going down,
The ancient worms eating up the sky.

2

Christ did not come to redeem our sins
The Christ Child was not obedient to his parents
The Kingdom of Heaven does not mean the next life
No one in business can be a Christian
The two worlds are both in this world

3

The saints rejoice out loud upon their beds!
Their song moves through the troubled sea
The way the holy tortoise moves
From dark blue into troubled green,
Or ghost crabs move above the dolomite.
The thieves are crying in the wild asparagus.

Six Winter Privacy Poems

1

About four, a few flakes.
I empty the teapot out in the snow,
       feeling shoots of joy in the new cold.
By nightfall, wind,
the curtains on the south sway softly.

2

My shack has two rooms; I use one.
The light falls on my table,
and I fly into one of my own poems—
I can't tell you where—
as if I appeared where I am now,
in a wet field, snow falling.

3

More of the fathers are dying each day.
It is time for the sons.
Bits of darkness are gathering around them.
The bits appear as flakes of light.

4

Sitting Alone

There is a solitude like black mud!
Sitting in the darkness singing
I can't tell if this joy
is from the body, or the soul, or a third place!

5

Listening to Bach

There is someone inside this music
who is not well described by the names
of Jesus, or Jehovah, or the Lord of Hosts!

6

When I woke, new snow had fallen.
I am alone, yet someone else is with me,
drinking coffee, looking out at the snow.

August Rain

After a month and a half without rain, at last, in late August, darkness comes at three in the afternoon, a cheerful thunder begins, and at last the rain. I set a glass out on a table to measure the rain, and suddenly buoyant and affectionate go indoors to find my children. They are upstairs, playing quietly alone in their doll-filled rooms, hanging pictures, thoughtfully moving "the small things that make them happy" from one side of the room to another. I feel triumphant, without need of money, far from the grave. I walk over the grass, watching the soaked chairs, and the cooled towels, and sit down on my stoop, dragging a chair out with me. The rain deepens. It rolls off the porch roof, making a great puddle near me. The bubbles slide toward the puddle edge, are crowded, and disappear. The black earth turns blacker, it absorbs the rain needles without a sound. The sky is low, everything silent, as when parents are angry. . . . What has failed and been forgiven—the leaves from last year unable to go on, lying near the foundation, dry under the porch, retreat farther into the shadow, they give off a faint hum, as of birds' eggs, or the tail of a dog.

The older we get the more we fail, but the more we fail the more we feel a part of the dead straw of the universe, the corners of barns with cowdung twenty years old, the chairs fallen back on their heads in deserted houses, the belts left hanging over the chairback after the bachelor has died in the ambulance on the way to the city, these objects also belong to us, they ride us as the child holding on to the dog's fur, these appear in our dreams, they are more and more near us, coming in slowly from the wainscoting, they make our trunks heavy, accumulating between trips, they lie against the ship's side, and will nudge the hole open that lets the water in at last.

Snowbanks North of the House

Those great sweeps of snow that stop suddenly six feet from the
house . . .
Thoughts that go so far.
The boy gets out of high school and reads no more books;
the son stops calling home.
The mother puts down her rolling pin and makes no more bread.
And the wife looks at her husband one night at a party, and loves him
no more.
The energy leaves the wine, and the minister falls leaving the church.
It will not come closer—
the one inside moves back, and the hands touch nothing, and are safe.

The father grieves for his son, and will not leave the room where the
coffin stands.
He turns away from his wife, and she sleeps alone.

And the sea lifts and falls all night, the moon goes on through the
unattached heavens alone.
The toe of the shoe pivots
in the dust . . .
And the man in the black coat turns, and goes back down the hill.
No one knows why he came, or why he turned away, and did not
climb the hill.

Visiting Emily Dickinson's
Grave with Robert Francis

A black iron fence closes the graves in, its ovals delicate as wine
stems. They resemble those chapel windows on the main Aran island,
made narrow in the 4th century so that not too much rain would drive in
. . . It is April, clear and dry. Curls of grass rise around the nearby
gravestones.

The Dickinson house is not far off. She arrived here one day, at 56,
Robert says, carried over the lots between by six Irish laboring men, when
her brother refused to trust her body to a carriage. The coffin was
darkened with violets and pine boughs, as she covered the immense
distance between the solid Dickinson house and this plot.

The distance is immense, the distances through which Satan and his
helpers rose and fell, oh vast areas, the distances between stars, between
the first time love is felt in the sleeves of the dress, and the death of the
person who was in that room . . . the distance between the feet and head
as you lie down, the distance between the mother and father, through
which we pass reluctantly.

My family "address an Eclipse every morning, which they call their 'Father.' " Each of us crosses that distance at night, arriving out of sleep on hands and knees, astonished we see a hump in the ground where we thought a chapel would be . . . it is a grassy knoll. And we clamber out of sleep, holding on to it with our hands . . .

Mourning Pablo Neruda

Water is practical
especially in
August.
Faucet water
that drops
into the buckets
I carry
to the young
willow trees
whose leaves have been eaten
off by grasshoppers.
Or this jar of water
that lies next
to me
on the carseat
as I drive to my shack.
When I look down,
the seat all
around the jar
is dark,
for water doesn't intend
to give, it gives
anyway,
and the jar of water
lies there
quivering
as I drive
through a countryside
of granite quarries,
stones
soon to be shaped
into blocks for the dead,
the only
thing they have
left that is theirs.

For the dead remain inside
us, as water
remains
inside granite—
hardly at all—
for their job is to go
away,
and not come back,
even when we ask them, but
water comes to us—
it doesn't care
about us, it goes
around us, on the way
to the Minnesota River,
to the Mississippi River,
to the Gulf,
always closer
to where
it has to be,
No one lays flowers
on the grave
of water,
for it is not
here,
it is
gone.

ROBERT BLY

Books

Twenty Poems of Georg Trakl (translations, with James Wright), 1961

Silence in the Snowy Fields, 1962

The Light Around the Body, 1967

Knut Hamsun, *Hunger* (translation), 1967

Tomas Tranströmer: Twenty Poems (translations), 1970

The Teeth Mother Naked at Last, 1970

Neruda and Vallejo: Selected Poems (translations, with John Knoepfle and James Wright), 1971

Sleepers Joining Hands, 1973

Lorca and Jiménez: Selected Poems (translations), 1973

Leaping Poetry (essays and translations), 1975

The Morning Glory, 1975

Friends, You Drank Some Darkness: Three Swedish Poets (translations), 1976

This Body is Made of Camphor and Gopherwood, 1977

The Kabir Book: Forty-Four of the Ecstatic Poems of Kabir (translations), 1977

Vicente Aleixandre: Twenty Poems (translations, with Lewis Hyde), 1977

This Tree Will Be Here for a Thousand Years, 1979

Rainer Maria Rilke: Selected Poems (translations), 1981

The Man in the Black Coat Turns, 1981

The Eight Stages of Translation, 1983

Antonio Machado, Times Alone: Selected Poems (translations), 1983

Loving a Woman in Two Worlds, 1985

Selected Poems, 1986

Tomas Tranströmer: Selected Poems, 1954–1986 (translations), 1987

Interviews, Criticism

George Lensing and Ronald Moran, *Four Poets of the Emotive Imagination: Robert Bly, James Wright, Louis Simpson and William Stafford*, 1976; *Talking All Morning: Collected Interviews and Conversations*, 1979; Howard Nelson, *Robert Bly: An Introduction to the Poetry*, 1984; Richard P. Sugg, *Robert Bly*, 1986; William H. Roberson, *Robert Bly: A Primary and Secondary Bibliography*, 1986.

Robert Creeley
(b. 1926)

Bruce Jackson

A New Englander by birth, and in his way a poetic descendent of Emily Dickinson, Robert Creeley was perhaps most formed as an artist by his experiences at Black Mountain College in North Carolina where, like Denise Levertov, he came under the influence of Charles Olson, edited the *Black Mountain Review*—one of several lively little magazines founded right after World War II that tried to change the nature and direction of American poetry—and mixed with other emerging American artists. Creeley has also lived on Mallorca, where he founded the Divers Press; in Mexico; and in Buffalo, New York, where he has taught for many years at the University of Buffalo.

Much has been made of Charles Olson's influential essay "Projective Verse," with its discussion of the "possibilities of the breath" as well as its focus on our "listenings," and it no doubt helped Creeley to his vision of the poem: a tightly orchestrated voice-print of intimate exchanges between speaker and listener; "things made of words," he likes to say. Having grown up on a farm, with a sense of all speech as saying what needs saying and no more, Creeley was ready to investigate the borders between speech and silence, an issue that has obsessed other contemporary poets, most notably the great European poet Paul Celan.

Looking for a minimal structure to explore language, as the painter Mark Rothko had explored the nature of color in his striped shapes, Creeley came to plow the same furrow again and again, planting within its narrow borders the most complicated exchanges on friendship, family, love, and death. Mixing sophisticated classical subjects (in "Damon & Pythias," for example) with nursery rhymes and rhythms, he achieves an effect at once tender and frightening: Heads seem to roll at the ends of phrases, and courses are set we hadn't counted on. In the midst of the these tales, their little structures squared off in a grid of sharp breaths, a peculiar, mad-singing voice keeps breaking the myth. "They are all dead now," the child who has had to grow up too fast announces in a frightening, matter-of-fact way. In "And," we hear strains of "boom, boom, all fall down," a kind of baby talk by way of Gertrude Stein and e.e. cummings with its strange but familiar syncopations and repetitions.

In "A Gift of Great Value," gift-horse (Trojan horse?), Freud, and Maurice Sendak all come together for the windy ride from birth to death. In "The Turn," a sleight-of-hand, now-you-see-it, now-you-don't strategy is behind the oddly holiday-like visit the voiceless, faceless humans pay to a land of harsh and illusory scenery, where they perform a mimetic dance armed with a stalk of celery as their only prop. Both "The City" and "The Statue" function in similar ways, almost as if Creeley had wound them up and set them off, creating moving tableaux vivants. In "Time," Creeley sets his poetic dictum clearly before us, in verse: "Each moment is / of such paradoxical / definition—a / waterfall that would / flow backward / if it could." This view of time has its own limits; it can only be played back and forth: As soon as we dig down to our ancestors (with that iron shovel, in "And"), we discover them dead and must turn around ("The Turn"), come back up, start all over again. Creeley's poems are not mere make-believe; they are a form of knowledge and, within their own propositions, true: "I propose to you / a body bleached, a body / which would be dead / were it not alive" ("The Statue").

SF

Damon & Pythias

When he got into bed,
he was dead.

Oh god, god, god, he said.
She watched him take off his shoes

and kneel there
to look for the change which had fallen

out of his pocket.
Old Mr. Jones

whom nobody loves
went to market for it,

and almost found it
under a table,

but by that time was unable.
And the other day two men,

who had been known as friends,
were said to be living together again.

After Lorca

for M. Marti

The church is a business, and the rich
are the business men.
                    When they pull on the bells, the
poor come piling in and when a poor man dies, he has a wooden
cross, and they rush through the ceremony.

But when a rich man dies, they
drag out the Sacrament
and a golden Cross, and go *doucement, doucement*
to the cemetery.

And the poor love it
and think it's crazy.

A Gift of Great Value

Oh that horse I see so high
when the world shrinks into its
relationships, my mother
sees as well as I.

She was born, but I bore with her.
This horse was a mighty occasion!
The intensity of its feet! The height
of its immense body!

Now then in wonder at evening, at
the last small entrance of the night,
my mother calls it, and I
call it *my father.*

With angry face, with no
rights, with impetuosity and
sterile vision—and a great
wind we ride.

And

A pretty party for people
to become engaged in, she was

twentythree, he
was a hundred and twentyseven times

all the times, over and over
and under and under she went

down stairs, thru doorways,
glass, alabaster, an iron shovel

stood waiting and
she lifted it to dig

back
and back to mother,

father and brother,
grandfather and grandmother—

They are all dead now.

The Turn

Each way the turn
twists, to be apprehended:
now she is
there, now she

is not, goes, but
did she, having gone,
went before
the eye saw

nothing. The tree
cannot walk, all its
going must
be violence. They listen

to the saw cut, the
roots scream. And in eating
even a stalk of celery
there will be pathetic screaming.

But what we want
is not what we get.
What we saw, we think
we will see again?

We will not. Moving,
we will
move, and then
stop.

The City

Not from that
could you get it,
nor can things
comprise a form

just to be made.
Again, let
each be this or
that, they, together,

are many whereas,
one by one,
each is a wooden
or metal or even

water, or vegetable,
flower, a crazy orange
sun, a windy
dirt, and here is

a place to sit
shaded by tall buildings
and a bed that
grows leaves on

all its branches
which are
boards I know
soon enough.

The Statue

I propose to you
a body bleached, a body
which would be dead
were it not alive.

We will stand it up
in the garden, which
we have taken such pains
to water. All the flowers

will grow at its feet,
and evenings it will
soften there as the darkness
comes down from such space.

Perhaps small sounds
will come from it, perhaps
the wind only, but its
mouth, could one see it,

will flutter. There will be
a day it walks just before
we come to look at it, but by then
it will have returned to its place.

Time

Moment to
moment the
body seems

to me to
be there: a
catch of

air, pattern
of space—Let's
walk today

all the way
to the beach,
let's think

of where we'll be
in two years'
time, of where

we *were*. Let
the days go.
Each moment is

of such paradoxical
definition—a
waterfall that would

flow backward
if it could. It
can? My time,

one thinks,
is drawing to
some close. This

feeling comes
and goes. No
measure ever serves

enough, enough—
so "finish it"
gets done, alone.

For W.C.W.

The rhyme is after
all the repeated
insistence.

There, you say, and
there, and there,
and *and* becomes

just so. And
what one wants is
what one wants,

yet complexly
as you
say.

Let's
let it go.
I want—

Then there is—
and,
I want.

Somebody Died

What shall we know we don't know,
that we know we know we don't know.

        *   *   *

The head walks
down the
street with
an umbrella.

        *   *   *

People
were walking
by.

        *   *   *

They will think of anything
next, the woman says.

Place

There was a path
through the field
down to the river,

from the house
a walk of
a half an hour.

Like that—
walking,
still,

to go swimming,
but only
if someone's there.

NOTES

Damon & Pythias. According to Roman legend, Damon was a Syracusan who barely escaped suffering the death penalty as a voluntary hostage for his friend Pythias.

After Lorca. Federico Garcia Lorca (1898–1936) was a Spanish poet and playwright; *doucement* means "softly" or "sweetly."

For W.C.W. W.C.W. is, of course, William Carlos Williams.

ROBERT CREELEY

Books

The Kind of Act of, 1953
A Form of Women, 1959
For Love: Poems 1950–1960, 1962
The Island (novel), 1963
The Gold Diggers and Other Stories, 1965
Words, 1967
Pieces, 1968
A Quick Graph: Collected Notes and Essays, 1970
A Day Book, 1972
Selected Poems, 1976
Hello: A Journal, February 29–May 3, 1976, 1978
Later, 1979
Charles Olson and Robert Creeley: The Complete Correspondence, 1980
The Collected Poems of Robert Creeley, 1945–1975, 1982
Mirrors, 1983
The Collected Prose of Robert Creeley, 1984
Memory Gardens, 1986

Criticism, Interviews

Martin Duberman, *Black Mountain: An Exploration in Community,* 1972; Mary Novik, *Robert Creeley: An Inventory, 1945–1970,* 1973; Donald Allen, *Contexts of Poetry: Interviews 1961–1971,* 1973; Charles Altieri, *Self and Sensibility in Contemporary American Poetry,* 1984; Robert Von Hallberg, *American Poetry and Culture,* 1985.

James
Dickey
(b. 1923)

William Stafford

The southerner's talent for storytelling and exaggeration that is familiar to us through the fiction of writers like William Faulkner, Eudora Welty, and Flannery O'Connor has been manifested less frequently in the work of poets. James Dickey surely exemplifies one way in which the southern imagination can be turned to the possibilities of poetry. In Dickey's poems, yarns, tall tales, and grotesque characters aspire to the universal condition of myth. The effort to bring them to that pitch and status can produce poems that seem labored and pretentious; but when the combination works, the result is exciting and fresh, not least for the way in which the ordinary and extraordinary interact. In "Bread," for example, the meal that celebrates the rescue of some World War II aviators whose bomber crashed in a swamp is both a miraculous feast shot through with associations of biblical miracle (manna, pentecostal fire, loaves and fishes, the Last Supper) and at the same time a very modest affair in a mess tent, consisting of standard armed forces fare: powdered eggs, canned fruit cocktail, and Spam. Similarly, in "Hedge Life," the tiny creatures (voles, shrews, wrens, snakes) that live in the hedge remain real and ordinary to us at the same time that their home gradually expands in meaning to become a mythical kingdom.

The selection of James Dickey's work presented here totals no more than three poems because we wanted to demonstrate, through one long poem, the way in which his storytelling abilities, vivid imagination, drive to create myth, and propensity for length can combine to produce a poem as potent and distinctive as "Falling." Dickey was a fighter pilot in World War II and Korea, and his imagination often responds best to stories that involve flight in some way. "Bread" illustrates this on a small scale, "Falling" on a large one. Starting from a news item about a stewardess who was accidentally sucked out through the emergency door of an airliner in flight, Dickey imagines himself into the experience in a way that re-creates it powerfully for his readers and achieves a memorable, expressive effect we can call mythic. As her terrible fall becomes an exhilarated skydive and striptease, a freeing of the self from ordinary restraints and the desperate allegiance to life, a Rilkean embrace of death and a fallen—or falling!—condition, the stewardess changes from an ordinary person to a kind of fertility goddess and scapegoat, a transformation made plausible and exciting by the poem's narrative drive and imaginative intensity. Especially when read aloud, this poem is both sure-fire entertainment and a distinctive literary achievement.

James Dickey's narrative talents are also evident in his novel, *Deliverance* (1970), which was a popular though not a critical success. After his military service, Dickey was for many years an advertising executive in Atlanta, Georgia, before turning full-time to writing. His role at Jimmy Carter's inaugural, and the popular appeal of his poems, especially through their narrative strength and relative accessibility, have made him one of our better-known poets. He lives in Columbia, South Carolina, where he teaches at the university. *Poems 1957–1967* brings together most of his strongest work, though there have been subsequent volumes (e.g., *The Strength of Fields* and *Puella*). A second novel, *Alnilam,* was published in 1987.

DY

Bread

Old boys, the cracked boards spread before
You, bread and spam   fruit cocktail   powder
Of eggs. I who had not risen, but just come down
From the night sky   knew always this was nothing
Like home   for under the table I was cut deep
      In the shoes

To make them like sandals no stateside store
Ever sold   and my shirtsleeves were ragged as
Though chopped off by propellers in the dark.
It was all our squadron, old boys: it was thus
I sat with you on your first morning
      On the earth,

Old boys newly risen from a B-25 sinking slowly
Into the swamps of Ceram. Patrick said
We got out   we got out on the wings
And lived there   we spread our weight
Thin as we could   arms and legs spread, we lay
      Down night and day,

We lived on the wings. When one of us got to one
Knee to spear a frog   to catch a snake
To eat, we lost another inch. O that water,
He said. O that water. Old boys, when you first
Rose, I sat with you in the mess-tent
      On solid ground,

At the unsinkable feast, and looked at the bread
Given to lizard-eaters. They set it down
And it glowed from under   your tongues
Fluttered   you reached   the scales fell
From your eyes   all of us weightless from living
      On wings so long

No one could escape   no one could sink or swim
Or fly. I looked at your yellow eyeballs
Come up   evolved   drawn out of the world's slime
Amphibious eyes   and Patrick said Bread
Is good   I sat with you in my own last war
      Poem   I closed my eyes

I ate the food I ne'er had eat.

Hedge Life

At morning we all look out
As our dwelling lightens; we have been somewhere.
With dew our porous home
Is dense, wound up like a spring,

Which is solid as motherlode
At night. Those who live in these apartments
Exist for the feeling of growth
As thick as it can get, but filled with

Concealment. When lightning
Strikes us, we are safe; there is nothing to strike, no bole
For all-fire's shattered right arm.
We are small creatures, surviving

On the one breath that grows
In our lungs in the complex green, reassured in the dawn-
silver heavy as wool. We wait
With crowded excitement

For our house to spring
Slowly out of night-wet to the sun; beneath us,
The moon hacked to pieces on the ground.
None but we are curled

Here, rising another inch,
Knowing that what held us solid in the moon is still
With us, where the outside flowers flash
In bits, creatures travel

Beyond us like rain,
The great sun floats in a fringed bag, all stones quiver
With the wind that moves us.
We trade laughters silently

Back and forth, and feel,
As we dreamed we did last night, our noses safe in our fur,
That what is happening to us in our dwelling
Is true: That on either side

As we sleep, as we wake, as we rise
Like springs, the house is winding away across the fields,
Stopped only momentarily by roads,
King-walking hill after hill.

Falling

*A 29-year-old stewardess fell . . . to her
death tonight when she was swept
through an emergency door that suddenly sprang open . . . The body . . .
was found . . . three hours after the
accident.*

NEW YORK TIMES

The states when they black out and lie there rolling   when they turn
To something transcontinental   move by   drawing moonlight out of
     the great
One-sided stone hung off the starboard wingtip   some sleeper next to
An engine is groaning for coffee   and there is faintly coming in
Somewhere the vast beast-whistle of space. In the galley with its racks
Of trays   she rummages for a blanket   and moves in her slim
     tailored
Uniform to pin it over the cry at the top of the door. As though she
     blew

The door down with a silent blast from her lungs   frozen   she is
     black
Out finding herself   with the plane nowhere and her body taking by
     the throat
The undying cry of the void   falling   living   beginning to be
     something
That no one has ever been and lived through   screaming without
     enough air
Still neat   lipsticked   stockinged   girdled by regulation   her hat
Still on   her arms and legs in no world   and yet spaced also
     strangely
With utter placid rightness on thin air   taking her time   she holds it
In many places   and now, still thousands of feet from her death she
     seems
To slow   she develops interest   she turns in her maneuverable body

To watch it. She is hung high up in the overwhelming middle of things
     in her
Self   in low body-whistling wrapped intensely   in all her dark
     dance-weight
Coming down from a marvellous leap   with the delaying,
     dumbfounding ease

Of a dream of being drawn   like endless moonlight to the harvest soil
Of a central state of one's country   with a great gradual warmth
     coming
Over her   floating   finding more and more breath in what she has
     been using
For breath   as the levels become more human   seeing clouds placed
     honestly
Below her left and right   riding slowly toward them   she clasps it
     all
To her and can hang her hands and feet in it in peculiar ways   and
Her eyes opened wide by wind, can open her mouth as wide   wider
     and suck
All the heat from the cornfields   can go down on her back with a
     feeling
Of stupendous pillows stacked under her   and can turn   turn as to
     someone
In bed   smile, understood in darkness   can go away   slant   slide
Off tumbling   into the emblem of a bird with its wings half-spread
Or whirl madly on herself   in endless gymnastics in the growing
     warmth
Of wheatfields rising toward the harvest moon.   There is time to live
In superhuman health   seeing mortal unreachable lights far down
     seeing
An ultimate highway with one late priceless car probing it   arriving
In a square town   and off her starboard arm the glitter of water
     catches
The moon by its one shaken side   scaled, roaming silver   My God it
     is good
And evil   lying in one after another of all the positions for love
Making   dancing   sleeping   and now cloud wisps at her no
Raincoat   no matter   all small towns brokenly brighter from inside
Cloud   she walks over them like rain   bursts out to behold a
     Greyhound
Bus shooting light through its sides   it is the signal to go straight
Down like a glorious diver   then feet first   her skirt stripped
     beautifully
Up   her face in fear-scented cloths   her legs deliriously bare   then
Arms out   she slow-rolls over   steadies out   waits for something
     great
To take control of her   trembles near feathers   planes head-down
The quick movements of bird-necks turning her head   gold eyes the
     insight-
eyesight of owls blazing into the hencoops   a taste for chicken
     overwhelming
Her   the long-range vision of hawks enlarging all human lights of cars
Freight trains   looped bridges   enlarging the moon racing slowly

Through all the curves of a river   all the darks of the midwest blazing
From above. A rabbit in a bush turns white   the smothering chickens
Huddle   for over them there is still time for something to live
With the steaming half-idea of a long stoop   a hurtling   a fall
That is controlled   that plummets as it wills   turns gravity
Into a new condition, showing its other side like a moon   shining
New Powers   there is still time to live on a breath made of nothing
But the whole night   time for her to remember to arrange her skirt
Like a diagram of a bat   tightly it guides her   she has this flying-
     skin
Made of garments   and there are also those sky-divers on TV
     sailing
In sunlight   smiling under their goggles   swapping batons back and
     forth
And He who jumped without a chute and was handed one by a diving
Buddy. She looks for her grinning companion   white teeth
     nowhere
She is screaming   singing hymns   her thin human wings spread out
From her neat shoulders   the air beast-crooning to her   warbling
And she can no longer behold the huge partial form of the world
     now
She is watching her country lose its evoked master shape   watching it
     lose
And gain   get back its houses and peoples   watching it bring up
Its local lights   single homes   lamps on barn roofs   if she fell
Into water she might live   like a diver   cleaving   perfect   plunge

Into another   heavy silver   unbreathable   slowing   saving
Element: there is water   there is time to perfect all the fine
Points of diving   feet together   toes pointed   hands shaped right
To insert her into water like a needle   to come out healthily dripping
And be handed a Coca-Cola   there they are   there are the waters
Of life   the moon packed and coiled in a reservoir   so let me begin
To plane across the night air of Kansas   opening my eyes
     superhumanly
Bright   to the dammed moon   opening the natural wings of my
     jacket
By Don Loper   moving like a hunting owl toward the glitter of water
One cannot just fall   just tumble screaming all that time   one must
     use
It   she is now through with all   through all   clouds   damp
     hair
Straightened   the last wisp of fog pulled apart on her face like wool
     revealing
New darks   new progressions of headlights along dirt roads   from
     chaos

And night   a gradual warming   a new-made, inevitable world of
    one's own
Country   a great stone of light in its waiting waters   hold   hold
    out
For water: who knows when what correct young woman must take up
    her body
And fly   and head for the moon-crazed inner eye of midwest
    imprisoned
Water   stored up for her for years   the arms of her jacket slipping
Air up her sleeves to go   all over her? What final things can be said
Of one who starts out sheerly in her body in the high middle of night
Air   to track down water like a rabbit where it lies like life itself
Off to the right in Kansas? She goes toward   the blazing-bare lake
Her skirts neat   her hands and face warmed more and more by the air
Rising from pastures of beans   and under her   under chenille
    bedspreads
The farm girls are feeling the goddess in them struggle and rise
    brooding
On the scratch-shining posts of the bed   dreaming of female signs
Of the moon   male blood like iron   of what is really said by the
    moan
Of airliners passing over them at dead of midwest midnight   passing
Over brush fires   burning out in silence on little hills   and will
    wake
To see the woman they should be   struggling on the rooftree to
    become
Stars: for her the ground is closer   water is nearer   she passes
It   then banks   turns   her sleeves fluttering differently as she rolls
Out to face the east, where the sun shall come up from wheatfields
    she must
Do something with water   fly to it   fall in it   drink it   rise
From it   but there is none left upon earth   the clouds have drunk it
    back
The plants have sucked it down   there are standing toward her only
The common fields of death   she comes back from flying to falling
Returns to a powerful cry   the silent scream with which she blew
    down
The coupled door of the airliner   nearly   nearly losing hold
Of what she has done   remembers   remembers the shape at the
    heart
Of cloud   fashionably swirling   remembers she still has time to die
Beyond explanation. Let her now take off her hat in summer air the
    contour
Of cornfields   and have enough time to kick off her one remaining
Shoe with the toes   of the other foot   to unhook her stockings
With calm fingers, noting how fatally easy it is to undress in midair

Near death   when the body will assume without effort any position
Except the one that will sustain it   enable it to rise   live
Not die   nine farms hover close   widen   eight of them separate,
     leaving
One in the middle   then the fields of that farm do the same   there is
     no
Way to back off   from her chosen ground   but she sheds the jacket
With its silver sad impotent wings   sheds the bat's guiding tailpiece
Of her skirt   the lightning-charged clinging of her blouse   the
     intimate
Inner flying-garment of her slip in which she rides like the holy ghost
Of a virgin   sheds the long windsocks of her stockings   absurd
Brassiere   then feels the girdle required by regulations squirming
Off her: no longer monobuttocked   she feels the girdle flutter   shake
In her hand   and float   upward   her clothes rising off her
     ascending
Into cloud   and fights away from her head the last sharp dangerous
     shoe
Like a dumb bird   and now will drop in   SOON   now will drop

In like this   the greatest thing that ever came to Kansas   down
     from all
Heights   all levels of American breath   layered in the lungs from
     the frail
Chill of space to the loam where extinction slumbers in corn tassels
     thickly
And breathes like rich farmers counting: will come among them after
Her last superhuman act   the last slow careful passing of her hands
All over her unharmed body   desired by every sleeper in his dream:
Boys finding for the first time their loins filled with heart's blood
Widowed farmers whose hands float under light covers to find
     themselves
Arisen at sunrise   the splendid position of blood unearthly drawn
Toward clouds   all feel something   pass over them as she passes
Her palms over _her_ long legs   _her_ small breasts   and deeply
     between
Her thighs   her hair shot loose from all pins   streaming in the wind
Of her body   let her come openly   trying at the last second to land
On her back   This is it   THIS
                                   All those who find her impressed
In the soft loam   gone down   driven well into the image of her body
The furrows for miles flowing in upon her where she lies very deep
In her mortal outline   in the earth as it is in cloud   can tell nothing
But that she is there   inexplicable   unquestionable   and remember
That something broke in them as well   and began to live and die
     more

When they walked for no reason into their fields to where the whole
    earth
Caught her   interrupted her maiden flight   told her how to lie   she
    cannot
Turn   go away   cannot move   cannot slide off it and assume
    another
Position   no sky-diver with any grin could save her   hold her in his
    arms
Plummet with her   unfold above her his wedding silks   she can no
    longer
Mark the rain with whirling women that take the place of a dead wife
Or the goddess in Norwegian farm girls   or all the back-breaking
    whores
Of Wichita. All the known air above her is not giving up quite one
Breath   it is all gone   and yet not dead   not anywhere else
Quite   lying still in the field on her back   sensing the smells
Of incessant growth try to lift her   a little sight left in the corner
Of one eye   fading   seeing something wave   lies believing
That she could have made it   at the best part of her brief goddess
State   to water   gone in headfirst   come out smiling
    invulnerable
Girl in a bathing-suit ad   but she is lying like a sunbather at the last
Of moonlight   half-buried in her impact on the earth   not far
From a railroad trestle   a water tank   she could see if she could
Raise her head from her modest hole   with her clothes beginning
To come down all over Kansas   into bushes   on the dewy sixth
    green
Of a golf course   one shoe   her girdle coming down fantastically
On a clothesline, where it belongs   her blouse on a lightning rod:

Lies in the fields   in *this* field   on her broken back as though on
A cloud she cannot drop through   while farmers sleepwalk without
Their women from houses   a walk like falling toward the far waters
Of life   in moonlight   toward the dreamed eternal meaning of their
    farms
Toward the flowering of the harvest in their hands   that tragic cost

Feels herself go   go toward   go outward   breathes at last fully
Not   and tries   less   once   tries   tries   AH, GOD—

JAMES DICKEY

Books

Into the Stone (in *Poets of Today*, VII), 1960

Drowning with Others, 1962

Helmets, 1964

The Suspect in Poetry (criticism), 1964

Buckdancer's Choice, 1965

Poems, 1957–1967, 1967

Babel to Byzantium (criticism), 1968

Deliverance (novel), 1970

The Eye-Beaters, Blood, Victory, Madness, Buckhead and Mercy, 1970

The Zodiac, 1976

The Strength of Fields, 1979

Puella, 1981

Alnilam (novel), 1987

Criticism, Interviews

Richard Howard, *Alone With America: Essays on the Art of Poetry in the United States Since 1950*, 1969, rev. 1980; *Self-Interviews.* 1970; John Graham, interview with Dickey in *The Writer's Voice: Conversations with Contemporary Writers*, ed. George Garrett, 1973; Norman Silverstein, "James Dickey's Muscular Eschatology," in *Contemporary Poetry in America*, ed. Robert Boyers, 1974; Richard J. Calhoun and Robert W. Hill, *James Dickey*, 1983; Bruce Weigl and T. R. Hummer, eds., *The Imagination as Glory*, 1984; Neal Bowers, *James Dickey: The Poet as Pitchman*, 1985.

Allen
Ginsberg
(b. 1926)

Robert Frank

A llen Ginsberg has achieved a legendary status that few poets experience in their lifetimes. Born in 1926 in Paterson, New Jersey, and educated at Columbia University, he worked for a while as a market analyst and wrote the kind of tight, metaphysical lyrics that were typical of the Fifties. Then, just short of thirty, he produced a long poem, "Howl," that caught the imagination of his generation and seemed to many to have permanently altered the course of American poetry. Ginsberg has remained a public figure ever since, known not only for his poetry—which he has recited to large audiences all over the world—but for his political activism in connection with the anti-war movement of the Sixties and for his deep interest in Eastern religions, especially Buddhism. He's a kind of international "clown prince" of poetry and mysticism, a figure who inspires affection even among those who feel that his literary reputation is based more on notoriety than on genuine accomplishment.

As an artist, Ginsberg is linked to William Carlos Williams, a sort of mentor, and to the group of writers known as "Beats," especially Jack Kerouac, Gregory Corso, Gary Snyder, and Philip Whalen. But he can also claim a distinctive heritage in the form of a tradition of ecstatic, "bardic" writing that has roots in the Bible, and representatives like Smart and Blake in the eighteenth century, Whitman and Rimbaud in the nineteenth, and Robinson Jeffers and Vladimir Mayakovsky in the twentieth. The poetry produced in this tradition is often characterized by a long line, repetitive phrasings, and the rhetoric of the Old Testament Psalms. When successful, it sustains a kind of pulsing energy that offsets the often prolix manner. Ginsberg could also invoke an artistic parallel to his poems in the improvisatory, spontaneous practices of American jazz musicians. He once characterized "Howl" as a kind of "jazz mass."

We have chosen to represent Ginsberg here with the entire text of "Howl," not only because it was his personal breakthrough from a more derivative and less expressive poetic style, but because it still carries, especially when read aloud, the almost volcanic intensity it registered on its first appearance. Other Ginsberg poems convey his wit, his spiritual and political values, his myriad experiences and preoccupations, but this one is still his grand "coming out" as a poet and his finest achievement, quivering with his indignation, compassion, and sense of artistic discovery. It helped bring American poetry into new areas of subject matter and altered attitudes toward poetic form.

There can be little doubt that a decision to write candidly about his own homosexuality contributed to Ginsberg's breakthrough. As he took on what was then taboo material, he began to feel less bound by orthodox modes of expression. He has said that he began "in solitude, diddling around with the form, thinking it couldn't be published anyway (queer content my parents shouldn't see, etc.) also it was out of my short-line line. But . . . I changed my mind about "measure" while writing it" ("From An Early Letter," as cited in *The New Naked Poetry,* ed. Berg and Mezey, 1976). New content and new form seem to have led each other on. And the combination of previously off-limit experiences—the underworld of drugs, gay pickups, hoboes, sailors, and bohemian artists—with the specialized "bardic" mode produced rhetorically effective results. Here was subject matter few dared to approach in the Fifties, treated not with circumspection or apology but ecstatically, in a style usually reserved for spiritual revelations and prophetic certainties.

The avalanche of detail the peom treats us to, moving relentlessly through the subterranean culture that fascinated Ginsberg, is largely a litany of loss. It catalogues wild pleasures and free spirits but it admits continuously to the self-destructive impulses by which its gifted but doubtful heroes are driven to snuff out their lives and dissipate their talents in a culture that can scarcely understand or value them. Besides the homosexuals, to whom he returns again and again, Ginsberg surveys radical activists (especially communists), drug addicts, mental patients, itinerants, and street people of every sort. Many of them are artists—former, would-be, and in a few cases genuine. By this association an interesting double shift is effected: art is brought down to the level of social misfits and dropouts, and at the same time the underworld drug culture and gay community are exalted to the level of art. Any good artist, the implication runs, will have to know and inhabit this ecstatic, hallucinatory world; its inhabitants, by converse implication, are all artists of a kind too. It is a simplistic formula, even a sentimental one, but it had, and still has, great power, especially when the aims of society and the aims of art are seriously opposed. They were deeply opposed in the Fifties, and Ginsberg blew the cover off the idea that art could be tame, safe, and less dangerous than crime or political subversion.

The first and longest section of "Howl" is mainly a list of characters whose wasted lives can affirm the catalogue of society's failures to redeem the individual and make a significant place for art. It brims with stirring details, and if it is overlong for what it accomplishes, one feels one wants to grant the poem's voice full scope for its woeful and sometimes grotesquely comic catalogue. The second section is mounted on a recurrent cry of accusation; we now learn that society's materialist greed is the root cause of which all these torn lives are symptoms. The third section is a kind of prayer and lullaby, affirming the love and brotherhood that can prevail in Ginsberg's strange underworld. It closes with a visionary moment that seems to combine sleep, escape, and apocalypse.

Ginsberg's remarkable accomplishment in this poem, and others, has earned him the celebrity status mentioned earlier, one that is compounded of shock, affection, admiration for his courage, and, by now, historical respect. He continues to lead an active life as a traveler, informal preacher, and spokesman for the value, meaning, and necessary freedom of art.

DY

Howl

For Carl Solomon

I

I saw the best minds of my generation destroyed by madness, starving
    hysterical naked,
dragging themselves through the negro streets at dawn looking for an
    angry fix,
angelheaded hipsters burning for the ancient heavenly connection to the
    starry dynamo in the machinery of night,
who poverty and tatters and hollow-eyed and high sat up smoking in the
    supernatural darkness of cold-water flats floating across the tops of
    cities contemplating jazz,
who bared their brains to Heaven under the El and saw Mohammedan
    angels staggering on tenement roofs illuminated,
who passed through universities with radiant cool eyes hallucinating
    Arkansas and Blake-light tragedy among the scholars of war,
who were expelled from the academies for crazy & publishing obscene
    odes on the windows of the skull,
who cowered in unshaven rooms in underwear, burning their money in
    wastebaskets and listening to the Terror through the wall,
who got busted in their pubic beards returning through Laredo with a belt
    of marijuana for New York,
who ate fire in paint hotels or drank turpentine in Paradise Alley, death,
    or purgatoried their torsos night after night
with dreams, with drugs, with waking nightmares, alcohol and cock and
    endless balls,
incomparable blind streets of shuddering cloud and lightning in the mind
    leaping toward poles of Canada & Paterson, illuminating all the
    motionless world of Time between,
Peyote solidities of halls, backyard green tree cemetery dawns, wine
    drunkenness over the rooftops, storefront boroughs of teahead joyride
    neon blinking traffic light, sun and moon and tree vibrations in the
    roaring winter dusks of Brooklyn, ashcan rantings and kind king light
    of mind,
who chained themselves to subways for the endless ride from Battery to
    holy Bronx on benzedrine until the noise of wheels and children
    brought them down shuddering mouth-wracked and battered bleak of
    brain all drained of brilliance in the drear light of Zoo,
who sank all night in submarine light of Bickford's floated out and sat
    through the stale beer afternoon in desolate Fugazzi's, listening to the
    crack of doom on the hydrogen jukebox,
who talked continuously seventy hours from park to pad to bar to
    Bellevue to museum to the Brooklyn Bridge,

a lost battalion of platonic conversationalists jumping down the stoops off
    fire escapes off windowsills off Empire State out of the moon,
yacketayakking screaming vomiting whispering facts and memories and
    anecdotes and eyeball kicks and shocks of hospitals and jails and
    wars,
whole intellects disgorged in total recall for seven days and nights with
    brilliant eyes, meat for the Synagogue cast on the pavement,
who vanished into nowhere Zen New Jersey leaving a trail of ambiguous
    picture postcards of Atlantic City Hall,
suffering Eastern sweats and Tangerian bone-grindings and migraines of
    China under junk-withdrawal in Newark's bleak furnished room,
who wandered around and around at midnight in the railroad yard
    wondering where to go, and went, leaving no broken hearts,
who lit cigarettes in boxcars boxcars boxcars racketing through snow
    toward lonesome farms in grandfather night,
who studied Plotinus Poe St. John of the Cross telepathy and bop
    kabbalah because the cosmos instinctively vibrated at their feet in
    Kansas,
who loned it through the streets of Idaho seeking visionary indian angels
    who were visionary indian angels,
who thought they were only mad when Baltimore gleamed in
    supernatural ecstasy,
who jumped in limousines with the Chinaman of Oklahoma on the
    impulse of winter midnight streetlight smalltown rain,
who lounged hungry and lonesome through Houston seeking jazz or sex
    or soup, and followed the brilliant Spaniard to converse about
    America and Eternity, a hopeless task, and so took ship to Africa,
who disappeared into the volcanoes of Mexico leaving behind nothing but
    the shadow of dungarees and the lava and ash of poetry scattered in
    fireplace Chicago,
who reappeared on the West Coast investigating the FBI in beards and
    shorts with big pacifist eyes sexy in their dark skin passing out
    incomprehensible leaflets,
who burned cigarette holes in their arms protesting the narcotic tobacco
    haze of Capitalism,
who distributed Supercommunist pamphlets in Union Square weeping
    and undressing while the sirens of Los Alamos wailed them down,
    and wailed down Wall, and the Staten Island ferry also wailed,
who broke down crying in white gymnasiums naked and trembling before
    the machinery of other skeletons,
who bit detectives in the neck and shrieked with delight in policecars for
    committing no crime but their own wild cooking pederasty and
    intoxication,
who howled on their knees in the subway and were dragged off the roof
    waving genitals and manuscripts,

who let themselves be fucked in the ass by saintly motorcyclists, and
   screamed with joy,
who blew and were blown by those human seraphim, the sailors, caresses
   of Atlantic and Caribbean love,
who balled in the morning in the evenings in rosegardens and the grass of
   public parks and cemeteries scattering their semen freely to
   whomever come who may,
who hiccuped endlessly trying to giggle but wound up with a sob behind
   a partition in a Turkish Bath when the blond & naked angel came to
   pierce them with a sword,
who lost their loveboys to the three old shrews of fate the one eyed shrew
   of the heterosexual dollar the one eyed shrew that winks out of the
   womb and the one eyed shrew that does nothing but sit on her ass
   and snip the intellectual golden threads of the craftsman's loom,
who copulated ecstatic and insatiate with a bottle of beer a sweetheart a
   package of cigarettes a candle and fell off the bed, and continued
   along the floor and down the hall and ended fainting on the wall
   with a vision of ultimate cunt and come eluding the last gyzym of
   consciousness,
who sweetened the snatches of a million girls trembling in the sunset,
   and were red eyed in the morning but prepared to sweeten the snatch
   of the sunrise, flashing buttocks under barns and naked in the lake,
who went out whoring through Colorado in myriad stolen night-cars,
   N.C., secret hero of these poems, cocksman and Adonis of Denver—
   joy to the memory of his innumerable lays of girls in empty lots &
   diner backyards, moviehouses' rickety rows, on mountaintops in
   caves or with gaunt waitresses in familiar roadside lonely petticoat
   upliftings & especially secret gas-station solipsisms of johns, &
   hometown alleys too,
who faded out in vast sordid movies, were shifted in dreams, woke on a
   sudden Manhattan, and picked themselves up out of basements
   hungover with heartless Tokay and horrors of Third Avenue iron
   dreams & stumbled to unemployment offices,
who walked all night with their shoes full of blood on the snowbank
   docks waiting for a door in the East River to open to a room full of
   steam-heat and opium,
who created great suicidal dramas on the apartment cliff-banks of the
   Hudson under the wartime blue floodlight of the moon & their heads
   shall be crowned with laurel in oblivion,
who ate the lamb stew of the imagination or digested the crab at the
   muddy bottom of the rivers of Bowery,
who wept at the romance of the streets with their pushcarts full of onions
   and bad music,
who sat in boxes breathing in the darkness under the bridge, and rose up
   to build harpsichords in their lofts,

who coughed on the sixth floor of Harlem crowned with flame under the
     tubercular sky surrounded by orange crates of theology,

who scribbled all night rocking and rolling over lofty incantations which
     in the yellow morning were stanzas of gibberish,

who cooked rotten animals lung heart feet tail borsht & tortillas dreaming
     of the pure vegetable kingdom,

who plunged themselves under meat trucks looking for an egg,

who threw their watches off the roof to cast their ballot for Eternity
     outside of Time, & alarm clocks fell on their heads every day for the
     next decade,

who cut their wrists three times successively unsuccessfully, gave up and
     were forced to open antique stores where they thought they were
     growing old and cried,

who were burned alive in their innocent flannel suits on Madison Avenue
     amid blasts of leaden verse & the tanked-up clatter of the iron
     regiments of fashion & the nitroglycerine shrieks of the fairies of
     advertising & the mustard gas of sinister intelligent editors, or were
     run down by the drunken taxicabs of Absolute Reality,

who jumped off the Brooklyn Bridge this actually happened and walked
     away unknown and forgotten into the ghostly daze of Chinatown
     soup alleyways & firetrucks, not even one free beer,

who sang out of their windows in despair, fell out of the subway window,
     jumped in the filthy Passaic, leaped on negroes, cried all over the
     street, danced on broken wineglasses barefoot smashed phonograph
     records of nostalgic European 1930s German jazz finished the
     whiskey and threw up groaning into the bloody toilet, moans in their
     ears and the blast of colossal steamwhistles,

who barreled down the highways of the past journeying to each other's
     hotrod-Golgotha jail-solitude watch or Birmingham jazz incarnation,

who drove crosscountry seventytwo hours to find out if I had a vision or
     you had a vision or he had a vision to find out Eternity,

who journeyed to Denver, who died in Denver, who came back to Denver
     & waited in vain, who watched over Denver & brooded & loned in
     Denver and finally went away to find out the Time, & now Denver is
     lonesome for her heroes,

who fell on their knees in hopeless cathedrals praying for each other's
     salvation and light and breasts, until the soul illuminated its hair for
     a second,

who crashed through their minds in jail waiting for impossible criminals
     with golden heads and the charm of reality in their hearts who sang
     sweet blues to Alcatraz,

who retired to Mexico to cultivate a habit, or Rocky Mount to tender
     Buddha or Tangiers to boys or Southern Pacific to the black
     locomotive or Harvard to Narcissus to Woodlawn to the daisychain or
     grave,

who demanded sanity trials accusing the radio of hypnotism & were left
   with their insanity & their hands & a hung jury,

who threw potato salad at CCNY lecturers on Dadaism and subsequently
   presented themselves on the granite steps of the madhouse with
   shaven heads and harlequin speech of suicide, demanding
   instantaneous lobotomy,

and who were given instead the concrete void of insulin Metrazol
   electricity hydrotherapy psychotherapy occupational therapy
   pingpong & amnesia,

who in humorless protest overturned only one symbolic pingpong table,
   resting briefly in catatonia,

returning years later truly bald except for a wig of blood, and tears and
   fingers, to the visible madman doom of the wards of the madtowns of
   the East,

Pilgrim State's Rockland's and Greystone's foetid halls, bickering with the
   echoes of the soul, rocking and rolling in the midnight solitude-bench
   dolmen-realms of love, dream of life a nightmare, bodies turned to
   stone as heavy as the moon,

with mother finally ******, and the last fantastic book flung out of the
   tenement window, and the last door closed at 4 A.M. and the last
   telephone slammed at the wall in reply and the last furnished room
   emptied down to the last piece of mental furniture, a yellow paper
   rose twisted on a wire hanger in the closet, and even that imaginary,
   nothing but a hopeful little bit of hallucination—

ah, Carl, while you are not safe I am not safe, and now you're really in
   the total animal soup of time—

and who therefore ran through the icy streets obsessed with a sudden
   flash of the alchemy of the use of the ellipse the catalog the meter &
   the vibrating plane,

who dreamt and made incarnate gaps in Time & Space through images
   juxtaposed, and trapped the archangel of the soul between 2 visual
   images and joined the elemental verbs and set the noun and dash of
   consciousness together jumping with sensation of Pater Omnipotens
   Aeterna Deus

to recreate the syntax and measure of poor human prose and stand before
   you speechless and intelligent and shaking with shame, rejected yet
   confessing out the soul to conform to the rhythm of thought in his
   naked and endless head,

the madman bum and angel beat in Time, unknown, yet putting down
   here what might be left to say in time come after death,

and rose reincarnate in the ghostly clothes of jazz in the goldhorn shadow
   of the band and blew the suffering of America's naked mind for love
   into an eli eli lamma lamma sabacthani saxophone cry that shivered
   the cities down to the last radio

with the absolute heart of the poem of life butchered out of their own
   bodies good to eat a thousand years.

II

What sphinx of cement and aluminum bashed open their skulls and ate
up their brains and imagination?

Moloch! Solitude! Filth! Ugliness! Ashcans and unobtainable dollars!
Children screaming under the stairways! Boys sobbing in armies! Old
men weeping in the parks!

Moloch! Moloch! Nightmare of Moloch! Moloch the loveless! Mental
Moloch! Moloch the heavy judger of men!

Moloch the incomprehensible prison! Moloch the crossbone soulless
jailhouse and Congress of sorrows! Moloch whose buildings are
judgment! Moloch the vast stone of war! Moloch the stunned
governments!

Moloch whose mind is pure machinery! Moloch whose blood is running
money! Moloch whose fingers are ten armies! Moloch whose breast is
a cannibal dynamo! Moloch whose ear is a smoking tomb!

Moloch whose eyes are a thousand blind windows! Moloch whose
skyscrapers stand in the long streets like endless Jehovahs! Moloch
whose factories dream and croak in the fog! Moloch whose
smokestacks and antennae crown the cities!

Moloch whose love is endless oil and stone! Moloch whose soul is
electricity and banks! Moloch whose poverty is the specter of genius!
Moloch whose fate is a cloud of sexless hydrogen! Moloch whose
name is the Mind!

Moloch in whom I sit lonely! Moloch in whom I dream Angels! Crazy in
Moloch! Cocksucker in Moloch! Lacklove and manless in Moloch!

Moloch who entered my soul early! Moloch in whom I am a
consciousness without a body! Moloch who frightened me out of my
natural ecstasy! Moloch whom I abandon! Wake up in Moloch! Light
streaming out of the sky!

Moloch! Moloch! Robot apartments! invisible suburbs! skeleton treasuries!
blind capitals! demonic industries! spectral nations! invincible
madhouses! granite cocks! monstrous bombs!

They broke their backs lifting Moloch to Heaven! Pavements, trees, radios,
tons! lifting the city to Heaven which exists and is everywhere about
us!

Visions! omens! hallucinations! miracles! ecstasies! gone down the
American river!

Dreams! adorations! illuminations! religions! the whole boatload of
sensitive bullshit!

Breakthroughs! over the river! flips and crucifixions! gone down the flood!
Highs! Epiphanies! Despairs! Ten years' animal screams and suicides!
Minds! New loves! Mad generation! down on the rocks of Time!

Real holy laughter in the river! They saw it all! the wild eyes! the holy
yells! They bade farewell! They jumped off the roof! to solitude!
waving! carrying flowers! Down to the river! into the street!

III

Carl Solomon! I'm with you in Rockland
  where you're madder than I am
I'm with you in Rockland
  where you must feel very strange
I'm with you in Rockland
  where you imitate the shade of my mother
I'm with you in Rockland
  where you've murdered your twelve secretaries
I'm with you in Rockland
  where you laugh at this invisible humor
I'm with you in Rockland
  where we are great writers on the same dreadful typewriter
I'm with you in Rockland
  where your condition has become serious and is reported on the
  radio
I'm with you in Rockland
  where the faculties of the skull no longer admit the worms of the
  senses
I'm with you in Rockland
  where you drink the tea of the breasts of the spinsters of Utica
I'm with you in Rockland
  where you pun on the bodies of your nurses the harpies of the
  Bronx
I'm with you in Rockland
  where you scream in a straightjacket that you're losing the game of
  the actual pingpong of the abyss
I'm with you in Rockland
  where you bang on the catatonic piano the soul is innocent and
  immortal it should never die ungodly in an armed madhouse
I'm with you in Rockland
  where fifty more shocks will never return your soul to its body again
  from its pilgrimage to a cross in the void
I'm with you in Rockland
  where you accuse your doctors of insanity and plot the Hebrew
  socialist revolution against the fascist national Golgotha
I'm with you in Rockland
  where you will split the heavens of Long Island and resurrect your
  living human Jesus from the superhuman tomb
I'm with you in Rockland
  where there are twentyfive thousand mad comrades all together
  singing the final stanzas of the Internationale
I'm with you in Rockland
  where we hug and kiss the United States under our bedsheets the
  United States that coughs all night and won't let us sleep

I'm with you in Rockland
> where we wake up electrified out of the coma by our own souls'
> airplanes roaring over the roof they've come to drop angelic bombs
> the hospital illuminates itself   imaginary walls collapse   O skinny
> legions run outside   O starry-spangled shock of mercy the eternal
> war is here   O victory forget your underwear we're free

I'm with you in Rockland
> in my dreams you walk dripping from a sea-journey on the highway
> across America in tears to the door of my cottage in the Western
> night

San Francisco, 1955–1956

ALLEN GINSBERG

Books

Howl and Other Poems, 1956

Empty Mirror: Early Poems, 1961

Kaddish and Other Poems, 1961

Reality Sandwiches, 1963

Planet News, 1968

The Fall of America: Poems of These States, 1968–1971

Mind Breaths, 1978

Collected Poems, 1984

The White Shroud, 1986

Interviews, Criticism

David Ossman, *The Sullen Art* (interview), 1963; Richard Howard, *Alone With America,* 1959; Thomas F. Merrill, *Allen Ginsberg,* 1969; James Breslin, "Allen Ginsberg: The Origins of 'Howl' and 'Kaddish,'" *Iowa Review* 8 (1977).

Donald
Hall
(b. 1928)

T he poems of Donald Hall show a remarkable variety of subjects and forms, but one of the constants that links them is a concern with the nature of time. Like many poets, past and present, Hall is fascinated by process and change, and his poems seek out those moments when time is transcended or understood. They might be described as a quest for such transcendence, a quest that turns up in metaphors of travel, like the river journey in "The Long River" or the last flight in "The Old Pilot." The sense of mystery involved in our confrontations with time is expressed in images as various as the accordion in "Wedding Party," the abandoned airfield in "An Airstrip in Essex, 1960," and the strange group of associations that come together in "Apples." Whether we call it change or mortality, the question of how we can reconcile our lives with this force remains an open one, but the sculptures of Henry Moore, as characterized in " 'Reclining Figure,' " with their representation of movement in a permanent form ("Then the knee of the wave / turned to stone"), suggest art's power to engineer such truces. Moore may also interest Hall by the fact of his productive old age; Hall has always been fascinated by longevity in artists and has interviewed and written about many elderly poets: Frost, Pound, Eliot, MacLeish. Father figures? Perhaps. But certainly successful creators over long spans, reflecting a harmonious existence in and with the temporal process.

Nature is another source of such harmony. In the poem "New Hampshire" the natural world, which includes the ruins of abandoned homesteads where "A bear sleeps in a cellar hole," exists as an accommodation of changelessness and change, and it can absorb even the anomalous wrecked aircraft, an image from other Hall poems where the combat aircraft of both world wars seem to stand for death and change. The natural energy that brings raspberries—"a quarrel of vines"—and bees from the "spilled body" of the wreck seems to argue for the restorative powers of nature. The poem is prophetic of Hall's own recent move to New Hampshire, where he has settled on his grandparents' farm and begun to write poems that investigate the timescapes in the rhythms and details of farm life. Hence the "ten thousand years" of man-sheep association witnessed in "The Black Faced Sheep."

Donald Hall was born and raised in Connecticut and educated at Harvard, Oxford, and Stanford. He taught for many years at the University of Michigan. His first book, *Exiles and Marriages* (1956), cultivated wit and formal elegance, primary values of the period that produced it, but in the 1960s his work began to change, reflecting the influence of American poetry's new preoccupation with surrealism and "deep image" poetry. Poems in this "middle" period sometimes experiment with the less noticed formal possibilities of syllabics, as in "The Long River," which uses a stanza with a set number of syllables to each line in the pattern 4-4-5-4-4, and "Apples," with its intricate stanza of 3-11-5-9 (or 7)-3-11. While a poem like "An Airstrip in Essex, 1960" shows Hall as a very successful practitioner of the laconic, mysterious "deep image" manner, a more expansive and discursive side of his nature, represented by "The Old Pilot" among the earlier poems included here, has characterized his recent work. From the volume *Kicking the Leaves* (1978), we have drawn two examples: "Ox Cart Man" and "The Black Faced Sheep." If these latest poems seem to lack some of the tension and concentration of earlier pieces, they rise to powerful and deeply felt statements and portraits by the intensity with which they fix themselves to their subjects and manage to be celebratory and elegiac at the same time.

Donald Hall has also been active as an anthologist, editor, critic, and writer of prose memoirs. *Remembering Poets* (1978) and *String Too Short to Be Saved* (reissued, 1979) are expertly written volumes of reflection and reminiscence.

DY

Wedding Party

The pock-marked player of the accordion
Empties and fills his squeeze box in the corner,
Kin to the tiny man who pours champagne,
Kin to the caterer. These solemn men,
Amid the sounds of silk and popping corks,
Stand like pillars. And the white bride
Moves through the crowd as a chaired relic moves.

Now all at once the pock-marked player grows
Immense and terrible beside the bride
Whose marriage withers to a rind of years
And curling photographs in a dry box;
And in the storm that hurls upon the room
Above the crowd he holds his breathing box
That only empties, fills, empties, fills.

The Long River

The musk-ox smells
in his long head
my boat coming. When
I feel him there,
intent, heavy,

the oars make wings
in the white night,
and deep woods are close
on either side
where trees darken.

I rowed past towns
in their black sleep
to come here. I rowed
by northern grass
and cold mountains.

The musk-ox moves
when the boat stops,
in hard thickets. Now
the wood is dark
with old pleasures.

An Airstrip in Essex, 1960

It is a lost road into the air.
It is a desert
among sugar beets.
The tiny wings
of the Spitfires of nineteen-forty-one
flake in the mud of the Channel.

Near the road a brick pillbox
totters under a load of grass,
where Home Guards waited
in the white fogs of the invasion winter.

Goodnight, old ruined war.

In Poland the wind rides on a jagged wall.
Smoke rises from the stones; no, it is mist.

The Old Pilot

in memory of Philip Thompson

He discovers himself on an old airfield.
He thinks he was there before,
but rain has washed out the lettering of a sign.
A single biplane, all struts and wires,
stands in the long grass and wildflowers.
He pulls himself into the narrow cockpit
although his muscles are stiff
and sits like an egg in a nest of canvas.
He sees that the machine gun has rusted.
The glass over the instruments
has broken, and the red arrows are gone
from his gas gauge and his altimeter.
When he looks up, his propeller is turning,
although no one was there to snap it.
He lets out the throttle. The engine catches
and the propeller spins into the wind.
He bumps over holes in the grass,
and he remembers to pull back on the stick.
He rises from the land in a high bounce
which gets higher, and suddenly he is flying again.
He feels the old fear, and rising over the fields
the old gratitude. In the distance, circling
in a beam of late sun like birds migrating,
there are the wings of a thousand biplanes.

New Hampshire

A bear sleeps in a cellar hole; pine needles
heap over a granite doorstep; a well brims
with acorns and the broken leaves of an oak
which grew where an anvil rusted in a forge.

Inside an anvil, inside a bear, inside a leaf,
a bark of rust grows on the tree of a gas pump;
EAT signs gather like leaves in the shallow
cellars of diners; a wildcat waits for deer

on the roof of a car. Blacktop buckled by frost
starts goldenrod from the highway. Fat honey bees
meander among raspberries, where a quarrel
of vines crawls into the spilled body of a plane.

Apples

They have gone
into the green hill, by doors without hinges,
or lifting city
manhole covers to tunnels
lined with grass,
their skin soft as grapes, their faces like apples.

The peacock
feather, its round eye, sees dancers underground.
The curved spot on this
apple is a fat camel, is a
fly's shadow,
is the cry of a marigold. Looking hard,

I enter:
I am caught in the web of a gray apple,
I struggle inside
an immense apple of blowing sand,
I blossom
quietly from a window-box of apples.

For one man
there are seven beautiful ladies with buns
and happy faces
in yellow dresses with green sashes
to bring him
whiskey. The rungs of a ladder tell stories

>to his friend.
Their voices like apples brighten in the wind.
Now they are dancing
with fiddles and ladies and trumpets
in the round
hill of the peacock, in the resounding hill.

"Reclining Figure"

from Henry Moore's sculpture

>Then the knee of the wave
turned to stone.

>By the cliff of her flank
I anchored,

>in the darkness of harbors
laid-by.

Ox Cart Man

>In October of the year,
he counts potatoes dug from the brown field,
counting the seed, counting
the cellar's portion out,
and bags the rest on the cart's floor.

>He packs wool sheared in April, honey
in combs, linen, leather
tanned from deerhide,
and vinegar in a barrel
hooped by hand at the forge's fire.

>He walks by ox's head, ten days
to Portsmouth Market, and sells potatoes,
and the bag that carried potatoes,
flaxseed, birch brooms, maple sugar, goose
feathers, yarn.

When the cart is empty he sells the cart.
When the cart is sold he sells the ox,
harness and yoke, and walks
home, his pockets heavy
with the year's coin for salt and taxes,

and at home by fire's light in November cold
stitches new harness
for next year's ox in the barn,
and carves the yoke, and saws planks
building the cart again.

The Black Faced Sheep

Ruminant pillows! Gregarious soft boulders!

If one of you found a gap in a stone wall,
the rest of you—rams, ewes, bucks, wethers, lambs;
mothers and daughters, old grandfather-father,
cousins and aunts, small bleating sons—
followed onward, stupid
as sheep, wherever
your leader's sheep-brain wandered to.

My grandfather spent all day searching the valley
and edges of Ragged Mountain,
calling "Ke-*day!*" as if he brought you salt,
"Ke-*day!* Ke-*day!*"

            *   *   *

When a bobcat gutted a lamb at the Keneston place
in the spring of eighteen-thirteen
a hundred and fifty frightened black faced sheep
lay in a stupor and died.

            *   *   *

When the shirt wore out, and darns in the woolen
shirt needed darning,
a woman in a white collar
cut the shirt into strips and braided it,
as she braided her hair every morning.

In a hundred years
the knees of her great-granddaughter
crawled on a rug made from the wool of sheep
whose bones were mud,
like the bones of the woman, who stares
from an oval in the parlor.

*   *   *

I forked the brambly hay down to you
in nineteen-fifty. I delved my hands deep
in the winter grass of your hair.

When the shearer cut to your nakedness in April
and you dropped black eyes in shame,
hiding in barnyard corners, unable to hide,
I brought grain to raise your spirits,
and ten thousand years
wound us through pasture and hayfield together,
threads of us woven
together, three hundred generations
from Africa's hills to New Hampshire's.

*   *   *

You were not shrewd like the pig.
You were not strong like the horse.
You were not brave like the rooster.

Yet none of the others looked like a lump of granite
that grew hair,
and none of the others
carried white fleece as soft as dandelion seed
around a black face,
and none of them sang such a flat and sociable song.

*   *   *

In November a bearded man, wearing a lambskin apron,
slaughtered an old sheep for mutton
and hung the carcass in north shade
and cut from the frozen sides all winter, to stew in a pot
on the fire that never went out.

*   *   *

Now the black faced sheep have wandered and will not return,
though I search the valleys
and call "Ke-*day*" as if I brought them salt.

Now the railroad draws
a line of rust through the valley. Birch, pine, and maple
lean from cellarholes
and cover the dead pastures of Ragged Mountain
except where machines make snow
and cables pull money up hill, to slide back down.

* * *

At South Danbury Church twelve of us sit—
cousins and aunts, sons—

where the great-grandfathers of the forty-acre farms
filled every pew.
I look out the window at summer places,
at Boston lawyers' houses
with swimming pools cunningly added to cowsheds,
and we read an old poem aloud, about Israel's sheep
—and I remember faces and wandering hearts,
dear lumps of wool—and we read

that the rich farmer, though he names his farm for himself,
takes nothing into his grave;
that even if people praise us, because we are successful,
we will go under the ground
to meet our ancestors collected there in the darkness;
that we are all of us sheep, and death is our shepherd,
and we die as the animals die.

DONALD HALL

Books

Exiles and Marriages, 1955

The Dark Houses, 1958

*String Too Short to Be Saved:
  Childhood Reminiscences* (prose),
  1961, 1979

A Roof of Tiger Lilies, 1964

Henry Moore (biography), 1966

*The Alligator Bride: Poems New and
  Selected*, 1969

The Yellow Room, 1971

The Town of Hill, 1975

*Goatfoot Milktongue Twinbird:
  Interviews, Essays, and Notes on
  Poetry, 1970–1976*, 1978

*Remembering Poets: Reminiscences
  and Opinions* (essays), 1978

Kicking the Leaves, 1978

*Oxford Book of American Literary
  Anecdotes*, 1981

The Happy Man, 1986

Criticism, Interviews

Robert Bly, "Some Notes on Donald Hall," *FIELD*, No. 2 (Spring 1970);
Scott Chisholm, "An Interview with Donald Hall," *Tennessee Poetry
Journal* 2 (Winter 1971); Ralph J. Mills, Jr., "Donald Hall's Poetry," *Iowa
Review* 2 (Winter 1971).

Richard
Hugo
(1923–1982)

William Stafford

R ichard Hugo grew up in Seattle and was educated at the University of Washington. He served as a bombardier during World War II and worked for Boeing for nearly thirteen years. Like Jarrell and Dickey, he drew heavily on his wartime experiences, but he wrote more with the fractured vision of, say, Vonnegut in *Slaughterhouse Five*. Hugo was an inveterate traveler, who kept going back to places that were important for him and discovered new ones as if they had been his real home all along. Part of his appeal lies in his ability to take us, physically and spiritually, to locations our heritage forces us to seek (a book published in 1975, *What Thou Lovest Well, Remains American,* points especially in this direction). Most of his poems explore the twin "rights" of freedom of self and freedom to travel that Americans prize so highly, concerns that link Hugo to other poets in this anthology, notably Stevens, Dickey, Stafford, and Kaufman.

Hugo taught at the University of Montana from 1964 until his death and served as the editor of the Yale Series of Younger Poets. His teaching and editing (particularly his interest in fostering young poets) went hand in hand with his writing, and he has been one of our most eloquent essayists on the problems of teaching writing. Since he had a deep sense of what he himself was up to, we do well to begin by looking at some statements in essays published under the title *The Triggering Town* (1979): "I came from a town with a bad reputation, too," he says. At the heart of the issues he raises is this parabolic view:

> The poem is always in your hometown, but you have a better chance of finding it in another. . . . At home, not only do you know that . . . the grocer is a newcomer who took over after the former grocer committed suicide, you have complicated emotional responses that defy sorting out. With the strange town, you can assume all knowns are stable, and you owe the details nothing emotionally. . . . However, not just any town will do. Though you've never seen it before, it must be a town you've lived in all your life.

In his typically tough-minded but soft-spoken way, Hugo goes on to isolate the fine distinction that he takes to be the central issue for contemporary poetry:

> With the private poet, and most good poets of the last century or so have been private poets, the words, at least certain key words, mean something to the poet they don't mean to the reader. A sensitive reader perceives this relation of poet to word and in a way that relation—the strange way the poet emotionally possesses his vocabulary—is one of the mysteries and preservative forces of the art.

Hugo's towns, or places, range the whole world, from Montana taverns to cemeteries on the Isle of Skye, off Scotland. They are stops on his private underground railway, where he pokes around in abandoned houses, quarries, and churches, or walks down old roads till they jump back to life and his "adequate self" emerges. Trying his hand at fiction for a spell, he said, "I settled back into poems for good . . . seemed to use poems to create some adequate self . . . I could be tough in a poem. . . ." If Hugo seems slightly obsessed by the quality of "toughness" (the word occurs often in his essays), it is not Hemingway we should think of. Hugo is talking about striking a balance between selves—which all good poems must manage—of finding the "right" relationship between things, as the title of a recent collection suggests: _The Right Madness on Skye_ (1980).

As he himself has warned, achieving this balance is difficult business; poems must "move and not contain more information than is necessary." At times, he crowds things together and seems to seek the most difficult ways for saying things, with a raspy energy that leaves the reader gasping. Haunted by his material, he plunges straight on, from fact to association to next fact to more associations to pure discourse and back to fact. This is not to suggest that he loses control of his material; indeed, though he is celebrated for his informal ways with words, he is in fact a master at iambic pentameter and syllabics, as a reading aloud of the poems in this selection will amply demonstrate. He also has full command of more formal structures, as witness his use of the demanding form of the villanelle to treat a difficult and heartbreaking subject, "The Freaks at Spurgin Road Field."

We have tried to represent almost all the major books Hugo has published over the past twenty years, since _A Run of Jacks_ (1961) appeared. However different his structures and moods seem from collection to collection, moving as he does from simple forms in the early poems to what would become a whole book of _31 Letters and 13 Dreams_, his approach is always of a man leaning your way, saying just for the two of you, as in "Open Country": "And you come back here / where land has ways of going on / and the shadow of a cloud / crawls like a freighter, no port in mind, / no captain, and the charts dead wrong." To test such stories by historical or personal experience would seem to be as mistaken as to try to prove the existence of "The Lady in Kicking Horse Reservoir" by dragging the water. There are no maps, no charts, save for what the mind's eye, the imagination, can see and tell of.

_SF_

1614 Boren

Room on room, we poke debris for fun,
chips of dolls, the union picnic flag,
a valentine with a plump girl in a swing
who never could grow body hair or old
in all that lace (her flesh the color
of a salmon egg), a black-edged scroll
regretting death: "whereas—Great Architect—
has seen it fit—the lesser aerie here—
great aerie in the sky—deep sympathy."
Someone could have hated this so much . . .
he owns a million acres in Peru.

What does the picture mean, hung where it is
in the best room? Peace, perhaps. The calm road
leading to the house half hid by poplars,
willows and the corny vines bad sketches used
around that time, the white canal in front
with two innocuous boats en route,
the sea suggested just beyond the bar;
the world of harm behind the dormant hill.

Why could room 5 cook and 7 not?
These dirty rooms were dirty even then,
the toilets ancient when installed,
and light was always weak and flat
like now, or stark from a bare bulb.
And the boarders when they spoke of this
used "place" and "house," the one with photos
of Alaska on his wall said "edifice."
This home could be a joke on the horizon—
bad proportions and the color of disease.

But the picture, where? The Netherlands
perhaps. There are Netherland canals.
But are they bleached by sky, or scorched
pale gray by an invader's guns?
It can't exist. It's just a sketcher's whim.
The world has poison and the world has sperm
and water looks like water, not like milk
or a cotton highway. There's a chance
a man who sweated years in a stale room,
probably one upstairs, left the picture here
on purpose, and when he moved believed
that was the place he was really moving from.

Napoli Again

Long before I hear it, Naples bright
with buildings trumpets from the hill.
A tugboat toots "*paisan*" and I am back.
That dock I sailed from eighteen years ago.
This bay had a fleet of half-sunk ships.
Where those dapper men are drinking wine,
a soldier beat an urchin with a belt.
Fountains didn't work. I remember stink.
Streets and buildings all seemed brown.

Romans hate such recent ruins,
bombed-out houses you do not repair.
Better pillars one must work to date.
Forget the innocent cut down,
cats gone crazy from the bombs
waiting down those alleys for delicious eyes.
Here, the glass replaced in *galleria* roofs,
cappuccino too high priced, it's hard
to go back years and feed the whores for free.

I'll never think of virgin angels here.
Did I walk this street before,
protesting: I am kind. You switch the menu,
gyp me on the bill. Remember me? My wings?
The silver target and the silver bomb?
Take the extra coin. I only came
to see you living and the fountains run.

The Lady in Kicking Horse Reservoir

Not my hands but green across you now.
Green tons hold you down, and ten bass curve
teasing in your hair. Summer slime
will pile deep on your breast. Four months of ice
will keep you firm. I hope each spring
to find you tangled in those pads
pulled not quite loose by the spillway pour,
stars in dead reflection off your teeth.

Lie there lily still. The spillway's closed.
Two feet down most lakes are common gray.
This lake is dark from the black blue Mission range
climbing sky like music dying Indians once wailed.
On ocean beaches, mystery fish

are offered to the moon. Your jaws go blue.
Your hands start waving every wind.
Wave to the ocean where we crushed a mile of foam.

We still love there in thundering foam
and love. Whales fall in love with gulls
and tide reclaims the Dolly skeletons
gone with a blast of aching horns to China.
Landlocked in Montana here
the end is limited by light, the final note
will trail off at the farthest point we see,
already faded, lover, where you bloat.

All girls should be nicer. Arrows rain
above us in the Indian wind. My future
should be full of windy gems, my past
will stop this roaring in my dreams.
Sorry. Sorry. Sorry. But the arrows sing:
no way to float her up. The dead sink
from dead weight. The Mission range
turns this water black late afternoons.

One boy slapped the other. Hard.
The slapped boy talked until his dignity
dissolved, screamed a single "stop"
and went down sobbing in the company pond.
I swam for him all night. My only suit
got wet and factory hands went home.
No one cared the coward disappeared.
Morning then: cold music I had never heard.

Loners like work best on second shift.
No one liked our product and the factory closed.
Off south, the bison multiply so fast
a slaughter's mandatory every spring
and every spring the creeks get fat
and Kicking Horse fills up. My hope is vague.
The far blur of your bones in May
may be nourished by the snow.

The spillway's open and you spill out
into weather, lover down the bright canal
and mother, irrigating crops
dead Indians forgot to plant.
I'm sailing west with arrows to dissolving foam
where waves strand naked Dollys.
Their eyes are white as oriental mountains
and their tongues are teasing oil from whales.

A Map of Montana in Italy

On this map white. A state thick as a fist
or blunt instrument. Long roads weave and cross
red veins full of rage. Big Canada, map maker's
pink, squats on our backs, planning bad winters
for years, and Glacier Park's green with my envy
of Grizzly Bears. On the right, antelope sail
between strands of barbed wire and never
get hurt, west, I think, of Plevna, say near
Sumatra, or more west, say Shawmut,
anyway, on the right, east on the plains.
The two biggest towns are dull deposits
of men getting along, making money, driving
to church every Sunday, censoring movies and books.
The two most interesting towns, Helena, Butte,
have the good sense to fail. There's too much
schoolboy in bars—I'm tougher than you—
and too much talk about money.
Jails and police are how you dream Poland—
odd charges, bad food and forms you must fill
stating your religion. In Poland say none.
With so few Negroes and Jews we've been reduced
to hating each other, dumping our crud
in our rivers, mistreating the Indians.
Each year, 4000 move, most to the west
where ocean currents keep winter in check.
This map is white, meaning winter, ice
where you are, helping children who may be
already frozen. It's white here too
but back of me, up in the mountains where
the most ferocious animals
are obsequious wolves. No one fights
in the bars filled with pastry. There's no
prison for miles. But last night the Italians
cheered the violence in one of our westerns.

The Freaks at Spurgin Road Field

The dim boy claps because the others clap.
The polite word, handicapped, is muttered in the stands.
Isn't it wrong, the way the mind moves back.

One whole day I sit, contrite, dirt, L.A.
Union Station, '46, sweating through last night.
The dim boy claps because the others clap.

Score, 5 to 3. Pitcher fading badly in the heat.
Isn't it wrong to be or not be spastic?
Isn't it wrong, the way the mind moves back.

I'm laughing at a neighbor girl beaten to scream
by a savage father and I'm ashamed to look.
The dim boy claps because the others clap.

The score is always close, the rally always short.
I've left more wreckage than a quake.
Isn't it wrong, the way the mind moves back.

The afflicted never cheer in unison.
Isn't it wrong, the way the mind moves back
to stammering pastures where the picnic should have worked.
The dim boy claps because the others clap.

In Your Bad Dream

Morning at nine, seven ultra-masculine men
explain the bars of your cage are silver
in honor of our emperor. They finger the bars
and hum. Two animals, too far to name,
are fighting. One, you are certain, is destined
to win, the yellow one, the one who from here
seems shaped like a man. Your breakfast
is snake but the guard insists eel. You say hell
I've done nothing. Surely that's not a crime.
You say it and say it. When men leave, their hum
hangs thick in the air as scorn. Your car's
locked in reverse and running. The ignition
is frozen, accelerator stuck, brake shot.
You go faster and faster back. You wait for the crash.
On a bleak beach you find a piano the tide
has stranded. You hit it with a hatchet.
You crack it. You hit it again and music
rolls dissonant over the sand. You hit it
and hit it driving the weird music from it.
A dolphin is romping. He doesn't approve.
On a clean street you join the parade. Women
line the streets and applaud, but only the band.

You ask to borrow a horn and join in.
The bandmaster says we know you can't play.
You are embarrassed. You pound your chest
and yell meat. The women weave into the dark
that is forming, each to her home. You know
they don't hear your sobbing crawling the street
of this medieval town. You promise money
if they'll fire the king. You scream a last promise—
Anything. Anything. Ridicule my arm.

Open Country

It is much like ocean the way it opens
and rolls. Cows dot the slow climb of a field
like salmon trawls dot swells, and here or there
ducks climb on no definite heading.
Like water it is open to suggestion,
electric heron, and every moon
tricky currents of grass.

                  Let me guess;
when you repair the damaged brain
of a beaten child or bring to a patient
news that will never improve, you need
a window not a wall to turn to.
And you come back here
where land has ways of going on
and the shadow of a cloud
crawls like a freighter, no port in mind,
no captain, and the charts dead wrong.

NOTES

1614 Boren. The street address of an abandoned roominghouse.
Napoli Again. "Napoli" refers to Naples, Italy. "Galleria" are arched or covered
    passageways, usually with shops on either side. "Cappuccino" is a special
    blend of Italian coffee, served with whipped cream. "Coin" refers to the coin
    one throws into the fountain for good luck.
The Lady in Kicking Horse Reservoir. "Dollys" are small locomotives, especially
    used in quarries or construction sites.

RICHARD HUGO

Books

A Run of Jacks, 1961

Death of the Kapowsin Tavern, 1965

Good Luck in Cracked Italian, 1969

The Lady in Kicking Horse Reservoir, 1973

What Thou Lovest Well, Remains American, 1975

31 Letters and 13 Dreams, 1977

Selected Poems, 1979

The Triggering Town (lectures and essays), 1979

White Center, 1980

The Right Madness on Skye, 1980

Death and the Good Life (mystery novel), 1981

Making Certain It Goes On: Collected Poems, 1984

The Real West Marginal Way: A Poet's Autobiography (edited by Ripley S. Hugo, Lois M. Welch, James Welch), 1986

Criticism

F. Garber, "Large Man in the Mountains: The Recent Work of Richard Hugo," *Western American Literature* 10 (November 1975); Michael S. Allen, *We Are Called Human: The Poetry of Richard Hugo*, 1982; Jonathan Holden, *Landscapes of the Self: The Development of Richard Hugo's Poetry*, 1984; Sanford Pinsker, *Three Pacific Northwest Poets: William Stafford, Richard Hugo, and David Wagoner*, 1987.

Donald
Justice
(b. 1925)

Brandy Kershner

Donald Justice is celebrated as a teacher of poets, and the control and precision of his poetry, as well as its range and experimentation, suggest how much he has had to offer his students. It is important not to neglect the teacher's work in favor of his pupils; this poet has quietly produced a body of work that puts him among the leading figures of his generation. His output has been modest because his standards are high, but the publication of his *Selected Poems* (1979), spanning some twenty-five years of writing, has made clear just how effective and original a poet he is.

Justice's poems have great depth as well as great concentration. Much of their power stems from his command of technique, reminding us that a deep interest in the musical and formal possibilities of language is no less likely to result in lasting work than the poems of writers with visionary, psychological, or philosophical preoccupations. A few details, cannily placed, as in the third section of "Dreams of Water," can speak volumes. A truly thoughtful rhyme can make language and reality meet in a way that is nothing short of magical. Short poems that capture the essence of large subjects (e.g., "On the Death of Friends in Childhood") are unforgettable.

Like many writers of his generation, Justice learned a great deal from W. H. Auden, the English poet whose presence in America from 1939 until his death in 1973 made his great influence inevitable if not always helpful. For many poets in that period, coming of age was a matter of attempting to retain the formal values and stylistic flair acquired through emulating Auden while ridding themselves of derivative mannnerisms and developing a personal vision. Among the poems selected here, "Dreams of Water" shows the influence of Auden most clearly (compare Auden's "Three Dreams"), but it is an uncharacteristic side of Auden—more suggestive, less discursive—and Justice has naturalized it splendidly for his own purposes. Indeed, the two-stress line of that poem, also found here in "Bus Stop," has been so effectively exploited by Justice for its dreamy and yet jerky rhythms that it can be said to be more his than Auden's. Auden would have made "Bus Stop" a clever bit of moralizing; Justice invests it with a sense of melancholy beauty that is as haunting as a painting by Edward Hopper.

A poem by Donald Justice may offer us fictive biographies like "A Dancer's Life," may cross musical with painterly possibilities, as in "Sonatina in Yellow," or may explore elegant variations on a theme, as in "White Notes." Even when its subject matter is personal, it drives toward an objective treatment of it, as in "Childhood," where the raw material may be Justice's own Florida boyhood but the aim is an artistic investigation of the "mythical childhood" explored by the earlier writers (Wordsworth, Rimbaud, Rilke, Hart Crane, Alberti) to whom it is dedicated. Whatever their form and mode, Justice's poems tend to become small, dreamlike worlds in which people face death, the fear of growing old, the unknown, and the mysteries of human isolation. Since these worlds are generally melancholy in their perceptions, we may wonder why they give us so much satisfaction until we realize that they are so truly and perfectly complete as artifacts that they tell us as much about pleasure as about pain.

As a teacher for many years at the Iowa Writers' Workshop, Donald Justice taught many of the poets included in this volume: Mark Strand, Charles Wright, Larry Levis, and David St. John. He continues this distinguished career now at the University of Florida, Gainesville. But Justice's career as a poet of craft, consistency, and rigorous attention to detail, as a student of human emotions and the human imagination, makes him an example to poets beyond his own classroom.

DY

Landscape with Little Figures

There were some pines, a canal, a piece of sky.
The pines are the houses now of the very poor,
Huddled together, in a blue, ragged wind.
Children go whistling their dogs, down by the mudflats,
Once the canal. There's a red ball lost in the weeds.
It's winter, it's after supper, it's goodbye.
O goodbye to the houses, the children, the little red ball,
And the pieces of sky that will go on falling for days.

On the Death of Friends in Childhood

We shall not ever meet them bearded in heaven,
Nor sunning themselves among the bald of hell;
If anywhere, in the deserted schoolyard at twilight,
Forming a ring, perhaps, or joining hands
In games whose very names we have forgotten.
Come, memory, let us seek them there in the shadows.

Dreams of Water

1

An odd silence
Falls as we enter
The cozy ship's-bar.

The captain, smiling,
Unfolds his spyglass
And offers to show you

The obscene shapes
Of certain islands,
Low in the offing.

I sit by in silence.

2

People in raincoats
Stand looking out from
Ends of piers.

A fog gathers;
And little tugs,
Growing uncertain

Of their position,
Start to complain
With the deep and bearded

Voices of fathers.

    3

The season is ending.
White verandas
Curve away.

The hotel seems empty
But, once inside,
I hear a great splashing.

Behind doors
Grandfathers loll
In steaming tubs,

Huge, unblushing.

Bus Stop

Lights are burning
In quiet rooms
Where lives go on
Resembling ours.

The quiet lives
That follow us—
These lives we lead
But do not own—

Stand in the rain
So quietly
When we are gone,
So quietly . . .

And the last bus
Comes letting dark
Umbrellas out—
Black flowers, black flowers.

And lives go on.
And lives go on.
Like sudden lights
At street corners

Or like the lights
In quiet rooms
Left on for hours,
Burning, burning.

A Dancer's Life

The lights in the theater fail. The long racks
Of costumes abandoned by the other dancers
Trouble Celeste. The conductor asks
If she is sad because autumn is coming on,

But when autumn comes she is merely pregnant and bored.
On her way back from the holidays, a man
Who appears to have no face rattles the door
To her compartment. *How disgusting*, she thinks;

How disgusting it always must be to grow old.
Dusk falls, and a few drops of rain.
On the train window trembles the blurred
Reflection of her own transparent beauty,

And through this, beautiful ruined cities passing,
Dark forests, and people everywhere
Pacing on lighted platforms, some
Beating their children, some apparently dancing.

The costumes of the dancers sway in the chill darkness.
Now sinking into sleep is like sinking again
Into the lake of her youth. Her parents
Lean from the rail of a ferryboat waving, waving,

As the boat glides farther out across the waves.
No one, it seems, is meeting her at the station.
The city is frozen. She warms herself
In the pink and scented twilight of a bar.

The waiter who serves her is young. She nods assent.
The conversation dies in bed. Later,
She hurries off to rehearsal. In the lobby,
Dizzy still with the weight of her own body,

She waits, surrounded by huge stills of herself
And bright posters announcing events to come.
Her life—she feels it closing about her now
Like a small theater, empty, without lights.

White Notes

1

Suddenly there was a dress,
Inhabited, in motion.

It contained a forest,
Small birds, rivers.

It contained the ivory
Of piano keys,
White notes.

Across the back of a chair
Skins of animals
Dried in the moon.

2

It happened.
Your body went out of your body.

It rose
To let the air in,
The night.

From the sheets it rose,
From the bare floor,
Floating.

Over roofs,
Smaller and smaller,
Lost.

Entangled now
In the cold arms
Of distant street lamps.

3

The city forgets where you live.
It wanders through many streets,
And the streets turn, confused,
Upon one another.

Parks have deserted themselves.
All night, awnings are whipped
And cannot remember.

O forgotten umbrella . . .
Darkness saw you, air
Displaced you, words
Erased you.

4

And afterwards,
After the quenching of the street lamps,
Long after the ivory could have been brought back to life by any touch.

Afterwards, when I might have told you
The address of your future.
Long after the future.

When the umbrella had been closed forever.
Then, when not even the moon
Would have the power to bruise you any more.

Then, in another time.

Sonatina in Yellow

Du schnell vergehendes Daguerrotyp
In meinen langsamer vergehenden Händen.

RILKE

The pages of the album,
As they are turned, turn yellow; a word,
Once spoken, obsolete,
No longer what was meant. Say it.
The meanings come, or come back later,
Unobtrusive, taking their places.

Think of the past. Think of forgetting the past.
It was an exercise requiring further practice;
A difficult exercise, played through by someone else.
Overheard from another room, now,
It seems full of mistakes.
                              So the voice of your father,
Rising as from the next room still
With all the remote but true affection of the dead,
Repeats itself, insists,
Insisting you must listen, rises
In the familiar pattern of reproof
For some childish error, a nap disturbed,
Or vase, broken or overturned;
Rises and subsides. And you do listen.
Listen and forget. Practice forgetting.

Forgotten sunlight still
Blinds the eyes of faces in the album.
The faces fade, and there is only
A sort of meaning that comes back,
Or for the first time comes, but comes too late
To take the places of the faces.

           Remember
The dead air of summer. Remember
The trees drawn up to their full height like fathers,
The underworld of shade you entered at their feet.
Enter the next room. Enter it quietly now,
Not to disturb your father sleeping there. _He stirs._
Notice his clothes, how scrupulously clean,
Unwrinkled from the nap; his face, freckled with work,
Smoothed by a passing dream. The vase
Is not yet broken, the still young roses
Drink there from perpetual waters. _He rises, speaks_ . . .

Repeat it now, no one was listening.
So your hand moves, moving across the keys,
And slowly the keys grow darker to the touch.

Childhood

J'ai heurté, savez-vous, d'incroyables Florides . . .

                             RIMBAUD

TIME: the thirties
PLACE: Miami, Florida

Once more beneath my thumb the globe turns—
And doomed republics pass in a blur of colors . . .
                  Winter mornings now, my grandfather,
Head bared to the mild sunshine, likes to spread
The Katzenjammers out around a white lawn chair
To catch the stray curls of citrus from his knife.
Chameleons quiver in ambush; wings
Of monarchs beat above bronze turds, feasting . . .
               And there are pilgrim ants
Eternally bearing incommensurate crumbs
Past slippered feet.—There,
In the lily pond, my own face wrinkles
With the slow teasings of a stick.
              The long days pass, days
Streaked with the colors of the first embarrassments . . .
And Sundays, among kin, happily ignored,
I sit nodding, somnolent with horizons:
             Myriad tiny suns
Drown in the deep mahogany polish of the chair-arms;
Bunched cushions prickle through starched cotton . . .

> Already
I know the pleasure of certain solitudes.
I can look up at a ceiling so theatrical
Its stars seem more aloof than the real stars;
And pre-depression putti blush in the soft glow
Of exit signs. Often I blink, re-entering
The world—or catch, surprised, in a shop window,
My ghostly image skimming across nude mannequins.
Drawbridges, careless of traffic, lean there
Against the low clouds—early evening . . .
> All day
There is a smell of ocean longing landward.
And, high on his frail ladder, my father
Stands hammering great storm shutters down
Across the windows of the tall hotels,
Swaying. Around downed wires, across broken fronds,
Our Essex steers, bargelike and slow . . .
> Westward now,
The smoky rose of oblivion blooms, hangs;
And on my knee a small red sun-glow, setting.
For a long time I feel, coming and going in waves,
The stupid wish to cry. I dream . . .
> And there are
Colognes that mingle on the barber's hands
Swathing me in his striped cloth Saturdays, downtown.
Billy, the midget haberdasher, stands grinning
Under the winking neon goat, his sign—
And Flagler's sidewalks fill. Slowly
The wooden escalator rattles upward
Towards the twin fountains of a mezzanine
Where boys, secretly brave, prepare to taste
The otherness trickling there, forbidden . . .
And then the warm cashews in cool arcades!
O counters of spectacles!—where the bored child first
Scans new perspectives squinting through strange lenses;
And the mirrors, tilting, offer back toy sails
Stiffening breezeless towards green shores of baize . . .
> How thin the grass looks of the new yards—
> And everywhere
The fine sand burning into the bare heels
With which I learn to crush, going home,
The giant sandspurs of the vacant lots.
Iridescences of mosquito hawks
Glimmer above brief puddles filled with skies,
Tropical and changeless. And sometimes,

Where the city halts, the cracked sidewalks
Lead to a coral archway still spanning
The entrance to some wilderness of palmetto—

Forlorn suburbs, but with golden names!

—Dedicated to the poets of a mythical childhood—
Wordsworth, Rimbaud, Rilke, Hart Crane, and Alberti

Nostalgia and Complaint
of the Grandparents

> Les morts
> C'est sous terre;
> Ça n'en sort
> Guère.

> J. LAFORGUE

Our diaries squatted, toadlike,
On dark closet ledges.
Forget-me-not and thistle
Decalcomaned the pages.
But where, where are they now,
    All the sad squalors
Of those between-wars parlors?—
Cut flowers; and the sunlight spilt like soda
    On torporous rugs; the photo
    Albums all outspread . . .
        The dead
Don't get around much anymore.

There was an hour when daughters
Practiced arpeggios;
Their mothers, awkward and proud,
Would listen, smoothing their hose—
Sundays, half past five!

Do you recall
How the sun used to loll,
Lazily, just beyond the roof,
Bloodshot and aloof?
We thought it would never set.
The dead don't get
Around much anymore.

Eternity resembles
One long Sunday afternoon.
No traffic passes; the cigar smoke
Coils in a blue cocoon.
Children, have you nothing
For our cold sakes?
No tea? No little tea cakes?
Sometimes now the rains disturb
Even our remote suburb.
There's a dampness underground.
The dead don't get around
Much anymore.

NOTES

A Dancer's Life. Justice notes, "Most of the details . . . were remembered, perhaps wrongly, from early Bergman movies, scripts, and criticism."

Sonatina in Yellow. The epigraph, from Rilke's poem on a youthful portrait of his father as a cadet, translates, "You quickly fading daguerreotype/In my more slowly fading hands."

Childhood. The epigraph, from Rimbaud's "The Drunken Boat," translates, "I've touched, you know, fantastic Floridas."

Nostalgia and Complaint of the Grandparents. The epigraph is translated by the refrain.

DONALD JUSTICE

Books

The Summer Anniversaries, 1960

Contemporary French Poetry (edited, with Alexander Aspel), 1965

Night Light, 1967

Departures, 1973

Selected Poems, 1979

Platonic Scripts (essays), 1984

The Sunset Maker, 1987

Criticism

Richard Howard, *Alone with America: Essays on the Art of Poetry in the United States Since 1950,* 1969, rev. 1980; Greg Simon, "On Donald Justice," *American Poetry Review* 2 (1976).

Shirley
Kaufman
(b. 1923)

Karen Benzian

The daughter of Eastern European immigrants, Shirley Kaufman grew up in Seattle and lived for many years in San Francisco before settling in Israel in 1973. She has always possessed, she says, a "west coast sensibility," and, like Jeffers, Snyder, and Duncan, she seeks strong visual experiences as beginnings for poems; eschews the narrative stance in favor of what she calls "related fragments"; is partial to open, less organized structures that "let incoherence spill over . . . so I can feel my way through a poem as it occurs, instead of adding it up afterward." This resolve has led her to be patient, to work for weeks at a time only to put poems aside for a fresh look still later, and it results finally in long, sustained landscapes that are about "different ways of looking at the same central theme." So it is particularly apt that our selection focuses on "Looking at Henry Moore's Elephant Skull Etchings in Jerusalem During the War," a poem that demonstrates her talent for making the long poem work. She lived through the October 1973 war and the ongoing disasters of the conflict in the Middle East, the daily watchfulness for bombs planted in buses and markets, and the agonizing over conflicting claims; and she has learned to control the difficult, sometimes excruciating subject matter by having learned from Olson and Williams about the rhythmic principles implicit in her own speech, her own breath. The result is utterances that pull the material apart into clear little shapes, *haiku*-like in their precision, true to the many irrational and unconnected feelings riding her:

> Simpson calls it impulse. The pulse inside. It's something physical. And yet. And yet. Who stops to think how he breathes? Or where the next breath's coming from? After the first gasp, entering the light, we go on breathing. And yet. There's more to life than breathing.
>
> (from an essay on "The Line")

Breathing marks the moment of birth. Many of Kaufman's poems center on the stirring of life from the skin of death: "It's my face / staring out of her picture / wrinkled and old / as a newborn infant // pushed there / ahead of myself" ("Nechama," a poem about her grandmother's death). And again, "if the thin membranes and the thick / weep in the naked bone // then the whole elephant can rise up / out of its flesh" ("Looking at Henry Moore's Elephant Skull Etchings")—and the startling metamorphosis that follows, the woman giving birth to the elephant so that the loss may be redeemed, and turning into what she gives birth to: "There's an elephant inside me / crowding me out / . . . I taste the coarse hairs / crowding the back of my mouth." In an essay on the use of place in contemporary poetry, Kaufman says, "Our bodies, or more precisely, our inner spaces, are the center of our experience. . . . Women are busy giving birth to themselves." The way Lowell or Hugo or James Wright returns to places to repossess them, Kaufman returns to *birth* places: "There is a way to enter / if you remember / where you came from"—the soft internal off-rhyme ("enter/remember") serving to rock us back to beginnings.

For Kaufman, though she often returns to the United States, beginnings have to do with questions like "What does it mean to be Jewish, to return to the Jewish homeland, to be an Israeli?" To deepen her ties to art in general, and the Israeli experience in particular, she has been learning Hebrew and translating Israeli poets like Kovner and Gilboa, learning with them to return to the Bible more steadfastly than she had before for stories about roots, exile, place, and displacement: "So I sit at my desk in Jerusalem, looking back at Seattle and San Francisco, looking back at the women in the Bible who keep getting into my poems, looking down through excavated layers . . . at the ruins . . . , the violent history of this country where I now live."

_SF_

His Wife

But it was right that she
looked back. Not to be
curious, some lumpy
reaching of the mind
that turns all shapes to pillars.
But to be only who she was
apart from them, the place
exploding, and herself
defined. Seeing them melt
to slag heaps and the flames
slide into their mouths.
Testing her own lips then,
the coolness, till
she could taste the salt.

Nechama

They changed her name
to Nellie. All the girls.
To be American.
And cut her hair.

She couldn't give up
what she thought she lost.

Streets like ceiling cracks
she looked up watching
where the same boy bicycled always
to the gate of her Russian house.
She saw him tremble
in the steam over her tea
after the samovar was gone.
She was Anna Karenina
married to somebody else.

      *   *   *

Oh she was beautiful. She could turn
into an egret with copper hair.
She could turn into a fig tree.
She could turn into a Siberian wolfhound.
She could turn into an opal
turning green. She could drown us
in the lake of her soft skin.

Rhythm of chopping garlic
motion as language in her wrists
warming her hands
rubbing it
over the leg of lamb.

            *   *   *

Leaving the kitchen she would cry
over pictures telling us
nothing new

till the small light by her bed
kept getting lost under the blanket
where she crawled looking
for something she forgot
or money in her old house
under the hankies looking
for spare parts.

She swallowed what we brought
because we said to.

            *   *   *

The rabbi knows
the 23rd psalm backwards
and he pretends he came for a wedding.

Do me a favor she still pleads
under the roses
begging for proof of faithfulness
or love. If I say yes
she might ask anything like
stay with me
or take me home.

            *   *   *

It's my face staring
out of her picture
wrinkled and old
as a newborn infant

pushed there
ahead of myself

or memorizing lines
over and over in a soundproof room
until the smile is stuck there
and the lips stay frozen
like a hole in the ice
where a child fell in.

Looking at Henry Moore's Elephant Skull Etchings in Jerusalem During the War

It wants to be somewhere else
remembering anything somewhere
private where it can lie down

floating in the warm belly
of the Dead Sea

so that the skull keeps
growing in the room

and the loose skin

until the whole head sees
its feet

from a great distance.

*   *   *

Heavy as earth is heavy
under its own weight

it's the same skin
wrinkled on the back of hills

grey in the early morning
on the Jericho Road.

*   *   *

The brain scooped out of it
lets in the light
we knew at the beginning

when our eyes were dazzled

pushed
without wanting to be pushed

out of the dark.

*   *   *

The mind of the elephant
has nothing to lose

        *   *   *

I was begging you
not to go
when you closed the door

and left me
watching the skull's
round openings

the eyelids gone.

         *   *   *

There are caverns
under our feet
with rivers running deep in them.

They hide
in the sides of cliffs
at Rosh Hanikra
where the sea breaks in.

There is a way to enter
if you remember
where you came from

how to breathe under water
make love in a trap.

       *   *   *

Step over the small bones
lightly when you feel them
tripping your feet.

       *   *   *

Fear hangs over your shoulder
like a gun it digs in my arm

but the live head knows
that the eyes get used to darkness

fingers learn how to read
the signs they touch.

    *   *   *

Ditches where bones stand up
and shake their fists at us

sons in the shadows
and the shadows flattened
like grass rolled over

one-eyed Cyclops
slit of a concrete bunker
we prowl through
looking for flowers.

    *   *   *

We are going down a long slide
into the secret chamber
we bought our tickets for the ride

the passage is narrow
and we can't find ourselves
in the trick mirrors

we lie down in the fetal position
back to back
each of us in his own eye socket

marvelous holes
the mind looked out of
filling with dust.

    *   *   *

My lips on the small
rise of forehead above your eyes

mouths of the women in Ramallah
who spit when the soldiers go by

huge head of an infant
shoved out of the birth canal

faces stretched over us like tents
wet bandages over burns

and the white skull balder
than rock under the smile.

*   *   *

If the smooth joining of the bone
makes arches from here to there

if the intricate structure yields
arms resting desert landscapes mother and child

if the thin membranes and the thick
weep in the naked bone

then the whole elephant can rise up
out of its flesh

as in the torso of Apollo

something is pulsing
in the vacant skull

making us change.

*   *   *

I don't want to stand
on our balcony with the lights out
black buildings
street lamps
and headlights turned off

and nothing
against the sky

the stars get closer
but it's not the same
as what you plug in.

*   *   *

There's an elephant inside me
crowding me out
he sees Jerusalem
through my eyes my skin
is stretched tight
over the elephant's skin his wrinkles
begin to break through
I taste the coarse hairs
crowding the back of my mouth
I fall down gagging over my four feet
my nose turns into a tongue with nostrils

it starts to grow.

*   *   *

I see bodies in the morning kneel
over graves and bodies under them
the skin burned off
their bones laid out in all the cold
tunnels under the world.

There is a photograph in the next room
of a dead child
withered against its mother
between the dry beans of her breasts

there is no blood
under the shrunk skin

their skulls are already visible.

*   *   *

The elephants come after us
in herds now

they will roll over us
like tanks

we are too sad to move

our skulls
much smaller than theirs
begin to shine.

The Dream of Completion

When asked for a sample of his work
Giotto took a red pencil,
drew a perfect circle
free hand
and sent it to the Pope.

What does it mean
to be that sure of anything?
The dream of completion.
We cross the field
with the small stones biting our sandals,
picking up shards.

Sometimes you finish
what I think I've said.

We take the clay fragments,
skin-colored, bits of them worn
or crumbling between our fingers,
and piece them together.
Something is always missing.

NOTES

His Wife. The reference is to Lot's wife, who was changed into a pillar of salt for
looking back during the flight from Sodom (Gen. 13:1−12, 19).

The Dream of Completion. Number 46 in a sequence of poems, 62 in all, printed as
one long poem, *Claims*.

SHIRLEY KAUFMAN

Books

The Floor Keeps Turning, 1969

Gold Country, 1973

Abba Kovner, *A Canopy in the*
Desert (translations), 1973

Amir Gilboa, *The Light of Lost Suns*
(translations), 1979

From One Life to Another, 1979

Claims, 1984

Abba Kovner, *My Little Sister*
(translations), 1986

Judith Herzberg, *But What*
(translations), 1988

Essays

"Here and There: The Use of Place in Contemporary Poetry," *FIELD*, No. 23
(Fall 1980)

Galway
Kinnell
(b. 1927)

William Stafford

I n a poem called "Spindrift" (not included here), Galway Kinnell sits on a beach, looking back the way he has come, noting that "My footprints / Slogging for the absolute / Already begin vanishing." The moment is typical in many ways. The poet presents himself as the protagonist of his poem, moving through a natural setting but preoccupied with metaphysical questions and concerned, not to say obsessed, with his own ephemerality. The edge of wry self-deprecation in the ironic distance between his romantic quest for the absolute and his very temporary impact on the world, as well as in the characterization implied by "slogging," is typical too. Kinnell is a visionary who is also perfectly capable of laughing at himself, though the humor does not so much undermine the seriousness as make it modern and palatable: Any poet who can introduce an experience of mystical knowledge with the phrase "Just now I had a funny sensation" ("Ruins Under the Stars") is someone we are apt to feel we can trust.

The poet-protagonist who walks beaches, climbs mountains, encounters animals, meditates in ruins, and stares at the night sky, "the old stars rustling and whispering," is looking for comforts in a harsh and violent universe, and they are few and far between. Civilization, for example a "SAC bomber . . . crawling across heaven," seems confused and purposeless much of the time. Wilderness, wildness, violence, the upsurge of primitive energies in the self and in nature: These are more real but they are also frightening, awesome. Art's role is to provide a little music, something to go with the crickets' shrilling, the elegies of birds, the crunch and crackle of porcupines, to cheer us up even as we are comsumed by the fires and energies of life, as we face the death that is a part of us ("the pre-trembling of a house that falls") as soon as we are born. Were it not for Kinnell's ability to create unlikely but convincing music, like the boys in "Freedom, New Hampshire" improvising on their tissue-covered combs, his world and his poems would be gloomy indeed.

The present selection, six poems, emphasizes Kinnell's musical talents. These lie partly in his ability to manipulate rich patterns of sound; reading the first section of "Ruins Under the Stars" aloud is a good place to start tasting and savoring his distinctive verbal music. But his musical gifts are organizational as well, and one can trace in these poems his development as a poet through experimentation with poems of musical structure, "suites" in which short lyrical sections accumulate around a major theme. The form is a descendant of the Romantic ode, and its great modern practitioners are Yeats and Stevens. Spiritually, Kinnell may be closer to some of his declared favorites—Villon, Rilke, Frost—but formally he is a successor to Yeats and Stevens, and the progress he has made with a poem organized like a musical composition is evident in the present selection. "Freedom, New Hampshire," his memorable elegy for his brother from his first volume, _What a Kingdom It Was_ (1960), gives us three sections in which we watch the two boys encountering birth, death, and the generative energies of nature in the country setting where they grew up. In the fourth section, these experiences are recapitulated as the poem moves on to the experience of human loss and grief; the bitter, beautiful conclusion is the stronger for our having been prepared by the sections preceding it, each with its own scenery, music, and movement.

Kinnell's investigation of the interaction of physical and spiritual, visible and invisible, is the main enterprise of the even more dazzling set of variations, "Flower Herding on Mount Monadnock," the title poem of the second collection (1964). By having as many as ten sections, by using the archetypal structure of the quest as a climb toward knowledge, with the poet as a kind of daft shepherd of the wildflowers, and by teasing us with narrative features, this poem invites our delight in its inventive play with contradictions and paradoxes. There is certainly no "slogging" here; the climb is more like an elated rise, an acceptance as well as a conquering of gravity and decay, accomplished by a strong musical sense and musical order, a dance up the mountainside.

The interest in longer poems that accumulate from shorter sections led Kinnell finally to the writing of a book-length poem in ten parts, modeled loosely on Rilke's *Duino Elegies,* each part a musical suite or sequence in seven sections, of the kind that earlier poems had developed so successfully. From that major effort, *The Book of Nightmares* (1971), we have included one sequence, the seventh of ten, "Little Sleep's-Head Sprouting Hair in the Moonlight." Any excerpting from *The Book of Nightmares* does it an injustice, since common lines of imagery and recurrent themes run through the entire poem, developing a cumulative meaning and force. Readers who wish to experience the full effect of "Little Sleep's-Head" are urged to read the whole poem from which it is taken. They will find it a fascinating and risky enterprise. In it the poet, thinking about his children and the fact of their mortality, seems less able to come to terms with death and change than he did in, say, "Freedom, New Hampshire," so that the book's appeal will be greatest to those readers most able to share its obsession with impermanence. At the same time, Kinnell pushes his characteristic humor and self-mockery into gothic and macabre regions where the excess is apt either to overwhelm the reader with admiration or produce a strong negative reaction. Still controversial, and still being digested and assessed fifteen years after its appearance, *The Book of Nightmares* is probably the most interesting poem of its kind since Hart Crane's *The Bridge* and Williams's *Paterson*. Since publishing it, Kinnell has produced two collections, *Mortal Acts, Mortal Words* (1980) and *The Past,* along with a *Selected Poems*.

Besides his influential and widely admired poetry, Galway Kinnell has published significant translations—of Villon, Yvan Goll, and Yves Bonnefoy—as well as a novel, *Black Light* (1966). He has taught at a number of universities as writer-in-residence and currently lives part of the year in Sheffield, Vermont, and part in New York, where he is heading a new writing program at NYU.

DY

Freedom, New Hampshire

1

We came to visit the cow
Dying of fever,
Towle said it was already
Shovelled under, in a secret
Burial-place in the woods.
We prowled through the woods
Weeks, we never

Found where. Other
Kids other summers
Must have found the place
And asked, Why is it
Green here? The rich
Guess a grave, maybe,
The poor think a pit

For dung, like the one
We shovelled in in the fall
That came up green
The next year, and that,
For all that shows, may as well
Have been the grave
Of a cow or something.

2

We found a cowskull once; we thought it was
From one of the asses in the Bible, for the sun
Shone into the holes through which it had seen
Earth as an endless belt carrying gravel, had heard
Its truculence cursed, had learned how sweat
Stinks, and had brayed—shone into the holes
With solemn and majestic light, as if some
Skull somewhere could be Baalbek or the Parthenon.

That night passing Towle's Barn
We saw lights. Towle had lassoed a calf
By its hind legs, and he tugged against the grip
Of the darkness. The cow stood by chewing millet.
Derry and I took hold, too, and hauled.
It was sopping with darkness when it came free.
It was a bullcalf. The cow mopped it awhile,
And we walked around it with a lantern,

And it was sunburned, somehow, and beautiful.
It took a dug as the first business
And sneezed and drank at the milk of light.
When we got it balanced on its legs, it went wobbling
Toward the night. Walking home in darkness
We saw the July moon looking on Freedom, New Hampshire,
We smelled the fall in the air, it was the summer,
We thought, Oh this is but the summer!

    3

Once I saw the moon
Drift into the sky like a bright
Pregnancy pared
From a goddess doomed
To keep slender to be beautiful—
Cut loose, and drifting up there
To happen by itself—
And waning, in lost labor;

As we lost our labor
Too—afternoons
When we sat on the gate
By the pasture, under the Ledge,
Buzzing and skirling on toilet-
papered combs tunes
To the rumble-seated cars
Taking the Ossipee Road

On Sundays; for
Though dusk would come upon us
Where we sat, and though we had
Skirled out our hearts in the music,
Yet the dandruffed
Harps we skirled it on
Had done not much better than
Flies, which buzzed, when quick

We trapped them in our hands,
Which went silent when we
Crushed them, which we bore
Downhill to the meadowlark's
Nest full of throats
Which Derry charmed and combed
With an Arabian air, while I
Chucked crushed flies into

Innards I could not see,
For the night had fallen

And the crickets shrilled on all sides
In waves, as if the grassleaves
Shrieked by hillsides
As they grew, and the stars
Made small flashes in the sky,
Like mica flashing in rocks

On the chokecherried Ledge
Where bees I stepped on once
Hit us from behind like a shotgun,
And where we could see
Windowpanes in Freedom flash
And Loon Lake and Winnipesaukee
Flash in the sun
And the blue world flashing.

     4

The fingerprints of our eyeballs would zigzag
On the sky; the clouds that came drifting up
Our fingernails would drift into the thin air;
In bed at night there was music if you listened,
Of an old surf breaking far away in the blood.

Kids who come by chance on grass green for a man
Can guess cow, dung, man, anything they want,
To them it is the same. To us who knew him as he was
After the beginning and before the end, it is green
For a name called out of the confusions of the earth—

Winnipesaukee coined like a moon, a bullcalf
Dragged from the darkness where it breaks up again,
Larks which long since have crashed for good in the grass
To which we fed the flies, buzzing ourselves like flies,
While the crickets shrilled beyond us, in July . . .

The mind may sort it out and give it names—
When a man dies he dies trying to say without slurring
The abruptly decaying sounds. It is true
That only flesh dies, and spirit flowers without stop
For men, cows, dung, for all dead things; and it is good, yes—

But an incarnation is in particular flesh
And the dust that is swirled into a shape
And crumbles and is swirled again had but one shape
That was this man. When he is dead the grass
Heals what he suffered, but he remains dead,
And the few who loved him know this until they die.

For my brother, 1925–1957

Ruins Under the Stars

1

All day under acrobat
Swallows I have sat, beside ruins
Of a plank house sunk up to its windows
In burdock and raspberry cane,
The roof dropped, the foundation broken in,
Nothing left perfect but axe-marks on the beams.

A paper in a cupboard talks about "Mugwumps,"
In a V-letter a farmboy in the Marines has "tasted battle . . ."
The apples are pure acid on the tangle of boughs,
The pasture has gone to popple and bush.
Here on this perch of ruins
I listen for the crunch of the porcupines.

2

Overhead the skull-hill rises
Crossed on top by the stunted apple,
Infinitely beyond it, older than love or guilt,
Lie the stars ready to jump and sprinkle out of space.

Every night under those thousand lights
An owl dies, or a snake sloughs its skin,
A man in a dark pasture
Feels a homesickness he does not understand.

3

Sometimes I see them,
The south-going Canada geese,
At evening, coming down
In pink light, over the pond, in great,
Loose, always-dissolving V's—
I go out into the field and listen
To the cold, lonely yelping
Of their tranced bodies in the sky.

4

This morning I watched
Milton Norway's sky-blue Ford
Dragging its ass down the dirt road
On the other side of the valley.

Later, off in the woods
A chainsaw was agonizing across the top of some stump.
A while ago the tracks of a little, snowy,
SAC bomber went crawling across heaven.

What of that little hairstreak
That was flopping and batting about
Deep in the goldenrod—
Did she not know, either, where she was going?

     5

Just now I had a funny sensation,
As if some angel, or winged star,
Had been perched nearby.
In the chokecherry bush
There was a twig just ceasing to tremble . . .

The bats come in place of the swallows.
In the smoking heap of old antiques
The porcupine-crackle starts up again,
The bone-saw, the pure music of our sphere,
And up there the stars rustling and whispering.

Flower Herding on Mount Monadnock

     1

I can support it no longer.
Laughing ruefully at myself
For all I claim to have suffered
I get up. Damned nightmarer!

It is New Hampshire out here,
It is nearly the dawn.
The song of the whippoorwill stops
And the dimension of depth seizes everything.

     2

The song of a peabody bird goes overhead
Like a needle pushed five times through the air,
It enters the leaves, and comes out little changed.

The air is so still
That as they go off through the trees
The love songs of birds do not get any fainter.

3

The last memory I have
Is of a flower which cannot be touched,

Through the bloom of which, all day,
Fly crazed, missing bees.

4

As I climb sweat gets up my nostrils,
For an instant I think I am at the sea,

One summer off Cap Ferrat we watched a black seagull
Straining for the dawn, we stood in the surf,

Grasshoppers splash up where I step,
The mountain laurel crashes at my thighs.

5

There is something joyous in the elegies
Of birds. They seem
Caught up in a formal delight,
Though the mourning dove whistles of despair.

But at last in the thousand elegies
The dead rise in our hearts,
On the brink of our happiness we stop
Like someone on a drunk starting to weep.

6

I kneel at a pool,
I look through my face
At the bacteria I think
I see crawling through the moss.

My face sees me,
The water stirs, the face,
Looking preoccupied,
Gets knocked from its bones.

7

I weighed eleven pounds
At birth, having stayed on
Two extra weeks in the womb.
Tempted by room and fresh air
I came out big as a policeman
Blue-faced, with narrow red eyes.
It was eight days before the doctor
Would scare my mother with me.

Turning and craning in the vines
I can make out through the leaves
The old, shimmering nothingness, the sky.

8

Green, scaly moosewoods ascend,
Tenants of the shaken paradise,

At every wind last night's rain
Comes splattering from the leaves,

It drops in flurries and lies there,
The footsteps of some running start.

9

From a rock
A waterfall,
A single trickle like a strand of wire,
Breaks into beads halfway down.

I know
The birds fly off
But the hug of the earth wraps
With moss their graves and the giant boulders.

10

In the forest I discover a flower.

The invisible life of the thing
Goes up in flames that are invisible
Like cellophane burning in the sunlight.

It burns up. Its drift is to be nothing.

In its covertness it has a way
Of uttering itself in place of itself,
Its blossoms claim to float in the Empyrean,

A wrathful presence on the blur of the ground.

The appeal to heaven breaks off.
The petals begin to fall, in self-forgiveness.
It is a flower. On this mountainside it is dying.

Little Sleep's-Head Sprouting Hair in the Moonlight

1

You cry, waking from a nightmare.

When I sleepwalk
into your room, and pick you up,
and hold you up in the moonlight, you cling to me
hard,
as if clinging could save us. I think
you think
I will never die, I think I exude
to you the permanence of smoke or stars,
even as
my broken arms heal themselves around you.

2

I have heard you tell
the sun, *don't go down*, I have stood by
as you told the flower, *don't grow old*,
don't die. Little Maud,

I would blow the flame out of your silver cup,
I would suck the rot from your fingernail,
I would brush your sprouting hair of the dying light,
I would scrape the rust off your ivory bones,
I would help death escape through the little ribs of your body,
I would alchemize the ashes of your cradle back into wood,
I would let nothing of you go, ever,

until washerwomen
feel the clothes fall asleep in their hands,
and hens scratch their spell across hatchet blades,
and rats walk away from the cultures of the plague,
and iron twists weapons toward the true north,
and grease refuses to slide in the machinery of progress,
and men feel as free on earth as fleas on the bodies of men,
and lovers no longer whisper to the one beside them in the dark,
    O you-who-will-no-longer-be . . .

And yet perhaps this is the reason you cry,
this the nightmare you wake crying from:
being forever
in the pre-trembling of a house that falls.

3

In a restaurant once, everyone
quietly eating, you clambered up
on my lap: to all
the mouthfuls rising toward
all the mouths, at the top of your voice
you cried
your one word, *caca! caca! caca!*
and each spoonful
stopped, a moment, in midair, in its withering
steam.

Yes,
you cling because
I, like you, only sooner
than you, will go down
the path of vanished alphabets,
the roadlessness
to the other side of the darkness,
your arms
like the shoes left behind,
like the adjectives in the halting speech
of very old men,
which used to be able to call up the forgotten nouns.

4

And you yourself,
some impossible Tuesday
in the year Two Thousand and Nine, will walk out
among the black stones
of the field, in the rain,

and the stones saying
over their one word, *ci-gît, ci-gît, ci-gît,*

and the raindrops
hitting you on the fontanel
over and over, and you standing there
unable to let them in.

5

If one day it happens
you find yourself with someone you love
in a café at one end
of the Pont Mirabeau, at the zinc bar
where white wine stands in upward opening glasses,

and if you commit then, as we did, the error
of thinking,
one day all this will only be memory,

learn to reach deeper
into the sorrows
to come—to touch
the almost imaginary bones
under the face, to hear under the laughter
the wind crying across the stones. Kiss
the mouth
which tells you, *here,*
here is the world. This mouth. This laughter. These temple bones.

The still undanced cadence of vanishing.

     6

In the light the moon
sends back, I can see in your eyes

the hand that waved once
in my father's eyes, a tiny kite
wobbling far up in the twilight of his last look,

and the angel
of all mortal things lets go the string.

     7

Back you go, into your crib.

The last blackbird lights up his gold wings: *farewell.*
Your eyes close inside your head,
in sleep. Already
in your dreams the hours begin to sing.

Little sleep's-head sprouting hair in the moonlight,
when I come back
we will go out together,
we will walk out together among
the ten thousand things,
each scratched in time with such knowledge, *the wages*
of dying is love.

The Angel

This angel, who mediates between us
and the world underneath us, trots ahead
so cheerfully. Now and then she bends
her spine down hard, like a dowser's branch,
over some, to her, well-known splashing spot
of holy water, of which she herself in turn
carefully besoms out a thrifty sprinkle.
Trotting ahead again, she scribbles her spine's
continuation into immaterial et cetera,
thus signaling that it is safe for us now
to go wagging our legs along vertically as we do,
across the ups and downs under which lie
ancestors dog-toothed millennia ago into oblivion.
Tonight she will crouch at the hearth,
where demons' breaths flutter up among the logs,
gnawing a freshly unearthed bone—bone of a dog,
if possible—making logs and bone together
cry through the room, *crack! splinter! groan!*

The Shroud

Lifted by its tuft
of angel hairs, a milkweed
seed dips-and-soars
across a meadow, chalking
in outline the rhythm
that waits in air all along,
like the bottom hem of nowhere.
Spinus tristis, who spends
his days turning gold
back into sod, rises-and-falls
along the same line the seed
just waved through the sunlight.
What sheet or shroud large enough
to hold the whole earth
are these seamstresses' chalks
and golden needles
stitching at so restlessly?
When will it ever be finished?

GALWAY KINNELL

Books

What a Kingdom It Was, 1960

Flower Herding on Mount Monadnock, 1964

Black Light (novel), 1965

The Poems of François Villon (translations), 1965, rev. 1977

Yves Bonnefoy, *On the Motion and Immobility of Douve* (translation), 1968

Body Rags, 1968

Yvan Goll, *Lackawanna Elegy* (translations), 1970

The Book of Nightmares, 1971

The Avenue Bearing the Initial of Christ into the New World: Poems 1946–64, 1974

Mortal Acts, Mortal Words, 1980

Selected Poems, 1982

The Past, 1985

Criticism, Interviews

Conrad Hilberry, "The Structure of Galway Kinnell's *The Book of Nightmares*," FIELD No. 12 (Spring 1975); Ralph Mills, *Cry of the Human*, 1975; *Walking Down the Stairs; Selections from Interviews*, 1978; James Guimond, *Seeing and Healing: A Study of the Poetry of Galway Kinnell*, 1985; Howard Nelson, *On the Poetry of Galway Kinnell: The Wages of Dying*, 1987; Lee Zimmerman, *Intricate and Simple Things: The Poetry of Galway Kinnell*, 1987.

Denise
Levertov
(b. 1923)

Judith McDowell

Few poets could lay claim to a more exotic heritage than Denise Levertov. Her father was a Russian Jew, descended from the founder of Habad Hasidism, who became an Anglican minister in England. Her mother, Beatrice Spooner-Jones, was a descendant of the Welsh tailor and mystic Angel Jones of Mold. She was educated at home and trained in classical ballet, and her first book, *The Double Image,* was published in England right after the war (1946). In 1947 she met and married the American writer Mitchell Goodman, and in 1948 she moved with him to the United States. Once settled here, she rapidly trained herself in the free verse tradition of William Carlos Williams, forming friendships with Robert Creeley, Charles Olson, and Robert Duncan, members of the Black Mountain "school." The notion of a school is confining for any good poet, however, and Denise Levertov's sense of kinship with writers of other persuasions, like Galway Kinnell, suggests that her values and allegiances are appropriately complex.

Levertov's mastery of free verse is clearly based on her ability to make it sing. Her Welsh-Russian-Jewish heritage informs her work with a sense of vision and celebration that takes the fullest advantage of the musical possibilities inherent in the English language in general and the movements of American speech in particular. "Six Variations," from her 1961 volume, *The Jacob's Ladder,* is both a declaration and a demonstration of her aesthetic. It finds beauty in unlikely places and activities, after the manner of Dr. Williams, but it also celebrates the transformation of such discovery into verbal form, the "intelligent music" of the dog's drinking "in irregular measure." The wedding of image and sound, as in "the fluted / cylinder of a new ashcan a dazzling silver," is her special gift and delight, and her early books are impressive demonstrations both of her growing technical virtuosity and of her powers of close observation and shrewd insight.

If "Six Variations" declares an aesthetic, the "Olga Poems" constitutes one of its finest validations, and we have left out many other excellent Levertov poems to make room for this masterpiece. This poem's tremendous effort of re-creation—of the past, of the bond between the estranged sisters, of Olga herself in a composite and moving portrait—is also a musical accomplishment of the most impressive kind, a suite of water music cascading and tumbling through its own images and emotions like the "falls and rapids of the music" of Olga's playing of Beethoven and the brown-gold brooks that recall her eyes.

As the poem suggests, Olga was a political radical and activist, and that seems to have been one source of difference between the two sisters. The writing of her elegy for her sister, as it happens, came just at the time (1964) when Denise Levertov was herself beginning to be deeply involved in the anti-war movement protesting America's role in Vietnam. In the years that followed, it was almost as though Olga's candle burned in her all over again, and her poetry changed appreciably. Given her passionate belief that poetry and life must interact constantly and directly, it was perhaps inevitable that a life absorbed by political issues would result in an "engaged" and more overtly didactic and polemical poetry, but this was a dilemma in which she was by no means alone among American poets in the late 1960s.

There has always been something of the teacher in the work of Denise Levertov. Her books have had titles like *O Taste and See,* and her early poems urge readers to make the most of the physical world and the senses. When that strain predominates, it can limit her effectiveness, but the two recent poems that conclude our selection, "Earliest Spring" and "Window-Blind," reaffirm the continuity and strength that have made her one of our finest and most interesting poets. They stress her ability to go out into the nature of things, to observe them with a clarity that renews their meaning for us, and to turn her observation into precise, resonant language, a poetry as natural and authentic as we could hope to have.

DY

Six Variations

i

We have been shown
how Basket drank—
and old man Volpe the cobbler
made up what words he didn't know
so that his own son, even,
laughed at him: but with respect.

ii

Two flutes! How close
to each other they move
in mazing figures,
never touching, never
breaking the measure,
as gnats dance in
summer haze all afternoon, over
shallow water sprinkled
with mottled blades of willow—
two flutes!

iii

Shlup, shlup, the dog
as it laps up
water
makes intelligent
music, resting
now and then to
take breath in irregular
measure.

iv

When I can't
strike one spark from you,
when you don't
look me in the eye,
when your answers
come

slowly, dragging
their feet, and furrows
change your face,
when the sky is a cellar
with dirty windows,
when furniture
obstructs the body, and bodies
are heavy furniture coated
with dust—time
for a lagging leaden pace,
a short sullen line,
measure
of heavy heart and
cold eye.

     v

The quick of the sun that gilds
broken pebbles in sidewalk cement
and the iridescent
spit, that defiles and adorns!
Gold light in blind love does not distinguish
one surface from another, the savor
is the same to its tongue, the fluted
cylinder of a new ashcan a dazzling silver,
the smooth flesh of screaming children a quietness, it is all
a jubilance, the light catches up
the disordered street in its apron,
broken fruitrinds shine in the gutter.

     vi

Lap up the vowels
of sorrow,
        transparent, cold
water-darkness welling
up from the white sand.
Hone the blade
of a scythe to cut swathes
of light sound in the mind.
Through the hollow globe, a ring
of frayed rusty scrapiron,
is it the sea that shines?
Is it a road at the world's edge?

Olga Poems

(Olga Levertoff, 1914–1964)

i

By the gas-fire, kneeling
to undress,
scorching luxuriously, raking
her nails over olive sides, the red
waistband ring—

(And the little sister
beady-eyed in the bed—
or drowsy, was I? My head
a camera—)

Sixteen. Her breasts
round, round, and
dark-nippled—

who now these two months long
is bones and tatters of flesh in earth.

ii

The high pitch of
nagging insistence, lines
creased into raised brows—

Ridden, ridden—
the skin around the nails
nibbled sore—

You wanted
to shout the world to its senses,
did you?—to browbeat

the poor into joy's
socialist republic—
What rage

and human shame swept you
when you were nine and saw
the Ley Street houses,

grasping their meaning as *slum*.
Where I, reaching that age,
teased you, admiring

architectural probity, circa
eighteen-fifty, and noted
pride in the whitened doorsteps.

Black one, black one,
there was a white
candle in your heart.

    iii

    i

Everything flows
            she muttered into my childhood,
pacing the trampled grass where human puppets
rehearsed fates that summer,
stung into alien semblances by the lash of her will—

everything flows—
I looked up from my Littlest Bear's cane armchair
and knew the words came from a book
and felt them alien to me

but linked to words we loved
                   from the hymnbook—*Time*
like an ever-rolling stream / bears all its sons away—

    ii

Now as if smoke or sweetness were blown my way
I inhale a sense of her livingness in that instant,
feeling, dreaming, hoping, knowing boredom and zest like anyone else—
a young girl in the garden, the same alchemical square
I grew in, we thought sometimes
too small for our grand destinies—
               But dread
was in her, a bloodbeat, it was against the rolling dark
oncoming river she raised bulwarks, setting herself
to sift cinders after early Mass all of one winter,

labelling her desk's normal disorder, basing
her verses on Keble's *Christian Year*, picking
those endless arguments, pressing on

to manipulate lives to disaster . . . To change,
to change the course of the river! What rage for order
disordered her pilgrimage—so that for years at a time

she would hide among strangers, waiting
to rearrange all mysteries in a new light.

    iii

Black one, incubus—
    she appeared
riding anguish as Tartars ride mares

over the stubble of bad years.

In one of the years
    when I didn't know if she were dead or alive
I saw her in a dream

haggard and rouged
      lit by the flare
from an eel- or cockle-stand on a slum street—

was it a dream? I had lost

all sense, almost, of
    who she was, what—inside of her skin,
under her black hair
          dyed blonde—

it might feel like to be, in the wax and wane of the moon,
in the life I feel as unfolding, not flowing, the pilgrim years—

    iv

On your hospital bed you lay
in love, the hatreds
that had followed you, a
comet's tail, burned out

as your disasters bred of love
burned out,
while pain and drugs
quarreled like sisters in you—

lay afloat on a sea
of love and pain—how you always
loved that cadence, 'Underneath
are the everlasting arms'—

all history
burned out, down
to the sick bone, save for

that kind candle.

    v

    i

In a garden grene whenas I lay—

you set the words to a tune so plaintive
it plucks its way through my life as through a wood.

As through a wood, shadow and light between birches,
gliding a moment in open glades, hidden by thickets of holly

your life winds in me.   In Valentines
a root protrudes from the greensward several yards from its tree

we might raise like a trapdoor's handle, you said,
and descend long steps to another country

where we would live without father or mother
and without longing for the upper world. *The birds*
sang sweet, O song, in the midst of the daye,

and we entered silent mid-Essex churches on hot afternoons
and communed with the effigies of knights and their ladies

and their slender dogs asleep at their feet,
the stone so cold—   *In youth*

is pleasure, in youth is pleasure.

        ii
Under autumn clouds, under white
wideness of winter skies you went walking
the year you were most alone

returning to the old roads, seeing again
the signposts pointing to Theydon Garnon
or Stapleford Abbots or Greensted,

crossing the ploughlands (whose color I named *murple*,
a shade between brown and mauve that we loved
when I was a child and you

not much more than a child) finding new lanes
near White Roding or Abbess Roding; or lost in Romford's
new streets where there were footpaths then—

frowning as you ground out your thoughts, breathing deep
of the damp still air, taking
the frost into your mind unflinching.

How cold it was in your thin coat, your down-at-heel shoes—
tearless Niobe, your children were lost to you
and the stage lights had gone out, even the empty theater

was locked to you, cavern of transformation where all
had almost been possible.
                        How many books
you read in your silent lodgings that winter,
how the plovers transpierced your solitude out of doors with their strange
    cries

I had flung open my arms to in longing, once, by your side
stumbling over the furrows—

Oh, in your torn stockings, with unwaved hair,
you were trudging after your anguish
over the bare fields, soberly, soberly.

    vi

Your eyes were the brown gold of pebbles under water.
I never crossed the bridge over the Roding, dividing
the open field of the present from the mysteries,
the wraiths and shifts of time-sense Wanstead Park held suspended,
without remembering your eyes. Even when we were estranged
and my own eyes smarted in pain and anger at the thought of you.
And by other streams in other countries; anywhere where the light
reaches down through shallows to gold gravel. Olga's
brown eyes. One rainy summer, down in the New Forest,
when we could hardly breathe for ennui and the low sky,
you turned savagely to the piano and sightread
straight through all the Beethoven sonatas, day after day—
weeks, it seemed to me. I would turn the pages some of the time,
go out to ride my bike, return—you were enduring in the
falls and rapids of the music, the arpeggios rang out, the rectory
trembled, our parents seemed effaced.
I think of your eyes in that photo, six years before I was born,
the fear in them. What did you do with your fear,
later? Through the years of humiliation,
of paranoia and blackmail and near-starvation, losing
the love of those you loved, one after another,
parents, lovers, children, idolized friends, what kept
compassion's candle alight in you, that lit you
clear into another chapter (but the same book) 'a clearing
in the selva oscura,
a house whose door
swings open, a hand beckons
in welcome'?
           I cross
so many brooks in the world, there is so much light
dancing on so many stones, so many questions my eyes
smart to ask of your eyes, gold brown eyes,
the lashes short but the lids
arched as if carved out of olivewood, eyes with some vision
of festive goodness in back of their hard, or veiled, or shining,
unknowable gaze . . .

May–August 1964

Earliest Spring

Iron scallops border the path, barely
above the earth; a purplish starling lustre.

Earth a different dark, scumbled, bare
between clumps of wintered-over stems.

Slowly, from French windows opened
to first, mild, pale, after-winter morning,

we inch forward, looking: pausing, examining
each plant. It's boring. The dry stalks
are tall as I, up to her thigh. But then—
"Ah! Look! A snowdrop!" she cries,
satisfied, and I see

thin sharp green darning-needles
stitch through the sticky gleam of dirt,

belled with white!
                "And another!
And here, look, and here."
                    A white carillon.
Then she stoops to show me precise
bright green check-marks

vivid on inner petals,
each outer petal
filing down to a point.

                    And more:
"Crocuses—yes, here they are . . ."

and these point upward, closed
tight as eyelids waiting a surprise,

egg-yoke gold or mauve;
and she brings my gaze

to filigree veins of violet
traced upon white, that make

the mauve seem. This is the earliest
spring of my life. Last year

I was a baby, and what I saw then
is forgotten. Now I'm a child. Now I'm not bored

at moving step by step,
slow, down the path. Each pause

brings us to bells or flames.

Window-Blind

Much happens when we're not there.
Many trees, not only that famous one, over and over,
fall in the forest. We don't see, but something sees,
or someone, a different kind of someone,
a different molecular model, or entities
not made of molecules anyway; or nothing, no one:
but something has taken place, taken space,
                   been present, absent,
returned. Much moves in and out of open windows
when our attention is somewhere else,
just as our souls move in and out of our bodies sometimes.
Everyone used to know this,
but for a hundred years or more
we've been losing our memories, moulting, shedding,
like animals or plants that are not well.
Things happen anyway,
whether we are aware or whether
the garage door comes down by remote control over our
recognitions, shuts off, cuts off—.
We are animals and plants that are not well.
We are not well but while we look away,
on the other side of that guillotine or through
the crack of day disdainfully left open below the blind
a very strong luminous arm reaches in,
or from an unsuspected place, in the room with us,
where it was calmly waiting, reaches outward.
And though it may have nothing at all to do with us,
and though we can't fathom its designs,
nevertheless our conditon thereby changes:
cells shift, a rustling barely audible as of tarlatan
flickers through closed books, one or two leaves
fall, and when we read them we can perceive,
if we are truthful, that we were not dreaming,
not dreaming but once more witnessing.

NOTES

Six Variations. "Basket" was Gertrude Stein's dog.

Olga Poems. "*Everything flows,*" the view of Heraclitus, the pre-Socratic philoso-
    pher. Final section—"The quoted lines—'a clearing / in the selva oscura
    . . .'—are an adaptation of some lines in "Selva Oscura" by the late Louis
    MacNeice, a poem much loved by my sister, Olga" (Levertov's note). *Selva
    oscura* means "dark wood," the place where Dante finds himself at the outset
    of *The Divine Comedy*.

DENISE LEVERTOV

Books

The Double Image, 1946

Here and Now, 1956

Overland to the Islands, 1958

With Eyes at the Back of Our Heads, 1960

The Jacob's Ladder, 1961

O Taste and See, 1964

The Sorrow Dance, 1967

Eugène Guillevic, Selected Poems (translations), 1969

Relearning the Alphabet, 1970

To Stay Alive, 1971

Footprints, 1972

The Poet in the World (essays), 1975

The Freeing of the Dust, 1975

Life in the Forest, 1978

Collected Earlier Poems: 1940–1960, 1979

Light Up the Cave (essays), 1981

Writing in the Dark, 1982

Candles in Babylon, 1982

Oblique Prayers, 1984

Breathing the Water, 1987

Criticism, Interviews

Linda Wagner, *Denise Levertov*, 1967; Robert Wilson, *A Bibliography of Denise Levertov*, 1972; Linda Wagner, ed., *Denise Levertov: In Her Own Province*, 1979; Rachel Blau DuPlessis, "The Critique of Consciousness and Myth in Levertov, Rich, and Rukeyser," in *Shakespeare's Sisters: Feminist Essays on Women Poets*, ed. Gilbert and Gubar, 1979.

Philip
Levine
(b. 1928)

Thomas Victor

The poems of Philip Levine are absorbed with the past. They write down every detail and do not flinch from the syntax and structure of prose if that is what it takes to sweep things up for a hard, close look at "facts." On reading the poems, it's as if we have waked from a heavy sleep; the remains of things seen, smelled, and touched continue to haunt us, and there are no hymns to pity or forgiveness in sight. In a much-quoted interview, Levine has said, "In a curious way, I'm not much interested in language. In my ideal poem, no words are noticed. You look through them into a vision of people, see the place . . . ." Any writer who gets in the way of vision, who uses language to call attention to itself, is on the wrong track, Levine goes on to imply.

Interviewed on numerous occasions, Levine has stressed again and again his identification with "men and women I met as an industrial worker and bum in America." A favorite among his own books is *The Names of the Lost* (1976), whose poems make it clear that he is not willing to forget his "heroes," the blacks and whites who have left their home towns for exhausting work in hostile cities, where their ways and language won't do. The title poem of his most praised collection, and one of the most celebrated poems of our time, "They Feed They Lion," not only pays homage to speech patterns Levine overheard on his jobs but invokes by its ritualizing structure and diction, with the biblical power of psalms, images of what oppressors have always done to oppressed. Pouncing on the phrase "they feed they lion," Levine rediscovers in its sprung rhythms the fresh, stark, serious power that spirituals evoke and achieves a kind of Blakean effect in the poem's orchestration. As in other Levine phrases that consider civilization's wholesale slaughter of livestock (e.g., "Not this Pig," "Angel Butcher," and "Animals Are Passing from Our Lives"), he addresses the horrifying fact that we destroy in order to eat. The poem closes on a composite biblical figure, a sort of avenging angel: "From they sack and they belly opened / And all that was hidden burning on the oil-stained earth / They feed they Lion and he comes." We have made an animal of our hunger, we have fed the anti-Christ, who will devour us.

Most Levine poems do not back away from the most brutal experiences that his "loners and losers" endure. As Hayden Carruth has remarked, Levine's poems "are about the kind of courage that people have when courage fails." Levine's gift lies in telling stories that have delighted and fascinated him in intimate, elegiac tones that keep obvious themes and standard rhetoric at bay. From early small-press books like *Silent in America: Vivas for Those Who Failed* (1965), to substantial, mid-career collections like *7 Years from Somewhere* (1979; a title with the ring of a contemporary ballad), *One for the Rose* (1981), and the more recent *Selected Poems* (1984) and *Sweet Will* (1985), Levine has remained a poet of the people, in the tradition of Whitman and Williams, who follows the fatal scent of his characters through the streets. Their redeeming feature is that they have, in Rimbaud's words, "more strengths than saints, more sense than explorers." Levine seems privy to their stories in the holy way of cellmates (see "Heaven"), and the poems stand as monuments to what humankind has suffered, from the Spanish Civil War through the Holocaust and beyond to the political prisons everywhere today. Levine, whose memory serves him well, writes of ultimate innocence.

While he seems preoccupied with dramatic and narrative voices in many poems, and has said he likes those poems best in which "the speaker is clearly not me," Levine is a master of many modes. Witness the incantatory rhythms of the delicate "Milkweed": slipping back into a sort of schoolboy reverie, the speaker finally realizes he is now, and only now, smart enough to see what didn't seem important before. Here, as in other poems, he sounds a major theme: we reclaim little but love it a lot.

Like other poets whose immigrant parents suffered during the Great Depression, Levine as a young man had to face World War II, industrial pollution, and the waste of land on a huge scale. On a smaller scale perhaps, but just as searing for him, was the personal disharmony he was witness to in the furious neighborhood arguments over socialism, communism, and anarchy. Levine graduated from Wayne State University and the Writers' Workshop at the University of Iowa and has been teaching undergraduates since 1958 at California State University at Fresno—teaching them, one suspects, in such a way as to ensure that they will know their first obligation as artists is to be true to what really happens.

SF

Heaven

If you were twenty-seven
and had done time for beating
your ex-wife and had
no dreams you remembered
in the morning, you might
lie on your bed and listen
to a mad canary sing
and think it all right to be
there every Saturday
ignoring your neighbors, the streets,
the signs that said join,
and the need to be helping.
You might build, as he did,
a network of golden ladders
so that the bird could roam
on all levels of the room;
you might paint the ceiling blue,
the floor green, and shade
the place you called the sun
so that things came softly to order
when the light came on.
He and the bird lived
in the fine weather of heaven;
they never aged, they
never tired or wanted
all through that war,
but when it was over
and the nation had been saved,
he knew they'd be hunted.
He knew, as you would too,
that he'd be laid off
for not being braver,
and it would do no good
to show how he had taken
clothespins and cardboard
and made each step safe.
It would do no good
to have been one of the few
that climbed higher and higher
even in time of war,
for now there would be the poor
asking for their share,
and hurt men in uniforms,

and no one to believe
that heaven was really here.

They Feed They Lion

Out of burlap sacks, out of bearing butter,
Out of black bean and wet slate bread,
Out of the acids of rage, the candor of tar,
Out of creosote, gasoline, drive shafts, wooden dollies,
They Lion grow.
           Out of the gray hills
Of industrial barns, out of rain, out of bus ride,
West Virginia to Kiss My Ass, out of buried aunties,
Mothers hardening like pounded stumps, out of stumps,
Out of the bones' need to sharpen and the muscles' to stretch,
They Lion grow.
           Earth is eating trees, fence posts,
Gutted cars, earth is calling in her little ones,
"Come home, Come home!" From pig balls,
From the ferocity of pig driven to holiness,
From the furred ear and the full jowl come
The repose of the hung belly, from the purpose
They Lion grow.
           From the sweet glues of the trotters
Come the sweet kinks of the fist, from the full flower
Of the hams the thorax of caves,
From "Bow Down" come "Rise Up,"
Come they Lion from the reeds of shovels,
The grained arm that pulls the hands,
They Lion grow.
           From my five arms and all my hands,
From all my white sins forgiven, they feed,
From my car passing under the stars,
They Lion, from my children inherit,
From the oak turned to a wall, they Lion,
From they sack and they belly opened
And all that was hidden burning on the oil-stained earth
They feed they Lion and he comes.

Clouds

1

Dawn. First light tearing
at the rough tongues of the zinnias,
at the leaves of the just born.

Today it will rain. On the road
black cars are abandoned, but the clouds
ride above, their wisdom intact.

They are predictions. They never matter.
The jet fighters lift above the flat roofs,
black arrowheads trailing their future.

     2

When the night comes small fires go out.
Blood runs to the heart and finds it locked.

Morning is exhaustion, tranquilizers, gasoline,
the screaming of frozen bearings,
the failures of will, the TV talking to itself.

The clouds go on eating oil, cigars,
housewives, sighing letters,
the breath of lies. In their great silent pockets
they carry off all our dead.

     3

The clouds collect until there's no sky.
A boat slips its moorings and drifts
toward the open sea, turning and turning.

The moon bends to the canal and bathes
her torn lips, and the earth goes on
giving off her angers and sighs

and who knows or cares except these
breathing the first rains,
the last rivers running over iron.

     4

You cut an apple in two pieces
and ate them both. In the rain
the door knocked and you dreamed it.
On bad roads the poor walked under cardboard boxes.

The houses are angry because they're watched.
A soldier wants to talk with God
but his mouth fills with lost tags.

The clouds have seen it all, in the dark
they pass over the graves of the forgotten
and they don't cry or whisper.

They should be punished every morning,
they should be bitten and boiled like spoons.

1933

My father entered the kingdom of roots
    his head as still as a stone
    (Laid out in black with a white tie
    he blinked
    and I told no one
    except myself over and over)
    laid out long and gray

The hands that stroked my head
    the voice in the dark asking
    he drove the car all the way to the river
      where the ships burned
    he rang with keys and coins
    he knew the animals and their names
      touched the nose of the horse
      and kicked the German dog away
    he brought Ray Estrada from Mexico in his 16th year
      scolded him like a boy, gave him beer money
      and commanded him to lift and push
    he left in October without his hat
    who answered to the name Father

Father, the world is different in many places
    the old Ford Trimotors are gone to scrap
    the Terraplane turned to snow
    four armies passed over your birthplace
      your house is gone
      all your tall sisters gone
      your fathers
      everyone
    Roosevelt ran again
    you would still be afraid

You would not know me now, I have a son taller than you
    I feel the first night winds catch in the almond
      the plum bend
      and I go in afraid of the death you are
    I climb the tree in the vacant lot
      and leave the fruit untasted
    I blink the cold winds in from the sea
      walking with Teddy, my little one
      squeezing his hand I feel his death
    I find the glacier and wash my face in Arctic dust

I shit handfuls of earth
I stand in the spring river pissing at stars
I see the diamond back at the end of the path
    hissing and rattling
    and will not shoot

The sun is gone, the moon is a slice of hope
    the stars are burned eyes that see
    the wind is the breath of the ocean
    the death of the fish is the allegory
        you slice it open and spill the entrails
        you remove the spine
        the architecture of the breast
        you slap it home
        the oils snap and sizzle.
        you live in the world
    you eat all the unknown deeps
    the great sea oaks rise from the floor
    the bears dip their paws in clear streams
        they hug their great matted coats
        and laugh in the voices of girls
    a man drops slowly like brandy or glue

In the cities of the world
    the streets darken with flies
    all the dead fathers fall out of heaven
        and begin again
    the angel of creation is a sparrow in the roadway
    storks rise slowly pulling the houses after them
    butterflies eat away the eyes of the sun
    the last ashes off the fire of the brain
    the last leavening of snow
    grains of dirt torn from under fingernails and eyes
    you drink these

There is the last darkness burning itself to death
    there are nine women come in the dawn with pitchers
    there is my mother
        a dark child in the schoolyard
        miles from anyone
        she has begun to bleed as her mother did
    there is my brother, the first born, the mild one
        his cold breath fogging the bombsight
    there is the other in his LTD
        he talks to the phone, he strokes his thighs
        he dismisses me

my mother waits for the horsecart to pass
my mother prays to become fat and wise
   she becomes fat and wise
the cat dies and it rains
the dog groans by the side door
the old hen flies up in a spasm of gold

My woman gets out of bed in the dark and washes her face
   she goes to the kitchen before we waken
   she picks up a skillet, an egg
   the kids go off to school without socks
   in the rain the worms come out to live
   my father opens the telegram under the moon
      Cousin Philip is dead
      my father stands on the porch in his last summer
      he holds back his tears
      he holds back my tears

Once in childhood the stars held still all night
   the moon swelled like a plum but white and silken
   the last train from Chicago howled through the ghetto
   I came downstairs
   my father sat writing in a great black book
   a pile of letters
   a pile of checks
   (he would pay his debts)
   the moon would die
   the stars jelly
   the sea freeze
   I would be a boy in worn shoes splashing through rain

Milkweed

Remember how unimportant
they seemed, growing loosely
in the open fields we crossed
on the way to school. We
would carve wooden swords
and slash at the luscious trunks
until the white milk started
and then flowed. Then we'd
go on to the long day after
day of the History of History
or the tables of numbers and order
as the clock slowly paid

out the moments. The windows
went dark first with rain
and then snow, and then the days,
then the years ran together and not
one mattered more than
another, and not one mattered.

Two days ago I walked
the empty woods, bent over,
crunching through oak leaves,
asking myself questions
without answers. From somewhere
a froth of seeds drifted by touched
with gold in the last light
of a lost day, going with
the wind as they always did.

Sweet Will

The man who stood beside me
34 years ago this night fell
on to the concrete, oily floor
of Detroit Transmission, and we
stepped carefully over him until
he wakened and went back to his press.

It was Friday night, and the others
told me that every Friday he drank
more than he could hold and fell
and he wasn't any dumber for it
so just let him get up at his
own sweet will or he'll hit you.

"At his own sweet will," was just
what the old black man said to me,
and he smiled the smile of one
who is still surprised that dawn
graying the cracked and broken windows
could start us all to singing in the cold.

Stash rose and wiped the back of his head
with a crumpled handkerchief and looked
at his own blood as though it were
dirt and puzzled as to how
it got there and then wiped the ends
of his fingers carefully one at a time

the way the mother wipes the fingers
of a sleeping child, and climbed back
on his wooden soda-pop case to
his punch press and hollered at all
of us over the oceanic roar of work,
addressing us by our names and nations—

"Nigger, Kike, Hunky, River Rat,"
but he gave it a tune, an old tune,
like "America the Beautiful." And he danced
a little two-step and smiled showing
the four stained teeth left in the front
and took another suck of cherry brandy.

In truth is was no longer Friday,
for night had turned to day as it
often does for those who are patient,
so it was Saturday in the year of '48
in the very heart of the city of man
where your Cadillac cars get manufactured.

In truth all those people are dead,
they have gone up to heaven singing
"Time on My Hands" or "Begin the Beguine,"
and the Cadillacs have all gone back
to earth, and nothing that we made
that night is worth more than me.

And in truth I'm not worth a thing
what with my feet and my two bad eyes
and my one long nose and my breath
of old lies and my sad tales of men
who let the earth break them back,
each one, to dirty blood or bloody dirt.

Not worth a thing! Just like it was said
at my magic birth when the stars
collided and fire fell from great space
into great space, and people rose one
by one from cold beds to tend a world
that runs on and on at its own sweet will.

NOTES

They Feed They Lion. It seems appropriate to recall the following quotation, from *New Testament Apocrypha*, by E. Hennecke, edited by W. Schneemelcher:

Jesus has said:
Blessed is the lion that
the man will devour, and the lion
will become man. And loathsome is the
man that the lion will devour,
and the lion will become man.

Gospel of Thomas, Logion 7,
translated by George Ogg

PHILIP LEVINE

Books

On the Edge, 1963

Silent in America: Vivas for Those Who Failed, 1965

Not This Pig, 1968

Red Dust, 1971

Pili's Wall, 1971

They Feed They Lion, 1972

1933, 1974

The Names of the Lost, 1976

Ashes: Poems Old and New, 1979

7 Years from Somewhere, 1979

Out of the Rose, 1981

Selected Poems, 1984

Off the Map: Selected Poems: By Gloria Fuertes (edited and translated by Philip Levine and Ada Long), 1984

Sweet Will, 1985

A Walk With Tom Jefferson, 1988

Interviews, Criticism

"And See If the Voice Will Enter You: An Interview with Philip Levine," *Ohio Review* 26 (Winter 1975); Charles Molesworth, "The Burned Essential Oil: The Poetry of Philip Levine," *Hollins Critic* 12 (December 1975); Calvin Bedient, "An Interview with Philip Levine," *Parnassus* 6 (1978); *Don't Ask* (interviews), 1981.

James
Merrill
(b. 1926)

Thomas Victor 1980

J ames Merrill has in recent years moved to a position of special eminence in American poetry. The eminence stems partly from the critical praise and attention showered on his remarkable long poem, *The Changing Light at Sandover,* a three-part work that rivals great poems of the past in its scope, length and complexity. It is also due to a more general recognition that Merrill has developed steadily from rather decorative beginnings into a poet whose mastery of technique recalls Richard Wilbur and whose inventive daring and cool melancholy bring to mind John Ashbery, among poets, and masters of modern fiction like Proust and Nabokov.

Merrill can be located first, perhaps, as a member of the "Auden generation." W. H. Auden's presence in this country after 1939 had an enormous influence, especially among east coast poets who were attracted to his sophisticated manner and accomplished handling of traditional forms. Some of the poets whose talents Auden recognized or influenced have since rebelled: one thinks of W. S. Merwin, Adrienne Rich, and John Ashbery. Others have remained more or less faithful: the names of John Hollander, Anthony Hecht, Richard Howard, and the late Howard Moss come to mind. This latter group does not really constitute a school, so they require no current leader, but the poet among them who has earned the largest praise and is now most widely acknowledged for his accomplishments is James Merrill.

For many poets of Merrill's generation, it could be said that the problem was how to resolve the tension between Auden's impersonal style and the native impulse to autobiography and personal candor represented by, among others, the confessional poets. Randall Jarrell has characterized Auden's later poetry mercilessly but candidly as ". . . a rhetoric mill grinding away at the bottom of Limbo . . . making little jokes, little plays on words, little rhetorical engines, as compulsively and unendingly and uneasily as a neurotic washes his hands" (*The Third Book of Criticism*). The manufacture of clever, hollow-hearted poems has been the curse that Auden bequeathed to his followers. Merrill does not always escape the dilemma, but insofar as he does his solution is to write about his own life more frankly and searchingly, not really in the manner of Berryman, Lowell, Plath, or Sexton, but still as a kind of concession to what they represent. Thus it is that his gigantic and ambitious trilogy is based on ouija-board sessions held over many years with his lover, the novelist David Jackson. In those sessions, Merrill and Jackson reputedly converse with the ghost of Auden (one way to exorcise an influence!), along with the Archangel Michael and various luminaries from the other world. It is slender stuff on which to rear a poem that has been likened to the accomplishments of Dante and Milton, and while it has the precedent of Yeats and his wife producing the materials for *A Vision* by means of automatic writing, it also risks the charge of triviality, a sort of cup-and-saucer metaphysics: huge questions of science, destiny, life and afterlife are cast into what sometimes sounds like witty tea-time chat.

The verdict on Merrill's trilogy is still perhaps not in, despite the lavish praise of some commentators, nor has Merrill's career yielded all the surprises it may have in store for us. What can be said with some confidence is that Merrill's use of his own life, in *Sandover* and in other poems of recent years, has been productive and intriguing. The example of Proust, mining his own life, not so much for revelations and agonies as for retrieved and investigated beauty, is relevant here. So is the intricate and pleasurable game that Nabokov makes for himself and his readers out of the problematic activities of memory. That Merrill has earned comparison with such admired fiction writers suggests how much his later accomplishments are grounded on the possibilities of narrative in poetry; that they are also both writers who are fascinated by the shifting boundaries of life and art helps illuminate the very sophisticated use Merrill makes of his own experience. He is a writer who needs control and distance, as realized in formal and technical mastery; his use of materials that risk the loss of control and the closing of the distance gives his work an excitement, a shimmer of risk, that keeps the drama of creativity constantly before us.

The way this works is very evident in the masterly long poem, "Lost in Translation" (from *Divine Comedies*, 1976), which we present here as the primary testimony to Merrill's accomplishment. Going back to one's own childhood to investigate the pathos of one's innocence and loneliness is a tricky business. Merrill handles it with a complex and comic sense of the risks and pleasures it entails. There's an implicit admission from the aging author that the difference between the little boy who delights in his puzzle and the poet who plays so happily with his art is very slight. Recapturing the past, like making the puzzle, may be self-indulgent play, but who would begrudge it, especially in a bewildering world that is fractured by different languages and the need to "translate" experience from other lives into our own before we can understand and sympathize? We are all pleasantly implicated in this poem, whether we had bilingual nannies and absent parents or not. Our weaknesses are the same as the boy/man Merrill's, and as we put the puzzle that is the poem together we can laugh, feel sorrow, make connections, and forgive the past and ourselves in a charmed harmony with the author.

Merrill's technical accomplishments—one can linger quite thoughtfully and profitably over the music, wordplay, and full meaning of lines like "An inchling, innocently branching palm" in "Lost in Translation"—are also illustrated in the two shorter poems included here, "The Pier: Under Pisces" and "In the Dark," both from his latest volume, *Late Settings* (1985). They show how Merrill's literate, obsessive verbal playing now tends to result in a sense of reality that is magical as well as aesthetic, a kind of metaphysical piercing of the normal obscurities of our existence, little rays of light in the gloom.

James Merrill has turned autobiography into vision, game playing into metaphysical research. In his long poem he has taken this either to his most accomplished, or to his most extravagant, level. Whatever the final assessment of that work, Merrill's accomplishment is by now substantial enough to place him among our leading poets.

DY

Lost in Translation

For Richard Howard

Diese Tage, die leer dir scheinen
und wertlos für das All,
haben Wurzeln zwischen den Steinen
und trinken dort überall.

A card table in the library stands ready
To receive the puzzle which keeps never coming.
Daylight shines in or lamplight down
Upon the tense oasis of green felt.
Full of unfulfillment, life goes on,
Mirage arisen from time's trickling sands
Or fallen piecemeal into place:
German lesson, picnic, see-saw, walk
With the collie who "did everything but talk"—
Sour windfalls of the orchard back of us.
A summer without parents in the puzzle,
Or should be. But the boy, day after day,
Writes in his Line-a-Day *No puzzle.*

He's in love, at least. His French Mademoiselle,
In real life a widow since Verdun,
Is stout, plain, carrot-haired, devout.
She prays for him, as does a curé in Alsace,
Sews costumes for his marionettes,
Helps him to keep behind the scene
Whose sidelit goosegirl, speaking with his voice,
Plays Guinevere as well as Gunmoll Jean.
Or else at bedtime in his tight embrace
Tells him her own French hopes, her German fears,
Her—but what more is there to tell?
Having known grief and hardship, Mademoiselle
Knows little more. Her languages. Her place.
Noon coffee. Mail. The watch that also waited
Pinned to her heart, poor gold, throws up its hands—
No puzzle! Steaming bitterness
Her sugars draw pops back into his mouth, translated:
"Patience, chéri. Geduld, mein Schatz."
(Thus, reading Valéry the other evening
And seeming to recall a Rilke version of "Palme,"
That sunlit paradigm whereby the tree
Taps a sweet wellspring of authority,
The hour came back. Patience dans l'azur.
Geduld im . . . Himmelblau? Mademoiselle.)

Out of the blue, as promised, of a New York
Puzzle-rental shop the puzzle comes—
A superior one, containing a thousand hand-sawn,
Sandal-scented pieces. Many take
Shapes known already—the craftsman's repertoire
Nice in its limitation—from other puzzles:
Witch on broomstick, ostrich, hourglass,
Even (surely not just in retrospect)
An inchling, innocently branching palm.
These can be put aside, made stories of
While Mademoiselle spreads out the rest face-up,
Herself excited as a child; or questioned
Like incoherent faces in a crowd,
Each with its scrap of highly colored
Evidence the Law must piece together.
Sky-blue ostrich? Likely story.
Mauve of the witch's cloak white, severed fingers
Pluck? Detain her. The plot thickens
As all at once two pieces interlock.

Mademoiselle does borders—(Not so fast.
A London dusk, December last.
Chatter silenced in the library
This grown man reenters, wearing grey.
A medium. All except him have seen
Panel slid back, recess explored,
An object at once unique and common
Displayed, planted in a plain tole
Casket the subject now considers
Through shut eyes, saying in effect:
"Even as voices reach me vaguely
A dry saw-shriek drowns them out,
Some loud machinery—a lumber mill?
Far uphill in the fir forest
Trees tower, tense with shock,
Groaning and cracking as they crash groundward.
But hidden here is a freak fragment
Of a pattern complex in appearance only.
What it seems to show is superficial
Next to that long-term lamination
Of hazard and craft, the karma that has
Made it matter in the first place.
Plywood, Piece of a puzzle." Applause
Acknowledged by an opening of lids
Upon the thing itself. A sudden dread—
But to go back. All this lay years ahead.)

Mademoiselle does borders. Straight-edge pieces
Align themselves with earth or sky
In twos and threes, naive cosmogonists
Whose views clash. Nomad inlanders meanwhile
Begin to cluster where the totem
Of a certain vibrant egg-yolk yellow
Or pelt of what emerging animal
Acts on the straggler like a trumpet call
To form a more sophisticated unit.
By suppertime two ragged wooden clouds
Have formed. In one, a Sheik with beard
And flashing sword hilt (he is all but finished)
Steps forward on a tiger skin. A piece
Snaps shut, and fangs gnash out at us!
In the second cloud—they gaze from cloud to cloud
With marked if undecipherable feeling—
Most of a dark-eyed woman veiled in mauve
Is being helped down from her camel (kneeling)
By a small backward-looking slave or page-boy
(Her son, thinks Mademoiselle mistakenly)
Whose feet have not been found. But lucky finds
In the last minutes before bed
Anchor both factions to the scene's limits
And, by so doing, orient
Them eye to eye across the green abyss.
The yellow promises, oh bliss,
To be in time a sumptuous tent.

Puzzle begun I write in the day's space,
Then, while she bathes, peek at Mademoiselle's
Page to the curé: ". . . cette innocente mère,
Ce pauvre enfant, que deviendront-ils?"
Her azure script is curlicued like pieces
Of the puzzle she will be telling him about.
(Fearful incuriosity of childhood!
"Tu as l'accent allemand," said Dominique.
Indeed. Mademoiselle was only French by marriage.
Child of an English mother, a remote
Descendant of the great explorer Speke,
And Prussian father. No one knew. I heard it
Long afterwards from her nephew, a UN
Interpreter. His matter-of-fact account
Touched old strings. My poor Mademoiselle,
With 1939 about to shake
This world where "each was the enemy, each the friend"

To its foundations, kept, though signed in blood,
Her peace a shameful secret to the end.)
"Schlaf wohl, chéri." Her kiss. Her thumb
Crossing my brow against the dreams to come.

This World that shifts like sand, its unforeseen
Consolidations and elate routine,
Whose Potentate had lacked a retinue?
Lo! it assembles on the shrinking Green.

Gunmetal-skinned or pale, all plumes and scars,
Of Vassalage the noblest avatars—
The very coffee-bearer in his vair
Vest is a swart Highness, next to ours.

Kef easing Boredom, and iced syrups, thirst,
In guessed-at glooms old wives who know the worst
Outsweat that virile fiction of the New:
"Insh'Allah, he will tire—" "—or kill her first!"

(Hardly a proper subject for the Home,
Work of—dear Richard, I shall let you comb
Archives and learned journals for his name—
A minor lion attending on Gérôme.)

While, thick as Thebes whose presently complete
Gates close behind them, Houri and Afreet
Both claim the Page. He wonders whom to serve,
And what his duties are, and where his feet,

And if we'll find, as some before us did,
That piece of Distance deep in which lies hid
Your tiny apex sugary with sun,
Eternal Triangle, Great Pyramid!

Then Sky alone is left, a hundred blue
Fragments in revolution, with no clue
To where a Niche will open. Quite a task,
Putting together Heaven, yet we do.

It's done. Here under the table all along
Were those missing feet. It's done.

The dog's tail thumping. Mademoiselle sketching
Costumes for a coming harem drama
To star the goosegirl. All too soon the swift
Dismantling. Lifted by two corners,
The puzzle hung together—and did not.
Irresistibly a populace
Unstitched of its attachments, rattled down.
Power went to pieces as the witch
Slithered easily from Virtue's gown.
The blue held out for time, but crumbled, too.

The city had long fallen, and the tent,
A separating sauce mousseline,
Been swept away. Remained the green
On which the grown-ups gambled. A green dusk.
First lightning bugs. Last glow of west
Green in the false eyes of (coincidence)
Our mangy tiger safe on his bared hearth.

Before the puzzle was boxed and readdressed
To the puzzle shop in the mid-Sixties,
Something tells me that one piece contrived
To stay in the boy's pocket. How do I know?
I know because so many later puzzles
Had missing pieces—Maggie Teyte's high notes
Gone at the war's end, end of the vogue for collies,
A house torn down; and hadn't Mademoiselle
Kept back her pitiful bit of truth as well?
I've spent the last days, furthermore,
Ransacking Athens for that translation of "Palme."
Neither the Goethehaus nor the National Library
Seems able to unearth it. Yet I can't
Just be imagining. I've seen it. Know
How much of the sun-ripe original
Felicity Rilke made himself forego
(Who loved French words—verger, mûr, parfumer)
In order to render its underlying sense.
Know already in that tongue of his
What Pains, what monolithic Truths
Shadow stanza to stanza's symmetrical
Rhyme-rutted pavement. Know that ground plan left
Sublime and barren, where the warm Romance
Stone by stone faded, cooled; the fluted nouns
Made taller, lonelier than life
By leaf-carved capitals in the afterglow.
The owlet umlaut peeps and hoots
Above the open vowel. And after rain
A deep reverberation fills with stars.

Lost, is it, buried? One more missing piece?

But nothing's lost. Or else: all is translation
And every bit of us is lost in it
(Or found—I wander through the ruin of S
Now and then, wondering at the peacefulness)
And in that loss a self-effacing tree,
Color of context, imperceptibly
Rustling with its angel, turns the waste
To shade and fiber, milk and memory.

The Pier: Under Pisces

The shallows, brighter,
Wetter than water,
Tepidly glitter with the fingerprint-
Obliterating feel of kerosene.

Each piling like a totem
Rises from rock bottom
Straight through the ceiling
Aswirl with suns, clear ones or pale bluegreen,

And beyond! where bubbles burst,
Sphere of their worst dreams,
If dream is what they do,
These floozy fish—

Ceramic-lipped in filmy
Peekaboo blouses,
Fluorescent body
Stockings, hot stripes,

Swayed by the hypnotic ebb and flow
Of supermarket Muzak,
Bolero beat the undertow's
Pebble-filled gourds repeat;

Jailbait consumers of subliminal
Hints dropped from on high
In gobbets none
Eschews as minced kin;

Who, hooked themselves—bamboo diviner
Bent their way
Vigorously nodding
Encouragement—

Are one by one hauled kisswise, oh
Into some blinding hell
Policed by leathery ex-
Justices each

Minding his catch, if catch is what he can,
If mind is what one means—
The torn mouth
Stifled by newsprint, working still. If . . . if . . .

The little scales
Grow stiff. Dusk plugs her dryer in,
Buffs her nails, riffles through magazines,
While far and wide and deep

Rove the great sharkskin-suited criminals
And safe in this lit shrine
A boy sits. He'll be eight.
We've drunk our milk, we've eaten our stringbeans,

But left untasted on the plate
The fish. An eye, a broiled pearl, meeting mine,
I lift his fork . . .
The bite. The tug of fate.

In the Dark

Come, try this exercise:
Focus a beam
Emptied of thinking, outward through shut eyes
On X, your "god" of long ago.

Wherever he is now the photons race,
A phantom, unresisting stream,

For nothing lights up. No
Sudden amused face,
No mote, no far-out figment, to obstruct
The energy—
                                 It just spends
And spends itself, and who will ever know

Unless he felt you aim at him   and ducked

Or you before the session ends
Begin to glow

NOTES

Lost in Translation. The epigraph translates, "These days that you think empty /
    and worthless for the universe, / have roots among the stones / and drink
    everywhere they can there."

JAMES MERRILL

Books

First Poems, 1951

The Seraglio (novel), 1957

The Country of a Thousand Years of
Peace, 1959

Water Street, 1962

The (Diblos) Notebook (novel), 1965

Nights and Days, 1966

The Fire Screen, 1969

Braving the Elements, 1972

The Yellow Pages, 1974

Divine Comedies, 1976

Mirabell: Books of Number, 1978

Scripts for the Pageant, 1980

From the First Nine: Poems 1946–
1976, 1982

The Changing Light at Sandover,
1982

Late Settings, 1985

Interviews, Criticism

David Kalstone, *Five Temperaments*, 1977; Helen Vendler, *Part of Nature, Part of Us*, 1980; "The Art of Poetry XXXI," interview with J. D. McClatchy, *Paris Review* 84 (Summer 1982); David Lehman and Charles Berger, eds., *James Merrill: Essays in Criticism*, 1983; Stephen Yenser, *The Consuming Myth: The Work of* James Merrill, 1987.

W. S.
Merwin
(b. 1927)

Paula Dunaway Merwin

A lthough W. S. Merwin was recognized as a promising poet during the 1950s, it was during the 1960s and 1970s that he gained a wide audience and grew to be one of our most original and most widely imitated poets. The first selection here, "Low Fields and Light," from his fourth collection, *The Drunk in the Furnace* (1960), shows his new style coming into being. The subject—a flat, monochromatic landscape that merges mysteriously with the sea—is disorienting because of the success with which the poem's language and manner seem to match it. The speaker is bemused, the language dazed and repetitive. In earlier poems Merwin had written about ancient myths and legendary places; here he begins to create myth, or a mythic sense of experience. We know that the sea-fields described here may be in Virginia, but we also recognize that their power for the speaker, as for us, derives from the way they seem to point beyond themselves. The poem looks ahead to Merwin's major work, a haunted and haunting poetry in which isolation and nullity are projected with an authority and specificity that remind us of myth.

The voice that has begun to emerge in "Low Fields and Light" is not that of an ordinary person. It is exalted and impersonal, the voice of someone who knows about or speaks from a mythic world. We could call it bardic, noting as we do that it is a voice most of Merwin's contemporaries have eschewed. Merwin can use it to create a character or even to invoke another culture, as in "The Last One," which seems to emanate from a primitive storyteller, a shaman recounting a myth of de-creation and desolation. Here the duality arises from our recognition that the story is at once deliberately timeless, a parable, and at the same time a modern political protest against the technological arrogance that has led to the defoliation of forests in Vietnam and to other forms of environmental misuse. "The Last One," along with the mordant "Caesar," reminds us that Merwin was one of the few poets to produce effective political poetry during the 1960s and 1970s. To realize that "Caesar" was written not long after John Kennedy's assassination is to be able to identify the raw historical reality behind it, but its power of survival presumably stems from the fact that it refuses to be tied to one politician's death, to Kennedy or to some Roman ruler, or even to one set of political attitudes. Whatever its occasion, it rises toward the expressive power to sum up large areas of human experience that we say myth possesses.

A mythmaker must be cautious about his use of particulars. Merwin's expert juggling of abstractions and concrete details is surely one secret of his distinctive style. It is almost as if they exchange roles, "Witnesses," for example, uses specific details—mouse, curtain, clock, gloves, knives—but it keeps them at a careful, generalized distance. Imagine them any more specific (e.g., "Windup mouse," "digital clock," "switchblade knives"), and you realize how much their deliberately generalized quality contributes to their characterization of evening as a sinister stranger with sinister accomplices. "The River of Bees" shows us, even in its title, how Merwin drains reality of substance in order to make it magical. A river is physical, bees are physical, but a river of bees is a combination so dreamlike and compelling that it points to another realm, whether metaphysical or of the imagination. The poem that follows can be described as a mingling of memory, dream, and meditation, but even its "messages"—"Men think they are better than grass" or "we were not born to survive/Only to live"—seem mysterious in a context that contains such ineffable details as "the noise of death drawing water." The poem's alternation between clarity and opacity keeps us off balance without completely frustrating us, and it remains one of the most memorable lyrics in *The Lice* (1967), Merwin's most influential collection.

To admit that stylistic and rhetorical formulas are at work in this style is not to dissipate its magic. Sometimes Merwin uses deliberate reversals, as in "We are the echo of the future" or the poem, not included here, titled "On the Anniversary of My Death" and beginning "Every year without knowing it I have passed the day. . . ." Even the notion of the spiders, in "The Broken," as trying to mend the air, can be seen to stem from a program in which norms are systematically turned inside out. But knowing how these effects may have been accomplished leaves us the more impressed by the way they attack our expectations and stir our emotions. The range of forms, from short lyric to dramatic monologue to verse narrative to prose text, is impressive too. From the first collection of Merwin's prose pieces, *The Miner's Pale Children* (1970), we have drawn "The Broken," which demonstrates the way in which Merwin extends his rhetoric of mythic absence and chilly narrative into small tales and dense prose texts.

One of our most literate writers, Merwin has demonstrated his wide interests and international affiliations by becoming the most active and successful translator of his generation. He has given us persuasive versions of older texts—Perseus, *The Song of Roland, The Poem of the Cid*—and of important modern writers like Neruda, Mandelstam, and Jean Follain. While some of these writers, Follain especially, may be thought of as influences, Merwin's style must be recognized as very much his own, a brilliant contribution to the best possibilities of modernism.

Unlike most of his contemporaries, Merwin has never taught regularly to support himself but has preferred to concentrate on writing and translating. His friendships with other writers are warm and extensive, going back to his undergraduate days at Princeton with Galway Kinnell. At present he lives most of the year in Hawaii.

DY

Low Fields and Light

I think it is in Virginia, that place
That lies across the eye of my mind now
Like a grey blade set to the moon's roundness,
Like a plain of glass touching all there is.

The flat fields run out to the sea there.
There is no sand, no line. It is autumn.
The bare fields, dark between fences, run
Out to the idle gleam of the flat water.

And the fences go on out, sinking slowly,
With a cow-bird half-way, on a stunted post, watching
How the light slides through them easy as weeds
Or wind, slides over them away out near the sky.

Because even a bird can remember
The fields that were there before the slow
Spread and wash of the edging line crawled
There and covered them, a little more each year.

My father never ploughed there, nor my mother
Waited, and never knowingly I stood there
Hearing the seepage slow as growth, nor knew
When the taste of salt took over the ground.

But you would think the fields were something
To me, so long I stare out, looking
For their shapes or shadows through the matted gleam, seeing
Neither what is nor what was, but the flat light rising.

Witnesses

Evening has brought its
Mouse and let it out on the floor,
On the wall, on the curtain, on
The clock. You with the gloves, in the doorway,
Who asked you to come and watch?

As the bats flower in the crevices
You and your brothers
Raise your knives to see by.
Surely the moon can find her way to the wells
Without you. And the streams
To their altars.

As for us, we enter your country
With our eyes closed.

The Last One

Well they'd made up their minds to be everywhere because why not.
Everywhere was theirs because they thought so.
They with two leaves they whom the birds despise.
In the middle of stones they made up their minds.
They started to cut.

Well they cut everything because why not.
Everything was theirs because they thought so.
It fell into its shadows and they took both away.
Some to have some for burning.

Well cutting everything they came to the water.
They came to the end of the day there was one left standing.
They would cut it tomorrow they went away.
The night gathered in the last branches.
The shadow of the night gathered in the shadow on the water.
The night and the shadow put on the same head.
And it said Now.

Well in the morning they cut the last one.
Like the others the last one fell into its shadow.
It fell into its shadow on the water.
They took it away its shadow stayed on the water.

Well they shrugged they started trying to get the shadow away.
They cut right to the ground the shadow stayed whole.
They laid boards on it the shadow came out on top.
They shone lights on it the shadow got blacker and clearer.
They exploded the water the shadow rocked.
They built a huge fire on the roots.
They sent up black smoke between the shadow and the sun.
The new shadow flowed without changing the old one.
They shrugged they went away to get stones.

They came back the shadow was growing.
They started setting up stones it was growing.
They looked the other way it went on growing.
They decided they would make a stone out of it.
They took stones to the water they poured them into the shadow.
They poured them in they poured them in the stones vanished.
The shadow was not filled it went on growing.
That was one day.

The next day was just the same it went on growing.
They did all the same things it was just the same.
They decided to take its water from under it.
They took away water they took it away the water went down.
The shadow stayed where it was before.
It went on growing it grew onto the land.
They started to scrape the shadow with machines.
When it touched the machines it stayed on them.
They started to beat the shadow with sticks.
Where it touched the sticks it stayed on them.
They started to beat the shadow with hands.
Where it touched the hands it stayed on them.
That was another day.

Well the next day started about the same it went on growing.
They pushed lights into the shadow.
Where the shadow got onto them they went out.
They began to stomp on the edge it got their feet.
And when it got their feet they fell down.
It got into eyes the eyes went blind.
The ones that fell down it grew over and they vanished.
The ones that went blind and walked into it vanished.
The ones that could see and stood still
It swallowed their shadows.
Then it swallowed them too and they vanished.
Well the others ran.

The ones that were left went away to live if it would let them.
They went as far as they could.
The lucky ones with their shadows.

Caesar

My shoes are almost dead
And as I wait at the doors of ice
I hear the cry go up for him Caesar Caesar

But when I look out the window I see only the flatlands
And the slow vanishing of the windmills
The centuries draining the deep fields

Yet this is still my country
The thug on duty says What would you change
He looks at his watch he lifts
Emptiness out of the vases
And holds it up to examine

So it is evening
With the rain starting to fall forever

One by one he calls night out of the teeth
And at last I take up
My duty

Wheeling the president past banks of flowers
Past the feet of empty stairs
Hoping he's dead

The River of Bees

In a dream I returned to the river of bees
Five orange trees by the bridge and
Beside two mills my house
Into whose courtyard a blind man followed
The goats and stood singing
Of what was older

Soon it will be fifteen years

He was old he will have fallen into his eyes

I took my eyes
A long way to the calendars
Room after room asking how shall I live

One of the ends is made of streets
One man processions carry through it
Empty bottles their
Image of hope
It was offered to me by name

Once once and once
In the same city I was born
Asking what shall I say

He will have fallen into his mouth
Men think they are better than grass

I return to his voice rising like a forkful of hay

He was old he is not real nothing is real
Nor the noise of death drawing water

We are the echo of the future

On the door it says what to do to survive
But we were not born to survive
Only to live

When You Go Away

When you go away the wind clicks around to the north
The painters work all day but at sundown the paint falls
Showing the black walls
The clock goes back to striking the same hour
That has no place in the years

And at night wrapped in the bed of ashes
In one breath I wake
It is the time when the beards of the dead get their growth
I remember that I am falling
That I am the reason
And that my words are the garment of what I shall never be
Like the tucked sleeve of a one-armed boy

The Broken

The spiders started out to go with the wind on its pilgrimage. At that time
they were honored among the invisibles—more sensitive than glass, lighter
than water, purer than ice. Even the lightning spoke well of them, and it
seemed as though they could go anywhere. But as they were travelling
between cold and heat, cracks appeared in them, appeared in their limbs,
and they stopped, it seemed they had to stop, had to leave the company of
the wind for a while and stay in one place until they got better, moving
carefully, hiding, trusting to nothing. It was not long before they gave up
trying to become whole again, and instead undertook to mend the air.
Neither life nor death, they said, would slip through it any more.

    After that they were numbered among the dust—makers of ghosts.
    The wind never missed them. There were still the clouds.

A Door

Do you remember how I beat on the door
kicked the door
as though I or the door were a bad thing
later it opened
I went in
nothing
starlight
snowing

an empty throne
snow swirling on the floor
around the feet

and on an instrument
we had been trying
to speak to each other
on which we had been trying to speak
to each other for long
for time
pieces lying apart there
giving off
echoes of words our last words *implor*
> *ing*
> *implor*
> *ing*
by deaf starlight for a moment

and you know we
have danced in such a room
I came in late and you
were far from the door
and I had to dance with
not you after not you before
I could reach you
but this was later than anyone
could have thought

thin
snow falling
in an empty bell
lighting that chair

could I turn at all

now should I kneel

and no door anywhere

The Black Jewel

In the dark
there is only the sound of the cricket

south wind in the leaves
is the cricket
so is the surf on the shore
and the barking across the valley

the cricket never sleeps
the whole cricket is the pupil of one eye
it can run it can leap it can fly
in its back the moon
crosses the night

there is only one cricket
when I listen

the cricket lives in the unlit ground
in the roots
out of the wind
it has only the one sound

before I could talk
I heard the cricket
under the house
then I remembered summer

mice too and the blind lightning
are born hearing the cricket
dying they hear it
bodies of light turn listening to the cricket
the cricket is neither alive nor dead
the death of the cricket
is still the cricket
in the bare room the luck of the cricket
echoes

Yesterday

My friend says I was not a good son
you understand
I say yes I understand

he says I did not go
to see my parents very often you know
and I say yes I know

even when I was living in the same city he says
maybe I would go there once
a month or maybe even less
I say oh yes

he says the last time I went to see my father
I say the last time I saw my father

he says the last time I saw my father
he was asking me about my life
how I was making out and he
went into the next room
to get something to give me

oh I say
feeling again the cold
of my father's hand the last time

he says and my father turned
in the doorway and saw me
look at my wristwatch and he
said you know I would like you to stay
and talk with me

oh yes I say

but if you are busy he said
I don't want you to feel that you
have to
just because I'm here

I say nothing

he says my father
said maybe
you have important work you are doing
or maybe you should be seeing
somebody I don't want to keep you

I look out the window
my friend is older than I am
he says and I told my father it was so
and I got up and left him then
you know

though there was nowhere I had to go
and nothing I had to do

W. S. MERWIN

Books

A Mask for Janus, 1952

The Dancing Bears, 1954

Green with Beasts, 1956

The Poem of the Cid (translation), 1959

The Drunk in the Furnace, 1960

The Satires of Perseus (translations), 1961

Spanish Ballads (translations), 1961

The Moving Target, 1963

The Song of Roland, 1963

The Lice, 1967

Selected Translations, 1948–1968, 1968

Transparence of the World: Poems of Jean Follain (translations), 1969

The Carrier of Ladders, 1970

The Miner's Pale Children (prose), 1970

Asian Figures (translations), 1973

Writings to an Unfinished Accompaniment, 1973

Selected Poems of Osip Mandelstam (translations, with Clarence Brown), 1974

The First Four Books of Poems, 1975

The Compass Flower, 1977

Houses and Travelers (prose), 1977

Selected Translations, 1968–1978, 1979

Finding the Islands, 1982

Unframed Originals (memoir), 1982

Opening the Hand, 1983

Selected Poems, 1988

The Rain in the Trees, 1988

Criticism

Richard Howard, *Alone with America,* 1969; Harvey Gross, "The Writing on the Void: The Poetry of W. S. Merwin," *Iowa Review* I (1970); Jan Gordon, "The Dwelling of Disappearance: W. S. Merwin's *The Lice,*" *Modern Poetry Studies* 3 (1972); Jarold Ramsey, "The Continuities of W. S. Merwin," *Massachusetts Review* 14 (1973); Laurence Lieberman, "The Church of Ash," in *Contemporary Poetry in America: Essays and Interviews,* ed. Robert Boyers, 1974; Cheri Davis, *W. S. Merwin,* 1981; Mark Christhilf, *W. S. Merwin, the Mythmaker,* 1986; Cary Nelson and Ed Folsom, eds., *W. S. Merwin: Essays on the Poetry,* 1987.

Frank
O'Hara
(1926–1966)

Ken Elinsue

B efore his untimely death in an accident—he was run over by a beach taxi one month past his fortieth birthday—Frank O'Hara could be said to have had a kind of charmed life as a poet. With a minimum of self-consciousness, *angst,* and ambition, he made poetry a part of his life and the lives of those around him in a fashion that was innovative, disarming, and thoroughly American. He jotted his poems down at work, at home, in transit, alone or in company, yielding to impulse, and fashioning, more by practice than by theory, an aesthetic of spontaneity and naturalness. He challenged the traditional notions of inspiration and significant occasion for the poem, and because he lived in a world where experimentation and impromptu expression in art were highly valued, the art scene of New York City in the 1950s and 1960s, he found the kind of support, encouragement, and enthusiasm that poets hope for but do not always receive. O'Hara was loved and appreciated in his milieu and deeply mourned at his death.

Educated at Harvard, O'Hara considered music as a career before turning to poetry, art criticism, and museum work. He worked for many years at the Museum of Modern Art, rising to Associate Curator despite his lack of formal training, and formed close friendships with many artists. His associations with other poets eventually led to the rather loosely conceived New York School of poets, which included John Ashbery, Barbara Guest, Kenneth Koch, and James Schuyler. Its values included humor, experimentation, spontaneity, and an alignment with modern French literature, including Surrealism, and with the postwar movements in American painting, especially action painting and pop art. If Ashbery would eventually emerge as the most important member of this group, it was O'Hara who seemed its prototypical figure, both in his life and in his art. He belonged, as this section of the anthology amply demonstrates, to a crowded generation, but he found his style and method early, so that by the time of his death a fairly substantial body of work was already in existence.

What O'Hara seems particularly to have accomplished, both by virtue of his easy temperament and the casual poetic style he forged, was to blur the distinction between life and art, perhaps a harder task with poetry than with some of the other arts. He seemed willing to include whatever happened to be at hand or in sight when the impulse to assemble a poem struck. The risks of doing this are obvious: they include triviality, chaos, and poems that are simply too private or subjective, reflecting the interests of the poet and his associates and leaving the reader disaffected or bored. O'Hara's poems escape none of these risks, but at their best they manage to transcend such limits, partly by means of a charm that seems to have been part of the poet's personality, partly by his finding ways to surprise us with significance where we least expected to find it. O'Hara is not afraid to mix large generalizations into his quick sketches of the living moment. It is as if he knows we will recognize that we live with these huge issues at our elbows all the time, whether they are in the foreground of our attention or not, just as we will also recognize that these questions coexist with particularities and trivialities that make the texture of existence slippery, bewildering, and, from the right perspective, comical.

A good example of the kind of subtle control and willingness to fail that characterize O'Hara's practice can be found in his famous elegy for Billie Holiday,

"The Day Lady Died." We can see how this poem behaves in relation to traditional poems of grief and commemoration; it turns their conventions inside out. O'Hara chooses to document the trivial events that led to the moment when he saw the newspaper headline and learned of the death, the moment when his reality shifted from idle happiness to sudden grief. He lets us infer his emotions, and he ends with an extremely delicate instant of aesthetic experience that resembles the death because "everyone and I stopped breathing." Marjorie Perloff, in her book on O'Hara, compares this ending to the close of Yeats's elegy, "In Memory of Major Robert Gregory," and the analogy is appropriate partly because Yeats himself was subverting the traditional formality and stylized lamentation of the elegy with a calculated spontaneity that depicted the way grief mixes into life and often attacks without warning. The point is not so much whether O'Hara was directly influenced by Yeats as that he was carrying forward tendencies of poetic modernism that were closely aligned with the ongoing experiments of his painter friends.

The fact that there is a significant occasion lurking behind the casual, sidelong manner of "The Day Lady Died," a pressure that brings it into existence and that we gradually discover, makes the poem less experimental, finally, than those which O'Hara assembles without having any momentous pretext for them. We have included a number of such poems in our selection because we feel that in their way they represent the extremes and accomplishments of this poet's art as fully, or more fully, than the better-known ones like "The Day Lady Died." The "spontaneity" can never be pure, of course; there will always be elements of rhetoric and manipulation in it. But O'Hara is taking larger risks when no special event or revelation privileges the act of writing other than the urge to capture the texture of experience and explore the possibilities of association and verbal play.

O'Hara's early death may have cut his career short, but it brought his poetry a larger audience and gave it the kind of legendary aura that hovers around the work of any promising artist who is cut off in his or her prime.

DY

An Image of Leda

The cinema is cruel
like a miracle. We
sit in the darkened
room asking nothing
of the empty white
space but that it
remain pure. And
suddenly despite us
it blackens. Not by
the hand that holds
the pen. There is
no message. We our-
selves appear naked
on the river bank
spread-eagled while
the machine wings
nearer. We scream
chatter prance and
wash our hair! Is
it our prayer or
wish that this
occur? Oh what is
this light that
holds us fast? Our
limbs quicken even
to disgrace under
this white eye as
if there were real
pleasure in loving
a shadow and caress-
ing a disguise!

Interior (With Jane)

The eagerness of objects to
be what we are afraid to do

cannot help but move us   Is
this willingness to be a motive

in us what we reject?   The
really stupid things, I mean

a can of coffee, a 35¢ ear
ring, a handful of hair, what

do these things do to us?   We
come into the room, the windows

are empty, the sun is weak
and slippery on the ice   And a

sob comes, simply because it is
coldest of the things we know

1951

Alone at night
in the wet city

the country's wit
is not memorable.

The wind has blown
all the trees down

but these anxieties
remain erect, being

the heart's deliberate
chambers of hurt

and fear whether
from a green apartment

seeming diamonds or
from an airliner

seeming fields. It's
not simple or tidy

though in rows of
rows and numbered;

the literal drifts
colorfully and

the hair is combed
with bridges, all

compromises leap
to stardom and lights.

If alone I am
able to love it,

the serious voices,
the panic of jobs,

it is sweet to me.
Far from burgeoning

verdure, the hard way
is this street.

In Hospital

These laboratories and those picnics
swing out over the bay
in a cradle of sleet

and seem indigenous, to the aged.
A bushel of cauliflower dirty
by the bed smells sweet,

like roses that were fed on snow.
Eyes, failing, call immense
suns a cow, a lemon,

and shrivelled lips, soon to be
smothered in earth, kiss men
whose youth's perennial

as letters from nieces. The morning
flows after twilight, a
luminous river,

and who steps ashore upon that
white sheet, need not
imagine permanence.

Homosexuality

So we are taking off our masks, are we, and keeping
our mouths shut? as if we'd been pierced by a glance!

The song of an old cow is not more full of judgment
than the vapors which escape one's soul when one is sick;

so I pull the shadows around me like a puff
and crinkle my eyes as if at the most exquisite moment

of a very long opera, and then we are off!
without reproach and without hope that our delicate feet

will touch the earth again, let alone "very soon."
It is the law of my own voice I shall investigate.

I start like ice, my finger to my ear, my ear
to my heart, that proud cur at the garbage can

in the rain. It's wonderful to admire oneself
with complete candor, tallying up the merits of each

of the latrines. 14th Street is drunken and credulous,
53rd tries to tremble but is too at rest. The good

love a park and the inept a railway station,
and there are the divine ones who drag themselves up

and down the lengthening shadow of an Abyssinian head
in the dust, trailing their long elegant heels of hot air

crying to confuse the brave "It's a summer day,
and I want to be wanted more than anything else in the world."

Blocks

1

Yippee! she is shooting in the harbor! he is jumping
up to the maelstrom! she is leaning over the giant's
cart of tears which like a lava cone let fall to fly
from the cross-eyed tantrum-tousled ninth grader's
splayed fist is freezing on the cement! he is throwing
up his arms in heavenly desperation, spacious Y of his
tumultuous love-nerves flailing like a poinsettia in
its own nailish storm against the glass door of the
cumulus which is withholding her from these divine
pastures she has filled with the flesh of men as stones!
O fatal eagerness!

2

O boy, their childhood was like so many oatmeal cookies.
I need you, you need me, yum, yum. Anon it became suddenly

3

like someone always losing something and never knowing what.
Always so. They were so fond of eating bread and butter and
sugar, they were slobs, the mice used to lick the floorboards
after they went to bed, rolling their light tails against
the rattling marbles of granulation. Vivo! the dextrose
those children consumed, lavished, smoked, in their knobby
candy bars. Such pimples! such hardons! such moody loves.
And thus they grew like giggling fir trees.

The Day Lady Died

It is 12:20 in New York a Friday
three days after Bastille day, yes
it is 1959 and I go get a shoeshine
because I will get off the 4:19 in Easthampton
at 7:15 and then go straight to dinner
and I don't know the people who will feed me

I walk up the muggy street beginning to sun
and have a hamburger and a malted and buy
an ugly NEW WORLD WRITING to see what the poets
in Ghana are doing these days
                                    I go on to the bank
and Miss Stillwagon (first name Linda I once heard)
doesn't even look up my balance for once in her life
and in the GOLDEN GRIFFIN I get a little Verlaine
for Patsy with drawings by Bonnard although I do
think of Hesiod, trans. Richmond Lattimore or
Brendan Behan's new play or *Le Balcon* or *Les Nègres*
of Genet, but I don't, I stick with Verlaine
after practically going to sleep with quandariness

and for Mike I just stroll into the PARK LANE
Liquor Store and ask for a bottle of Strega and
then I go back where I came from to 6th Avenue
and the tobacconist in the Ziegfeld Theatre and
casually ask for a carton of Gauloises and a carton
of Picayunes, and a NEW YORK POST with her face on it
and I am sweating a lot by now and thinking of
leaning on the john door in the 5 SPOT
while she whispered a song along the keyboard
to Mal Waldron and everyone and I stopped breathing

Poem

I don't know as I get what D. H. Lawrence is driving at
when he writes of lust springing from the bowels
or do I
it could be the bowels of the earth
to lie flat on the earth in spring, summer or winter is sexy
you feel it stirring deep down slowly up to you
and sometimes it gives you a little nudge in the crotch
that's very sexy
and when someone looks sort of raggedy and dirty like Paulette
    Goddard

in *Modern Times* it's exciting, it isn't usual or attractive
perhaps D.H.L. is thinking of the darkness
certainly the crotch is light
and I suppose
any part of us that can only be seen by others
is a dark part
I feel that about the small of my back, too and the nape of my neck
they are dark

they are erotic zones as in the tropics
whereas Paris is straightforward and bright about it all
a coal miner has kind of a sexy occupation
though I'm sure it's painful down there
but so is lust
of light we can never have enough
but how would we find it
unless the darkness urged us on and into it
and I am dark
except when now and then it all comes clear
and I can see myself
as others luckily sometimes see me
in a good light

Answer to Voznesensky & Evtushenko

We are tired of your tiresome imitations of Mayakovsky
we are tired
                of your dreary tourist ideas of our Negro selves
our selves are in far worse condition than the obviousness
of your color sense
                your general sense of Poughkeepsie is
a gaucherie no American poet would be guilty of in Tiflis
thanks to French Impressionism
                                we do not pretend to know more
than can be known
                how many sheets have you stained with your semen
oh Tartars, and how many
                of our loves have you illuminated with
your heart your breath
                as we poets of America have loved you
your countrymen, our countrymen, our lives, your lives, and
the dreary expanses of your translations
                                your idiotic manifestos
and the strange black cock which has become ours despite your envy

we do what we feel
                              you do not even do what you must or can
I do not love you any more since Mayakovsky died and Pasternak
theirs was the death of my nostalgia for your tired ignorant race
since you insist on race
                              you shall not take my friends away from me
because they live in Harlem
                                        you shall not make Mississippi into
          Sakhalin
you came too late, a lovely talent doesn't make a ball
          I consider myself to be black and you not even part
where you see death
                         you see a dance of death
                                                  which is
imperialist, implies training, requires techniques
our ballet does not employ
                              you are indeed as cold as wax
as your progenitor was red, and how greatly we loved his redness
in the fullness of our own idiotic sun! what
"roaring universe" outshouts his violent triumphant sun!
          you are not even speaking
                              in a whisper
          Mayakovsky's hat worn by a horse

FRANK O'HARA

Books

Meditations in an Emergency, 1957   *Lunch Poems*, 1965
Odes, 1965   *The Collected Poems*, 1971

Criticism

Richard Howard, *Alone With America*, 1969; Charles Molesworth, "The
Clear Architecture of the Nerves," *Iowa Review* 6 (1975); Marjorie Perloff,
Frank O'Hara: Poet Among Painters, 1977.

Adrienne
Rich
(b. 1929)

William Stafford

rom 1954 on, Adrienne Rich began dating her poems. "Writing is tentative and exploratory," she said, "and one needs to allow poems to speak for their moment." Somewhat later, and more tellingly, she added, "The meaning of a poem becomes clear to me only as I see what happens in my life; poems are more like premonitions than conclusions." These statements characterize her formal break with the past. Early books had brought her considerable recognition; impressed by her technical control and mastery of forms, Auden selected *A Change of World* for the 1951 Yale Series of Younger Poets Award, and Jarrell praised her second collection, *The Diamond Cutters,* for similar reasons. She herself says that these first poems were mere exercises for poems she hadn't written; that while she learned her craft from various male poets all the way from Yeats and Thomas to Stevens and Frost, she realized that "formalism was part of the strategy: like asbestos gloves it allowed me to handle materials I couldn't pick up bare-handed."

But her life, and the nation's life, were starting to come apart. The 1950s and the early 1960s, with their sit-ins and marches, political assassinations and anti-war movement, were painful and unbalancing. Married and committed to raising her children during those years, she could only read "in fierce snatches, scribble in notebooks, write poetry in fragments . . . but felt that politics was not something 'out there' but something 'in here' and of the essence of my condition." A revolution was also going on in *Sexual Politics,* as Kate Millett's book defined it, and women everywhere were "awakening." In Rich's thoughtful essay, "When We Dead Awaken: Writing as Re-Vision" (on her own poem as well as Ibsen's play by the same name, which raises issues about how the male artist uses women in creating culture), she asks passionate, searching questions about men–women relationships and probes into matters she had addressed in her third book of poems. *Snapshots of a Daughter-in-Law* (1963) is an album of candid accounts of how women have been led to treat other women. From this time on, in forms that are beginning to open up, Rich's poems focus on the destructiveness women face in our society, and one of her central means is to mix moral and political issues with her art.

"After Dark" (dated 1964) is a poem about her relationship with her father, who had supported and encouraged her (too much? too soon?). It also reflects her personal and historical struggle to achieve a whole new "psychic geography" (her term), which would be made up of a language and images for the experiences women were only becoming aware of. The poem works through initial angers that many a poet has stopped at (Plath, for example)—where both father and daughter ("Blood is a sacred poison") were in prison—and moves to a tranquil place where both can give each other what they need. Though death finally comes for the father ("the blunt barge // bumps along the shore"), the poem ends on a dream that frees them of their fears. Rich has discovered, she says, that "poems are like dreams, in them you put what you don't know you know."

What Rich was on the way to knowing emerges even more clearly from a spirited exchange she had with Galway Kinnell, whose essay "Poetry, Personality and Death" prompted her to write a response she called "Poetry, Personality and Wholeness." She agreed with Kinnell that certain male poets were on the right track in moving beyond mere personality toward a persona or an abstract "I," but she felt that these were still an evasion. Only an inward look would authenticate the "I," rather than idealize it, she argued. She mentions Emily Dickinson as a model, whose muse was "The Soul," a power unto itself. Rich believes it is the acceptance of the loneliness implicit in this notion that will make for a healthier poetry. She continued to pursue these matters in a remarkable collection of essays, *On Lies, Secrets and Silence* (1979), as well as in a book of poems, *The Dream of a Common Language* (1977), whose title points to her ultimate goal.

The Will to Change (1971), from which "The Burning of Paper Instead of Children" is taken, shows her coming into her own. The woman in the poem is distressed by other things than her neighbor, "a scientist and art-collector." Burning books is one matter, but what if the whole nature of human relationships, in its sexual and political dimensions, has been corrupted by "the oppressor's language," a language that has no means left to talk of wholeness, to talk with "joy instead of dread"? Working with montage techniques common to the films and theater of the period, Rich explores breaks in the double helix of love-talk and love-making: "you enter without knowing / what it is you enter." The implicit danger, which she describes with fierce images, is that all speech will burn up ("my mouth is burning") and disappear for any woman or man: "In America we have only the present tense. I am in danger. You are in danger." The language has taken on the quality of a military manual, and it can only sound rote now.

In *Diving into the Wreck* (1973), one of the most famous books of the decade, whose title poem has become a shibboleth for the feminist movement , Rich breaks down the artificial barriers "between private and public, between Vietnam and lover's bed, between the deepest images we carry out of our dreams and the most daylight events 'out in the world.'" While remaining in this mode of a heightened sort of feminism for more than a decade since, continuing her extraordinary productivity with books of poems and essays issuing regularly, she nonetheless seems to be looking elsewhere for what she has recently called "a new time of poetry—I have had to fight very hard for it, and then there is the question of learning to do it all over again." "In the Wake of Home" and, more especially, "Children Playing Checkers at the Edge of the Forest" give more than a hint of where she is now headed: reconciling the innocence and the "dreadfulness," which may come only if we look up from the game (not being played after all!) to see the tree we all step from, even the deer. Talking is still the issue, but no longer the talk of woman versus man, or even woman to woman. It's the talking we need to learn to get past all pretending, the realization that we are all worthy of noticing temptation.

Currently Adrienne Rich teaches feminist theory, as well as poetry and poetics, at Stanford University.

SF

After Dark

1

You are falling asleep and I sit looking at you
old tree of life
old man whose death I wanted
I can't stir you up now.
Faintly a phonograph needle
whirs round in the last groove
eating my heart to dust.
That terrible record! how it played

down years, wherever I was
in foreign languages even
over and over, *I know you better*
than you know yourself   I know

you better than you know
yourself   I know
you   until, self-maimed,
I limped off, torn at the roots,

stopped singing a whole year,
got a new body, new breath,
got children, croaked for words,
forgot to listen

or read your *mene tekel* fading on the wall,
woke up one morning
and knew myself your daughter.
Blood is a sacred poison.

Now, unasked, you give ground.
We only want to stifle
what's stifling us already.
Alive now, root to crown, I'd give

—oh,—something—not to know
our struggles now are ended.
I seem to hold you, cupped
in my hands, and disappearing.

When your memory fails—
no more to scourge my inconsistencies—
the sashcords of the world fly loose.
A window crashes

suddenly down. I go to the woodbox
and take a stick of kindling
to prop the sash again.
I grow protective toward the world.

2

Now let's away from prison—
Underground seizures!
I used to huddle in the grave
I'd dug for you and bite

my tongue for fear it would babble
—Darling—
I thought they'd find me there
someday, sitting upright, shrunken,

my hair like roots and in my lap
a mess of broken pottery—
wasted libation—
and you embalmed beside me.

No, let's away. Even now
there's a walk between doomed elms
(whose like we shall not see much longer)
and something—grass and water—

an old dream-photograph.
I'll sit with you there and tease you
for wisdom, if you like,
waiting till the blunt barge

bumps along the shore.
Poppies burn in the twilight
like smudge pots.
I think you hardly see me

but—this is the dream now—
your fears blow out,
off, over the water.
At the last, your hand feels steady.

1964

The Burning of Paper Instead of Children

I was in danger of
verbalizing my moral
impulses out of existence.

DANIEL BERRIGAN,

ON TRIAL IN BALTIMORE

1. My neighbor, a scientist and art-collector, telephones me in a state
of violent emotion. He tells me that my son and his, aged eleven and
twelve, have on the last day of school burned a mathematics textbook in

the backyard. He has forbidden my son to come to his house for a week,
and has forbidden his own son to leave the house during that time. "The
burning of a book," he says, "arouses terrible sensations in me, memories
of Hitler; there are few things that upset me so much as the idea of burning
a book."

Back there: the library, walled
with green Britannicas
Looking again

in Dürer's *Complete Works*
for MELANCOLIA, the baffled woman

the crocodiles in Herodotus
the Book of the Dead
the *Trial of Jeanne d'Arc*, so blue
I think, It is her color

and they take the book away
because I dream of her too often

love and fear in a house
knowledge of the oppressor
I know it hurts to burn

2. To imagine a time of silence
or few words
a time of chemistry and music

the hollows above your buttocks
traced by my hand
or, *hair is like flesh,* you said

an age of long silence

relief
from this tongue   this slab of limestone
or reinforced concrete
fanatics and traders
dumped on this coast wildgreen clayred
that breathed once
in signals of smoke
sweep of the wind

knowledge of the oppressor
this is the oppressor's language

yet I need it to talk to you

3. *People suffer highly in poverty and it takes dignity and intelligence to
overcome this suffering. Some of the suffering are: a child did not had
dinner last night: a child steal because he did not have money to buy it: to
hear a mother say she do not have money to buy food for her children and
to see a child without cloth it will make tears in your eyes.*

(the fracture of order
the repair of speech
to overcome this suffering)

4. We lie under the sheet
after making love, speaking
of loneliness
relieved in a book
relived in a book
so on that page
the clot and fissure
of it appears
words of a man
in pain
a naked word
entering the clot
a hand grasping
through bars:

deliverance

What happens between us
has happened for centuries
we know it from literature

still it happens

sexual jealousy
outflung hand
beating bed

dryness of mouth
after panting

there are books that describe all this
and they are useless

You walk into the woods behind a house
there in that country
you find a temple
built eighteen hundred years ago
you enter without knowing
what it is you enter

so it is with us

no one knows what may happen
though the books tell everything

burn the texts   said Artaud

5. I am composing on the typewriter late at night, thinking of today. How well we all spoke. A language is a map of our failures. Frederick Douglass wrote an English purer than Milton's. People suffer highly in poverty. There are methods but we do not use them. Joan, who could not read, spoke some peasant form of French. Some of the suffering are: it is hard to tell the truth; this is America; I cannot touch you now. In America we have only the present tense. I am in danger. You are in danger. The burning of a book arouses no sensation in me. I know it hurts to burn. There are flames of napalm in Catonsville, Maryland. I know it hurts to burn. The typewriter is overheated, my mouth is burning, I cannot touch you and this is the oppressor's language.

1968

In the Wake of Home

1

You sleep in a room with bluegreen curtains
posters   a pile of animals on the bed
A woman and a man who love you
and each other   slip the door ajar
you are almost asleep   they crouch in turn
to stroke your hair   you never wake

This happens every night for years.
This never happened.

2

Your lips   steady   never say
It should have been this way
That's not what you say
You   so carefully not asking, *Why?*
Your eyes   looking straight in mine
remind me of a woman's
auburn hair   my mother's hair
but you never saw that hair

The family coil   so twisted, tight and loose
anyone trying to leave
has to strafe the field
burn the premises down

3

The home houses
mirages   memory fogs the kitchen panes
the rush-hour traffic outside
has the same old ebb and flow
Out on the darkening block
somebody calls you home
night after night   then never again
Useless for you to know
they tried to do what they could
before they left for good

4

The voice that used to call you home
has gone off on the wind
beaten into thinnest air
whirling down other streets
or maybe the mouth was burnt to ash
maybe the tongue was torn out
brownlung has stolen the breath
or fear has stolen the breath
maybe under another name
it sings on AM radio:
And if you knew, what would you know?

5

But you will be drawn to places
where generations lie
side by side with each other:
fathers, mothers and children
in the family prayerbook
or the country burying-ground
You will hack your way back through the bush
to the *Jodensavanne*
where the gravestones are black with mould
You will stare at old family albums
with their smiles   their resemblances
You will want to believe that nobody
wandered off   became strange
no woman dropped her baby and ran
no father took off for the hills
no axe splintered the door
—that once at least it was all in order
and nobody came to grief

6

Any time you go back
where absence began
the kitchen faucet sticks in a way you know
you have to pull the basement door
in before drawing the bolt
the last porch-step is still loose
the water from the tap
is the old drink of water
Any time you go back
the familiar underpulse
will start its throbbing: *Home, home!*
and the hole torn and patched over
will gape unseen again

7

Even where love has run thin
the child's soul musters strength
calling on dust-motes   song on the radio
closet-floor of galoshes
stray cat   piles of autumn leaves
whatever comes along
—the rush of purpose to make a life
worth living past abandonment
building the layers up again
over the torn hole   filling in

8

And what of the stern and faithful aunt
the fierce grandmother   the anxious sister
the good teacher   the one
who stood at the crossing when you had to cross
the woman hired to love you
the skeleton who held out a crust
the breaker of rules   the one
who is neither a man nor a woman
who warmed the liquid vein of life
and day after day whatever the need
handed it on to you?
You who did and had to do
so much for yourself   this was done for you
by someone who did what they could
when others left for good

9

You imagine an alley   a little kingdom
where the mother-tongue is spoken
a village of shelters   woven
or sewn of hides   in a long-ago way
a shanty standing up
at the edge of sharecropped fields
a tenement where life is seized by the teeth
a farm battened down on snowswept plains
a porch with rubber-plant and glider
on a steep city street
You imagine the people would all be there
fathers mothers and children
the ones you were promised would all be there
eating   arguing   working
trying to get on with life
you imagine this used to be
for everyone   everywhere

10

What if I told you your home
is this continent of the homeless
of children sold   taken by force
driven from their mothers' land
killed by their mothers to save from capture
—this continent of changed names and mixed-up blood
of languages tabooed
diasporas unrecorded
undocumented refugees
underground railroads   trails of tears
What if I tell you your home
is this planet of warworn children
women and children standing in line or milling
endlessly calling each others' names
What if I tell you, you are not different
it's the family albums that lie
—will any of this comfort you
and how should this comfort you?

11

The child's soul carries on
in the wake of home
building a complicated house
a tree-house without a tree
finding places for everything

the song   the stray cat   the skeleton
The child's soul musters strength
where the holes were torn
but there are no miracles:
even children become exhausted
And how shall they comfort each other
who have come young to grief?
Who will number the grains of loss
and what would comfort be?

1983

Children Playing Checkers
at the Edge of the Forest

Two green-webbed chairs
                    a three-legged stool between
Your tripod
           Spears of grass
                     longer than your bare legs
cast shadows on your legs
              drawn up
                   away from the squared
red-and-black cardboard
            the board of rules
                 the board of play
But you're not playing, you're talking
               It's midsummer
and greater rules are breaking
            it's the last
innocent summer you will know
           and I
will go on awhile pretending that's not true
When I have done pretending
            I can see this:
the depth of the background
           shadows
              not of one moment only
erased and charcoaled in again
             year after year
I can see how the tree looms back behind you
the first tree of the forest
           the last tree

from which the deer step out
from protection
                    The first tree
into dreadfulness
                    The last and the first tree

1987

NOTES

After Dark. "Mene tekel" is from "mene, mene, tekel, upharsin" —numbered, numbered, weighed and divided—from the Bible (Daniel 5:25): the writing on the wall, interpreted by Daniel to mean that God had weighed Belshazzar and his kingdom and found them wanting.

Two Shakespearean references weight this poem with glances at other fathers and daughters. "Our struggles now are ended" recalls Prospero's speech beginning "Our revels now are ended," after the interruption of Miranda's wedding masque. In 2, "Now let's away from prison" reverses King Lear's "Come, let's away to prison," after he and Cordelia have been reunited and arrested.

In the Wake of Home. "Jodensavanne" is where the Cayenne Jews erected the second synagogue in the colony, outside the largest city in Surinam. The year was 1685.

ADRIENNE RICH

Books

A Change of World, 1951

The Diamond Cutters, 1955

Snapshots of a Daughter-in-Law: Poems, 1954–1962, 1963, 1967

Necessities of Life: Poems 1962–1965, 1966

Leaflets: Poems 1965–1968, 1969

The Will to Change: Poems 1968–1970, 1971

Diving into the Wreck: Poems 1971–1972, 1973

Poems: Selected and New, 1950–1974, 1975

Twenty-One Love Poems, 1976

Of Woman Born: Motherhood as Experience and Institution (prose), 1976

The Dream of a Common Language: Poems 1974–1977, 1978

On Lies, Secrets and Silence: Selected Prose 1966–1978, 1979

A Wild Patience Has Taken Me This Far: Poems 1978–1981, 1981

The Fact of a Doorframe, 1984

Your Native Land, Your Life, 1986

Essays, Criticism

Barbara C. Gelpi and Albert Gelpi, eds., *Adrienne Rich's Poetry: A Norton Critical Edition*, 1975; David Kalstone, *Five Temperaments*, 1977; Rachel Blau DuPlessis, "The Critique of Consciousness and Myth in Levertov, Rich, and Rukeyser," in *Shakespeare's Sisters: Feminist Essays on Women Poets*, ed. Gilbert and Gubar, 1979.

Anne
Sexton
(1928–1974)

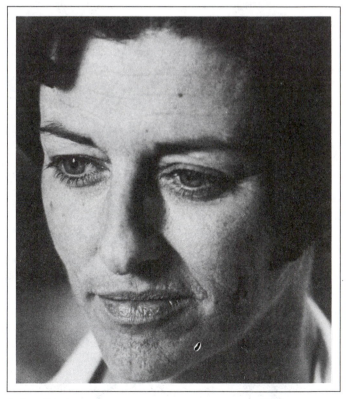

Arthur Furst

Anne Sexton led a complicated, troubled life, beset by numerous episodes of mental instability from which she could not ultimately recover. Many have noted that "her life became her poetry," by way of suggesting that in her case perhaps too much life had entered the poems. That she had trouble transcending her subject matter at times and seemed to ignore her technical capacities in her last years, pushing unfinished poems to publication, by now goes without saying. In a careful, moving essay ("How It Was"), Maxine Kumin draws the salient facts together and comments sensitively on the important issues raised by such art and such a life. Clearly, art can and must be separated from life lived, and, as Denise Levertov suggests in her essay, "Light Up the Cave," Sexton did release enough of her material sufficiently for us to focus on the work itself and give her now her artistic due.

From early encounters with a few, great poet-teachers, among them John Holmes, Robert Lowell, and W. D. Snodgrass, on through her extensive relationships with many other writers, chiefly in letters, Sexton more than made up for what was at best a junior college education. We know from her correspondence what a great reader she became, drawn along by her quick mind and a driving sense of what it would take to develop her own abilities. Not only was she passionately committed to practicing poetry as one might practice medicine, she was possessed of a sense of the ideal, never mind her struggles to live up to it. She wrote, "I keep feeling there isn't one poem being written by any one of us—the whole product—is one long poem—it's God's poem perhaps. Or God's people's poem." This view, coupled with her earthy, self-aware sense of humor (an aspect many of her critics miss), helped her step outside herself on occasion and take the necessary skeptical look at what would otherwise be merely repugnant.

As in our selections from Sylvia Plath, we're representing Sexton poems that are more muted, more touching and suggestive, and less declamatory than most in her canon, because we sense that these characteristics may be undervalued and even overlooked. Even poems like "The Abortion" and "Sylvia's Death" are not the loud statements they might have become by virtue of Sexton's respect for the material as well as the reader, and an uncanny sense of how to treat her most difficult subjects and concerns: she can adopt a gentle, mothering tone, not far from the lullaby voice of fairy tale, and include herself as co-witness to whatever might lie in store. Later, in the book _Transformations,_ in which she takes on Grimm's fairy tales, she would force this method to extremes in search of underlying connections between myth and human behavior.

"The Abortion" is set in what might be called the Grimm brothers' Pennsylvania, the place the narrator goes to "have it done." The deceptively simple, haunting refrain, "Somebody who should have been born / is gone" is interwoven with the rhymed tercets and leads to a cumulative melody that washes away the implicit terror and horror, save for the moment of self-knowledge in the final stanza (". . . Or say what you meant, / you coward . . ."). She handles the terza rima as well as most practitioners who have employed it since _The Divine Comedy,_ and she pays her respects to tradition along with Donne, Herrick, Shelley, and, in our own time, William Carlos Williams. Incidentally, other texts in this selection, "What's That,"

"The Truth the Dead Know" (one of her earliest successes with traditional forms), and even "Sixth Psalm," bear witness to Sexton's dedication to, and mastery of, traditional forms.

In a poem like "The Fury of Overshoes" we can see another dimension to Sexton's ways with tale, set, as was her wont, in some childhood time (it was no accident that she would co-author, with Maxine Kumin, lovely children's books and delight in their making). In a way, we remain prisoners of childhood's ring around us, as Rilke noted, and Sexton is almost alone among contemporary poets—one does think of Roethke—in summoning up the tiny fears we've never escaped for having been made to give up "your nightlight / and your teddy / and your thumb"—fears that remain and thicken. The final "oh" of course has to do with the much larger fear that our own most intimate objects cannot know us, which is another way of saying we will drift away—"The world wasn't / yours."

Our final selection, "Rowing," represents Sexton's bravest and perhaps most flawed book, *The Awful Rowing Toward God* (published posthumously, as were several other collections). "La-de-da," she wrote in a letter, "is making fun of myself, is calling attention to the absurdity of the poet reaching for God. . . ." In this fitful collection, as indeed in most of her other work, she takes on Life and Meaning with Sisyphean results. There's a dizzying amount of detached imagery that doesn't always resonate within the poems, but when she relocates the source of her anguish, where she needs to head—the island that is God, say—the poems finally wind up being an act she commits herself to: "This story ends with me still rowing."

Anne Sexton was praised and honored in her lifetime—she won a Pulitzer Prize and was elected a Fellow of the Royal Society of Literature, for instance—as much, one suspects, for moving readers to feel and think about serious matters not much written about in "serious" poetry of late, as for the spirited poetic ways in which she schooled herself for carrying her messages.

SF

The Truth the Dead Know

For My Mother, Born March 1902,
Died March 1959
And My Father, Born February 1900,
Died June 1959

Gone, I say and walk from church,
refusing the stiff procession to the grave,
letting the dead ride alone in the hearse.
It is June. I am tired of being brave.

We drive to the Cape. I cultivate
myself where the sun gutters from the sky,
where the sea swings in like an iron gate
and we touch. In another country people die.

My darling, the wind falls in like stones
from the whitehearted water and when we touch
we enter touch entirely. No one's alone.
Men kill for this, or for as much.

And what of the dead? They lie without shoes
in their stone boats. They are more like stone
than the sea would be if it stopped. They refuse
to be blessed, throat, eye and knucklebone.

What's That

Before it came inside
I had watched it from my kitchen window,
watched it swell like a new balloon,
watched it slump and then divide,
like something I know I know—
a broken pear or two halves of the moon,
or round white plates floating nowhere
or fat hands waving in the summer air
until they fold together like a fist or a knee.
After that it came to my door. Now it lives here.
And of course: it is a soft sound, soft as a seal's ear,
that was caught between a shape and a shape and then returned to me.

You know how parents call
from sweet beaches anywhere, *come in come in,*
and how you sank under water to put out
the sound, or how one of them touched in the hall
at night: the rustle and the skin
you couldn't know, but heard, the stout
slap of tides and the dog snoring. It's here
now, caught back from time in my adult year—
the image we did forget: the cranking shells on our feet
or the swing of the spoon in soup. It is as real
as splinters stuck in your ear. The noise we steal
is half a bell. And outside cars whisk by on the suburban street

and are there and are true.
What else is this, this intricate shape of air?
calling me, calling you.

The Abortion

Somebody who should have been born
is gone.

Just as the earth puckered its mouth,
each bud puffing out from its knot,
I changed my shoes, and then drove south.

Up past the Blue Mountains, where
Pennsylvania humps on endlessly,
wearing, like a crayoned cat, its green hair,

its roads sunken in like a gray washboard;
where, in truth, the ground cracks evilly,
a dark socket from which the coal has poured,

Somebody who should have been born
is gone.

the grass as bristly and stout as chives,
and me wondering when the ground would break,
and me wondering how anything fragile survives;

up in Pennsylvania, I met a little man,
not Rumpelstiltskin, at all, at all . . .
he took the fullness that love began.

Returning north, even the sky grew thin
like a high window looking nowhere.
The road was as flat as a sheet of tin.

*Somebody who should have been born
is gone.*

Yes, woman, such logic will lead
to loss without death. Or say what you meant,
you coward . . . this baby that I bleed.

Sylvia's Death

for Sylvia Plath

O Sylvia, Sylvia,
with a dead box of stones and spoons,

with two children, two meteors
wandering loose in the tiny playroom,

with your mouth into the sheet,
into the roofbeam, into the dumb prayer,

(Sylvia, Sylvia,
where did you go
after you wrote me
from Devonshire
about raising potatoes
and keeping bees?)

what did you stand by,
just how did you lie down into?

Thief!—
how did you crawl into,

crawl down alone
into the death I wanted so badly and for so long,

the death we said we both outgrew,
the one we wore on our skinny breasts,

the one we talked of so often each time
we downed three extra dry martinis in Boston,

the death that talked of analysts and cures,
the death that talked like brides with plots,

the death we drank to,
the motives and then the quiet deed?

(In Boston
the dying
ride in cabs,
yes death again,
that ride home
with our boy.)

O Sylvia, I remember the sleepy drummer
who beat on our eyes with an old story,

how we wanted to let him come
like a sadist or a New York fairy

to do his job,
a necessity, a window in a wall or a crib,

and since that time he waited
under our heart, our cupboard,

and I see now that we store him up
year after year, old suicides

and I know at the news of your death,
a terrible taste for it, like salt.

(And me,
me too.
And now, Sylvia,
you again
with death again,
that ride home
with our boy.)

And I say only
with my arms stretched out into that stone place,

what is your death
but an old belonging,

a mole that fell out
of one of your poems?

(O friend,
while the moon's bad,
and the king's gone,
and the queen's at her wit's end
the bar fly ought to sing!)

O tiny mother,
you too!
O funny duchess!
O blonde thing!

Sixth Psalm

For America is a lady rocking on a porch in an unpainted house on an unused road but Anne does not see it.

For America is a librarian in Wichita coughing dust and sharing sourballs with the postman.

For America is Dr. Abraham passing out penicillin and sugar pills to the town of Woolrich, Pennsylvania.

For America is an old man washing his feet in Albion, Michigan. Drying them carefully and then applying Dr. Scholl's foot powder. But Anne does not see it. Anne is locked in.

For America is a reformed burglar turned locksmith who pulls up the shades of his shop at nine A.M. daily (except Sunday when he leaves his phone number on the shop door).

For America is a fat woman dusting a grand piano in English Creek, New Jersey.

For America is a suede glove manufacturer sitting in his large swivel chair feeling the goods and assessing his assets and debits.

For America is a bus driver in Embarrass, Minnesota, clocking the miles and watching the little cardboard suitcases file by.

For America is a land of Commies and Prohibitionists but Anne does not see it. Anne is locked in. The Trotskyites don't see her. The Republicans have never tweaked her chin for she is not there. Anne hides inside folding and unfolding rose after rose. She has no one. She has Christopher. They sit in their room pinching the dolls' noses, poking the dolls' eyes. One time they gave a doll a ride in a fuzzy slipper but that was too far, too far wasn't it. Anne did not dare. She put the slipper with the doll inside it as in a car right into the closet and pushed the door shut.

For America is the headlight man at the Ford plant in Detroit, Michigan, he of the wires, he of the white globe, all day, all day, all year, all his year's headlights, seventy a day, improved by automation but Anne does not.

For America is a miner in Ohio, slipping into the dark hole and bringing forth cat's eyes each night.

For America is only this room . . . there is no useful activity.

For America only your dolls are cheerful.

The Fury of Overshoes

They sit in a row
outside the kindergarten,
black, red, brown, all
with those brass buckles.
Remember when you couldn't
buckle your own
overshoe
or tie your own
shoe
or cut your own meat
and the tears
running down like mud
because you fell off your
tricycle?
Remember, big fish,
when you couldn't swim
and simply slipped under
like a stone frog?
The world wasn't
yours.
It belonged to
the big people.
Under your bed
sat the wolf
and he made a shadow
when cars passed by
at night.
They made you give up
your nightlight
and your teddy
and your thumb.
Oh overshoes,
don't you
remember me,
pushing you up and down
in the winter snow?
Oh thumb,
I want a drink,
it is dark,
where are the big people,
when will I get there,
taking giant steps

all day,
each day
and thinking
nothing of it?

Rowing

A story, a story!
(Let it go. Let it come.)
I was stamped out like a Plymouth fender
into this world.
First came the crib
with its glacial bars.
Then dolls
and the devotion to their plastic mouths.
Then there was school,
the little straight rows of chairs,
blotting my name over and over,
but undersea all the time,
a stranger whose elbows wouldn't work.
Then there was life
with its cruel houses
and people who seldom touched—
though touch is all—
but I grew,
like a pig in a trenchcoat I grew,
and then there were many strange apparitions,
the nagging rain, the sun turning into poison
and all of that, saws working through my heart,
but I grew, I grew,
and God was there like an island I had not rowed to,
still ignorant of Him, my arms and my legs worked,
and I grew, I grew,
I wore rubies and bought tomatoes
and now, in my middle age,
about nineteen in the head I'd say,
I am rowing, I am rowing
though the oarlocks stick and are rusty
and the sea blinks and rolls
like a worried eyeball,
but I am rowing, I am rowing

though the wind pushes me back
and I know that that island will not be perfect,
it will have the flaws of life,
the absurdities of the dinner table,
but there will be a door
and I will open it
and I will get rid of the rat inside of me,
the gnawing pestilential rat.
God will take it with his two hands
and embrace it.

As the African says:
This is my tale which I have told,
if it be sweet, if it be not sweet,
take somewhere else and let some return to me.
This story ends with me still rowing.

ANNE SEXTON

Books

To Bedlam and Part Way Back, 1960
All My Pretty Ones, 1962
Live or Die, 1966
Love Poems, 1969
Transformations, 1971
The Book of Folly, 1972
The Death Notebooks, 1974
The Awful Rowing Toward God, 1975

45 Mercy Street, 1976
Anne Sexton: A Self-Portrait in Letters, 1977
Words for Dr. Y.: Uncollected Poems, 1978
The Collected Poems of Anne Sexton, 1981

Essays, Criticism

Elaine Showalter and Carol Smith, "A Nurturing Relationship: A Conversation with Anne Sexton and Maxine Kumin, April 15, 1974," *Women's Studies* (April 1976); J. D. McClatchey, ed., *Anne Sexton—The Poet and Her Critics*, 1978; Richard Howard, *Alone with America: Essays on the Art of Poetry in the United States Since 1950*, rev. 1980; David Cowart, "Anne Sexton," in *Dictionary of Literary Biography*, 1980; Susan Resneck Parr, "Anne Sexton," *American Writers* (Supplement II, 1981); Maxine Kumin, "How It Was," Preface to *The Collected Poems of Anne Sexton*, 1981.

Gerald
Stern
(b. 1925)

Stefani Karakas

Like quite a few other contemporary American poets, Gerald Stern has recently published a collection of essays on his, and by extension our age's, poetic constitution, touching on many matters of genuine interest. Among them are the values of reading and writing poetry in a society that, in its current focus on feelings, would seem to have lost sight of Eliot's notion that "feeling and emotion are particular, whereas thought is general." While Gerald Stern wears his heart on his heart in these personal essays, he is tough-minded as well, and careful to follow even the slightest clues to our true moral and social character as revealed by our artistic accomplishments. In "Some Secrets," his moving account of his own development in which he traces his journey all the way from rank isolation to a readiness to "believe in everything," we learn that even early on "poetry had to be serious and lyrical and personal and approach the sublime" for him and the few friends he started out with, who also "lived and studied without direction." Though he would work his way up the academic ladder almost to a Ph.D., with time spent in France for even more exposure to world literature, he has remained a largely self-taught artist, driven by early patterns of "loss and failure." A sort of Wandering Jew, he has made his way with a poetry that laments without bitterness, a poetry of steady affirmation and deep loyalties, born of the endless struggle to keep going, to keep art both celebratory and measured, a bulwark against the rest of life ("Do not regret your little bout with life in the morning").

Disarmingly ingenuous at crucial moments, but mostly working "like a dog" in his poems, Stern enters them as just another character, a sort of Woody Allen breeziness and naiveté about him, with regard for all those who have come before in the encyclopedia of human struggle. Stern sacrifices artifice for articulate emotion, and even when he works in shorter lines and definite stanzaic forms, his medium is the full phrase, with no short-cuts or enjambments to speak of, and he is particularly fond of simple connections between statements, as he sets up what can be called a multiple consciousness, eloquent in its suppositions, acted out by characters in search of wisdom and justice for all. "I do the crow walking clumsily over his meat, / I do the child sitting for his dessert, / I do the poet asleep at the table,"—I do, I do, the poems pronounce, over and over, not to a single reader, but to an audience. Stern's eloquence is fostered by a rich sense of humor, an ability to laugh at himself at the center, and as we respond to the joking, we are vulnerable to the intelligent, judicious comments that Stern, the philosopher, levels at us. His eloquence is also fostered by music, and it's no accident that music is one of Stern's major themes. There are all sorts of musicians as major characters in the poems, from the one "banging my pencil on the iron fences, / whistling Bach and Muczynski through the closed blinds," to "the great Stern himself / dragging his heart from one ruined soul to another," with Isaac the violinist nicely outshadowing his poetic counterpart.

An even larger theme, or subject, is of course what has happened to the Eastern European world of Stern's forebears, by way of all the disasters visited upon them in our time. The way Isaac B. Singer has sat in his New York cafeteria, telling stories for all who did not make it over the breach (one thinks particularly of a collection called *My Friend Kafka*), Stern has sat "a thousand times . . . in restaurant windows," which might as well be the "birch forests" partisans fought their way through to survival, keeping the old stories, the "news," alive. And one way to read these poems is as columns appearing in something like a neighborhood paper. Even in a poem as apparently different in tone and substance as "Kissing Stieglitz Goodbye," the figure of the girl "standing against the wall" conjures up other figures against other walls who were shot. We shake, with the poet himself, after the image is invoked. While "The Expulsion" may be added up in biblical terms, it's also clear that our age has provided equally horrifying metaphors for expulsion, for the smaller scale the world seems balanced on now. The way out, in Stern's terms, through "the long and brutal corridor / down which we sometimes shuffle, and sometimes run," is still not an exit to anything resembling innocence and full knowledge; the knowledge is of a kind that is accurate only as far as it can go.

Having taught in a variety of places over the years, Gerald Stern seems finally to have put an end to his own wanderings and to have settled in at the Writers' Workshop at Iowa, where he teaches in the graduate program.

SF

Romania, Romania

I stand like some country crow across the street
from the Romanian Synagogue on Rivington Street
singing songs about Moldavia and Bukovina.
I am a walking violin, screeching
a little at the heights, vibrating a little
at the depths, plucking sadly on my rubber guts.
It's only music that saves me. Otherwise
I would be keeping the skulls forever, otherwise
I would be pulling red feathers from my bloody neck.
It's only music, otherwise I would be white
with anger or giving in to hatred
or turning back to logic and religion—
the Brahms Concerto, hills and valleys of gold,
the mighty Kreutzer, rubies piled over rubies,
a little Bartók, a little ancient Bach—
but more for the thin white tablecloths under the trees
than for Goga and his Christians,
and more for the red petticoats and the cold wine and the garlic
than the railroad station and the submachine guns,
and more for the little turn on Orchard Street
and the life of sweetness and more for the godly Spanish
and the godly Chinese lined up for morning prayers,
and much much more for the leather jackets on sticks
and the quiet smoke
and the plush fire escapes,
and much much more for the silk scarves in the windows
and the cars in the streets
and the dirty invisible stars—
Yehudi Menuhin
wandering through the hemlocks,
Jascha Heifetz
bending down over the tables,
the great Stern himself
dragging his heart from one ruined soul to another.

There Is Wind, There Are Matches

A thousand times I have sat in restaurant windows,
through mopping after mopping, letting the ammonia clear
my brain and the music from the kitchens

ruin my heart. I have sat there hiding
my feelings from my neighbors, blowing smoke
carefully into the ceiling, or after I gave
that up, smiling over my empty plate
like a tired wolf. Today I am sitting again
at the long marble table at Horn and Hardart's,
drinking my coffee and eating my burnt scrapple.
This is the last place left and everyone here
knows it; if the lights were turned down, if the
heat were turned off, if the banging of dishes stopped,
we would all go on, at least for a while, but then
we would drift off one by one toward Locust or Pine.
—I feel this place is like a birch forest
about to go; there is wind, there are matches, there is snow,
and it has been dark and dry for hundreds of years.
I look at the chandelier waving in the glass
and the sticky sugar and the wet spoon.
I take my handkerchief out for the sake of the seven
years we spent in Philadelphia and the
steps we sat on and the tiny patches of lawn.
I believe now more than I ever did before
in my first poems and more and more I feel
that nothing was wasted, that the freezing nights
were not a waste, that the long dull walks and
the boredom, and the secret pity, were
not a waste. I leave the paper sitting,
front page up, beside the cold coffee,
on top of the sugar, on top of the wet spoon,
on top of the grease. I was born for one thing,
and I can leave this place without bitterness
and start my walk down Broad Street past the churches
and the tiny parking lots and the thrift stores.
There was enough justice, and there was enough wisdom,
although it would take the rest of my life—the next
two hundred years—to understand and explain it;
and there was enough time and there was enough affection
even if I did tear my tongue
begging the world for one more empty room
and one more window with clean glass
to let the light in on my last frenzy.
—I do the crow walking clumsily over his meat,
I do the child sitting for his dessert,
I do the poet asleep at his table,
waiting for the sun to light up his forehead.
I suddenly remember every ruined life,

every betrayal, every desolation,
as I walk past Tasker toward the city of Baltimore,
banging my pencil on the iron fences,
whistling Bach and Muczynski through the closed blinds.

Morning Harvest

     Pennsylvania spiders
not only stretch their silk between the limbs
of our great trees but hang between our houses
and pull their sheets across the frantic eyes
of cats and the soft chests of men.
Some are so huge they move around like mammals,
waddling slowly over the rough cement
and into the bushes to nurse their young or feed
on berries and crunch on bones.
But it is the ones that live on the iron bridge
going across to Riegelsville, New Jersey,
that are the most artistic and luxurious.
They make their webs between the iron uprights
and hang them out in the dew above the river
like a series of new designs on display,
waiting for you to choose the one most delicate,
waiting for you just to touch the sticky threads
as you look at their soft silk, as you love them.

If your mind is already on business,
even if your mind is still into your dream,
you will be shocked by their beauty and you will sit there
two minutes, two hours, a half a century you will sit there
until the guards begin to shout, until they rush up in confusion
and bang on your window and look at you in fear.
You will point with your left finger at the sun
and draw a tracery in the cold air,
a dragline from door handle to door handle,
foundation lines inside the windows,
long radials from the panel to the headrest
and gluey spirals turning on the radials;
and you will sit in the center of your web
like a rolled-up leaf or a piece of silent dirt,
pulling gently on your loose trapline.
They will scream in your ear,

they will tear desperately at the sheets,
they will beg for air
before you finally relieve them by starting your engine
and moving reluctantly over the small bridge.

Do not regret your little bout with life in the morning.
If you drive slowly you can have almost one minute
to study the drops of silver hanging in the sun
before you turn the corner past the gatehouse
and down the road beside the railroad cars
and finally over the tracks and up the hill
to the morning that lies in front of you like one more design.
It is the morning I live in and travel through,
the morning of children standing in the driveways,
of mothers wrapping their quilted coats around them
and yellow buses flashing their lights like berserk police cars.
It is lights that save us, lights that light the way,
blue lights rushing in to help the wretched,
red lights carrying twenty pounds of oxygen down the highway,
white lights entering the old Phoenician channels
bringing language and mathematics and religion into the darkness.

The Dancing

In all these rotten shops, in all this broken furniture
and wrinkled ties and baseball trophies and coffee pots
I have never seen a post-war Philco
with the automatic eye
nor heard Ravel's "Bolero" the way I did
in 1945 in that tiny living room
on Beechwood Boulevard, nor danced as I did
then, my knives all flashing, my hair all streaming,
my mother red with laughter, my father cupping
his left hand under his armpit, doing the dance
of old Ukraine, the sound of his skin half drum,
half fart, the world at last a meadow,
the three of us whirling and singing, the three of us
screaming and falling, as if we were dying,
as if we could never stop—in 1945—
in Pittsburgh, beautiful filthy Pittsburgh, home
of the evil Mellons, 5,000 miles away
from the other dancing—in Poland and Germany—
oh God of mercy, oh wild God.

Kissing Stieglitz Goodbye

Every city in America is approached
through a work of art, usually a bridge
but sometimes a road that curves underneath
or drops down from the sky. Pittsburgh has a tunnel—

you don't know it—that takes you through the rivers
and under the burning hills. I went there to cry
in the woods or carry my heavy bicycle
through fire and flood. Some have little parks—

San Francisco has a park. Albuquerque
is beautiful from a distance; it is purple
at five in the evening. New York is Egyptian,
especially from the little rise on the hill

at 14-C; it has twelve entrances
like the body of Jesus, and Easton, where I lived,
has two small floating bridges in front of it
that brought me in and out. I said goodbye

to them both when I was 57. I'm reading
Joseph Wood Krutch again—the second time.
I love how he lived in the desert. I'm looking at the skull
of Georgia O'Keeffe. I'm kissing Stieglitz goodbye.

He was a city, Stieglitz was truly a city
in every sense of the word; he wore a library
across his chest; he had a church on his knees.
I'm kissing him goodbye; he was, for me,

the last true city; after him there were
only overpasses and shopping centers,
little enclaves here and there, a skyscraper
with nothing near it, maybe a meaningless turf

where whores couldn't even walk, where nobody sits,
where nobody either lies or runs; either that
or some pure desert: a lizard under a boojum,
a flower sucking the water out of a rock.

*   *   *

What is the life of sadness worth, the bookstores
lost, the drugstores buried, a man with a stick
turning the bricks up, numbering the shards,
dream twenty-one, dream twenty-two. I left

with a glass of tears, a little artistic vial.
I put it in my leather pockets next
to my flask of Scotch, my golden knife and my keys,
my joyful poems and my T-shirts. Stieglitz is there

beside his famous number; there is smoke
and fire above his head; some bowlegged painter
is whispering in his ear; some lady-in-waiting
is taking down his words. I'm kissing Stieglitz

goodbye, my arms are wrapped around him, his photos
are making me cry; we're walking down Fifth Avenue;
we're looking for a pencil; there is a girl
standing against the wall—I'm shaking now

when I think of her; there are two buildings, one
is in blackness, there is a dying poplar;
there is a light on the meadow; there is a man
on a sagging porch. I would have believed in everything.

The Expulsion

I'm working like a dog here, testing my memory,
my mouth is slightly open, my eyes are closed,
my hand is lying under the satin pillow.
My subject is loss, the painter is Masaccio,
the church is the Church of the Carmine, the narrow panel
is on the southwest wall, I make a mouth
like Adam, I make a mouth like Eve, I make
a sword like the angel's. Or Schubert; I hear him howling
too, there is a touch of the Orient
throughout the great C Major. I'm thinking again
of poor Jim Wright and the sheet of tissue paper
he sent me. Lament, lament, for the underlayer
of wallpaper, circa 1935.
Lament for the Cretans, how did they disappear?
Lament for Hannibal. I'm standing again
behind some wires, there are some guns, my hand
is drawing in the eyes, I'm making the stripes,
I'm lying alone with water falling down
the left side of my face. That was our painting.
We stood in line to see it, we loved the cry
that came from Eve's black mouth, we loved the grief
of her slanted eyes, we loved poor Adam's face

half buried in his hands, we loved the light
on the shoulder and thighs, we loved the shadows, we loved
the perfect sense of distance. Lament, lament,
for my sister. It took ten years for the flesh to go,
she would be twenty then, she would be sixty
in 1984. Lament for my father,
he died in Florida, he died from fear, apologizing
to everyone around him. I walked through three feet
of snow to buy a suit; it took a day
to get to the airport. Lament, lament. He had
fifty-eight suits, and a bronze coffin; he lay
with his upper body showing, a foot of carpet.
He came to America in 1905, huge wolves
snapped at the horse's legs, the snow was on the ground
until the end of April. The angel is red,
her finger is pointing, she floats above the gate,
her face is cruel, she isn't like the angels
of Blake, or Plato, she is an angry mother,
her wings are firm. Lament, lament, my father
and I are leaving Paradise, an angel
is shouting, my hand is on my mouth, my father
is on the edge of his bed, he uses a knife
for a shoe horn, he is in Pittsburgh, the sky is black,
the air is filthy, he bends half over to squeeze
his foot into his shoe, his eyes are closed,
he's moaning. I miss our paradise, the pool
of water, the flowers. Our lives are merging, our shoes
are not that different. The angel is rushing by,
her lips are curled, there is a coldness, even
a madness to her, Adam and Eve are roaring,
the whole thing takes a minute, a few seconds,
and we are left on somebody's doorstep, one of
my favorites, three or four marble steps and a simple
crumbling brick—it could be Baltimore,
it could be Pittsburgh, the North Side or the Hill.
Inside I know there is a hall to the left
and a living room to the right; no one has modernized
it yet, there are two plum trees in the back
and a narrow garden, cucumbers and tomatoes.
We talk about Russia, we talk about the garden,
we talk about Truman, and Reagan. Our hands are rubbing
the dusty marble, we sit for an hour. "It is
a crazy life," I say, "after all the model
homes we looked at, I come back to the old
row house, I do it over and over." "My house"—

he means his father's—"had a giant garden
and we had peppers and radishes; my sister
Jenny made the pickles." We start to drift
at 5 o'clock in the evening, the cars from downtown
are starting to poison us. It is a paradise
of two, maybe, two at the most, the name
on the mailbox I can't remember, the garden
is full of glass, there is a jazzy door
on the next house over, and louvered windows. It is
a paradise, I'm sure of it. I kiss
him goodbye, I hold him, almost like the kiss
in 1969, in Philadelphia,
the last time I saw him, in the Russian manner
his mouth against my mouth, his arms around me—
we could do that once before he died—
the huge planes barely lifting off the ground,
the families weeping beside us, the way they do,
the children waving goodbye, the lovers smiling,
the way they do, all our loss, everything
we know of loneliness there, their minds already
fixed on the pain, their hands already hanging,
under the shining windows, near the yellow tiles,
the secret rooms, the long and brutal corridor
down which we sometimes shuffle, and sometimes run.

GERALD STERN

Books

The Pineys, 1971	*Paradise Poems,* 1984
The Naming of Beasts, 1972	*Lovesick,* 1987
Rejoicings, 1973	*New and Selected Poems,* 1988
Lucky Life, 1977	*Selected Essays,* 1988
The Red Coal, 1981	

Essays, Criticism

Mark Hillringhouse, "An Interview with Gerald Stern," *American Poetry Review* (March-April 1984); Jane Somerville, "Gerald Stern," *The Literary Review* (Fall 1984); Ed Hirsch, "A Late, Ironic Whitman," *The Nation* (January 10, 1985); David Walker, "Chekhov in America," *FIELD,* no. 38 (Spring, 1988).

Richard
Wilbur
(b. 1921)

Rhoda Nathans

Richard Wilbur was recognized early as a poet of exceptional skill and consistency. In his first book, *The Beautiful Changes* (1947), he seemed more fully formed and in command of what he wanted than most young poets. In retrospect we can see that that book was full of influences not yet fully absorbed— Hopkins, Marianne Moore, John Crowe Ransom, Auden, Stevens—and that the poet was still feeling his way toward what would be his mature style; but it is also true that the level of technical skill was unusually high. In an era when formal values were especially prized, it was a dazzling debut.

"A Black November Turkey," from Wilbur's third collection, *Things of This World* (1956), reveals his poetic strengths and preferences very clearly. The subject is a barnyard scene, but one such as few of us have experienced, so tranformed is it by what the poet has chosen to emphasize. Experience is here aesthetic, and reality is aesthetically seen. The chickens become an illustration of the wonderful phenomenon of light. The turkey is an opportunity for imaginative comparisons: his body its own cortege, then a cloud and a ship, his feathers ashes, his head a shepherd's crook and a saint's death mask. When Wilbur is through with him, the turkey is a natural wonder, part of a reality that is enigmatic as to meaning but unmistakable as to beauty, not least in its way of balancing the turkey's "timeless" look with the "clocking" (note the fragrant pun on "clucking") hens and roosters. It is partly that the world provides us with such brilliant contrasts—black and white, timeless and clocking, superb and vulgar—and partly, of course, that the artist finds or makes them, since we would scarcely have made all this from turkey and hens on our own.

The power of reality to assert its beauty can be as succinctly observed as it is in "Transit" and "Stop." It can be the product of a naturalist's close interest in the details of a plant's structure and foliage, as in "Thyme Flowering among Rocks." At the close of "Stop" the poet invokes Greek mythology to complete his comparison, bringing together the unlikely beauty of the baggage truck with the distant legends of a dim and glowing underworld. "Thyme Flowering among Rocks" ends with a reference to Bashō, the great Japanese writer of haiku, and the spirit that finds the world "Truer than it seems" is certainly one that the American poet can be said to share with his Japanese counterpart.

More complex treatments of this view of the world as hard to fathom but easy to admire and love can be found in "Beasts" and "The Mind-Reader." The "tracking" of "Beasts"—how it gets from one image to another—is intriguing and mysterious. It is a kind of nocturne, a mapping of the night that moves from beasts to the man-beast threshold where the werewolf is giving himself up to the sharper senses that seem the very basis of the poem's own alert survey. The latter half of the poem shows us romantic idealists, "suitors of excellence," whose dreams seem at first to separate them sharply from the beast's world until we realize that their construings of "the painful/Beauty of heaven, the lucid moon/And the risen hunter" bring them and us back round to the animal world once more. It is hard to imagine a more civilized and witty celebration of the powerful connections we have to the animals, to "bestiality." "The Mind-Reader," the longest selection here, treats dream, imagination, the unsounded depths of the self, and life itself with a mesmerizing and urbane penetration that grows cumulatively more engrossing as the poem unwinds.

Noting that some of these poems rhyme and that most of them employ meter in original and masterful ways does not really tell us as much about Wilbur the poet as we might think. More to the point, perhaps, is the impression that their detachment, completeness, and control make upon us. This poet does not write about his life and feelings in the way that so many do. His witty and impersonal manner runs through all his work, so that for the three decades covered by this anthology he has remained consistent in his commitments and artistic preferences, a choice that deserves understanding and respect. It has made him a stable point in a world where artistic and political currents have often swirled confusingly, and he has always had good lessons to teach young poets who have sent themselves to school among his poems, where the eye for detail and the ear for graceful music have never faltered.

Richard Wilbur taught for many years at Wesleyan University. An expert translator, he is famous for his versions of Molière's comedies. That stage experience may have led to his successful venture as a writer of song lyrics for the musical *Candide*. His program as a poet remains what he declared it to be in 1950: "an effort to articulate relationships not quite seen, to make or discover some pattern in the world" (*Mid-Century Poets*, ed. John Ciardi). This makes him an aesthete in the best sense, as Stevens was, and the uncertainty about whether the pattern is being discovered or imposed is one of the things that keeps his poems exciting. He currently serves as America's Poet Laureate at the Library of Congress.

DY

A Black November Turkey

to A.M. and A.M.

Nine white chickens come
With haunchy walk and heads
Jabbing among the chips, the chaff, the stones
    And the cornhusk-shreds,

And bit by bit infringe
A pond of dusty light,
Spectral in shadow until they bobbingly one
    By one ignite.

Neither pale nor bright,
The turkey-cock parades
Through radiant squalors, darkly auspicious as
    The ace of spades,

Himself his own cortège
And puffed with the pomp of death,
Rehearsing over and over with strangled râle
    His latest breath.

The vast black body floats
Above the crossing knees
As a cloud over thrashed branches, a calm ship
    Over choppy seas,

Shuddering its fan and feathers
In fine soft clashes
With the cold sound that the wind makes, fondling
    Paper-ashes.

The pale-blue bony head
Set on its shepherd's-crook
Like a saint's death-mask, turns a vague, superb
    And timeless look

Upon these clocking hens
And the cocks that one by one,
Dawn after mortal dawn, with vulgar joy
    Acclaim the sun.

Beasts

Beasts in their major freedom
Slumber in peace tonight. The gull on his ledge
Dreams in the guts of himself the moon-plucked waves below,

And the sunfish leans on a stone, slept
By the lyric water,

In which the spotless feet
Of deer make dulcet splashes, and to which
The ripped mouse, safe in the owl's talon, cries
Concordance. Here there is no such harm
And no such darkness

As the selfsame moon observes
Where, warped in window-glass, it sponsors now
The werewolf's painful change. Turning his head away
On the sweaty bolster, he tries to remember
The mood of manhood,

But lies at last, as always,
Letting it happen, the fierce fur soft to his face,
Hearing with sharper ears the wind's exciting minors,
The leaves' panic, and the degradation
Of the heavy streams.

Meantime, at high windows
Far from thicket and pad-fall, suitors of excellence
Sigh and turn from their work to construe again the painful
Beauty of heaven, the lucid moon
And the risen hunter,

Making such dreams for men
As told will break their hearts as always, bringing
Monsters into the city, crows on the public statues,
Navies fed to the fish in the dark
Unbridled waters.

Stop

In grimy winter dusk
We slowed for a concrete platform;
The pillars passed more slowly;
A paper bag leapt up.

The train banged to a standstill.
Brake-steam rose and parted.
Three chipped-at blocks of ice
Sprawled on a baggage-truck.

Out in that glum, cold air
The broken ice lay glintless,
But the truck was painted blue
On side, wheels, and tongue,

A purple, glowering blue
Like the phosphorus of Lethe
Or Queen Persephone's gaze
In the numb fields of the dark.

Thyme Flowering among Rocks

This, if Japanese,
Would represent grey boulders
Walloped by rough seas

So that, here or there,
The balked water tossed its froth
Straight into the air.

Here, where things are what
They are, it is thyme blooming,
Rocks, and nothing but—

Having, nonetheless,
Many small leaves implicit,
A green countlessness.

Crouching down, peering
Into perplexed recesses,
You find a clearing

Occupied by sun
Where, along prone, rachitic
Branches, one by one,

Pale stems arise, squared
In the manner of *Mentha*,
The oblong leaves paired.

One branch, in ending,
Lifts a little and begets
A straight-ascending

Spike, whorled with fine blue
Or purple trumpets, banked in
The leaf-axils. You

Are lost now in dense
Fact, fact which one might have thought
Hidden from the sense,

Blinking at detail
Peppery as this fragrance,
Lost to proper scale

As, in the motion
Of striped fins, a bathysphere
Forgets the ocean.

It makes the craned head
Spin. Unfathomed thyme! The world's
A dream, Basho said,

Not because that dream's
A falsehood, but because it's
Truer than it seems.

The Mind-Reader

Lui parla.

for Charles and Eula

Some things are truly lost. Think of a sun-hat
Laid for the moment on a parapet
While three young women—one, perhaps, in mourning—
Talk in the crenellate shade. A slight wind plucks
And budges it; it scuffs to the edge and cartwheels
Into a giant view of some description:
Haggard escarpments, if you like, plunge down
Through mica shimmer to a moss of pines
Amidst which, here or there, a half-seen river
Lobs up a blink of light. The sun-hat falls,
With what free flirts and stoops you can imagine,
Down through that reeling vista or another,
Unseen by any, even by you or me.
It is as when a pipe-wrench, catapulted
From the jounced back of a pick-up truck, dives headlong
Into a bushy culvert; or a book
Whose reader is asleep, garbling the story,
Glides from beneath a steamer chair and yields
Its flurried pages to the printless sea.

It is one thing to escape from consciousness
As such things do, another to be pent
In the dream-cache or stony oubliette
Of someone's head.
                         They found, when I was little,
That I could tell the place of missing objects.
I stood by the bed of a girl, or the frayed knee
Of an old man whose face was lost in shadow.

When did you miss it?, people would be saying,
Where did you see it last? And then those voices,
Querying or replying, came to sound
Like cries of birds when the leaves race and whiten
And a black overcast is shelving over.
The mind is not a landscape, but if it were
There would in such case be a tilted moon
Wheeling beyond the wood through which you groped,
Its fine spokes breaking in the tangled thickets.
There would be obfuscations, paths which turned
To dried-up stream-beds, hemlocks which invited
Through shiny clearings to a groundless shade;
And yet in a sure stupor you would come
At once upon dilapidated cairns,
Abraded moss, and half-healed blazes leading
To where, around the turning of a fear,
The lost thing shone.

                  Imagine a railway platform—
The long cars come to a cloudy halt beside it,
And the fogged windows offering a view
Neither to those within nor those without.
Now, in the crowd—forgive my predilection—
Is a young woman standing amidst her luggage,
Expecting to be met by you, a stranger.
See how she turns her head, the eyes engaging
And disengaging, pausing and shying away.
It is like that with things put out of mind,
As the queer saying goes: a lost key hangs
Trammeled by threads in what you come to see
As the webbed darkness of a sewing-basket,
Flashing a little; or a photograph,
Misplaced in an old ledger, turns its bled
Oblivious profile to rebuff your vision,
Yet glistens with the fixative of thought.
What can be wiped from memory? Not the least
Meanness, obscenity, humiliation,
Terror which made you clench your eyes, or pulse
Of happiness which quickened your despair.
Nothing can be forgotten, as I am not
Permitted to forget.

              It was not far
From that to this—this corner café table
Where, with my lank grey hair and vatic gaze,
I sit and drink at the receipt of custom.

They come here, day and night, so many people:
Sad women of the quarter, dressed in black,
As to a black confession; blinking clerks
Who half-suppose that Taurus ruminates
Upon their destinies; men of affairs
Down from Milan to clear it with the magus
Before they buy or sell some stock or other;
My fellow-drunkards; fashionable folk,
Mocking and ravenously credulous,
And skeptics bent on proving me a fraud
For fear that some small wonder, unexplained,
Should leave a fissure in the world, and all
Saint Michael's host come flapping back.

                         I give them
Paper and pencil, turn away and light
A cigarette, as you have seen me do;
They write their questions; fold them up; I lay
My hand on theirs and go into my frenzy,
Raising my eyes to heaven, snorting smoke,
Lolling my head as in the fumes of Delphi,
And then, with shaken, spirit-guided fingers,
Set down the oracle. All that, of course,
Is trumpery, since nine times out of ten
What words float up within another's thought
Surface as soon in mine, unfolding there
Like paper flowers in a water-glass.
In the tenth case, I sometimes cheat a little.
That shocks you? But consider: what I do
Cannot, so most conceive, be done at all,
And when I fail, I am a charlatan
Even to such as I have once astounded—
Whereas a tailor can mis-cut my coat
And be a tailor still. I tell you this
Because you know that I have the gift, the burden.
Whether or not I put my mind to it,
The world usurps me ceaselessly; my sixth
And never-resting sense is a cheap room
Black with the anger of insomnia,
Whose wall-boards vibrate with the mutters, plaints,
And flushings of the race.

                   What should I tell them?
I have no answers. *Set your fears at rest,*
I scribble when I must. *Your paramour*
Is faithful, and your spouse is unsuspecting.

You were not seen, that day, beneath the fig-tree.
Still, be more cautious. When the time is ripe,
Expect promotion. I foresee a message
From a far person who is rich and dying.
You are admired in secret. If, in your judgment,
Profit is in it, you should take the gamble.
As for these fits of weeping, they will pass.

It makes no difference that my lies are bald
And my evasions casual. It contents them
Not to have spoken, yet to have been heard.
What more do they deserve, if I could give it,
Mute breathers as they are of selfish hopes
And small anxieties? Faith, justice, valor,
All those reputed rarities of soul
Confirmed in marble by our public statues—
You may be sure that they are rare indeed
Where the soul mopes in private, and I listen.
Sometimes I wonder if the blame is mine,
If through a sullen fault of the mind's ear
I miss a resonance in all their fretting.
Is there some huge attention, do you think,
Which suffers us and is inviolate,
To which all hearts are open, which remarks
The sparrow's weighty fall, and overhears
In the worst rancor a deflected sweetness?
I should be glad to know it.

                          Meanwhile, saved
By the shrewd habit of concupiscence,
Which, like a visor, narrows my regard,
And drinking studiously until my thought
Is a blind lowered almost to the sill,
I hanker for that place beyond the sparrow
Where the wrench beds in mud, the sun-hat hangs
In densest branches, and the book is drowned.
Ah, you have read my mind. One more, perhaps . . .
A mezzo-litro. Grazie, professore.

Transit

A woman I have never seen before
Steps from the darkness of her town-house door
At just that crux of time when she is made
So beautiful that she or time must fade.

What use to claim that as she tugs her gloves
A phantom heraldry of all the loves
Blares from the lintel? That the staggered sun
Forgets, in his confusion, how to run?
Still, nothing changes as her perfect feet
Click down the walk that issues in the street,
Leaving the stations of her body there
As a whip maps the countries of the air.

RICHARD WILBUR
Books

The Beautiful Changes and Other
  Poems, 1947

Ceremony and Other Poems, 1950

A Bestiary (compilation), 1955

Molière, The Misanthrope
  (translation), 1955

Things of This World, 1956

Poems, 1943–1956, 1957

Candide: A Comic Operetta Based
  on Voltaire's Satire (lyrics by
  Wilbur, book by Hellman, score by
  Bernstein), 1957

Poe: Complete Poems (editor), 1959

Advice to a Prophet and Other
  Poems, 1961

Molière, Tartuffe (translation), 1963

The Poems of Richard Wilbur, 1963

Walking to Sleep, New Poems and
  Translations, 1969

Molière, The School for Wives
  (translation), 1972

Opposites, 1973

The Mind-Reader, 1976

Responses: Prose Pieces, 1953–1976
  (criticism), 1976

Molière, The Learned Ladies
  (translation), 1978

The Whale: Uncollected
  Translations, 1980

Racine, Andromache (translation),
  1982

Racine, Phaedra (translation), 1986

Interviews, Criticism

Donald Hall, "The New Poetry: Notes on the Past Fifteen Years in America," in *New World Writing*, 1955; David Curry, "An Interview with Richard Wilbur," *Trinity Review* 17 (December 1962); Robert Frank and Stephen Mitchell, "Richard Wilbur: An Interview," *Amherst Library Magazine* 10 (Summer 1964); Ralph J. Mills, Jr., *Contemporary American Poetry*, 1965; Donald Hill, *Richard Wilbur*, 1967; John Field, *Richard Wilbur: A Bibliographical Checklist*, 1971; Edward Honig, "A Conversation with Richard Wilbur," *Modern Language Notes* 91 (October 1976); Peter Stitt, Ellesa High, Helen McCoy, "The Art of Poetry," *Paris Review* 19 (Winter 1977); Wendy Salinger, ed., *Richard Wilbur's Creation*, 1983; Peter Stitt, *The World's Hieroglyphic Beauty: Five American Poets*, 1985.

James
Wright
(1927–1980)

John Unterecker

A broad vein of compassion and social concern runs through the poetry of James Wright. Growing up in Martins Ferry, an industrial town on the Ohio River, and raised in a working-class family amid the considerable poverty of the Great Depression, he developed a sympathy for criminals, derelicts, minorities, and the uneducated poor that never left him. A note of sorrow, even of anguish, is never far away in his poems, though they can ring with celebration and reverberate with humor.

Educated at Kenyon College, where he studied with John Crowe Ransom, and at the University of Washington, where Theodore Roethke was his teacher and friend, James Wright began in the 1950s, like so many poets of his generation, writing poems of a formal cast. "Mutterings over the Crib of a Deaf Child," from his first collection, *The Green Wall* (1957), demonstrates this early manner at its most delicate and successful, in a poem that combines qualities of song with a dramatic exchange between two voices. "Saint Judas," the title poem of his second collection (1959), is technically impressive both as a sonnet and as a dramatic monologue. What makes it characteristically Wright's is the emphasis on suffering—even Judas cannot be free of compassion—along with the idea that altruism should involve no bargaining. Since he feels already "banished from heaven," Judas expects no reward for his kindness; he holds the man "for nothing" and presumably out of an empathy born of his own hopelessness.

After *Saint Judas*, Wright's style changed markedly. He had already moved to Minneapolis, and his friendship with another Minnesota poet, Robert Bly, as well as his interest in translation, brought the work of foreign poets to bear on his poetry in a dramatic way. Classical Chinese poetry, German expressionist poetry, especially Georg Trakl's, and Spanish surrealism, particularly as found in the work of Vallejo and Neruda—these influences enabled Bly and Wright to break sharply with their previous poems and forge a new style. The resulting poetry had a plainness, directness, and candor that made a considerable impact on American poetry during the 1960s. What is especially curious about this shift in Wright's case (Bly's too) is that it enabled the poet to write his most indelibly American poetry. Wright's earlier work had been mildly influenced by Robert Frost and Edward Arlington Robinson, but the new style, with its wild mixture of foreign influences, took Wright into his most impressive accounts of American settings and American experience. "Stages on a Journey Westward" is an obvious example of this, and "Twilights" is an even more interesting one: It behaves very much like a German expressionist or Spanish surrealist poem, but its maple leaves, shopping centers, steel mills, and barns make it indubitably American. The same observation can be made about "Outside Fargo, North Dakota," "Milkweed," "Two Hangovers," and "The Life." All these poems manage to capture scenes and feelings that are characteristic of American life but that had never gotten into our poetry before. They may be as mythic in cast as "The Life," which mentions Etruscans but is deeply American in its voice, movement, mood, and details—a poem that could come from no other culture. They may be as haunting and picturesque as "Outside Fargo, North Dakota," where middlewestern loneliness and the somber beauty of the Great Plains are caught in a breathtaking poem modeled after the Chinese lyric. And they may draw specifically on Wright's own experience growing up in Ohio, as the first part of "Two Hangovers" does. In their range and music, these poems of the 1960s had an effect on American poetry that is still to be fully assessed.

In the 1970s, living and teaching in New York City and traveling often to Europe, Wright began to produce poems that reflect a newfound fascination with the Mediterranean world, as the poems that conclude our selection tend to demonstrate. He could still treat American subjects effectively, as in the bitter "Ohioan Pastoral," but the poem "A Winter Daybreak above Vence" is much more typical of his last three volumes. Sometimes the poems of this phase make deliberate connections with the classical world, but they are mainly romantic lyrics, more celebratory and happy than the work of Wright's early and middle years. "A Winter Daybreak above Vence" is an extraordinary account of a dawn that is comic, theatrical, dreamlike, mystical, and tender, all at the same time.

In 1980, shortly after he had completed his final collection of poems, _This Journey_, James Wright died in New York City.

_DY_

Mutterings over the Crib of a Deaf Child

"How will he hear the bell at school
Arrange the broken afternoon,
And know to run across the cool
Grasses where the starlings cry,
Or understand the day is gone?"

Well, someone lifting curious brows
Will take the measure of the clock.
And he will see the birchen boughs
Outside sagging dark from the sky,
And the shade crawling upon the rock.

"And how will he know to rise at morning?
His mother has other sons to waken,
She has the stove she must build to burning
Before the coals of the nighttime die;
And he never stirs when he is shaken."

I take it the air affects the skin,
And you remember, when you were young,
Sometimes you could feel the dawn begin,
And the fire would call you, by and by,
Out of the bed and bring you along.

"Well, good enough. To serve his needs
All kinds of arrangements can be made.
But what will you do if his finger bleeds?
Or a bobwhite whistles invisibly
And flutes like an angel off in the shade?"

He will learn pain. And, as for the bird,
It is always darkening when that comes out.
I will putter as though I had not heard,
And lift him into my arms and sing
Whether he hears my song or not.

Saint Judas

When I went out to kill myself, I caught
A pack of hoodlums beating up a man.
Running to spare his suffering, I forgot
My name, my number, how my day began,
How soldiers milled around the garden stone
And sang amusing songs; how all that day

Their javelins measured crowds; how I alone
Bargained the proper coins, and slipped away.

Banished from heaven, I found this victim beaten,
Stripped, kneed, and left to cry. Dropping my rope
Aside, I ran, ignored the uniforms:
Then I remembered bread my flesh had eaten,
The kiss that ate my flesh. Flayed without hope,
I held the man for nothing in my arms.

Stages on a Journey Westward

1

I began in Ohio.
I still dream of home.
Near Mansfield, enormous dobbins enter dark barns in autumn,
Where they can be lazy, where they can munch little apples,
Or sleep long.
But by night now, in the bread lines my father
Prowls, I cannot find him: So far off,
1500 miles or so away, and yet
I can hardly sleep.
In a blue rag the old man limps to my bed,
Leading a blind horse
Of gentleness.
In 1932, grimy with machinery, he sang me
A lullaby of a goosegirl.
Outside the house, the slag heaps waited.

2

In western Minnesota, just now,
I slept again.
In my dream, I crouched over a fire.
The only human beings between me and the Pacific Ocean
Were old Indians, who wanted to kill me.
They squat and stare for hours into small fires
Far off in the mountains.
The blades of their hatchets are dirty with the grease
Of huge, silent buffaloes.

3

It is dawn.
I am shivering,
Even beneath a huge eiderdown.
I came in last night, drunk,
And left the oil stove cold.

I listen a long time, now, to the flurries.
Snow howls all around me, out of the abandoned prairies.
It sounds like the voices of bums and gamblers,
Rattling through the bare nineteenth-century whorehouses
In Nevada.

    4

Defeated for re-election,
The half-educated sheriff of Mukilteo, Washington,
Has been drinking again.
He leads me up the cliff, tottering.
Both drunk, we stand among the graves.
Miners paused here on the way up to Alaska.
Angry, they spaded their broken women's bodies
Into ditches of crab grass.
I lie down between tombstones.
At the bottom of the cliff
America is over and done with.
America,
Plunged into the dark furrows
Of the sea again.

Twilights

The big stones of the cistern behind the barn
Are soaked in whitewash.
My grandmother's face is a small maple leaf
Pressed in a secret box.
Locusts are climbing down into the dark green crevices
Of my childhood. Latches click softly in the trees. Your hair is gray.

The arbors of the cities are withered.
Far off, the shopping centers empty and darken.

A red shadow of steel mills.

Two Hangovers

NUMBER ONE
I slouch in bed.
Beyond the streaked trees of my window,
All groves are bare.
Locusts and poplars change to unmarried women
Sorting slate from anthracite
Between railroad ties:
The yellow-bearded winter of the depression
Is still alive somewhere, an old man
Counting his collection of bottle caps

In a tarpaper shack under the cold trees
Of my grave.
I still feel half drunk,
And all those old women beyond my window
Are hunching toward the graveyard.

Drunk, mumbling Hungarian,
The sun staggers in,
And his big stupid face pitches
Into the stove.
For two hours I have been dreaming
Of green butterflies searching for diamonds
In coal seams;
And children chasing each other for a game
Through the hills of fresh graves.
But the sun has come home drunk from the sea,
And a sparrow outside
Sings of the Hanna Coal Co. and the dead moon.
The filaments of cold light bulbs tremble
In music like delicate birds.
Ah, turn it off.

NUMBER TWO: I TRY TO WAKEN AND GREET THE WORLD ONCE AGAIN
In a pine tree,
A few yards away from my window sill,
A brilliant blue jay is springing up and down, up and down,
On a branch.
I laugh, as I see him abandon himself
To entire delight, for he knows as well as I do
That the branch will not break.

Milkweed

While I stood here, in the open, lost in myself,
I must have looked a long time
Down the corn rows, beyond grass,
The small house,
White walls, animals lumbering toward the barn.
I look down now. It is all changed.
Whatever it was I lost, whatever I wept for
Was a wild, gentle thing, the small dark eyes
Loving me in secret.
It is here. At a touch of my hand,
The air fills with delicate creatures
From the other world.

Outside Fargo, North Dakota

Along the sprawled body of the derailed Great Northern freight car,
I strike a match slowly and lift it slowly.
No wind.

Beyond town, three heavy white horses
Wade all the way to their shoulders
In a silo shadow.

Suddenly the freight car lurches.
The door slams back, a man with a flashlight
Calls me good evening.
I nod as I write good evening, lonely
And sick for home.

The Life

Murdered, I went, risen,
Where the murderers are,
That black ditch
Of river.

And if I come back to my only country
With a white rose on my shoulder,
What is that to you?
It is the grave
In blossom.

It is the trillium of darkness,
It is hell, it is the beginning of winter,
It is a ghost town of Etruscans who have no names
Any more.

It is the old loneliness.
It is.
And it is
The last time.

Ohioan Pastoral

On the other side
Of Salt Creek, along the road, the barns topple
And snag among the orange-rinds,
Oil cans, cold balloons of lovers.
One barn there

Sags, sags and oozes
Down one side of the copperous gulley.
The limp whip of a sumac dangles
Gently against the body of a lost
Bathtub, while high in the flint-cracks
And the wild grimed trees, on the hill,
A buried gas-main
Long ago tore a black gutter into the mines.
And now it hisses among the green rings
On fingers in coffins.

A Winter Daybreak above Vence

The night's drifts
Pile up below me and behind my back,
Slide down the hill, rise again, and build
Eerie little dunes on the roof of the house.
In the valley below me,
Miles between me and the town of St.-Jeannet,
The road lamps glow.
They are so cold, they might as well be dark.
Trucks and cars
Cough and drone down there between the golden
Coffins of greenhouses, the startled squawk
Of a rooster claws heavily across
A grove, and drowns.
The gumming snarl of some grouchy dog sounds,
And a man bitterly shifts his broken gears.
True night still hands on,
Mist cluttered with a racket of its own.

Now on the mountainside,
A little way downhill among turning rocks,
A square takes form in the side of a dim wall.
I hear a bucket rattle or something, tinny,
No other stirring behind the dim face
Of the goatherd's house. I imagine
His goats are still sleeping, dreaming
Of the fresh roses
Beyond the walls of the greenhouse below them
And of lettuce leaves opening in Tunisia.

I turn, and somehow
Impossibly hovering in the air over everything,

The Mediterranean, nearer to the moon
Than this mountain is,
Shines. A voice clearly
Tells me to snap out of it. Galway
Mutters out of the house and up the stone stairs
To start the motor. The moon and the stars
Suddenly flicker out, and the whole mountain
Appears, pale as a shell.

Look, the sea has not fallen and broken
Our heads. How can I feel so warm
Here in the dead center of January? I can
Scarcely believe it, and yet I have to, this is
The only life I have. I get up from the stone.
My body mumbles something unseemly
And follows me. Now we are all sitting here strangely
On top of the sunlight.

JAMES WRIGHT

Books

The Green Wall, 1957

Saint Judas, 1959

Twenty Poems of Georg Trakl
(translations, with Robert Bly),
1961

The Branch Will Not Break, 1963

The Rider on the White Horse:
Selected Short Fiction of Theodor
Storm (translations), 1964

Shall We Gather at the River, 1968

Poems by Hermann Hesse
(translations), 1970

Collected Poems, 1971

Neruda and Vallejo: Selected Poems
(translations, with Robert Bly and
John Knoepfle), 1971

Wandering: Notes and Sketches by
Hermann Hesse (translations, with
Franz Wright), 1972

Two Citizens, 1973

To a Blossoming Pear Tree, 1977

This Journey, 1982

Collected Prose, 1983

A Secret Field (journals), 1985

Interviews, Criticism

William Heyen and Jerome Mazzaro, "Something to be Said for the Light:
A Conversation with James Wright," *Southern Humanities Review* 6
(1972); Interview, *Paris Review* 62 (1975); "Letters from Europe, Two
Notes from Venice, Remarks on Two Poems, and Other Occasional
Prose," in *American Poets in 1976,* ed. William Heyen, 1976; George
Lensing and Ronald Moran, *Four Poets of the Emotive Imagination:*
Robert Bly, James Wright, Louis Simpson and William Stafford, 1976;
Michael Cuddihy, ed., *Ironwood: James Wright/A Special Issue,* vol. 5,
no. 2 (1977); Dave Smith, ed., *The Pure Clear Word: Essays on the Poetry*
of James Wright, 1982; Peter Stitt, *The World's Hieroglyphic Beauty: Five*
American Poets, 1985; David C. Dougherty, *James Wright,* 1987.

Twelve Poets
Born Between
1930 and 1940

Margaret
Atwood
(b. 1939)

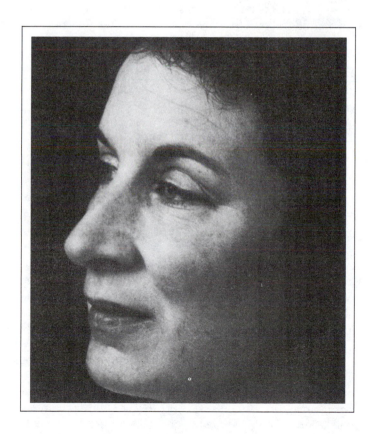

M argaret Atwood, like few other writers of our time, has produced a large and widely differing range of poems that show her working at the same high, serious level in poetry as in the other forms she practices. Extremely active as a fiction writer, with a steady succession of impressive, important novels and an increasing body of vibrant short fiction to her credit, she has also managed to serve as critic, essayist, and anthologist, with special focus on other Canadian writers and their role in shaping contemporary literature.

While some critics seem put off by the sheer amount of her production and complain about a tendency to glibness, most readers eagerly look forward to whatever Atwood will do next because she has managed to speak to many issues and many constituencies in, as Marilyn French has observed, "a taut, limpid style that combines powerful introspection, honesty, and satire." A very *inclusive* writer, with poetic gifts for controlling the effects of her prose more acutely, Atwood has always seemed to begin somewhere off the page, not quite focused, not in any hurry to announce large themes or insights, which she herself has warned are likely to do any writer in: "It's a lot more like walking in the dark: you move one step at a time, you depend on sound and touch, and you can't see where you're going, though you may guess." It's in the guessing that she surprises and moves us. In "Game After Supper" the narrator follows this advice and, to our relief, is not punished (by murder, or rape . . .) for her willingness to risk the other's, the stranger's, approach, which may of course be a figment, a sort of inner-mirror vision that all is not right within. In most of the work, the many mysteries—whether of the missing father in the novel *Surfacing*, or in such poems as "The Robber Bridegroom" and "Damside"—ultimately hinge on how much trust and courage can be summoned up ("If this were a poem I'd trust the river"), even though one realizes the journey may end in destruction or oblivion.

Moments of transcendence, which Atwood seems to work toward again and again, can come only in shared, human experience ("which includes both of us"—see "Damside"), episodes in which one cannot survive alone, or at least one needs to review what has happened with someone, or something, else. And so even "The Woman Who Could Not Live with Her Faulty Heart" is at heart a listener ("it forces me to listen"), someone who, in Atwood's view, is willing to go beyond individual fantasies to a point of communion with "the other." Whether it takes the form of one's own heart, or creatures like "Vultures" or the "Landcrab," or fellow travelers on the "Trainride, Vienna—Bonn," who in another time might become executioners (again), Atwood goes to the core of our existence, the interdependency with other beings. This is what obviates what in other writers might be a tendency to allow similar characters to be victimized. Whatever the potshots, and on a deeper level the deprecation, they are self-dealt; Atwood's worry is with the duality of all human nature, not the narrower concerns of who does what to whom.

Atwood has said she works toward "the most dangerous point of the poem," the place where her characters realize they're back at square one and a new response is called for, or else! Their only advantage may be that "they've been around once" (from an interview); it's as if in the circling (a common theme, from the early collection, *The Circle Game,* on through the most recent poem cycles) some crack might emerge, some way out of the predicament. In "Last Poem," with characteristic wit, even a wink, Atwood the poet can truthfully have it both ways for herself: each poem _is_ after all one's last. More to the point of this revealing poem is the poet's knowledge, as she wonders "how to say / goodbye gracefully and not merely snivel," that she must accept the hand out of the rubble, "one action that shines like pure luck." There's a sort of Schopenhauerian stasis achieved at this moment, when "Because there's nothing more I can do I do nothing." It may result in stagnation, to be sure, and evolve into pessimism, but if the energies are calmed, at the core of our being, an individual may just reverse the path she's on toward inertia, and life start up again. As the closing moment of "The Robber Bridegroom" has it, even as we are shocked by the nature of the romance and glad the bride survives ("only a little frightened"), she will dream of him "as he is." It is a pointed way of saying all life is sacred, and, as some of Atwood's poems imply, the more so when we can't figure out why.

Having grown up "in and out of the bush" and not having attended school until the eighth grade, Atwood has enjoyed generous measures of private and public experience—in many jobs, as cashier, waitress, market researcher, and in studies beyond the M.A. (Radcliffe) in English literature—that have provided her with many lenses to look through. Withal, with customary sagacity, she has recently said, "Life begins with geology and with geography," and even in her most invented landscapes (see the recent novel, _The Handmaid's Tale_) one knows exactly where one is on her map, rooted in lived-in land, ready to look around.

_SF_

Game After Supper

This is before electricity,
it is when there were porches.

On the sagging porch an old man
is rocking. The porch is wooden,

the house is wooden and grey;
in the living room which smells of
smoke and mildew, soon
the woman will light the kerosene lamp.

There is a barn but I am not in the barn;
there is an orchard too, gone bad,
its apples like soft cork
but I am not there either.

I am hiding in the long grass
with my two dead cousins,
the membrane grown already
across their throats.

We hear crickets and our own hearts
close to our ears;
though we giggle, we are afraid.

From the shadows around
the corner of the house
a tall man is coming to find us:

he will be an uncle,
if we are lucky.

Vultures

Hung there in the thermal
whiteout of noon, dark ash
in the chimney's updraft, turning
slowly like a thumb pressed down
on target; indolent V's; flies, until they drop.

Then they're hyenas, raucous
around the kill, flapping their black
umbrellas, the feathered red-eyed widows
whose pot bodies violate mourning,
the snigger at funerals,
the burp at the wake.

They cluster, like beetles
laying their eggs on carrion,
gluttonous for a space, a little
territory of murder: food
and children.

Frowsy old saint, bald-
headed and musty, scrawny-
necked recluse on your pillar
of blazing air which is not
heaven: what do you make
of death, which you do not
cause, which you eat daily?

I make life, which is a prayer.
I make clean bones.
I make a grey zinc noise
which to me is a song.

Well, heart, out of all this
carnage, could you do better?

Landcrab

A lie, that we come from water.
The truth is we were born
from stones, dragons, the sea's
teeth, as you testify,
with your crust and jagged scissors.

Hermit, hard socket
for a timid eye,
you're a soft gut scuttling
sideways, a blue skull,
round bone on the prowl.
Wolf of treeroots and gravelly holes,
a mouth on stilts,
the husk of a small demon.

Attack, voracious
eating, and flight:

it's a sound routine
for staying alive on edges.

Then there's the tide, and that dance
you do for the moon
on wet sand, claws raised
to fend off your mate,
your coupling a quick
dry clatter of rocks.
For mammals
with their lobes and bulbs,
scruples and warm milk,
you've nothing but contempt.

Here you are, a frozen scowl
targeted in flashlight,
then gone: a piece of what
we are, not all,
my stunted child, my momentary
face in the mirror,
my tiny nightmare.

The Robber Bridegroom

He would like not to kill. He would like
what he imagines other men have,
instead of this red compulsion. Why do the women
fail him and die badly? He would like to kill them gently,
finger by finger and with great tenderness, so that
at the end they would melt into him
with gratitude for his skill and the final pleasure
he still believes he could bring them
if only they would accept him,
but they scream too much and make him angry.
Then he goes for the soul, rummaging
in their flesh for it, despotic with self-pity,
hunting among the nerves and the shards
of their faces for the one thing
he needs to live, and lost
back there in the poplar and spruce forest
in the watery moonlight, where his young bride,
pale but only a little frightened,
her hands glimmering with his own approaching
death, gropes her way towards him
along the obscure path, from white stone

to white stone, ignorant and singing,
dreaming of him as he is.

The Woman Who Could Not
Live With Her Faulty Heart

I do not mean the symbol
of love, a candy shape
to decorate cakes with,
the heart that is supposed
to belong or break;

I mean this lump of muscle
that contracts like a flayed biceps,
purple-blue, with its skin of suet,
its skin of gristle, this isolate,
this caved hermit, unshelled
turtle, this one lungful of blood,
no happy plateful.

All hearts float in their own
deep oceans of no light,
wetblack and glimmering,
their four mouths gulping like fish.
Hearts are said to pound:
this is to be expected, the heart's
regular struggle against being drowned.

But most hearts say, I want, I want,
I want, I want. My heart
is more duplicitous,
though no twin as I once thought.
It says, I want, I don't want, I
want, and then a pause.
It forces me to listen,

and at night it is the infra-red
third eye that remains open
while the other two are sleeping
but refuses to say what it has seen.

It is a constant pestering
in my ears, a caught moth, limping drum,
a child's fist beating
itself against the bedsprings:

I want, I don't want.
How can one live with such a heart?

Long ago I gave up singing
to it, it will never be satisfied or lulled.
One night I will say to it:
Heart, be still,
and it will.

Trainride, Vienna–Bonn

i

It's those helmets we remember,
the shape of a splayed cranium,
and the faces under them,
ruthless & uniform

But these sit on the train
clean & sane, in their neutral
beige & cream: this girl smiles,
she wears a plastic butterfly, and the waiter gives
a purple egg to my child
for fun. Kindness abounds.

ii

Outside the windows the trees flow
past in a tender mist,
lightgreen & moist with buds

What I see though is the black trunks,
a detail from Breughel:
the backs of three men returning
from the hunt, their hounds following,
stark lines against the snow.

Damside

This used to be a dam;
now everything thrown
in washes over, continuous
and shining like hair.

The children scramble on the rim.
For them it's something for fishing
in and spitting into.
They trail barbed hooks in the water,
jigging for some doomed mouth.

We walk downstream
and up again. Pinecones and the first green
antennae spiralling through the stubble
by the pathside, wet breadcrusts
and greasy rubbish
that the just-born flies revel in.

The river's brown
and not something you'd drink
unless you thought you were dying.

If this were a poem I'd trust the river,
kneel and cup my hands
around its liquid ice, its ozone-
blue. If this were a poem you'd live forever.

As it is, I can offer you
only this poor weather:
my chilled hands, the fragments
of a noon in early spring,
an east wind which includes
both of us, and the stained river,
a prayer, a sewer, a prayer.

Last Poem

Tonight words fall away from me like shed clothing
thrown casually on the floor as if there's no
tomorrow, and there's no tomorrow.

One day halfway up the mountain or down the freeway,
air in any case whistling by,
you stop climbing or driving and know you will never get there.

I lie on a blue sofa and suck icecubes
while my friends and the friends of my friends and women
I hardly know get cancer.
There's one a week, one a minute; we all discuss it.

I'm a plague worker, I brush finger to finger,
hoping it's not catching, wondering how to say
goodbye gracefully and not merely snivel.
There are small mercies, granted, but not many.

Meanwhile I sit here futureless with you:
in one second something will wrench like a string or a zipper
or time will slide on itself like the granite sides of a fissure
and houses, chairs, lovers collapse in a long tremor.

That's your hand sticking out of the rubble.
I touch it, you're still living;
to have this happen I would give anything,
to keep you alive with me despite the wreckage.

I hold this hand as if waiting for the rescue
and that one action shines like pure luck.
Because there's nothing more I can do I do nothing.

What we're talking about is a table and two glasses,
two hands, a candle, and outside the curtained window
a charred landscape with the buildings and trees still smouldering.
Each poem is my last and so is this one.

MARGARET ATWOOD

Books

Double Persephone, 1961

The Circle Game, 1966

The Animals in That Country, 1968

The Edible Woman (novel), 1969

The Journals of Susanna Moodie, 1970

Procedures for Underground, 1970

Power Politics, 1972

Surfacing (novel), 1972

Survival (criticism), 1972

You Are Happy, 1974

Lady Oracle (novel), 1976

Selected Poems 1965–1975, 1976

Two-headed Poems, 1978

Up in the Tree, 1978

Life Before Man (novel), 1979

True Stories, 1981

Bodily Harm (novel), 1982

Second Words (criticism), 1982

Dancing Girls and Other Stories, 1982

Murder in the Dark (short prose), 1983

Bluebeard's Egg and Other Stories, 1986

The Handmaid's Tale (novel), 1986

Selected Poems II: Poems Selected and New: 1976–1986, 1987

Criticism, Interview

Barbara Rigney, *Madness and Sexual Politics in the Feminist Novel*, 1978; Arnold E. Davidson, ed., *The Art of Margaret Atwood*, 1981; Sherrill B. Grace, ed., *Margaret Atwood: Language, Text, and System*, 1983; Jerome Rosenberg, *Margaret Atwood*, 1984; Frank Davey, *Margaret Atwood: A Feminist Poetics*, 1984; Earl G. Ingersoll, "Evading the Pigeonholers: A Conversation with Margaret Atwood," *Midwest Quarterly* (Summer 1987).

Russell
Edson
(b. 1935)

C oming across the work of Russell Edson for the first time, the reader is likely to wonder, are these poems or aren't they? Or, whatever they are, how do they manage to be so simple and mysterious at once? What forces are unleashed through them? One way out of this befuddlement is to read the pieces aloud to others. People will gradually begin to laugh, steadily, helplessly, realizing they are in the grip of something both ferocious and serene, something that reminds them of games of logic or conundrums.

No discussion of Edson should go very far without recalling that he is a student of philosophy, with a love for argument about large questions. He feels that human intelligence is born out of a vast mindlessness and that therefore, like Kafka, we must look upon our situation as absurd. He builds his texts on this notion, calling them "islands of memory surrounded by nothing." Nor can one ignore the form he has been working with, passionately and relentlessly, for the past twenty-five years. From early collections that he designed and printed himself (he is an accomplished printmaker), to the later work issued by major publishers, Edson has, as he says, been singularly devoted to "feeding and caring for" the prose poem, a term that critics have settled on but one with which he himself is not entirely comfortable. In revealing and funny interviews, letters, and essays—especially the important "Portrait of the Writer as a Fat Man," from which most of the quotes used here are taken—he has had much to say about the fable form he has inherited, from Aesop on down to such other modern masters as George Ade and Thurber.

Central to his unique vision of the fable is his belief that the writer must "grow his own writing, his own meditation." Meditation is a useful term for what Edson is up to, but in a typically Edsonian gesture he immediately qualifies his remark to mean "the shape of a meditation, upon which surface pictures and speculations play." Underlying this is a preference for prose that is free from the self-consciousness of poetry, "a prose more compact than the storyteller's, removed from the formalities of *literature*." With no formal schooling to speak of, having learned to draw and printmake first and foremost (Edson's father was a well-known cartoonist), largely self-taught in language and literature, Edson has virtually isolated himself in his home in Connecticut with only occasional forays into the world of poetry readings, lecture circuits, and teaching. This lifestyle has provided him with a certain freedom to grow on his own, and he adds that he even desires to be free from himself, his own expectations of where his work might lead.

This isolation has led him to texts that depend entirely on their own geometries, proceeding as they do from their own givens to their own proofs, exploring inner life for itself and not for "private expression or public anger," which Edson feels poetry has fallen prey to. He speaks with fervor of a shared responsibility for "imagining the universe," for mapping "the vague descriptions of the mind drifting through its own interior." His characters often maneuver their way through these pieces, from the old captain in "The Pilot," whose room has become his ship, to the odd folk in "The Wheelbarrow," who steer their cows around. Edson keeps his language simple and his images direct, so that "the reader comes to recognitions long before consciousness of what has happened sets in." A key word is "intuition," and a key volume *The Intuitive Journey and Other Works* (1976), from which some of the texts presented here are taken. But even intuition is not enough, Edson feels, unless it is driven by the humor of "the deep, uncomfortable metaphor." Such humor not only will get us to laugh but will likely sink us in deep reservoirs of sadness. In "The Fall" the young man's parents conclude he is right, that is, they take him literally: "But his parents said look it is fall." It is too late to go back, once we accept the given; the man has told his parents he _is_ a tree. The "situation" can only advance, inexorably, toward its logical conclusion. Edson's genius lies in tracking the emotional formations that have a compact psychological life of their own. The parents say things like "then go" and "do not grow" and "as your roots," which bespeak their admonishing power and control. The life has long left their son when he says, "I was fooling I am not a tree. . . ." Edson concentrates events that soon reach a peak on which all reconciliation is shattered. He is right to disclaim those formal means for developing pieces that other poets rely on (e.g., mood, tone, and sound), settling instead for "the rough vision of discovery" we already feel upon reading the first line of a text by Edson.

Edson says he often works from first lines, the full meaning of which he's not sure of, but generally senses something "quaint and horrible at once about them" (from an essay on "Counting Sheep"). Second lines come "obbligato to the first, as attempts to repair the loss of scale" (that the sheep have suffered, in this instance), and further lines come as logical responses to the moves on the board. Moving in an opposite direction from the surrealists, who used irrational language to scorn rational thought, Edson keeps finding perfectly rational language to construct his irrational scenes. He can take on the nonsense of his stories because the language itself makes so much sense. Against much contemporary poetry that seems to insist on lack of content, Edson's style is to make something of nothing, to pull a whole little story out of an odd, dreamlike recollection of how something might have evolved: "I was combing some long hair coming out of a tree" ("In the Forest"); "A man had just married an automobile" ("The Automobile"); "A huge shoe mounts up from the horizon" ("The Wounded Breakfast"). Recently he put this style into Edson-like perspective: "We ask not necessarily to understand, in fact in most cases we'd rather not, we ask only to believe. . . . Art makes us believe what we cannot understand."

_SF_

The Fall

There was a man who found two leaves and came indoors holding them out saying to his parents that he was a tree.

To which they said then go into the yard and do not grow in the living-room as your roots may ruin the carpet.

He said I was fooling I am not a tree and he dropped his leaves.

But his parents said look it is fall.

In the Forest

I was combing some long hair coming out of a tree . . .
I had noticed long hair coming out of a tree, and a comb on the ground by the roots of that same tree.
The hair and the comb seemed to belong together. Not so much that the hair needed combing, but the reassurance of the comb being drawn through it . . .
I stood in the gloom and silence that many forests have in the pages of fiction, combing the thick womanly hair, the mammal-warm hair; even as the evening slowly took the forest into night . . .

A Journey Through the Moonlight

In sleep when an old man's body is no longer aware of its boundaries, and lies flattened by gravity like a mere of wax in its bed . . . It drips down to the floor and moves there like a tear down a cheek . . . Under the back door into the silver meadow, like a pool of sperm, frosty under the moon, as if in his first nature, boneless and absurd.

The moon lifts him up into its white field, a cloud shaped like an old man, porous with stars.
He floats through high dark branches, a corpse tangled in a tree on a river.

The Wheelbarrow

Cows they had, many, like heavy clouds drifting in the meadow.
But they didn't have the wheelbarrow that they thought they had been promised. They had studied catalogs and prayed; but no wheel barrow.

So at last they tied wheels to the front hooves of a cow and had a couple of stout gentlemen lift the hind legs and wheel the cow about the farm.

Although they admitted the cow made a very poor wheelbarrow, a make-do at best, still, they had done long enough without a wheelbarrow not to really need one, and could now relax in decorative values, for, as they said, time has long decayed utility from actual need.

The other cows look around at this new farm equipment; then turning they drift out like heavy clouds into the meadow.

The Pilot

Up in a dirty window in a dark room is a star which an old man can see. He looks at it. He can see it. It is the star of the room; an electrical freckle that has fallen out of his head and gotten stuck in the dirt on the window.

He thinks he can steer by that star. He thinks he can use the back of a chair as a ship's wheel to pilot this room through the night.

He says to himself, brave Captain, are you afraid?

Yes, I am afraid; I am not so brave.

Be brave, my Captain.

And all night the old man steers his room through the dark . . .

An Old Man's Son

There was an old man who had a kite for a son, which he would let up into the air attached to a string, when he had need to be alone.

. . . And would watch this high bloom of himself, as something distant that will be close again . . .

The Wounded Breakfast

A huge shoe mounts up from the horizon, squealing and grinding forward on small wheels, even as a man sitting to breakfast on his veranda is suddenly engulfed in a great shadow almost the size of the night.

He looks up and sees a huge shoe ponderously mounting out of the earth. Up in the unlaced ankle-part an old woman stands at a helm behind the great tongue curled forward; the thick laces dragging like ships' rope on the ground as the huge thing squeals and grinds forward; children everywhere, they look from the shoelace holes, they crowd about the old woman, even as she pilots this huge shoe over the earth . . .

Soon the huge shoe is descending the opposite horizon, a monstrous snail squealing and grinding into the earth . . .

The man turns to his breakfast again, but sees it's been wounded, the yolk of one of his eggs is bleeding . . .

The Automobile

A man had just married an automobile.

But I mean to say, said his father, that the automobile is not a person because it is something different.

For instance, compare it to your mother. Do you see how it is different from your mother? Somehow it seems wider, doesn't it? And besides, your mother wears her hair differently.

You ought to try to find something in the world that looks like mother.

I have mother, isn't that enough of a thing that looks like mother? Do I have to gather more mothers?

They are all old ladies who do not in the least excite any wish to procreate, said the son.

But you cannot procreate with an automobile, said father.

The son shows father an ignition key. See, here is a special penis which does with the automobile as the man with the woman; and the automobile gives birth to a place far from this place, dropping its puppy miles as it goes.

Does that make me a grandfather? said father.

That makes you where you are when I am far away, said the son.

Father and mother watch an automobile with a *just married* sign on it growing smaller in a road.

Counting Sheep

A scientist has a test tube full of sheep. He wonders if he should try to shrink a pasture for them.

They are like grains of rice.

He wonders if it is possible to shrink something out of existence.

He wonders if the sheep are aware of their tininess, if they have any sense of scale? Perhaps they just think the test tube is a glass barn . . .

He wonders what he should do with them; they certainly have less meat and wool than ordinary sheep. Has he reduced their commercial value?

He wonders if they could be used as a substitute for rice, a sort of woolly rice . . . ?

He wonders if he just shouldn't rub them into a red paste between his fingers?

He wonders if they're breeding, or if any of them have died.

He puts them under a microscope and falls asleep counting them . . .

The Death of an Angel

Being witless it said no prayer. Being pure it withered like a flower.

They could not tell its sex. It had neither anal nor genital opening.

The autopsy revealed no viscera, neither flesh nor bone. It was stuffed with pages from old Bibles and cotton.

When they opened the skull it played *Tales from the Vienna Woods;* instead of brain they found a vagina and a penis, testicles and an anus, packed in sexual hair.

Ah, that's better! cried one of the doctors.

The Amateur

There was a man who wanted to be an amateur animal. He could never hope to be a professional. Besides, he had rather keep his amateur standing in case the animal should become extinct. In that case he could quickly switch and pretend to know nothing of his former animal.
Then, if questioned, he could say, me? no, I'm just an amateur.
Are you sure you're not an extinct professional?
I swear . . .

The Long Picnic

An official document blows through a forest between the trees over the heads of the picnickers.
It is the end of summer, and there is only the snow to be looked forward to. The photosynthetic world is collapsing.
Those who have been picnicking all summer in the forest see that their food has gone bad. The blackberry jam is tar, the picnic baskets are full of bones wrapped in old newspapers.
A young man turns to his sweetheart. She's an old woman with white hair; her head bobs on her neck.
The picnickers try to catch the document as it flies over their heads. But the wind carries it away.
What is written on it is that *the summer is over* . . .

A Cottage in the Wood

He has built himself a cottage in a wood, near where the insect rubs its wings in song.

Yet, without measure, or proper sense of scale, he has made the cottage too small. He realizes this when only his hand will fit through the door. He tries the stairs to the second floor with his fingers, but his arm wedges in the entrance. He wonders how he will cook his dinner. He might get his hands through the kitchen windows. But even so, he will not be able to cook enough on such a tiny stove.

He shall also lie unsheltered in the night, even though a bed with its covers turned down waits for him in the cottage.

He lies down and curls himself around the cottage, listening to the insect that rubs its wings in song.

Darwin Descending

Do you believe in evolution, oh, thing of easy answers?

Do you believe Darwin was descended from a thing more jaw than head?

. . . Imagine an early Darwin roving the trees, nostalgic for the future . . .

A female Darwin slaps him on the back of his small, but promising head; whatcha thinking about, ya brainless brute? she peeps.

I was just wondering about the origin of species, he twitters.

You haven't the brains of a modern chimpanzee, she screeches.

Yeah, but I think that's where I'm evolving; a large-brained primate with an opposable thumb, with which I shall oppose all of nature, twitters Darwin.

Oh, stop it, you're hardly on to tools; why, you haven't even fooled with fire yet, she hoots.

Yeah, but one day, Darwinette, I'm gonna talk good, and even learn how to write *talking* with a fountain pen . . .

Promises, promises . . .

But, as we all know, Darwin did descend.

It was at a cocktail party, and he had been roving the upstairs halls looking for the indoor plumbing.

And now he was returning via the carpeted stairway.

Everyone turned and applauded: look, the descent of Darwin!

NOTES

A Journey Through the Moonlight. "Mere" (in the second line) has the archaic meaning of "lake" or "pond"—akin to Latin *mare*, sea.

RUSSELL EDSON

Books

The Very Thing That Happens, 1964

What a Man Can See, 1969

The Childhood of an Equestrian, 1973

The Clam Theater, 1973

The Reason Why the Closet-Man Is Never Sad, 1974

The Falling Sickness: Four Plays, 1975

The Intuitive Journey and Other Works, 1976

The Wounded Breakfast, 1985

Essay

"Portrait of the Writer as a Fat Man: Some Subjective Ideas or Notions on the Care & Feeding of Prose Poems," in *A FIELD Guide to Contemporary Poetry and Poetics*, ed. Friebert and Young, 1980.

Michael
Harper
(b. 1938)

Stephen Friebert

Michael Harper grew up in a home in Brooklyn where musicians like Billie Holiday regularly came and went, bringing their blues and jazz. When the Harper family moved to Los Angeles in 1951, he started a dizzying collection of jobs and school experiences that saw him trying everything from postal clerking to playing professional football under an assumed name. Along the way he managed to read voraciously and write a good deal, trying his hand first on plays and fiction. He earned degrees from Los Angeles State and the University of Iowa, where he studied at the Writers' Workshop. In the 1960s he began publishing poems and journeyed to far-off places to deepen his understanding of the poetry and culture of other lands, the better to mirror "the wealth of human materials in my own life, its ethnic richness, complexity of language and stylization, the tension between stated moral idealism and brutal historical realities."

Working with landscapes rich in history and lore, he shapes his texts toward figurative moments marked by images of personal pain and loss. To arrive at these images, he sometimes strains after the right turn of phrase, but there are no false notes on where he stands, who he is, what he has to say, and how he says it. While Harper writes as passionately as anyone of the threats to our civilization and of our duty to struggle, to resist, his most affecting poems deal directly with family matters and center around the loss of a son (see especially "Nightmare Begins Responsibility" and "We Assume: On the Death of Our Son, Reuben Masai Harper"). This loss is a nightmare that Harper confronts again and again, in some kind of "ritualistic search for the presence and images of (all our?) children 'torn away,' " as the critic Robert Stepto sees it ("After Modernism, After Hibernation: Michael Harper, Robert Hayden, and Jay Wright"). "The Dance of the Elephants" is a poignant example of how Harper looks with bifocal vision at the horrors of holocaust the world would just as soon forget, and the ironic comfort our children find in the tiny possessions they take along for what may be the final journey. Our humanity persists, the poem suggests, in our taking with us whatever words and objects are almost ours, even to the grave. Before Harper will tackle this powerful, even debilitating subject matter, he always starts by "finding a pattern for the poem at conception, a means of balancing form and content in formal rather than traditional lines" (from an essay on "Grandfather").

The ballad form suggested itself for "Grandfather," and of late Harper has been writing more and more ballads. Originally intended for preserving critical information orally, the ballad, or story-song, is dramatic and economical and thus attracts a poet like Harper, who has a lot of misinformation to correct—in the case of "Grandfather," the warped picture of a black family that D. W. Griffith's classic film *The Birth of a Nation* presented—and a lot of new information to pass on about such seemingly diverse matters as music, economics, railroads (above and underground, Harper is quick to note), history, race relations, hospital rooms, landfills, and rocking chairs. One of his strengths is his ability to bring much of this information together under one roof and send it spinning by like a carousel of human history. In his words, the struggle is "to portray clear images of heroic stances against adversity." A closer look reveals that Harper turns the ballad form inside out, fashioning of it a modern instrument that can carry today's tunes; his stories focus on several (not single) crucial episodes at once, begin frequently after (not before) the action that has resulted in catastrophe, and play back events in fractured fragments that match the complexity of the issues. But whatever the final forms of the poems, Harper makes sure he includes a persuasive amount of "circumstantial" detail, and uses subjective attitudes if he must. All this parallels the way contemporary black musicians play with traditional forms to discover dimensions hitherto unexplored. New forms emerge that are not tied to stock themes and standard rhetoric, with their rhythms loosened to accommodate human speech alongside poetic diction: "A woman who'd lost her first son / consoled us with an angel gone ahead / to pray for our family— / gone into that sky / seeking oxygen, / gone into autopsy, / a fine brown powdered sugar, a disposable cremation."

While the titles of Harper's major collections underline the seriousness of his mission—*History Is Your Own Heartbeat* (1971), *Debridement* (1973), *Nightmare Begins Responsibility* (1975), and the selected poems, *Images of a Kin* (1977)—many of the poems strike a beneficent chord, and there is a lighter side to his art that is just as affecting for the ways he can tune a tiny song to the sounds of others who have come before.

SF

The Dance of the Elephants

Part I

The trains ran through the eleven
nights it took to vacate the town;
relatives and lovers tacked in a row
on the button-board sidings,
wails of children tossed in a pile
wails of women tossed in a salad
to be eaten with soap and a rinse.
Those who took all they had to the borders,
those who took their bottles
three centuries old, those who
thought only of language, the written
word, are forgiven.
One daughter is riding on the train
above her mother, above her mother,
into the tunnel of the elephants.

Culture tells us most about its animals
singing our children asleep, or let them
slip into a room as smoothly as
refrigeration.

Part II

To be comforted by Swiss music
is a toy elephant in a box,
skimming the nickelplated air.
Beethoven's a passion dance
forgotten in a stamped coin—
it is magic—it is magic—

We dance the old beast round the fireplace,
coal engines fuming in a row,
elephant chimes in a toy rain—
human breath skimming the air.

We skim the air—
it is magic—the engines
smelling the chimes,
Beethoven chiming the magic—
we escape it on a train.

Sung in America,
the song some telescopic sight,
a nickelplated cream,
a small girl cuddles her elephant,
the song in the streets
leaping the train windows,
and what love as the elephant chimes.

Homage to the New World

Surrounded by scientists in a faculty
house, the trees wet with hot rain,
grass thickening under the trees,
welcomers come, ones and twos,
gifts of shoehorns, soap, combs,
half a subscription to the courier,
some news about changing
plates, the nearest market,
how to pick up the trash, a gallon
of milk twice a week, ok?

On the third day here,
a friend came in the night to announce
a phone call and a message,
and heard the shell go in
and the rifle cocking,
our next-door animal-vet neighbor,
and cried out, "Don't shoot,"
and walked away to remember the phone
and the message, the crickets,
and the rifle cocking,
grass and hot rain.

I write in the night air
of the music of Coltrane,
the disc of his voice in this
contralto heart, my wife;
so what! Kind of Blue,
these fatherless whites
come to consciousness
with a history of the gun—
the New World, if misery had
a voice, would be a rifle cocking.

for Agnes & Ed Brandabur

Kin

When news came that your mother'd
smashed her hip, both feet caught
in rungs of the banquet table,
our wedding rebroken on the memory
of the long lake of silence
when the stones of her body
broke as an Irish fence of stones,
I saw your wet dugs drag
with the weight of our daughter
in the quick of her sleep
to another feeding;
then the shoulders dropped
their broken antenna branches
of fear at the knife
running the scars
which had borne into the colon
for the misspent enema,
the clubbed liver unclean
with the stones of the gall bladder,
and the broken arch of hip
lugging you to the lake,
the dough inner tube of lading
swollen with innerpatching.

I pick you up from the floor
of your ringing fears, the floor
where the photographs you have worked
into the cool sky of the gray you love,
and you are back at the compost pile
where the vegetables burn,
or swim in the storm of your childhood,
when your father egged you on with his
open machinery, the exhaust choking your sisters,
and your sisters choked still.

Now his voice stops you in accusation,
and the years pile up on themselves
in the eggs of your stretched sons,
one born on his birthday, both dead.
I pull you off into the sanctuary
of conciliation, of quiet tactics,
the uttered question, the referral,

which will quiet the condition you have seen
in your mother's shadow, the crutches
inching in the uncut grass,
and the worn body you will carry
as your own birthmark of his scream.

Grandfather

In 1915 my grandfather's
neighbors surrounded his house
near the dayline he ran
on the Hudson
in Catskill, NY
and thought they'd burn
his family out
in a movie they'd just seen
and be rid of his kind:
the death of a lone black
family is *the Birth*
of a Nation,
or so they thought.
His 5'4" waiter gait
quenched the white jacket smile
he'd brought back from watered
polish of my father
on the turning seats,
and he asked his neighbors
up on his thatched porch
for the first blossom of fire
that would burn him down.

They went away, his nation,
spittooning their torched necks
in the shadows of the riverboat
they'd seen, posse decomposing;
and I see him on Sutter
with white bag from your
restaurant, challenged by his first
grandson to a foot-race
he will win in white clothes.

I see him as he buys galoshes
for his railed yard near Mineo's
metal shop, where roses jump
as the el circles his house

toward Brooklyn, where his rain fell;
and I see cigar smoke in his eyes,
chocolate Madison Square Garden chews
he breaks on his set teeth,
stitched up after cancer,
the great white nation immovable
as his weight wilts
and he is on a porch
that won't hold my arms,
or the legs of the race run
forwards, or the film
played backwards on his grandson's eyes.

Nightmare Begins Responsibility

I place these numbed wrists to the pane
watching white uniforms whisk over
him in the tube-kept
prison
fear what they will do in experiment
watch my gloved stickshifting gasolined hands
breathe *boxcar-information-please* infirmary tubes
distrusting white-pink mending paperthin
silkened end hairs, distrusting tubes
shrunk in his *trunk-skincapped*
shaven head, in thighs
distrusting-white-hands-picking-baboon-light
on this son who will not make his second night
of this wardstrewn intensive airpocket
where his father's asthmatic
hymns of *night-train,* train done gone
his mother can only know that he has flown
up into essential calm unseen corridor
going boxscarred home, *mamaborn, sweetsonchild*
gonedowntown into *researchtestingwarehousebatteryacid*
mama-son-done-gone/me telling her 'nother
train tonight, no music, no breathstroked
heartbeat in my infinite distrust of them:

and of my distrusting self
white-doctor-who-breathed-for-him-all-night
say it for two sons gone,
say nightmare, say it loud
panebreaking heartmadness:
nightmare begins responsibility.

We Assume: On the Death of
Our Son, Reuben Masai Harper

We assume
that in 28 hours,
lived in a collapsible isolette,
you learned to accept pure oxygen
as the natural sky;
the scant shallow breaths
that filled those hours
cannot, did not make you fly—
but dreams were there
like crooked palmprints on
the twin-thick windows of the nursery—
in the glands of your mother.

We assume
the sterile hands
drank chemicals in and out
from lungs opaque with mucus,
pumped your stomach,
eeked the bicarbonate in
crooked, green-winged veins,
out in a plastic mask;

A woman who'd lost her first son
consoled us with an angel gone ahead
to pray for our family—
gone into that sky
seeking oxygen,
gone into autopsy,
a fine brown powdered sugar,
a disposable cremation:

We assume
you did not know we loved you.

Landfill

Loads of trash and we light the match;
what can be in a cardboard box
can be in the bed of the pickup
and you jostle the containers onto the side road.
A match for this little road,
and a match for your son riding next to you firing,
and a match for the hole in the land filled with trees.

I will not mention concrete because theirs is the meshed
wire of concrete near the docks, and the concrete
of burned trees cut in cords of change-sawing,
and we will light a match to this too.

Work in anger for the final hour of adjustment
to the surveyors, and to the lawyers speaking of squatting,
and the land burning to no one.
This building of scrap metal, high as the storm that will
break it totally in the tornado dust,
and to the animals that have lived in the wheathay of their bedding
will beg for the cutting edge, or the ax,
or the electrified fencing that warms them in summer rain.

My son coughs on the tarred scrubble of cut trees,
and is cursed by the firelight, and beckoned to me to the pickup,
and washed off the soot of his sootskinned face,
and the dirt at the corners of my daughter's mouth will be
    trenchmouth;
and the worn moccasin of my woman will tear into the bulbed big toe,
and the blood will be black as the compost pile burning,
and the milk from her dugs will be the balm for the trenchmouth,
as she wipes her mouth from the smoke of the landfill filled with fire,
and these loads of trash will be the ashes for her to take:
and will be taken to the landfill, and filled, and filled.

Last Affair: Bessie's Blues Song

Disarticulated
arm torn out,
large veins cross
her shoulder intact,
her tourniquet
her blood in all-white big bands:

Can't you see
what love and heartache's done to me
I'm not the same as I used to be
this is my last affair

Mail truck or parked car
in the fast lane,
afloat at forty-three
on a Mississippi road,
Two-hundred-pound muscle on her ham bone,
'nother nigger dead 'fore noon:

Can't you see
what love and heartache's done to me
I'm not the same as I used to be
this is my last affair

Fifty-dollar record
cut the vein in her neck,
fool about her money
toll her black train wreck,
white press missed her fun'ral
in the same stacked deck:

Can't you see
what love and heartache's done to me
I'm not the same as I used to be
this is my last affair

Loved a little blackbird
heard she could sing,
Martha in her vineyard
pestle in her spring,
Bessie had a bad mouth
made my chimes ring:

Can't you see
what love and heartache's done to me
I'm not the same as I used to be
this is my last affair

NOTES

Grandfather. "Sutter" is a street name.
Last Affair: Bessie's Blues Song. "Bessie" was the great blues singer Bessie Smith.

MICHAEL HARPER

Books

Dear John, Dear Coltrane, 1970
History Is Your Own Heartbeat, 1971
Song: I Want a Witness, 1972
Debridement, 1973

Nightmare Begins Responsibility, 1975
Images of Kin, 1977
Healing Song for the Inner Ear, 1985

Criticism, Interviews

J. O'Brien, ed., *Interviews with Black Writers*, 1973; Robert Stepto, "After Modernism, After Hibernation," in *Chant of Saints*, 1979; James Randall, "An Interview with Michael Harper," *Ploughshares* 7, no. 1 (1981).

Sylvia
Plath
(1932–1963)

Rollie McKenna

T he career of Sylvia Plath, a deeply unhappy and greatly gifted poet, was over before most people realized it had begun. Her major collection, *Ariel* (1965), appeared more than a year after she took her life in London. There are two other posthumous collections, *Crossing the Water* and *Winter Trees*. Only her first book of poems, *The Colossus* (1960), appeared while she was still alive. To have a poet of brilliance come to notice in such circumstances was both disorienting and fascinating to most readers, and it is not surprising that a kind of cult has grown up around Sylvia Plath. She has been variously seen as a feminist martyr, as a type of the romantic prodigy who burns out and dies young, and as a psychotic whose poetry was a helpless, aberrant offshoot of her condition. While there is a grain of truth in each of these views, the actuality is more complex than any single label would suggest, though no less melancholy, and we may never fully understand how and why Sylvia Plath had to destroy herself.

What does seem clear from the poems is that she lived on a knife-edge, in the presence of a tremendous attraction to death and nothingness. This attraction informs her poems, giving them spiritual strength and adventurousness on the one hand, and psychological dislocation and occasional perversity on the other. To read Plath is to be first dazzled by her technical virtuosity and the flashing reach of her imagination; then, as the constant death wish, the romance of suicide, becomes clear, the reader is apt to react with dismay. Eventually, one adjusts to the intense negativity and tries to balance it with what is positive in the poems. The present selection aims to reflect the full range of her imaginative preoccupations without losing sight of the fact that her finest work is balanced between her fascination with death and her ability to observe and celebrate life. Her shrillest poems (e.g., "Daddy" and "Lady Lazarus") are not included here; their frequent appearance in anthologies has already tended to obscure her best accomplishment.

The first two poems of this selection, early pieces from *The Colossus,* show how her balance can operate. In "The Manor Garden" a mother addresses her unborn child, and the poem is marked by her consciousness that birth is also the onset of dying. Similarly, in "Watercolor of Grantchester Meadows," nature seems quaint and wholesome to the undergraduates boating in the springtime countryside, but the speaker is aware of the way that nature implies death and destruction too, and sees the students' black gowns as foreshadowing the night when "The owl shall stoop from his turret, the rat cry out."

These comparatively early poems also show Sylvia Plath's gifts for musical language and strong, resonant images, gifts she shared with her husband, Ted Hughes, the English poet, and her sometime teacher, Robert Lowell. The poems from *Ariel* (the rest of our selection, with the exception of "Winter Trees") suggest how distinctively she began to use those gifts in her last phase. "Sheep in Fog" is remarkable for the way it compresses the vision of "Watercolor" into something more powerful and mysterious, a tranquil landscape through which a dimension beyond life, both threatening and enticing, is thrillingly glimpsed. It is also an astonishing sequence, eccentric but absolutely precise in movement, a deftly sketched metaphor for existence—are we not all sheep in fog?—in which each detail rises inexorably but surprisingly from the last. Imagination, the image-making faculty, is the poet's special province, and the gift of thinking in images, sequences of astonishing links and leaps, is one that marks the greatest poetic talents. The sureness of "Sheep in Fog," a quality found again and again in *Ariel,* is perhaps Sylvia Plath's strongest hallmark as a poet. Sometimes, as in "The Couriers" and "Words," her track can be hard to follow, but we learn to trust her imagination as it moves among the things of this world, haunted and questing, for its sense of deep relations and illuminating connections. She sees the world with sharp clarity—the poppies in "Poppies in July" are flames, then mouths, then skirts, then wounds—and its color and vitality hurt her until she longs for transparency and nothingness. Agonizing, to have such a gift for observation and to receive so little solace from it!

Several of these poems, carrying on from "The Manor Garden," are about motherhood: "Morning Song," "The Night Dances," "Nick and the Candlestick." Again, their great originality with the subject can be seen to stem partly from the poet's consciousness of death in life. The mother's bemusement at the child's beauty and simplicity is colored by a sense of the coexistence and appeal of nothingness; birth, growth, and innocence are shadowed by their opposites. At the same time, that tension of opposites would mean nothing without its brilliant embodiment in poetic imagery: the watch, the museum, the cloud and puddle, the cow and cat and balloons of "Morning Song"; the cosmic trance of "The Night Dances," where lilies and snowflakes interact with comets and stars, all of them summoned to reflect a baby's random joy of movement; and the uncanny cave, both tomb and womb, that is so hauntingly and convincingly set forth in "Nick and the Candlestick."

Readers who are curious about Sylvia Plath's thirty-one years of life can learn more from her autobiographical novel, *The Bell Jar* (1963), from the fascinating collection of her letters, and from her published journals. But the best homage we can pay to her poetry is to recognize it as the accomplishment of a poet whose control and balance, however precarious, enabled her to produce poems of great beauty under tremendous pressure, like carbon turning to diamond. The existence of these poems is independent now of the life that produced them, and they can enter our own lives, becoming our strange and precious possessions, and troubling our complacency.

DY

Watercolor of Grantchester Meadows

There, spring lambs jam the sheepfold. In air
Stilled, silvered as water in a glass
Nothing is big or far.
The small shrew chitters from its wilderness
Of grassheads and is heard.
Each thumb-size bird
Flits nimble-winged in thickets, and of good color.

Cloudwrack and owl-hollowed willows slanting over
The bland Granta double their white and green
World under the sheer water
And ride that flux at anchor, upside down.
The punter sinks his pole.
In Byron's pool
Cattails part where the tame cygnets steer.

It is a country on a nursery plate.
Spotted cows revolve their jaws and crop
Red clover or gnaw beetroot
Bellied on a nimbus of sun-glazed buttercup.
Hedging meadows of benign
Arcadian green
The blood-berried hawthorn hides its spines with white.

Droll, vegetarian, the water rat
Saws down a reed and swims from his limber grove,
While the students stroll or sit,
Hands laced, in a moony indolence of love—
Black-gowned, but unaware
How in such mild air
The owl shall stoop from his turret, the rat cry out.

The Manor Garden

The fountains are dry and the roses over.
Incense of death. Your day approaches.
The pears fatten like little buddhas.
A blue mist is dragging the lake.

You move through the era of fishes,
The smug centuries of the pig—
Head, toe and finger
Come clear of the shadow. History

Nourishes these broken flutings,
These crowns of acanthus,
And the crow settles her garments.
You inherit white heather, a bee's wing,

Two suicides, the family wolves,
Hours of blankness. Some hard stars
Already yellow the heavens.
The spider on its own string

Crosses the lake. The worms
Quit their usual habitations.
The small birds converge, converge
With their gifts to a difficult borning.

Morning Song

Love set you going like a fat gold watch.
The midwife slapped your footsoles, and your bald cry
Took its place among the elements.

Our voices echo, magnifying your arrival. New statue.
In a drafty museum, your nakedness
Shadows our safety. We stand round blankly as walls.

I'm no more your mother
Than the cloud that distils a mirror to reflect its own slow
Effacement at the wind's hand.

All night your moth-breath
Flickers among the flat pink roses. I wake to listen:
A far sea moves in my ear.

One cry, and I stumble from bed, cow-heavy and floral
In my Victorian nightgown.
Your mouth opens clean as a cat's. The window square

Whitens and swallows its dull stars. And now you try
Your handful of notes;
The clear vowels rise like balloons.

Poppies in July

Little poppies, little hell flames,
Do you do no harm?

You flicker. I cannot touch you.
I put my hands among the flames. Nothing burns.

And it exhausts me to watch you
Flickering like that, wrinkly and clear red, like the skin of a mouth.

A mouth just bloodied.
Little bloody skirts!

There are fumes that I cannot touch.
Where are your opiates, your nauseous capsules?

If I could bleed, or sleep!—
If my mouth could marry a hurt like that!

Or your liquors seep to me, in this glass capsule,
Dulling and stilling.

But colourless. Colourless.

Ariel

Stasis in darkness.
Then the substanceless blue
Pour of tor and distances.

God's lioness,
How one we grow,
Pivot of heels and knees!—The furrow

Splits and passes, sister to
The brown arc
Of the neck I cannot catch,

Nigger-eye
Berries cast dark
Hooks—

Black sweet blood mouthfuls,
Shadows.
Something else

Hauls me through air—
Thighs, hair;
Flakes from my heels.

White
Godiva, I unpeel—
Dead hands, dead stringencies.

And now I
Foam to wheat, a glitter of seas.
The child's cry

Melts in the wall.
And I
Am the arrow,

The dew that flies
Suicidal, at one with the drive
Into the red

Eye, the cauldron of morning.

Poppies in October

Even the sun-clouds this morning cannot manage such skirts.
Nor the woman in the ambulance
Whose red heart blooms through her coat so astoundingly—

A gift, a love gift
Utterly unasked for
By a sky

Palely and flamily
Igniting its carbon monoxides, by eyes
Dulled to a halt under bowlers.

O my God, what am I
That these late mouths should cry open
In a forest of frost, in a dawn of cornflowers.

Nick and the Candlestick

I am a miner. The light burns blue.
Waxy stalactites
Drip and thicken, tears

The earthen womb
Exudes from its dead boredom.
Black bat airs

Wrap me, raggy shawls,
Cold homicides.
They weld to me like plums.

Old cave of calcium
Icicles, old echoer.
Even the newts are white,

Those holy Joes.
And the fish, the fish—
Christ! They are panes of ice,

A vice of knives,
A piranha
Religion, drinking

Its first communion out of my live toes.
The candle
Gulps and recovers its small altitude,

Its yellows hearten.
O love, how did you get here?
O embryo

Remembering, even in sleep,
Your crossed position.
The blood blooms clean

In you, ruby.
The pain
You wake to is not yours.

Love, love,
I have hung our cave with roses,
With soft rugs—

The last of Victoriana.
Let the stars
Plummet to their dark address,

Let the mercuric
Atoms that cripple drip
Into the terrible well,

You are the one
Solid the spaces lean on, envious.
You are the baby in the barn.

The Couriers

The word of a snail on the plate of a leaf?
It is not mine. Do not accept it.

Acetic acid in a sealed tin?
Do not accept it. It is not genuine.

A ring of gold with the sun in it?
Lies. Lies and a grief.

Frost on a leaf, the immaculate
Cauldron, talking and crackling

All to itself on the top of each
Of nine black Alps.

A disturbance in mirrors,
The sea shattering its grey one—

Love, love, my season.

The Night Dances

A smile fell in the grass.
Irretrievable!

And how will your night dances
Lose themselves. In mathematics?

Such pure leaps and spirals—
Surely they travel

The world forever, I shall not entirely
Sit emptied of beauties, the gift

Of your small breath, the drenched grass
Smell of your sleeps, lilies, lilies.

Their flesh bears no relation.
Cold folds of ego, the calla,

And the tiger, embellishing itself—
Spots, and a spread of hot petals.

The comets
Have such a space to cross,

Such coldness, forgetfulness.
So your gestures flake off—

Warm and human, then their pink light
Bleeding and peeling

Through the black amnesias of heaven.
Why am I given

These lamps, these planets
Falling like blessings, like flakes

Six-sided, white
On my eyes, my lips, my hair

Touching and melting.
Nowhere.

Death & Co.

Two, of course there are two.
It seems perfectly natural now—
The one who never looks up, whose eyes are lidded
And balled, like Blake's,
Who exhibits

The birthmarks that are his trademark—
The scald scar of water,
The nude
Verdigris of the condor.
I am red meat. His beak

Claps sidewise: I am not his yet.
He tells me how badly I photograph.
He tells me how sweet
The babies look in their hospital
Icebox, a simple

Frill at the neck,
Then the flutings of their Ionian
Death-gowns,
Then two little feet.
He does not smile or smoke.

The other does that,
His hair long and plausive.
Bastard
Masturbating a glitter,
He wants to be loved.

I do not stir.
The frost makes a flower,

The dew makes a star,
The dead bell,
The dead bell.

Somebody's done for.

Winter Trees

The wet dawn inks are doing their blue dissolve.
On their blotter of fog the trees
Seem a botanical drawing—
Memories growing, ring on ring,
A series of weddings.

Knowing neither abortions nor bitchery,
Truer than women,
They seed so effortlessly!
Tasting the winds, that are footless,
Waist-deep in history—

Full of wings, otherworldliness.
In this, they are Ledas.
O mother of leaves and sweetness
Who are these pietàs?
The shadows of ringdoves chanting, but easing nothing.

Sheep in Fog

The hills step off into whiteness.
People or stars
Regard me sadly, I disappoint them.

The train leaves a line of breath.
O slow
Horse the color of rust,

Hooves, dolorous bells—
All morning the
Morning has been blackening,

A flower left out.
My bones hold a stillness, the far
Fields melt my heart.

They threaten
To let me through to a heaven
Starless and fatherless, a dark water.

Words

Axes
After whose stroke the wood rings,
And the echoes!
Echoes travelling
Off from the center like horses.

The sap
Wells like tears, like the
Water striving
To re-establish its mirror
Over the rock

That drops and turns,
A white skull,
Eaten by weedy greens.
Years later I
Encounter them on the road—

Words dry and riderless,
The indefatigable hoof-taps.
While
From the bottom of the pool, fixed stars
Govern a life.

NOTES

Watercolor of Grantchester Meadows. A favorite boating spot for Cambridge students (e.g., Lord Byron), who pole long flat boats called punts. A cygnet is a young swan.

Ariel. The title is the name of a favorite horse, and the poem is an account of a horseback ride at dawn; but the glance at the name of Prospero's familiar spirit, agent of his magic, in Shakespeare's *The Tempest,* is surely intentional.

Nick and the Candlestick. Nick: the second of Sylvia Plath's and Ted Hughes's two children.

The Night Dances. The poem is spoken by a mother who is watching her baby's random movements as it sleeps in its crib.

Death & Co. "Like Blake's": one of the personifications of Death resembles the death mask of the poet William Blake. The pair seem to be visiting the speaker in a hospital ward.

SYLVIA PLATH

Books

The Colossus, 1960

The Bell Jar (novel, written under the name of Victoria Lucas), 1963

Ariel, 1965

Crossing the Water, 1971

Winter Trees, 1972

Johnny Panic and The Bible of Dreams: Short Stories, Prose and Diary Excerpts (edited by Ted Hughes), 1979

The Collected Poems (edited by Ted Hughes), 1981

The Journals of Sylvia Plath, 1982

Letters, Criticism

Charles Newman, ed., *The Art of Sylvia Plath*, 1970; A. Alvarez, *The Savage God*, 1972; Eileen Aird, *Sylvia Plath: Her Life and Work*, 1973; Aurelia Plath, ed., *Letters Home*, 1975; Edward Butscher, *Sylvia Plath: Method and Madness*, 1976; David Holbrook, *Sylvia Plath: Poetry and Existence*, 1976; Judith Kroll, *Chapters in a Mythology: The Poetry of Sylvia Plath*, 1976; Gary Lane, ed., *Sylvia Plath: New Views on the Poetry*, 1979; Jon Rosenblatt, *Sylvia Plath: The Poetry of Initiation*, 1979; Linda Wagner, ed., *Critical Essays on Sylvia Plath*, 1984; Edward Butscher, ed., *Sylvia Plath: The Woman and the Work*, 1985; Linda Wagner-Martin, *Sylvia Plath: A Biography*, 1987; Harold Bloom, ed., *Sylvia Plath*, 1988.

Stanley
Plumly
(b. 1939)

Brigitta Shroyer

W hat could an iron lung and a wildflower have in common? Nothing, you might say, until you begin to read Stanley Plumly. This poet hymns unlikely things, finding beauty and grace where they were overlooked, so that a frightful contraption like an iron lung can become a miraculous vehicle for "out-of-the-body travel," the major metaphor as well as the title of Plumly's finest collection (1977). In the same way, wildflowers we may have scarcely noticed, like meadow-rue and peppergrass, are shown to have the same kind of unlikely and stirring beauty. Stirring, perhaps, *because* unlikely, rescued from a modest oblivion to enhance our sense of life.

One way that Plumly gets us to see his objects of praise in new ways is by strange and compelling associations. In "Out-of-the-Body Travel" the father's soulful violin playing and his careful slaughtering of a bull are seen as the same act, and as they mirror each other they also express the boy's ambivalence and shape the images of distance and closeness, harm and tenderness, that close the poem. "For Esther," dedicated to the poet's mother, shows a similar linking on a larger scale. It is about trains and railroads and a boy's fascination with them; but how, we wonder, does it also manage to be a poem about, and for, the boy's mother? The fact that mother and son share the memories might suffice as a reason for joining their uneasy love to images of railroads, but the connection goes much deeper. It touches on the mutual desire to be together and to be away from each other; the second possibility is represented both literally and metaphorically by the trains that pass through the little town where they live.

Writing about one's childhood and parents is never easy. The necessary perspective is hard to achieve, and the common temptation to make of childhood a lost paradise often lures us into nostalgia and sentimentality. Perhaps because his childhood was unhappy enough to resist idealization, and certainly because he writes with great honesty about all the divided feelings in his life and the lives of his family, Plumly achieves an elegiac tenderness about his past without falling into self-indulgence or self-pity. His poems are deeply personal and wonderfully impersonal at the same time. The past as he sees it is no less mixed in character and value than the present; the difference is that our having survived it gives us a calm perspective on it, a power over it—"Recovery is memory. / I never broke my arm"—and allows us to see its value, even in things as unlikely as iron lungs.

Not all these poems deal with memory and personal experience. They may tackle general subjects, as "Wildflower" does, or arise from a contemplation of art and the imagination, as "After Whistler" seems to. But "Wildflower" contains a memory ("the summer I picked everything"), and "After Whistler" brings the painter's puzzling techniques into an alignment with the story of how the speaker's grandmother saved his life and then launched him toward the future by her love. It's as if this poet were slowly furnishing a museum made up of the most cherished and sustaining objects he can find. Some come from "pain remembered" ("Out-of-the-Body Travel"); some from pain imagined (Plumly is not, after all, the speaker of "The Iron Lung"); but others center on minor and solitary pleasures such as being alone, and the simple joy of naming and identifying expressed in "Wildflower."

Stanley Plumly grew up in Ohio and Virginia and was educated at Wilmington College in Ohio and at Ohio University. He taught for a number of years at Ohio University, where he helped found the *Ohio Review,* and he has been a visiting writer at a number of other institutions, including Iowa, Princeton, Columbia, and the University of Washington. At present, he teaches in the writing program at the University of Maryland.

DY

Out-of-the-Body Travel

1

And then he would lift this finest
of furniture to his big left shoulder
and tuck it in and draw the bow
so carefully as to make the music

almost visible on the air. And play
and play until a whole roomful of the sad
relatives mourned. They knew this was
drawing of blood, threading and rethreading

the needle. They saw even in my father's
face how well he understood the pain
he put them to—his raw, red cheek
pressed against the cheek of the wood . . .

2

And in one stroke he brings the hammer
down, like mercy, so that the young bull's
legs suddenly fly out from under it . . .
While in the dream he is the good angel

in Chagall, the great ghost of his body
like light over the town. The violin
sustains him. It is pain remembered.
Either way, I know if I wake up cold,

and go out into the clear spring night,
still dark and precise with stars,
I will feel the wind coming down hard
like his hand, in fever, on my forehead.

The Iron Lung

So this is the dust that passes through porcelain,
so this is the unwashed glass left over from supper,
so this is the air in the attic, in August,
and this the down on the breath of the sleeper . . .

If we could fold our arms, but we can't.
If we could cross our legs, but we can't.
If we could put the mind to rest . . .
But our fathers have set this task before us.

My face moons in the mirror, weightless,
without air, my head propped like a penny.
I'm dressed in a shoe, ready to walk out
of here. I'm wearing my father's body.

I remember my mother standing in the doorway
trying to tell me something. The day is thick
with the heat rising from the road. I am
too far away. She looks like my sister.

And I am dreaming of my mother in a doorway
telling my father to die or go away.
It is the front door, and my drunken father falls
to the porch on his knees like one of his children.

It is precisely at this moment I realize
I have polio and will never walk again.
And I am in the road on my knees, like my father,
but as if I were growing into the ground

I can neither move nor rise.
The neighborhood is gathering, and now
my father is lifting me into the ambulance
among the faces of my family. His face is

a blur or a bruise and he holds me
as if I had just been born. When I wake
I am breathing out of all proportion to myself.
My whole body is a lung; I am floating

above a doorway or a grave. And I know
I am in this breathing room as one
who understands how breath is passed
from father to son and passed back again.

At night, when my father comes to talk,
I tell him we have shared this body long enough.
He nods, like the speaker in a dream.
He knows that I know we're only talking.

Once there was a machine for breathing.
It would embrace the body and make a kind of love.
And when it was finished it would rise
like nothing at all above the earth

to drift through the daylight silence.
But at dark, in deep summer, if you thought you heard
something like your mother's voice calling you home,
you could lie down where you were and listen to the dead.

Peppergrass

Nothing you could know, or name, or say
in your sleep, nothing you'd remember,
poor-man's-pepper, wildflower, weed—
what the guidebook calls *the side
of the road*—as from the moon the earth
looks beautifully anonymous, this field
pennycress, this shepherd's purse, nothing
you could see: summer nights we'd look up
at the dark, the stars, and turn like toys . . .

Nothing you could hold on to
but the wet grass, cold as morning.

We were windmills where the wind came from,
nothing, nothing you could name,
blowing the lights out, one by one.

For Esther

     1

From the back it looks like a porch,
portable, the filigree railing French.

And Truman, Bess and the girl each come out
waving, in short sleeves, because the heat
is worse than Washington.

The day is twelve hours old, Truman is talking.
You tell me to pay attention,
                      so I have my ball-
cap in my hands when he gets to the part that the sun

is suicidal, his dry voice barely audible above the train.

It makes a noise like steam.
He says, he says, he says.

His glasses silver in the sun. He says
there is never enough, and leans down to us.

2

Shultz and I put pennies on the track to make
the train jump. It jumps.

Afternoons you nap—one long pull of the body
through the heat.

                I go down to the depot
against orders; it's practically abandoned
except for the guy who hangs out

the mail and looks for pennies. He's president
of this place, he says. We pepper his B & O
brick building with tar balls when he's gone.

You hate the heat and sleep and let
your full voice go when I get caught.

You can't stand my noise or silence.
And I can hear a train in each bent coin.

You're thirty. I still seem to burden that young body.

3

Light bar, dark bar, all the way down. The trick is
if a train comes there is room for only the river.

I look down between the crossties at the Great Miami.
Three miles back, near home,

Kessler has already climbed to his station.
The trick is waiting for the whistle.

                I remember
your dream about bridges: how, as a child, they shook
you off, something the wind compelled.

You woke up holding on. And now this August morning

I don't know enough to be afraid or care.
I do my thinking here,

looking down at the long ladder on the water,
forty feet below.

4

The engine at idle, coasting in the yard, the call bell
back and forth, back and forth above the lull . . .

I hang on like the mail as the cars lock in
to one another, couple, and make a train.

The time I break my arm you swear
me to the ground—no more rivers,
no more side-car rides—

                        and stay up half
the night to rub my legs to sleep.

Sometimes you talk as if Roosevelt

were still alive. Recovery is memory.
I never broke my arm.

                    Back and forth. The names
of the states pass every day in front of us, single-file.

5

If a house were straw there'd be a wind,
if a house were wood there'd be a fire,

if a house were brick there'd be a track
and a train to tell the time.

                  I wish each passage
well—wind, fire, time, people on a train.
From here to there, three minutes, whistle-stop.

And the speech each night, the seconds clicking off.

The whole house shakes—or seems to. At intervals,
the ghost smoke fills

all the windows on the close-in side.
It's our weather. It's what we hear all night,
between Troy and anywhere, what you meant

to tell me, out of the body, out of the body travel.

Wildflower

Some—the ones with fish names—grow so north
they last a month, six weeks at most.
Some others, named for the fields they look like,
last longer, smaller.

And these, in particular, whether trout- or corn-lily,
onion or bellwort, just cut
this morning and standing open in tapwater in the kitchen
will close with the sun.

It is June, wildflowers on the table.
They are fresh an hour ago, like sliced lemons,
with the whole day ahead of them.
They could be common mayflower lilies-of-the-valley,

day-lilies, or the clustering Canada, large, gold,
long-stemmed as pasture roses, belled out over the vase—
or maybe solomon's-seal, the petals
ranged in small toy pairs

or starry, tipped at the head like weeds.
They could be anonymous as weeds.
They are, in fact, the several names of the same thing,
lilies of the field, butter-and-eggs,

toadflax almost, the way the whites and yellows juxtapose,
and have "the look of flowers that are looked at,"
rooted as they are in water, glass, and air.
I remember the summer I picked everything,

flower and wildflower, singled them out in jars
with a name attached. And when they had dried as stubborn
as paper I put them on pages and named them again.
They were all lilies, even the hyacinth,

even the great pale flower in the hand of the dead.
I picked it, kept it in the book for years
before I knew who she was,
her face lily-white, kissed and dry and cold.

After Whistler

In his portrait of Carlyle, Whistler builds
from the color out: he calls it an arrangement
in gray and black and gives it a number in order
to commit us to the composition—to the foreground
first, in profile, before we go on to a wall
that seems to be neutral but is really the weather.
Carlyle is tired, beyond anger, and beautiful,
his white head tilted slightly toward the painter.
He is wearing a long coat and rests his hat on his knees.

When I was born I came out holding my breath, blue.
The cord had somehow rotted at the navel—
I must have lain alone for hours before they would let
my father's mother, the other woman there, give blood.
She still had red hair and four years to live.
The place on my arm where they put the needles in
I call my mortality scar. When I think of my grand-
mother lifting me all the way to the kitchen counter
I think of the weight by which we are doubled or more

through the lives of others. I followed her
everywhere, or tried to. I was her witness.
When I look at Whistler's portrait of Carlyle
I think of how the old survive: we make them up.
In the vegetable garden, therefore, the sun is gold
as qualified in pictures. She is kneeling in front
of the light in such a way I can separate skin from bone.
She is an outline, planting or preparing the ground.
For all I know she will never rise from this green place.

Even the painter's mother is staring into the future,
as if her son could paint her back into her body.
I was lucky. In nineteen thirty-nine they still
believed blood was family. In a room real
with walls the color of buckwheat she would sit out
the afternoon dressed up, rocking me to sleep.
It would be Sunday, slow, no one else at home.
And I would wake that way, small in her small arms,
hers, in the calendar dark, my head against her heart.

NOTES

For Esther. The first stanza recalls Harry Truman's whistlestop campaign in the
summer and fall of 1948.

Wildflower. The quote "the look of flowers that are looked at" is from T. S. Eliot's
Four Quartets ("Burnt Norton," I).

STANLEY PLUMLY

Books

In the Outer Dark, 1970   *Out-of-the-Body Travel*, 1977

Giraffe, 1974   *Summer Celestial*, 1983

Interviews, Essays

"The One Thing," in *American Poets in 1976*, ed. William Heyen, 1976;
"The Path of Saying: An Interview with Stanley Plumly," *Poetry Miscellany* 9 (December 1979); "Interview with Stanley Plumly," *Ohio Review* 25 (Fall 1980); David Young, "Out Beyond Rhetoric: Four Poets and One Critic," *FIELD*, No. 29 (Spring 1984).

Dennis Schmitz
(b. 1937)

Anne Schmitz

Dennis Schmitz writes poems that let you know right away you have a challenge on your hands. The subject matter is often grotesque, the tone is dry and reticent, and the verse has a high specific density. In the absence of punctuation and capitalization the reader must make constant decisions about where one syntactical unit ends and another begins. Details crowd into the text in a dazzling and often bewildering succession. You take a deep breath before and after you read a Schmitz poem. In between, you call on quick wits and close attention.

Such efforts are well rewarded. The difficulties of these texts are not superficial features but muscle, sinew, and bone. Every element in a poem by Dennis Schmitz contributes to a well-constructed and compact whole. The reader doesn't have to supply order, just discover it. One acquaints oneself with these poems in the same way that one explores a well-made building, a process that can take time. In "A Letter to Ron Silliman on the Back of a Map of the Solar System," Greek myth and scientific fact are brought together in a fantastic combination that becomes a metaphor for our condition, or for the way we sometimes feel its weight and weirdness. Nothing in the poem, we realize upon pondering it closely, is incidental or casual. It is a thing to walk around and contemplate with astonishment, both as architecture and as music.

The pair of Chicago-based poems that follow, "Star & Garter Theater" and "Queen of Heaven Mausoleum," confirm the impression that Schmitz's poems are dense, complex structures to which we orient ourselves gradually and with growing delight. Both touch on the human need to create by constructing. The striptease and horror-movie world of the first is one where a monster is built ("my arm is sewn to your shoulder") and sex is a cumbersome assemblage ("now the fat ladies of the night // are lowered into the lace / stockings & strapped into their black / apparatus"). The poem's deft joinings become a superior reflection of the obsessive combinations of its subject. The construction worker who speaks in "Queen of Heaven Mausoleum" about the dreamlike work of finishing crypts is likewise a close cousin of the poet/maker who sketches his character's parodies of death and birth in a condensed, elegant style. Two later manifestations of the construction theme may be found in this selection: "Making a Door," in which a father and daughter work together on a dollhouse; and "Making Chicago," the most complex and explicit treatment of the human urge to build that Schmitz has yet undertaken.

The dry humor and deadpan manner of these poems keep them impersonal. Thus "Mile Hill," which is about Schmitz and his family, does not differ significantly in effect from "String," which generalizes our human experience before focusing on a pathetic wino whose song tells us that privacy is mostly an illusion. It is as though the poles of what is personal and what is impersonal are reversed in Schmitz so that an excess of objectivity is what can take him into the subjective. His ability to move imaginatively into the lives and inner worlds of others is also illustrated by "A Picture of Okinawa." From a photograph and a few childhood memories of a distant war he is able to leap into the psyche of "the last Japanese soldier," who surrendered only thirty years later, having lived among the trees of the jungle. The poem is funny, touching, and grotesque; it makes us marvel at the poet's ability to combine imaginative sympathy with fierce powers of objectification.

Dennis Schmitz's vision, which is ultimately religious in character, is the greatest source of unity in his poetry. The human condition in an imperfect, fallen world is his chief preoccupation. He sees us as grounded or trapped in the physical world and in our bodies, yearning for some kind of transcendence. As "Mile Hill" puts it, "we are on our knees / everyday to find on the ground / what we'd lost to the sky." Knowing that the subject of any given Schmitz poem is apt to be the fallen world and the human search for transcendence, the reader will have an easier time with complex pieces like "Making Chicago" and "Bird-Watching." It is not that Schmitz writes the same poem over and over but that he brings, as all good artists do, a specific vision to bear on the world around him, a definite point of view. Locating the center of that vision or viewpoint is a logical step in coming to terms with the poet's work.

Dennis Schmitz grew up on a farm near Dubuque, Iowa. He was educated at Loras College and the University of Chicago and lived and worked for a number of years in Chicago before moving to California, where since 1966 he has taught writing and literature at California State University at Sacramento.

DY

A Letter to Ron Silliman on the Back of a Map of the Solar System

I weigh 486 lbs on Jupiter
    I can't tell you why
I am crying why
        whole ridges of the memory
pull loose this immense gravity
keeps us down
under the slide I discarded first
    my old father who weighed more
here on my back a smaller hump somehow
my penis came out
    wrong or a strangely distended
heart girls touch for luck I threw
    down my weapons too what use
I said poor Aeneas is the afternoon
when distance turns our atmosphere
to frozen gas & shadows the gods give
        a discernible half-life
winks by the best
of our instruments the father
Jupiter ate the most promising
    of his children the Latin myths say

little that they were not grateful
to the sly Greeks a fallen
    city was given curiously foreign
buildings with supports constructed
    on heavenly principles Cassandra
for instance screamed & the water-clocks
ran faster in our color bands
   sodium insects & our smaller
life take on a radiance &
become explosive when it rains we know
it is a warning
    do not even cry the atmosphere
is unstable keep it under sawdust wet
with oil the moist armpits & loins
    are unstable for our use only
the subtle dust that drifts
    down when the last of the fallen memory
settles & Jupiter surrenders
a final disguise for our mothers

were raped & we grow up half-gods in turn
to eat or forget our real origins

Star & Garter Theater

for Roger Aplon

it is always night here
faces close but never heal
only the eyes develop

scabs when we sleep & head
by head the dream is drained
into the white pool

of the screen. we go on rehearsing
THE REVENGE OF FRANKENSTEIN:
my arm is sewn to your shoulder.
your father's awful hand
& an actual criminal brain

take root under the projector's
cold moon. I wanted to do
only good. I planted my mouth
& kisses grew all over skid row.
now the fat ladies of the night

are lowered into the lace
stockings & strapped into their black
apparatus. this body is grafted
to theirs. alone we are helpless,

but put together winos, whores
& ambivalent dead we walk the daytime
world charged with our beauty.

Queen of Heaven Mausoleum

white as coal-ash pressed
again in veins, fuel for the living
I lay all summer in the fourth

floor crypts chipping
the excess we poured in the footings
for the dead. the foreman kneels

to hand in the tools
his face framed by this inner
world square as an oven
in which my flesh warmed
death's inspired
ingredients. which was my hand
& which the dead hand wanting to pry
open for future, the concrete

forms a dead father reinforces
as he fills his son's
teetering flesh. after a moment
my eyes film, magnify
sparks dropping from the darkness
like snowflakes. I fall
back into the frozen position

of the dead or the foetus I once saw
in the clear icy jacket of a jar.
around my ankles something tightens
& pulls my legs straight
in this second more awkward birth
when the grinning foreman slaps
me from my faint, will I cry

to be buried or gratefully begin
to nurse at the world I thirsted for?

Making a Door

a weedy creek
peeled from cornfields,
the whole countryside
where I grew up
thaws from the front
windows of this dollhouse

we are making together.
my daughter kneels
to chalk night
on the back windows,
wanting for this one house
all that our family lived
her eight years—
even dreams reduced
to the neat minimum

of her bedroom.
I ask to enter
the doll's world,
tell in altered size
what I dreamed

in my half of the house:
how I reached speech
through a series of dahs,
made my face a welt
on the five senses—
I go on distributing
myself over the assigned parts.
the house is almost done.

I hand her the saw.

Mile Hill

December: the trees chafing.
instead of a hole
at the horizon the focused light
of a welder's torch: the sun

& the iridescent this-world fuse.
6 days' drive, Calif to the cramped Iowa
farms. by the roadside we stretch
as I explain where my family

grew. below,
small preserved Dubuque bristles
in '90s plain-face
brick across the uneven hills,
circles where the river does

south to slough water.
Sara picks up
snow; molds it to her small hand,
tinges it with her pink

flesh: concomitant beauty
the bloodspot on the egg
we are on our knees
everyday to find on the ground
what we'd lost to the sky.

String

no one knows the way out of his mother
except as she leads him
the final knot is his head
which drags the nerves
along the spine like doublestitch
up the reverse
of the body & outside the soft fabric
currents which pucker
erogenous zones. no other joy

but this string, this dorsal string
one end shit, the other end tongue.
who has not asked the way back?
who is not guilty of graceless longing,
& alone? watch that man who

puppet-dances through noon
traffic skinning light
off the chrome. though his hands
are broken his quarrel
goes on. his pants front soaked, shamed,

he sings for pedestrians.
his mouth will bunch with old stitches
but he will sing, "privacy is only

contraction, heavy
body, dangle of shriveled nuts . . ."

Making Chicago

We cannot take a single step toward
heaven. It is not in our power to travel
in a vertical direction. If however we
look heavenward for a long time, God
comes and takes us up. He raises us
easily.

SIMONE WEIL

let it end here where the blueprint
shows a doorway,
where it shows all of Chicago
reduced to a hundred prestressed floors,
fifty miles of conduit & ductwork

the nerve-impulse climbs to know God.
every floor we go up is one more down
for the flashy suicide, *for blessèd man who*
by thought might lift himself

to angel. how slowly we become only men!
I lift the torch away, push up the opaque
welder's lens to listen for the thud
& grind as they pour aggregate,

extrapolating the scarred forms resisting
all that weight & think
the years I gave away to reflexive anger,

to bad jobs, do not count
for the steps the suicide
divides & subdivides in order not to reach

the roof's edge. I count the family years
I didn't grow older with the stunted
locust trees in Columbus Park,
the ragweed an indifferent ground crew
couldn't kill, no matter the poison.
now I want to take up death more often

& taste it a little—
by this change I know I am not what I was:
the voice is the voice of Jacob
but the hands are the hands of Esau—
god & antigod mold what I say,

make me sweat inside the welding gloves,
make what I thought true turn heavy.
but there must be names
in its many names the concrete can't take.
what future race in the ruins
will trace out our shape from the bent

template of the soul,
find its orbit in the clouded atmosphere
of the alloy walls we used as a likeness

for the sky? the workmen stagger
under the weight of the window's nuptial
sheet—in its white reflected clouds
the sun leaves a virgin spot

of joy.

A Picture of Okinawa

Out of adult hearing
the birds stammer this place
the animals intact
the remembered trees mismade
because a child painted them

from radio news & the interdicted
marsh back of Catfish Slough—
no GI drab but the Rousseau greens
snakes shed in their turnings

from heaven-held aquas & cerulean.
When the last Japanese soldier
gave up thirty years late
crashed down in some islander's

backyard, the sniper webbings cradling
his navel to the bandoliers
& commando knife with the four
metal knuckle-rings, I still looked
for my soldier uncle in this picture

my aunt never sent
to show how I imagined the enemy
condemned to eat close to heaven
the lonely madness for another's flesh,
his greenish waste wrapped in leaves

& stabbed on treeforks,
one mottled arm reaching for birds,
leaf by leaf making himself
innocent of his weapons—
only thirty years to come down human.

Bird-Watching

Across the channel, Mare Island welders cut
bulkheads & winch up
riveted slabs of the WW II

mine-tender. I can see
the torches flash against visualized rust;
I can see so far
back that the war cruelties are camouflaged

as feats of scruple.
The binoculars sweat rings around my eyes,
& when my arms tire, it's the sky that comes down

fuzzy through the Zeiss
26 × 10 lens into debris—the shoe, paper news
& condoms, the "beauty

from brevity derived" I can't catalog.
I'm on the flyway for marbled
godwits, scooters & loons,
but taxidermy might have devised what I think

is only a dead heron peppered with grit,
marshgrass poking
out the bird's buggy eyeholes.

I want to get down,
include myself in the focus: the war,

all epithets, between memory & present things
memory can't yet reach.
Though the marsh is a constant

madras-bleed between old soda bottles
that slash grids in the earthbound
walker's boots & the heuristic dieback

of the grass, I'm on one knee
to this Bird-in-the-volleys-of-lesser-birds,
praising glut but lifting
binoculars once more to distance myself

from it. Idolatry begins in one's fear
of being the only thing, saying
to detritus, *let it linger, let even just the feathers*

of it stay—that is why I pick
up my glasses with the little men still in them.
They are so intent on forgetting;

they are so self-contained & innocent,

lit both by the small
circles of sky & by the torches they stroke
against the steel that arches over them.

DENNIS SCHMITZ

Books

We Weep for Our Strangeness, 1969   *String*, 1980
Double Exposures, 1971   *Singing*, 1985
Goodwill, Inc., 1976

Criticism

David Young, "Dennis Schmitz and Charles Simic," *FIELD*, No. 24
(Spring 1981).

Charles
Simic
(b. 1938)

©Thomas Victor, 1980

The poems of Charles Simic tend to be clear, compact, and mysteriously resonant. Some are quite short, others accumulate short sections as deliberate variations on a theme (e.g., "Bestiary for the Fingers of My Right Hand"). The reader senses the presence of distillation, as though large subjects had been reduced to pungent microcosms. We can conclude that Simic is a master of archetypes, but we need to remember that our sense of the archetypal is usually produced by a writer's careful manipulation of context. A loaf of bread can be just a loaf of bread in one poem, while in another it may summon powerful associations from history, myth, and the Bible. Simic's sense of the power of simple objects—tables, doors, brooms, stones—stems in part from his East European heritage (he spent the first ten years of his life in Yugoslavia) and in part from his careful study of folklore and myth while he was forming himself as a poet.

A glance at the first poem in our selection, "Butcher Shop," will serve to illustrate some of Simic's techniques. A place that most of us would pass without much thought is called back to our attention. A special time is invoked—"late at night"—and an atmosphere of suspense and drama is established by an ingenious comparison: "There is a single light in the store / Like the light in which the convict digs his tunnel." We are ready to look again at butcher shops, and as further figures of speech appear—the blood map on the apron, the church comparison in the third stanza—they lead us on into a sense of how fully the butcher shop can represent the dark side of our civilization, a place of destruction and nourishment that is as mysterious as any temple. The poet is not interested in judging the butcher or our habits of eating meat and slaughtering animals. Only a nonjudgmental attitude will take him as far as he wishes to go toward an encounter "Where I am fed, / Where deep in the night I hear a voice." Whose voice it is and what it says are left for the reader to decide, but the interlocking of life and death, creation and destruction that the poem envisions is one that most of us can respond to with a combination of terror and delight. It is part of the "gothic" side of our literature, akin to horror movies and monster myths, that cultivates this playing with our worst fears, and Simic is perfectly aware of his link with that side of the imagination. The poems crackle with a dark merriment about the whole human urge to the gothic and monstrous, and they bear titles like "Begotten of the Spleen" to make that allegiance clear.

"Butcher Shop" is set "late at night" and imagines "great continents" and "great rivers and oceans of blood." That expansion of horizon is also typical of Simic's cunning microcosms. In "Tapestry" we learn that the object (of which the poem seems a miniature replica), a tapestry out of Breughel or Bosch, "hangs from heaven to earth." "Psalm" discovers a woman who is a forest "standing at the beginning of time." The fork in "Fork" seems to have "crept / Right out of hell," while the city in "The Marvels of the City" tends to be every city that has ever existed, in history or in the imagination. Roads in Simic poems tend to be "long as sleep," and language is "as old as rain," while a stretch of tundra may be "on the scale of the universe." The poems reach out specifically to the vast areas of space and time they attempt to represent in miniature, and their dramatic changes in scale keep our imaginations wide open, reminding us constantly that we need to be in touch with the timeless and the unchanging. It is with delight that we consent to recognize that forks, for example, give us ready links with the distant past and with realities beyond the everyday. Such recognitions reopen our ties to the ancient world of the peasant in which life and death, birth and growth, exist in a coherent fabric. The modern world stands in danger of losing touch with this sense of existence. Other poets have sought to rescue and prize it—one thinks of Jarrell's fairy-tale poems—as have writers of fiction like Singer, Garcia Marquez, and Calvino. Simic, among the poets of his generation, is the authoritative imagination when it comes to the tradition that is also manifested in nursery rhymes, proverbs, riddles, and spells—in short, the world of magic.

A writer with such allegiances and of such mastery might not need to develop or change, but Simic, careful to avoid artistic stagnation, has experimented continually with new variations on the rich artistic possibilities of his material. The poems in the second half of our selection, drawn from his two recent volumes, *Classic Ballroom Dances* (1980) and *Unending Blues* (1986), continue to reflect the "peasant" tradition of lively myth and folklore, but they cross it with history and personal recollection: the "small, provincial city" ("Empire of Dreams"), the "floodlights / in the guard towers" ("Begotten of the Spleen"), the "dancefloor of the Union Hall" ("Classic Ballroom Dances"), the idling truck in "Dark Farmhouses." These are not mythic or folkloric archetypes but direct manifestations of twentieth-century history as it has made itself felt in the world in which Simic grew up (Eastern Europe during and after the Second World War) and in the lives and imaginations of all of us. The "cross-ventilating" of the mythic world by the historical and personal has protected Simic from simply repeating earlier successes and has opened his poems up to new horizons.

Charles Simic came to the United States in 1949 and settled in Chicago where he attended Oak Park High School and the University of Chicago. After a stint in the army he completed his B.A. at New York University, where he also did graduate work. He has had jobs of all kinds, but has for some years been a teacher, first in California and, since 1974, at the University of New Hampshire. Besides his numerous books of poetry (e.g., *Dismantling the Silence, Return to a Place Lit by a Glass of Milk, Charon's Cosmology*), he has been an active translator of French, Russian, and Yugoslav poetry, most notably the work of the Yugoslav poet Vasko Popa in two collections: *The Little Box* (1970), and *Homage to the Lame Wolf* (1979, 1987). The absence of self-indulgence in Simic's poetry, a reflection of his urge to reach out to the lives and concerns of ordinary people, has helped win him a wide audience of enthusiastic readers.

DY

Butcher Shop

Sometimes walking late at night
I stop before a closed butcher shop.
There is a single light in the store
Like the light in which the convict digs his tunnel.

An apron hangs on the hook:
The blood on it smeared into a map
Of the great continents of blood,
The great rivers and oceans of blood.

There are knives that glitter like altars
In a dark church
Where they bring the cripple and the imbecile
To be healed.

There is a wooden slab where bones are broken,
Scraped clean:—a river dried to its bed
Where I am fed,
Where deep in the night I hear a voice.

Tapestry

It hangs from heaven to earth.
There are trees in it, cities, rivers,
small pigs and moons. In one corner
snow is falling over a charging cavalry,
in another women are planting rice.

You can also see:
a chicken carried off by a fox,
a naked couple on their wedding night,
a column of smoke,
an evil-eyed woman spitting into a pail of milk.

What is behind it?
—Space, plenty of empty space.

And who is talking now?
—A man asleep under a hat.

And when he wakes up?
—He'll go into the barbershop.
They'll shave his beard, nose, ears and hair
To look like everyone else.

Psalm

1

Old ones to the side.

If there's a tailor, let him sit
With his legs crossed.
My suit will arrive in a moment.

All priests into mouse-holes.
All merchants into pigs. We'll cut their throats later.

To the beggars a yawn,
We'll see how they'll climb into it.

To the one who thinks, to the one between yes and no,
A pound of onions to peel.

To the mad ones crowns, if they still want them.
To the soldier a manual to turn into a flea.

No one is to touch the children.
No one is to shovel out the dreamers.

2

I'm Joseph of the Joseph of the Joseph who rode on a donkey,
A wind-mill on the tongue humming with stars,
Columbus himself chained to a chair,
I'm anyone looking for a broom-closet.

3

You must understand that I write this at night
Their sleep surrounds me like an ocean.
Her name is Mary, the most mysterious of all.
She's a forest, standing at the beginning of time.
I'm somebody lying within it. This light is our sperm.
The forest is old, older than sleep.
Older than this psalm I'm singing right to the end.

Bestiary for the Fingers of My Right Hand

1

Thumb, loose tooth of a horse.
Rooster to his hens.
Horn of a devil. Fat worm
They have attached to my flesh
At the time of my birth.
It takes four to hold him down,
Bend him in half, until the bone
Begins to whimper.

Cut him off. He can take care
Of himself. Take root in the earth,
Or go hunting with wolves.

2

The second points the way.
True way. The path crosses the earth,
The moon and some stars.
Watch, he points further.
He points to himself.

3

The middle one has backache.
Stiff, still unaccustomed to this life;
An old man at birth. It's about something
That he had and lost,
That he looks for within my hand,
The way a dog looks
For fleas
With a sharp tooth.

4

The fourth is mystery.
Sometimes as my hand
Rests on the table
He jumps by himself
As though someone called his name.

After each bone, finger,
I come to him, troubled.

5

Something stirs in the fifth
Something perpetually at the point
Of birth. Weak and submissive,
His touch is gentle.
It weighs a tear.
It takes the mote out of the eye.

Fork

This strange thing must have crept
Right out of hell.
It resembles a bird's foot
Worn around the cannibal's neck.

As you hold it in your hand,
As you stab with it into a piece of meat,
It is possible to imagine the rest of the bird:
Its head which like your fist
Is large, bald, beakless and blind.

Ballad

What's that approaching like dusk like poverty
A little girl picking flowers in a forest
The migrant's fire of her long hair
Harm's way she comes and also the smile's round about way

In another life in another life
Aunt rain sewing orphan's buttons to each stone
Solitude's stitch
Let your horns out little stone

Screendoor screeching in the wind
Mother-hobble-gobble baking apples
Wooden spoons dancing ah the idyllic life of wooden spoons
I need a table to spread these memories on

Little girl fishing using me as bait
Me a gloomy woodcutter in the forest of words
I am going to say one thing and mean another
I'll tuck you in a matchbox like a hornet

In another life in another life
Dandelion and red poppy grow in the back yard
Shoes in the rain bark at the milkman
Little girl alone playing blindman's buff

The words want to bring back more—
You are *it* she says laughing and is gone
Divination by one's own heartbeat
Draw near to what doesn't say yes or no

And she had nothing under her dress
Star like an eye the gamecocks have overlooked
Tune up your fingers and whistle
On a trail lined with elms she hides herself behind a tree

I tread the sod you walked on with kindness
Not even the wind blew to remind me of time
Approaches that which they insist on calling happiness
The nightbird says its name

On a tripod made of limbs hoist this vision
At eveningtime when they examine you in love
Glancing back on the road long as sleep
Little girl skipping the owl's hushed way.

Animal Acts

A bear who eats with a silver spoon.
Two apes adept at grave-digging.
Rats who do calculus.
A police dog who copulates with a woman,
Who takes undertaker's measurements.

A bedbug who suffers, who has doubts
About his existence. The miraculous
Laughing dove. A thousand-year-old turtle
Playing billiards. A chicken who
Cuts his own throat, who bleeds.

The trainer with his sugar-cubes,
With his chair and whip. The evenings
When they all huddle in a cage,
Smoking cheap cigars, lazily
Marking the cards in the new deck.

Empire of Dreams

On the first page of my dreambook
It's always evening
In an occupied country.
Hour before the curfew.
A small provincial city.
The houses all dark.
The store-fronts gutted.

I am on a street corner
Where I shouldn't be.
Alone and coatless
I have gone out to look
For a black dog who answers to my whistle.
I have a kind of halloween mask
Which I am afraid to put on.

Begotten of the Spleen

The Virgin Mother walked barefoot
among the land mines.
She carried an old man in her arms.
The dove on her shoulder

barked at the moon.
The earth was an old people's home.
Judas was the night nurse.
He kept emptying bedpans into river Jordan.

The old man had two stumps for legs.
He was on a dog-chain. St. Peter pushed a cart
loaded with flying carpets.
They weren't flying carpets.

They were bloody diapers.
It was a cock-fighting neighborhood.
The Magi stood on street corners
cleaning their nails with German bayonets.

The old man gave Mary Magdalena
a mirror. She lit a candle,
and hid in the outhouse. When she got thirsty,
she licked the mist off the glass.

That leaves Joseph. Poor Joseph.
He only had a cockroach
to load his bundles on.
Even when the lights came on she wouldn't run
into her hole.

And the lights came on:
The floodlights
in the guard towers.

Classic Ballroom Dances

Grandmothers who wring the necks
Of chickens; old nuns
With names like Theresa, Marianne,
Who pull schoolboys by the ear;

The intricate steps of pickpockets
Working the crowd of the curious
At the scene of an accident; the slow shuffle
Of the evangelist with a sandwich-board;

The hesitation of the early morning customer
Peeking through the window-grille
Of a pawnshop; the weave of a little kid
Who is walking to school with eyes closed;

And the ancient lovers, cheek to cheek,
On the dancefloor of the Union Hall,
Where they also hold charity raffles
On rainy Monday nights of an eternal November.

Harsh Climate

The brain itself in its skull
Is very cold,
According to
Albertus Magnus.

Something like a stretch of tundra
On the scale of the universe.
Galactic wind.
Lofty icebergs in the distance.

Polar night.
A large ocean liner caught in the ice.
A few lights still burning on the deck.
Silence and fierce cold.

The Marvels of the City

For Bata

I went down the tree-lined street of false gods
The cobbled street of two wise monkeys
The street of roasted nightingales
The small twisted street of the insomniacs
The street of those who feather their beds

That's right—the street of the dog's metaphysics
The dark alley of the Emperor's favorite barber
With its fountain and stone lion
The closed shutters on the street of the hundred-year-old harlot
The flag-bedecked courthouses and banks
On the square of the betrayed revolution

Here at last I thought feeling a rush of blood
The street of eternal recurrence and its proof
The tavern at the sign of the Pig and Seraphim
Erudite salamanders sipping wine of arctic vintage
Hamlet's wine the wine of stargazers
Loveless couples the wine of idiot savants

We are solely of the mind said one
Beyond Good and Evil said another
But the waiters black hair growing out of their ears
Just took our orders and said nothing

Dark Farmhouses

Windy evening,
Chinablue snow,
The old people are shivering
In their kitchens.

Truck without lights
Idling on the highway,
Is it a driver you require?
Wait a bit.

There's coal to load up,
A widow's sack of coal.

Is it a shovel you need?
Idle on,
A shovel will come by and by
Over the darkening plain.

A shovel,
And a spade.

Promises of Leniency and Forgiveness

Orphanage in the rain,
Empty opera house with its lights dimmed,
Thieves' market closed for the day,
O evening sky with your cloudy tableaus!

Incurable romantics marrying eternal grumblers.
Life haunted by its more beautiful sister-life—
Always, always . . . we had nothing
But the way with words. Someone rising to eloquence

After a funeral, or in the naked arms of a woman
Who has her head averted because she's crying,
And doesn't know why. Some hairline fracture of the soul
Because of these razor-backed hills, bare trees and bushes,

Sea-blackened rocks inscrutable as card players . . .
One spoke then of the structure of the inquirer himself,
Of blues in my bread, of great works and little faith.
Above the clouds the firm No went on pacing.

The woman had a tiny smile and an open umbrella,
Since now it had started to rain in a whisper,
The kind of rain that must have whispered in some other life
Of which we know nothing anymore except

That someone kept watching it come down softly,
Already soot-colored to make them think of
Serious children at play, and of balls of lint in a dark dark corner
Like wigs, fright wigs for the infinite.

CHARLES SIMIC

Books

What the Grass Says, 1967

Somewhere Among Us A Stone Is Taking Notes, 1969

I. Lalic, *Fire Garden* (translations, with C. W. Truesdale), 1970

Vasko Popa, *The Little Box* (translations), 1970

Four Modern Yugoslav Poets (translations), 1970

White, 1970

Dismantling the Silence, 1971

Return to a Place Lit by a Glass of Milk, 1974

Another Republic (anthology, edited with Mark Strand), 1976

Charon's Cosmology, 1977

Vasko Popa, *Homage to the Lame Wolf* (translations), 1979, 1987

Classic Ballroom Dances, 1980

Austerities, 1982

Weather Forecast for Utopia & Vicinity, 1983

Selected Poems, 1985

The Uncertain Certainty: Interviews, Essays, and Notes on Poetry, 1985

Unending Blues, 1986

I. Lalic, *Rollcall of Mirrors: Selected Poems* (translations), 1988

Criticism

David Walker, "O What Solitude," and James Carpenter, "Charles Simic's White," *Ironwood* 7/8 (1976); *Manassas Review* 1, no. 2 (Winter 1978) issues devoted to Simic, with interview, six articles, and bibliography; Peter Schmidt, "Charles Simic's Pocket Epic," *Contemporary Literature* 23, 4 (1982); David Young, "Dennis Schmitz and Charles Simic," *FIELD*, No. 24 (Spring 1981); David Young, "The Naturalizing of Surrealism," *FIELD*, No. 36 (Spring 1987).

Gary
Snyder
(b. 1930)

© Layle Silbert, 1977

T he poems of Gary Snyder have large and long perspectives. They bring together different cultures (e.g., "Hitch Haiku") and survey vast tracts of history and geography (e.g., "Mother Earth: Her Whales"). A poet's values, as Snyder has noted, go back to the Neolithic: "the fertility of the soil, the magic of animals, the power-vision in solitude, the terrifying initiation and rebirth, the love and ecstasy of the dance, the common work of the tribe." When Snyder can make the past and the present jump together, as he does, for example, in "Above Pate Valley," there is a sense of enlightenment, of opening vistas, that is exhilarating. The speaker's sense of community expands to include those long-ago makers of arrowheads who were drawn to the same mountain meadow. A comparable lift comes from the sudden uniting of man and nature in "Water," where the comic encounters with rattlesnake and trout (the magic of animals) carry the reader, along with the speaker, into a kind of *satori,* awakening, the Zen term for sudden spiritual understanding that also brings a oneness with the universe.

"Above Pate Valley" and "Water" are from Gary Snyder's first collection *Riprap* (1959), which reflects his experiences as a logger, firewatcher, and moun- taineer in the western states—California and Oregon—where he grew up. It also reflects his interest in Chinese poetry, which he studied and translated in those years (especially Han Shan, *Cold Mountain Poems,* published in a joint edition with *Riprap* in 1965). A work experience and a literary interest coming together is typical of Gary Snyder's poetry. He brings the attention of an anthropologist, a student of human culture and languages, to bear on his subjects, but he also draws directly, again and again, on his own active life, his own experience of "the work and play of the tribe."One must be both a sailor and a geographer to arrive at the realization, in "Hitch Haiku," that scrap brass dumped from the ship when it is crossing the Mindinao Deep will be "falling six miles." This same character reads Blake during a Japanese typhoon. He has traveled widely, worked a lot with his hands, read voraciously, and pondered deeply. Involved in a casual game of hopscotch on the beach, he does not try to suppress his knowledge that the game is an ancient divining ritual, a way of foretelling one's life and fate. The work and play of the tribe can come to the same thing, and children's games are one more meaningful way of learning and knowing. Enlightenment can come from standing on the deck of an oil tanker or noticing some arrowhead chippings in a mountain meadow or reading a long-dead English poet in an Oriental cowshed. We learn not to despise the means by which the world makes itself known to us.

Studying Zen in Japan might have tempted Gary Snyder to withdraw from the world, but he is too much a naturalist and activist, with a deep concern for our good and bad ways with the planet. Seeing what was happening to Japan made him decide to return to the nation the Japanese were emulating. If pollution, environmental problems, and misuse of technology were to be confronted directly, it made the most sense to come home to the heart of the problem. He settled back in California in the late 1960s and has been active ever since in the conservation movement, not simply protesting the misuse of resources and pointing out our civilization's errors, but trying to help educate Americans to new styles of living and thinking, new ways of valuing themselves and the world around them. He continues, it might be noted, in the native tradition of Emerson and Thoreau. The awareness he wants to share—of ecosystems, cycles, primitive wisdom about holistic ways of seeing the world—is not always easy to put into poems, and Snyder is willing to risk the didactic in the interest of making his poetry of a piece with the rest of his life and beliefs. Recent poems, represented here by "Song of the Taste" and "Mother Earth: Her Whales," are explicit about the nature of his commitments.

It is difficult to represent Gary Snyder's work with a selection of poems because some of his best efforts have gone into the writing of two long poems. _Myths and Texts_ (1960), from which anthologists sometimes excerpt portions, is much better read in its entirety. An even more ambitious conception, _Mountains and Rivers Without End,_ based on the form of a Chinese scroll unrolling horizontally, has had many of its projected forty sections appear in print but has yet to see full completion. The reader is urged to investigate these longer texts and to sample Snyder's essays, as represented by collections like _The Real Work_ (1980). In his energy and resourcefulness, Gary Snyder is properly a particular inspiration to young people. They share his concerns and his ideals and can respond readily to the openness and directness of his poems.

_DY_

Above Pate Valley

We finished clearing the last
Section of trail by noon,
High on the ridge-side
Two thousand feet above the creek—
Reached the pass, went on
Beyond the white pine groves,
Granite shoulders, to a small
Green meadow watered by the snow,
Edged with Aspen—sun
Straight high and blazing
But the air was cool.
Ate a cold fried trout in the
Trembling shadows. I spied
A glitter, and found a flake
Black volcanic glass—obsidian—
By a flower. Hands and knees
Pushing the Bear grass, thousands
Of arrowhead leavings over a
Hundred yards. Not one good
Head, just razor flakes
On a hill snowed all but summer,
A land of fat summer deer,
They came to camp. On their
Own trails. I followed my own
Trail here. Picked up the cold-drill,
Pick, singlejack, and sack
Of dynamite.
Ten thousand years.

Water

Pressure of sun on the rockslide
Whirled me in dizzy hop-and-step descent,
Pool of pebbles buzzed in a Juniper shadow,
Tiny tongue of a this-year rattlesnake flicked,
I leaped, laughing for little boulder-color coil—
Pounded by heat raced down the slabs to the creek
Deep tumbling under arching walls and stuck
Whole head and shoulders in the water:
Stretched full on cobble—ears roaring
Eyes open aching from the cold and faced a trout.

Hitch Haiku

They didn't hire him
      so he ate his lunch alone:
the noon whistle

          *   *   *

Cats shut down
      deer thread through
men all eating lunch

          *   *   *

Frying hotcakes in a dripping shelter
      Fu Manchu
Queets Indian Reservation in the rain

          *   *   *

A truck went by
      three hours ago:
Smoke Creek desert

         *   *   *

Jackrabbit eyes all night
  breakfast in Elko.

       *   *   *

Old kanji hid by dirt
on skidroad Jap town walls
      down the hill
to the Wobbly hall

                   Seattle

       *   *   *

Spray drips from the cargo-booms
a fresh-chipped winch
      spotted with red lead
young fir—
      soaking in summer rain

       *   *   *

Over the Mindanao Deep

Scrap brass
      dumpt off the fantail
falling six miles

       *   *   *

[The following two were written on classical
themes while traveling through Sappho, Washington.
The first is by Thomas L. Hoodlatch.]

Moonlight on the burned-out temple—
            wooden horse shit.

Sunday dinner in Ithaca—
            the twang of a bowstring

       *   *   *

After weeks of watching the roof leak
           I fixed it tonight
by moving a single board

       *   *   *

A freezing morning in October in the high
Sierra crossing Five Lakes Basin to the
Keweahs with Bob Greensfelder and Claude Dalenburg

Stray white mare
            neck rope dangling
forty miles from farms.

       *   *   *

Back from the Keweahs

Sundown, Timber Gap
            —sat down—
               dark firs.
   dirty;   cold;
too tired to talk

      *   *   *

Cherry blossoms at Hood river
            rusty sand near Tucson
mudflats of Willapa Bay

      *   *   *

Pronghorn country

Steering into the sun
            glittering jewel-road
shattered obsidian

                    *   *   *
The mountain walks over the water!
Rain down from the mountain!
            high bleat of a
cow elk
            over blackberries

                    *   *   *

A great freight truck
            lit like a town
through the dark stony desert

                    *   *   *

Drinking hot saké
                toasting fish on coals
    the motorcycle
out   parked in the rain.

                    *   *   *

Switchback

turn, turn,
and again,   hard-
scrabble
steep travel a-
head.

Hop, Skip, and Jump

for Jim and Annie Hatch

    the curvd lines toe-drawn, round cornerd squares
bulge out doubles from its single pillar line, like,
Venus of the Stone Age.
she takes stone,
with a white quartz band for her lagger.
                                    she
    takes a brown-staind salt-sticky cigarette
                            butt.
he takes a mussel shell. he takes a clamshell. she takes
a stick.

he is tiny, with a flying run & leap—
shaggy blond—misses all the laggers,
                tumbles from one foot.
                they are dousing
a girl in a bikini down the beach
                first with cold seawater
                        then with wine.
double-leg single-leg   stork stalk turn
on the end-square—hop, fork, hop, scoop the lagger,
        we have all trippt and fallen.
        surf rough and full of kelp,
    all the ages—
draw a line on another stretch of sand—
                                and—
                        everybody try
to do the hop, skip, and jump.

                                4.X.1964 Muir Beach

It

(Reading Blake in a cowshed during a typhoon on an island in the East China Sea)

Cloud—cloud—cloud—   hurls
        up and on over;
Bison herds stamp-
eding   on Shantung

Fists of rain
        flail half down the length of the floor
Bamboo hills
        bend and regain;
                fields follow the laws of waves.

        puppy scuds in wet
        squats on the slat bed
                —on the edge of a spiral
centered five hundred miles southwest.

Reading in English:
        the way the words join
        the weights, the warps

        I know what it means.

my language is home.

mind-fronts meeting
bite back at each other,
whirl up a Mother Tongue.
one hundred knot gusts dump palms
over somebody's morning cream—

Cowshed skull
Its windows open
swallows and strains
gulfs of wild-slung
quivering ocean air.
breathe it;
taste it;	how it

Feeds the brain.

Song of the Taste

Eating the living germs of grasses
Eating the ova of large birds

the fleshy sweetness packed
around the sperm of swaying trees

The muscles of the flanks and thighs of
soft-voiced cows
the bounce in the lamb's leap
the swish in the ox's tail

Eating roots grown swoll
inside the soil

Drawing on life of living
clustered points of light spun
out of space
hidden in the grape.

Eating each other's seed
eating
ah, each other.

Kissing the lover in the mouth of bread:
lip to lip.

Mother Earth: Her Whales

An owl winks in the shadows
A lizard lifts on tiptoe, breathing hard
Young male sparrow stretches up his neck,
      big head, watching—

The grasses are working in the sun. Turn it green.
Turn it sweet. That we may eat.
Grow our meat.

Brazil says "sovereign use of Natural Resources"
Thirty thousand kinds of unknown plants.
The living actual people of the jungle
      sold and tortured—
And a robot in a suit who peddles a delusion called "Brazil"
      can speak for *them?*

        The whales turn and glisten, plunge
          and sound and rise again,
        Hanging over subtly darkening deeps
        Flowing like breathing planets
          in the sparkling whorls of
            living light—

    And Japan quibbles for words on
      what kinds of whales they can kill?
    A once-great Buddhist nation
      dribbles methyl mercury
      like gonorrhea
        in the sea.

    Père David's Deer, the Elaphure,
    Lived in the tule marshes of the Yellow River
    Two thousand years ago—and lost its home to rice—
    The forests of Lo-yang were logged and all the silt &
    Sand flowed down, and gone, by 1200 AD—

Wild Geese hatched out in Siberia
      head south over basins of the Yang, the Huang,
      what we call "China"
On flyways they have used a million years.
Ah China, where are the tigers, the wild boars,
      the monkeys,
        like the snows of yesteryear
Gone in a mist, a flash, and the dry hard ground
Is parking space for fifty thousand trucks.
IS man most precious of all things?

—then let us love him, and his brothers, all those
Fading living beings—

North America, Turtle Island, taken by invaders
       who wage war around the world.
May ants, may abalone, otters, wolves and elk
Rise! and pull away their giving
       from the robot nations.

Solidarity. The People.
Standing Tree People!
Flying Bird People!
Swimming Sea People!
Four-legged, two-legged, people!

How can the head-heavy power-hungry politic scientist
Government two-world Capitalist-Imperialist
Third-world Communist paper-shuffling male
     non-farmer jet-set bureaucrats
Speak for the green of the leaf? Speak for the soil?

(Ah Margaret Mead . . . do you sometimes dream of Samoa?)

The robots argue how to parcel out our Mother Earth
To last a little longer
      like vultures flapping
Belching, gurgling,
     near a dying Doe.

"In yonder field a slain knight lies—
We'll fly to him and eat his eyes
    with a down
  derry derry derry down down."

    An Owl winks in the shadow
    A lizard lifts on tiptoe
      breathing hard
    The whales turn and glisten
      plunge and
    Sound, and rise again
    Flowing like breathing planets

    In the sparkling whorls

    Of living light.

              Stockholm: Summer Solstice 40072

GARY SNYDER

Books

Riprap, 1959

Myths and Texts, 1960, 1978

Riprap and Cold Mountain Poems,
1965

Six Sections from Mountains and
Rivers Without End, 1965, 1970

Three Worlds, Three Realms, Six
Roads, 1966

The Back Country, 1968

Earth House Hold (essays), 1969

Regarding Wave, 1970

Turtle Island, 1974

The Old Ways, 1977

The Real Work (essays), 1980

Axe Handles, 1983

Passage Through India (prose), 1983

Left Out in the Rain, 1985

Interviews, Criticism

Kenneth Rexroth, *American Poetry in the Twentieth Century*, 1971; Bob
Steuding, *Gary Snyder*, 1976; Charles Molesworth, *Gary Snyder's
Vision*, 1983; Katherine McNeil, *Gary Snyder, A Bibliography*, 1983;
Sherman Paul, *In Search of the Primitive*, 1986.

Mark
Strand
(b. 1934)

Jack Driscoll

Mark Strand, one of the best-known poets of his generation, writes poems that explore silence, absence, and nullity. In this he somewhat resembles W. S. Merwin, but Strand's world is more painterly and his gothic sense more playful. His landscapes are mysterious without necessarily being austere. They remind us of silent movies, old photographs, and the work of atmospheric painters of loneliness like Edward Hopper: "When somebody spoke, there was no answer. / Clouds came down / And buried the buildings along the water. / And the water was silent. / The gulls stared" ("Elegy for My Father," 1). In one sense, this is a perfectly natural scene with fog and a calm sea, but the insistence on solitude is unmistakable. Strand's initial efforts to become a painter were not wasted. Just as the landscapes tend to be deserted and mysterious, so the people in these poems tend to move about like ghosts or robots: "They mourn for you. / They lead you back into the empty house. / They carry the chairs and tables inside. / They sit you down and teach you to breathe. / And your breath burns" ("Elegy for My Father," 5). There is contact here, but it does not break the essential sense of isolation. The sleepwalking people belong to the hushed and dreamlike landscapes, and both project an existential bleakness that is fascinating and troubling.

The style that makes such projections so powerful is based on a rhetoric of simple forms. Short, declarative sentences abound. Repetition is frequent. Questions and answers sound like a primer or a language-learning manual, in "Elegy for My Father," heightening the strangeness of the interview of a dead father by a living son. Everywhere in Strand's poetry language tends to slow down and grow rigid, eschewing its lusher and suppler ways. The result reminds us of ritualized language as we know it from the Bible and other primitive texts in which chant and psalm, proverb and catalogue, express an obsessive and supernatural version of reality.

The primitive rhythms and wooden constructions are of course very self-conscious; we are meant to share in the artist's deliberate sense of exploring extremes. "The Prediction" is partly a poem about itself, its own validation, and whether its self-contained quality is a strength or a weakness is left for the reader to decide. Sophisticated readers will surely appreciate the poem's rueful acknowledgement of the limits of its magic: It can "predict," but only within its own frame. The "Elegy for My Father," centerpiece of our selection from Strand, is a poem that seems as intent on an exploration of the aesthetics of grief as on the expression of grief itself. In a way, it makes the emotion more powerful by muting and muffling it. It also seems able to acknowledge that our emotions are seldom unmixed. In approaching a work of art called an elegy, for example, we are in search of aesthetic pleasure as much as pain or grief. Since art is artful, why not acknowledge that (the analogy of John Ashbery's work is useful here) and let the reader share the poet's sense of the task before him? As a son, Strand grieves profoundly for his father. As an artist, he is fascinated with the way a stylized treatment, a rhetoric of chant and repetition, may help re-create the experience and emotion of grief. Both son and artist are before us in the "Elegy," and the result is one of the most distinctive poems of the 1970s. Call it, if you like, the first great postmodern elegy.

One of the sections of the "Elegy" concerns the fate of the father's shadow, and that use of the shadow, the archetype of the dark and unknown part of the self, serves to remind us how much Strand shares an interest in magic with contemporaries like Simic, Merwin, and Willard. ''The Prediction,'' after all, deals with a vivid experience of premonition. The conversation in the second section of the ''Elegy'' is like part of a seance or a strange recasting of the ghost scene in _Hamlet_. Other moments in that poem remind us of rituals of exorcism. ''Where Are the Waters of Childhood?'' guides us on a dream journey to life's beginnings. While these ventures into the extraordinary and the supernatural are tinged with self-consciousness and a hint of self-mockery, it remains Strand's special knack that he can produce effects of having released secret forces or penetrated to the heart of certain mysteries, so that his poems carry both authority and fascination.

Born in Prince Edward Island, Canada, Mark Strand grew up in various parts of Canada and the United States and attended Antioch College and, for a time, the Yale Art School. He has taught widely, at schools such as Iowa, Yale, Brandeis, and Columbia. He lived for a number of years in New York City before moving to Utah, where he is writer-in-residence at the University of Utah in Salt Lake City. The publication of his _Selected Poems_ in 1980 clarified the nature and extent of his achievement as a poet, and his recent experiments with fiction suggest a new direction for his very special artistry.

_DY_

Keeping Things Whole

In a field
I am the absence
of field.
This is
always the case.
Wherever I am
I am what is missing.

When I walk
I part the air
and always
the air moves in
to fill the spaces
where my body's been.

We all have reasons
for moving.
I move
to keep things whole.

The Prediction

That night the moon drifted over the pond,
turning the water to milk, and under
the boughs of the trees, the blue trees,
a young woman walked, and for an instant

the future came to her:
rain falling on her husband's grave, rain falling
on the lawns of her children, her own mouth
filling with cold air, strangers moving into her house,

a man in her room writing a poem, the moon drifting into it,
a woman strolling under its trees, thinking of death,
thinking of him thinking of her, and the wind rising
and taking the moon and leaving the paper dark.

The Dance

The ghost of another comes to visit and we hold
communion while the light shines.
While the light shines, what else can we do?
And who doesn't have one foot in the grave?

I notice how the trees seem shaggy with leaves
and the steam of insects engulfs them.
The light falls like an anchor through the branches.
And which one of us is not being pulled down constantly?

My mind floats in the purple air of my skull.
I see myself dancing. I smile at everybody.
Slowly I dance out of the burning house of my head.
And who isn't borne again and again into heaven?

Elegy for My Father

(Robert Strand 1908–68)

1 The Empty Body

The hands were yours, the arms were yours,
But you were not there.
The eyes were yours, but they were closed and would not open.
The distant sun was there.
The moon poised on the hill's white shoulder was there.
The wind on Bedford Basin was there.
The pale green light of winter was there.
Your mouth was there,
But you were not there.
When somebody spoke, there was no answer.
Clouds came down
And buried the buildings along the water,
And the water was silent.
The gulls stared.
The years, the hours, that would not find you
Turned in the wrists of others.
There was no pain. It had gone.
There were no secrets. There was nothing to say.
The shade scattered its ashes.
The body was yours, but you were not there.
The air shivered against its skin.
The dark leaned into its eyes.
But you were not there.

2 Answers

Why did you travel?
Because the house was cold.
Why did you travel?
Because it is what I have always done between sunset and sunrise.

What did you wear?
I wore a blue suit, a white shirt, yellow tie, and yellow socks.
What did you wear?
I wore nothing. A scarf of pain kept me warm.
Who did you sleep with?
I slept with a different woman each night.
Who did you sleep with?
I slept alone. I have always slept alone.
Why did you lie to me?
I always thought I told the truth.
Why did you lie to me?
Because the truth lies like nothing else and I love the truth.
Why are you going?
Because nothing means much to me anymore.
Why are you going?
I don't know. I have never known.
How long shall I wait for you?
Do not wait for me. I am tired and I want to lie down.
Are you tired and do you want to lie down?
Yes, I am tired and I want to lie down.

3 Your Dying

Nothing could stop you.
Not the best day. Not the quiet. Not the ocean rocking.
You went on with your dying.
Not the trees
Under which you walked, not the trees that shaded you.
Not the doctor
Who warned you, the white-haired young doctor who saved you once.
You went on with your dying.
Nothing could stop you. Not your son. Not your daughter
Who fed you and made you into a child again.
Not your son who thought you would live forever.
Not the wind that shook your lapels.
Not the stillness that offered itself to your motion.
Not your shoes that grew heavier.
Not your eyes that refused to look ahead.
Nothing could stop you.
You sat in your room and stared at the city
And went on with your dying.
You went to work and let the cold enter your clothes.
You let blood seep into your socks.
Your face turned white.
Your voice cracked in two.

You leaned on your cane.
But nothing could stop you.
Not your friends who gave you advice.
Not your son. Not your daughter who watched you grow small.
Not fatigue that lived in your sighs.
Not your lungs that would fill with water.
Not your sleeves that carried the pain of your arms.
Nothing could stop you.
You went on with your dying.
When you played with children you went on with your dying.
When you sat down to eat,
When you woke up at night, wet with tears, your body sobbing,
You went on with your dying.
Nothing could stop you.
Not the past.
Not the future with its good weather.
Not the view from your window, the view of the graveyard.
Not the city. Not the terrible city with its wooden buildings.
Not defeat. Not success.
You did nothing but go on with your dying.
You put your watch to your ear.
You felt yourself slipping.
You lay on the bed.
You folded your arms over your chest and you dreamed of the world
     without you,
Of the space under the trees.
Of the space in your room,
Of the spaces that would now be empty of you,
And you went on with your dying.

Nothing could stop you.
Not your breathing. Not your life.
Not the life you wanted.
Not the life you had.
Nothing could stop you.

4 Your Shadow

You have your shadow.
The places where you were have given it back.
The hallways and bare lawns of the orphanage have given it back.
The Newsboys Home has given it back.
The streets of New York have given it back and so have the streets of
     Montreal.
The rooms in Belém where lizards would snap at mosquitos have given it
     back.

The dark streets of Manaus and the damp streets of Rio have given it
    back.
Mexico City where you wanted to leave it has given it back.
And Halifax where the harbor would wash its hands of you has given it
    back.
You have your shadow.
When you traveled the white wake of your going sent your shadow
        below, but when you arrived it was there to greet you. You had your
        shadow.
The doorways you entered lifted your shadow from you and when you
        went out, gave it back. You had your shadow.
Even when you forgot your shadow, you found it again; it had been with
        you.
Once in the country the shade of a tree covered your shadow and you
        were not known.
Once in the country you thought your shadow had been cast by
        somebody else. Your shadow said nothing.
Your clothes carried your shadow inside; when you took them off, it
        spread like the dark of your past.
And your words that float like leaves in an air that is lost, in a place no
        one knows, gave you back your shadow.
Your friends gave you back your shadow.
Your enemies gave you back your shadow. They said it was heavy and
        would cover your grave.
When you died your shadow slept at the mouth of the furnace and ate
        ashes for bread.
It rejoiced among ruins.
It watched while others slept.
It shone like crystal among the tombs.
It composed itself like air.
It wanted to be like snow on water.
It wanted to be nothing, but that was not possible.
It came to my house.
It sat on my shoulders.
Your shadow is yours. I told it so. I said it was yours.
I have carried it with me too long. I give it back.

5 Mourning

They mourn for you.
When you rise at midnight,
And the dew glitters on the stone of your cheeks,
They mourn for you.
They lead you back into the empty house.
They carry the chairs and tables inside.
They sit you down and teach you to breathe.

And your breath burns,
It burns the pine box and the ashes fall like sunlight.
They give you a book and tell you to read.
They listen and their eyes fill with tears.
The women stroke your fingers.
They comb the yellow back into your hair.
They shave the frost from your beard.
They knead your thighs.
They dress you in fine clothes.
They rub your hands to keep them warm.
They feed you. They offer you money.
They get on their knees and beg you not to die.
When you rise at midnight they mourn for you.
They close their eyes and whisper your name over and over.
But they cannot drag the buried light from your veins.
They cannot reach your dreams.
Old man, there is no way.
Rise and keep rising, it does no good.
They mourn for you the way they can.

6 The New Year

It is winter and the new year.
Nobody knows you.
Away from the stars, from the rain of light,
You lie under the weather of stones.
There is no thread to lead you back.
Your friends doze in the dark
Of pleasure and cannot remember.
Nobody knows you. You are the neighbor of nothing.
You do not see the rain falling and the man walking away,
The soiled wind blowing its ashes across the city.
You do not see the sun dragging the moon like an echo.
You do not see the bruised heart go up in flames,
The skulls of the innocent turn into smoke.
You do not see the scars of plenty, the eyes without light.
It is over. It is winter and the new year.
The meek are hauling their skins into heaven.
The hopeless are suffering the cold with those who have nothing to hide.
It is over and nobody knows you.
There is starlight drifting on the black water.
There are stones in the sea no one has seen.
There is a shore and people are waiting.
And nothing comes back.
Because it is over.
Because there is silence instead of a name.
Because it is winter and the new year.

Where Are the Waters of Childhood?

See where the windows are boarded up,
where the gray siding shines in the sun and salt air
and the asphalt shingles on the roof have peeled or fallen off,
where tiers of oxeye daisies float on a sea of grass?
That's the place to begin.

Enter the kingdom of rot,
smell the damp plaster, step over the shattered glass,
the pockets of dust, the rags, the soiled remains of a mattress,
look at the rusted stove and sink, at the rectangular stain
on the wall where Winslow Homer's *Gulf Stream* hung.

Go to the room where your father and mother
would let themselves go in the drift and pitch of love,
and hear, if you can, the creak of their bed,
then go to the place where you hid.

Go to your room, to all the rooms whose cold, damp air you breathed,
to all the unwanted places where summer, fall, winter, spring,
seem the same unwanted season, where the trees you knew have died
and other trees have risen. Visit that other place
you barely recall, that other house half hidden.

See the two dogs burst into sight. When you leave,
they will cease, snuffed out in the glare of an earlier light.
Visit the neighbors down the block; he waters his lawn,
she sits on her porch, but not for long.
When you look again they are gone.

Keep going back, back to the field, flat and sealed in mist.
On the other side, a man and a woman are waiting;
they have come back, your mother before she was gray,
your father before he was white.

Now look at the North West Arm, how it glows a deep cerulean blue.
See the light on the grass, the one left burning, the cloud
that flares. You're almost there, in a moment your parents
will disappear, leaving you under the light of a vanished star,
under the dark of a star newly born. Now is the time.

Now you invent the boat of your flesh and set it upon the waters
and drift in the gradual swell, in the laboring salt.
Now you look down. The waters of childhood are there.

MARK STRAND

Books

Reasons for Moving, 1968

The Contemporary American Poets:
American Poetry Since 1940
(anthology, ed.), 1969

Darker, 1970

New Poetry of Mexico (anthology,
ed.), 1970

The Story of Our Lives, 1973

The Owl's Insomnia: Selected Poems
of Rafael Alberti (translations),
1973

Souvenir of the Ancient World:
Carlos Drummond de Andrade
(translations), 1976

Another Republic: 17 European &
South American Writers (edited
with Charles Simic), 1976

The Late Hour, 1978

The Monument (prose), 1978

Selected Poems, 1980

Mr. and Mrs. Baby (stories), 1985

Interviews, Criticism

Richard Howard, *Alone with America: Essays on the Art of Poetry in the United States Since 1950*, 1969; Harold Bloom, "Dark and Radiant Peripheries: Mark Strand and A. R. Ammons," *Southern Review*, new series 8 (Winter 1972); "A Conversation with Mark Strand," *Ohio Review* 13 (Winter 1972); Mark Strand, "The Need to Change or the Anxiety of Self-Influence," *FIELD*, No. 16 (Spring 1977); *Strand: A Profile* (Profile Editions, Grilled Flowers Press; with an interview, critical essays, poems and prose by Mark Strand, and a select bibliography), 1980.

Jean
Valentine
(b. 1934)

In his essay "Word Against Object," George Steiner discusses what he calls "the tactic of silence" that has come about in modern poetry, he feels, because of a discrepancy between "individual perception and the frozen generalities of speech." Writers fall silent at terrible moments in history, when language has been so corrupted by despotic, demonic forces as to defy attempts to cleanse it. "Rather silence than a betrayal of felt meanings," Steiner concludes, citing Wittgenstein's remark that what one does *not* write at such times is the important part of a writer's contribution. More than any other poet in this anthology, perhaps, Jean Valentine seeks refuge in a language of silence, or extreme privacy, choosing as she does to provide so little exposition or context for her poems that some readers complain of inscrutability. Words like "spare, brilliant," but also "baffling, mysterious" are used to characterize her style, which admittedly depends on eerie juxtapositions, floating images, dizzying leaps, and enigmatic structures that leave the lazy reader behind. If one word can be helpful, perhaps Hayden Carruth's adjective "notational" best gets at Valentine's strategies for dealing with the intimate spheres of dream and reality that have merged in our nightmarish world. By noting things, by relying on an abbreviated system, a kind of shorthand, she is able to track things as fast as they happen, from words countered by other words to objects that displace other objects.

If we relax our need for instant understanding and participate with Valentine as she locates her poems visually before us, we have a better chance of following her poetic process. It is a process that insists on the inherent, tenuous quality of things and requires her to sort her way among the contradictions of what we say and mean to say, what we see and mean to see. This struggle with intention and implication is ultimately provocative because as she merely sketches but never fully colors in her landscapes, the reader must provide additional images to help develop the picture. Glimpses of things seen, snatches of conversation overheard, are filtered through scrims that soften their outlines as they alter our perspectives. In effect, the poems permit one last look at a past that can only be imagined now, in part because it was so horrible, in part because there are few survivors. We encounter these ghostly figures in luminous, ominous landscapes reminiscent of Bergman films: "He pointed at the window, the trees, or the snow, / or our silver auditorium" ("The Forgiveness Dream: Man from the Warsaw Ghetto"). These are kin who "are here. / Were here." Because the poet never tells us what to feel or think, we sometimes grow frightened, but this is a poetry that frees the mind and reassures us that we are capable of spiritual powers with which to face our visions. We must only keep looking, listening, and speaking, however fitfully, to ourselves, or our lost selves, to our friends, family and lovers, and on back to our beginnings, for "our lives have been a minute, a feather, our sex was chaff" ("The Field").

Jean Valentine's first collection, *Dream Barker,* won the Yale Series of Younger Poets Award in 1965. Of all its poems, "The Second Dream" most closely resembles what has continued to absorb her: some sort of destructive force approaches, from an unlikely place—"the planes were out / And coming, from a friendly country." The briefest time remains, what can one do? Nothing, perhaps, save use that brief moment to locate our spiritual center, acknowledge our love for those around us, and thus preserve whatever humanity is left in the world. In poem after poem, we see life from its most fragile to its most resolute, in one sweeping motion. Survivors will forgive us, if we can't forgive ourselves, for doing "nothing" but turning inward, living with our grief: "I said to him in English, 'I've lived the whole time / here, in peace. A private life.' 'In shame,' / I said." The old man understands, ". . . he nodded, / and wrote in my notebook—'Let it be good' " ("The Forgiveness Dream").

Pilgrims, Valentine's second book, appeared in 1969. Almost all the poems, especially the remarkable title poem with its quiet, deliberate circling over accepted destiny, reach such compact, final form that one can understand why she waited five years to publish her next book, *Ordinary Things* (1974). Valentine found a way out of the finality that *Pilgrims* had achieved by sacrificing some of her previous range and going deeper in one direction. *Ordinary Things* is a treatise on developing contemplative powers to deal with what has been called the "aesthetic surfaces" in our lives. Straining to regard things as simple as a coffee cup, or "a child's handprint in a clay plate," Valentine argues for a contemplation that in its intensity will train us for the spiritual problems we face in troubled times. In *The Messenger* (1979), her most recent collection, the stakes are higher still. With an archaeologist's care she digs up "The Field," and comes across the last room: "Incised on stone, bronze, silver, / eyes, belly, mouth, circle on circle." The room in which love is made, children are born, is also the tomb. Prefigured in the early poems, called "an opened ground" in "Pilgrims," and "a northern still life" in "December 21st," this place, this room of Valentine's own, with its look down at our beginnings, and its glance up to what we still face, is finally where life can start up again. Jean Valentine likes to quote from a letter Sarah Orne Jewett wrote to Willa Cather: "You must find a quiet place. You must find your own quiet center of life and write from that." It is the only hope.

Jean Valentine was born and raised in Chicago. While studying at Radcliffe, she worked closely with the poet and playwright William Alfred. She has taught at a variety of places, such as Barnard, Swarthmore, Yale, and Hunter, and has been teaching on and off at Sarah Lawrence College since 1974.

SF

The Second Dream

We all heard the alarm. The planes were out
And coming, from a friendly country. You, I thought,
Would know what to do. But you said,
"There is nothing to do. Last time
The bodies were like charred trees."

We had so many minutes. The leaves
Over the street left the light silver as dimes.
The children hung around in slow motion, loud,
Liquid as butterflies, with nothing to do.

Orpheus and Eurydice

> *What we spent, we had.*
> *What we had, we have.*
> *What we lost, we leave.*
>
> —EPITAPH FOR HIS WIFE AND HIMSELF,
> BY THE DUKE OF DEVON, 12TH CENTURY

i

You. You running across the field.

A hissing second, not a word,
and there it was, our underworld:
behind your face another, and another,
and I

away.

—And you alive: staring,
almost smiling;

hearing them come down, tearing
air from air.

ii
"This dark is everywhere"
we said, and called it light,
coming to ourselves.
                         Fear
has at me, dearest. Even this night
drags down. The moon's gone. Someone
shakes an old black camera-cloth
in front of our eyes.
Yours glint like a snowman's eyes.
We just look on, at each other.

What we had, we have. They circle down.
You draw them down like flies.
You laugh, we run
over a red field, turning at the end to blue air,—
you turning, turning again! the river
tossing a shoe up, a handful of hair.

Pilgrims

Standing there they began to grow skins
dappled as trees, alone in the flare
of their own selves: the fire
died down in the open ground

and they made a place for themselves.
It wasn't much good,
they'd fall, and freeze,

some of them said
Well, it was all they could,

some said it was beautiful, some days,
the way the little ones took to the water,
and some lay smoking, smoking,

and some burned up for good,
and some waited,
lasting, staring
over each other's merciful shoulders,
listening:
           only high in a sudden January thaw
or safe a second in some unsmiling eyes
they'd known always

whispering
Why are we in this life.

After Elegies

Almost two years now I've been sleeping,
a hand on a table that was in a kitchen.

Five or six times you have come by
the window; as if I'd been on a bus

sleeping through the Northwest, waking up,
seeing old villages pass in your face,

sleeping.
                    A doctor and his wife, a doctor too, are in the kitchen
area, wide awake. We notice things
differently: a child's handprint in a clay plate, a geranium, aluminum
balconies rail to rail, the car horns of a wedding,

blurs of children in white. *LIFE* shots
of other children.   Fire to paper; black

faces, judge faces, Asian faces; flat
earth   your face   fern   coal

The Forgiveness Dream:
Man from the Warsaw Ghetto

He looked about six or seven, only much too thin.
It seemed right he would be there, but everything,
every lineation, was slow . . . He was speaking in Polish,
I couldn't answer him.
He pointed at the window, the trees, or the snow,
or our silver auditorium.

I said to him in English, "I've lived the whole time
here, in peace. A private life."   "In shame,"
I said. He nodded. He was old now, kind,
my age, or my mother's age: He nodded,
and wrote in my notebook—"Let it be good."

He frowned, and stopped,
as if he'd forgotten something,
and wrote again,
"Let it."

I walk, and stop, and walk—
touch the birchbark   shining, powdery, cold:
taste the snow, hot on my tongue—
pure cold, licked from the salt of my hand;
This quiet, these still unvisitable stars
move with choices.
Our kin are here.
Were here.

The Field

Chemicals in peat bogs keep
bodies so nearly perfectly, that
men cutting peat, who have
come across them, have supposed
these people, dead for as
long as 2000 years, were just
recently drowned or murdered.

A sculpture in a bare white gallery:
Pike jaws arch, in a shining transparent space
without locality: levels of peat, sand, air.
Bones. Teeth.
Fine, thin white jaws: the willingness to do harm—Odysseus
leaving—

At forty we have always been parents; we hold each other's sex
in a new tenderness . . . As we were; hardly breathing
over the pulse in the infant's lucent temple—

Our breath comes shorter,
our lives have been a minute, a feather, our sex is chaff . . .

Sleep: the room
breaks up into blue and red
film, long muscles crossing bones, raw pelvis pulled
to birth: Incised on stone, bronze, silver,
eyes, belly, mouth, circle on circle—

Look, by morning noises, in this city island flickering with blue flame,
These photographs.
The Tollund man. The Windeby girl. The goddess
Nerthus.

In the middle of a light wood   of tall forked trees stripped white
at the edge of a bog, in Denmark,
we walk   slowly out to the field   walk slowly by
the hacked-out cots of silk
bog children.

Silences: A Dream of Governments

From your eyes I thought
we could almost move   almost speak
But the way your face
held there, in the yellow air,
And that hand, writing down our names—
And the way the sun
shone right through us
Done with us

    Then
the plain astonishment—the air
broken open: just ourselves
sitting, talking; like always;
the kitchen window
propped open by the same
blue-gray dictionary.
August. Rain. A Tuesday.

Then, absence. The open room
suspended   The long street
gone off   quiet, dark.
The ocean floor. Slow
shapes glide by

Then, day
keeps beginning again: the same
stubborn pulse against the throat,
the same
listening for a human voice—
your name, my name

Living Together

Dawn, streaks of rose-brown, dry—
A car starts up. A needle veers,
an hour, a summer . . . Day
settles back, on the last
century, our trying, our Biblical
conviviality.

This should, should not, happen, these
two people met, or not then, not now;
or now.

Out in the white Judaic light
you move like figures in a lesson;

You open your life like a book.
Still I hear your story
like a parable, where every word is simple,
but how does this one
go with the one before, the next . . .

December 21st

How will I think of you
"God-with-us"
a name: a word

and trees paths stars this earth
how will I think of them

and the dead I love   and all absent friends
here-with-me

and table: hand: white coffee mug:
a northern still life:

and you
without a body

quietness

and the infant's red-brown mouth   a star
at the star of the girl's nipple . . .

NOTES

Orpheus and Eurydice. Orpheus was given a lyre he learned to play so well that
rivers stopped flowing and savage beasts grew tame. He married Eurydice,
who died from a serpent's bite. Disconsolate, Orpheus visited the infernal
regions to recover her and Pluto consented to return Eurydice if Orpheus
agreed not to look back while leaving. Orpheus forgot his promise, and as he
turned to look at Eurydice, she vanished.

The Forgiveness Dream: Man from the Warsaw Ghetto. On April 19, 1943, the
Jews in the Warsaw Ghetto (Poland) rose against the Germans, and after a few
weeks of fierce fighting, the whole area was razed and the Jews annihilated.

December 21st. The words in quotations, "God-with-us," are a literal translation of "Emmanuel" and the next phrase, "a name: a word" recalls Jesus Christ. The "girl" offering her nipple to the infant is Mary.

JEAN VALENTINE

Books

Dream Barker, 1965   Ordinary Things, 1974
Pilgrims, 1969   The Messenger, 1979

Criticism

Philip Booth, "Jean Valentine's *The Messenger*," *American Poetry Review* (January–February 1980).

Nancy
Willard
(b. 1936)

Eric Lindbloom

To use Roethke's phrase, "we hark back to the condition of the child" in the poems of Nancy Willard. It is a condition that encourages beliefs in many things, from angels to talking hens and vegetable saints, made real by Willard's sharp eye for detail; her witty, crafty ways of making things talk; and natural speech rhythms (which some critics have called psalmic) that present startling and strange elements in matter-of-fact tones. In addition, she has an uncanny feeling for the "magic" in ordinary things, turning them over and over until they take on a living presence—an egg will never be the same after "How the Hen Sold Her Eggs to the Stingy Priest"—or scooping out their essences, as she does with the pumpkin in "Saint Pumpkin." Children turn up frequently and easily in these pieces, because, like Willard, they love things for themselves and are more interested in how they look and work and fit together than in our presuppositions or notions of them. An early poem, "Picture Puzzles," darkly celebrates a family's joint enterprise of assembling Fra Angelico's *Nativity,* or "how the shapes of our healing lie / dumb in our hand."

Willard's critical study, *Testimony of the Invisible Man* (1970), a collection of essays on Ponge, Rilke, Williams, and Neruda, examines how these modern masters place objects (in all their myriad forms) at the center of their poetic worlds. One is reminded of what the German poet Günter Eich added to this dialogue: "Real language is a falling together of the word and the object. Our task is to translate from the language that is around us but not 'given.' . . . I must admit . . . I am still not beyond the 'thing-word' or noun . . . like a child who says 'tree,' 'moon,' 'mountain' and thus orients himself" (from "Some Remarks on Literature and Reality"). Nancy Willard has written many books for and about children, all of which center on similar definitions, naming things that have been badly named or that must still be named. As one of her characters reports, "Naming things we already know wouldn't change a thing." Similarly, many of the poems have to do with seeing things for the first time. There is "the first strawberry" of "Original Strawberry." Insects we thought we knew, seen through the microscope of Willard's encyclopedic imagination, become something "that does not belong to the habits / of our globe" ("The Insects"). And moons and pumpkins need to be seen without the "false face" we give them, "a light of our own making" ("Saint Pumpkin").

While Willard mentions in an essay that many of her poems start from common or domestic experiences, "working in the kitchen, picking up toys, bringing a bottle to a child at night," they quickly turn to large matters of faith and belief, which they explore in oracular ways. In both the poems and prose, her characters search for "faith and greater faith" as they "lie down in white pastures" ("Angels in Winter") or move among the signs and symbols of the complicated laws of life. Her story "The Hucklebone of a Saint," begins, "In my father's house, moral ambiguity was not allowed." If the child drops her knife, her father commands her to pick it up, while her mother adds, "A man is coming"—and if she were to drop a spoon, "A child is coming." As the mother in this story demonstrates that "faith takes root in the insignificant," it is frequently a mother figure in the poems who helps a child make sense of the "innocent" power of animals and objects encountered on the journey from birth to death. Mother and child develop, with delicate wordplay in parablelike exchanges, their imaginary powers as they heighten their sense of self in a world in which nothing human survives (see especially, "Questions My Son Asked Me, Answers I Never Gave Him"). Willard's most recent poems move toward even more complex, involved relationships with other spirits in the world, exploring the nature of deities we must make room for in our minds or perish. Willard's odd assortment of characters seem destined to roam some sort of purgatory until they find the right language to describe things.

Nancy Willard was born in Michigan and received a Ph.D. from the University of Michigan. She has lived in Oslo and Paris and now makes her home in Poughkeepsie, New York, where she teaches at Vassar College. In addition to more than a dozen children's books, she has published several collections of stories and poems and a novel, *Things Invisible to See*. *Skin of Grace* won the Devins Memorial Award for poetry in 1967.

SF

The Insects

They pass like a warning of snow,
        the dragonfly, mother of millions,
the scarab, the shepherd spider,
        the bee. Our boundaries break
on their jeweled eyes,
        blind as reflectors.
The black beetle
        under the microscope wears the
blue of Chartres. The armored
        mantis, a tank in clover,
folds its wings like a flawless
        inlay of wood, over and over.

"There is something about insects
        that does not belong to the habits
of our globe," said Maeterlinck,
        touching the slick
upholstery of the spider,
        the watchspring and cunning
tongue of the butterfly, blown out
        like a paper bugle. Their humming
warns us of sickness, their silence
        of honey and frost. Asleep
in clapboards and rafters,
        their bodies keep

the cost of our apples and wool,
        A hand smashes their wings,
tearing the veined
        landscape of winter trees.
In the slow oozing of our days
        who can avoid remembering
their silken tents on the air,
        the spiders wearing their eggs
like pearls, born on muscles
        of silk, the pulse of a rose, baiting
the fly that lives for three hours,
        lives only for mating?

Under a burning glass, the creature
    we understand disappears. The dragonfly
is a hawk, the roach
    cocks his enormous legs at your acre,
eyes like turrets piercing
    eons of chitin and shale. Drummers
under the earth, the cicadas
    have waited for seventeen summers
to break their shell,
    shape of your oldest fear
of a first world
    of monsters. We are not here.

Original Strawberry

The first strawberry:
plain as a teething ring.
And God blessed the strawberry
and eying the future made it
three-leaved for the Trinity
and red for His son's blood.

The strawberry was tasty but sad.
Lord, why make me so low?
And God decreed that the meek
should inherit the earth.

But has a strawberry ears?

On the seventh day it seceded
from creation like a grieving nun.
On the eighth, stars pocked its body
(my sky at sunset, said the strawberry)
and a green sun grew on its north pole
(my vernal equinox, said the strawberry).

Pick a strawberry as if you were paying court.
From which constellation shall you sail
to the mandala
that only a knife can find?

Angels in Winter

Mercy is whiter than laundry,
great baskets of it, packed like snowmen.
In the cellar I fold and sort and watch
through a squint in the dirty window
the plain bright snow.

Unlike the earth, snow is neuter.
Unlike the moon, it stays.
It falls, not from grace, but a silence
which nourishes crystals.
My son catches them on his tongue.

Whatever I try to hold perishes.
My son and I lie down in white pastures
of snow and flap like the last survivors
of a species that couldn't adapt to the air.
Jumping free, we look back at

angels, blurred fossils of majesty and justice
from the time when a ladder of angels
joined the house of the snow
to the houses of those whom it covered
with a dangerous blanket or a healing sleep.

As I lift my body from the angel's,
I remember the mad preacher of Indiana
who chose for the site of his kingdom
the footprint of an angel and named the place
New Harmony. Nothing of it survives.

The angels do not look backward
to see how their passing changes the earth,
the way I do, watching the snow,
and the waffles our boots print on its unleavened face,
and the nervous alphabet of the pheasant's feet,

and the five-petaled footprint of the cat,
and the shape of snowshoes, white and expensive as tennis,
and the deep ribbons tied and untied by the sleds.
I remember the millions who left the earth;
it holds no trace of them,

as it holds of us, tracking through snow,
so tame and defenseless
even the air could kill us.

How the Hen Sold Her Eggs to the Stingy Priest

An egg is a grand thing for a journey.

It will make you a small meal on the road
and a shape most serviceable to the hand

for darning socks, and for barter
a purse of gold opens doors anywhere.

If I wished for a world better than this one
I would keep, in an egg till it was wanted,

the gold earth floating on a clear sea.
If I wished for an angel, that would be my way,

the wings in gold waiting to wake,
the feet in gold waiting to walk,

and the heart that no one believed in
beating and beating the gold alive.

Questions My Son Asked Me, Answers I Never Gave Him

1. Do gorillas have birthdays?
   Yes. Like the rainbow they happen,
   like the air they are not observed.

2. Do butterflies make a noise?
   The wire in the butterfly's tongue
   hums gold.
   Some men hear butterflies
   even in winter.

3. Are they part of our family?
   They forgot us, who forgot how to fly.

4. Who tied my navel? Did God tie it?
   God made the thread: O man, live forever!
   Man made the knot: enough is enough.

5. If I drop my tooth in the telephone
   will it go through the wires and bite someone's ear?
   I have seen earlobes pierced by a tooth of steel.
   It loves what lasts.
   It does not love flesh.
   It leaves a ring of gold in the wound.

6. If I stand on my head
   will the sleep in my eye roll up into my head?
   Does the dream know its own father?
   Can bread go back to the field of its birth?

7. Can I eat a star?
   Yes, with the mouth of time
   that enjoys everything.

8. Could we xerox the moon?
   This is the first commandment:
   I am the moon, thy moon.
   Thou shalt have no other moons before thee.

9. Who invented water?
   The hands of the air, that wanted to wash each other.

10. What happens at the end of numbers?
    I see three men running toward a field.
    At the edge of the tall grass, they turn into light.

11. Do the years ever run out?
    God said, I will break time's heart.
    Time ran down like an old phonograph.
    It lay flat as a carpet.
    At rest on its threads, I am learning to fly.

Night Light

The moon is not green cheese.
It is china and stands in this room.
It has a ten-watt bulb and a motto:
Made in Japan.

Whey-faced, doll-faced,
it's closed as a tooth
and cold as the dead are cold
till I touch the switch.

Then the moon performs
its one trick:
it turns into a banana.
It warms to its subjects,

it draws us into its light,
just as I knew it would
when I gave ten dollars
to the pale clerk

in the store that sold
everything.
She asked, did I have a car?
She shrouded the moon in tissue

and laid it to rest in a box.
The box did not say *Moon*.
It said *This side up*.
I tucked the moon into my basket

and bicycled into the world.
By the light of the sun
I could not see the
moon under my sack of apples,

moon under slab of salmon,
moon under clean laundry,
under milk its sister
and bread its brother,

moon under meat.
Now supper is eaten.
Now laundry is folded away.
I shake out the old comforters.

My nine cats find their places
and go on dreaming where they left off.
My son snuggles under the heap.
His father loses his way in a book.

It is time to turn on the moon.
It is time to live by a different light.

Saint Pumpkin

Somebody's in there.
Somebody's sealed himself up
in this round room,
this hassock upholstered in rind,
this padded cell.
He believes if nothing unbinds him
he'll live forever.

Like our first room
it is dark and crowded.
Hunger knows no tongue
to tell it.
Water is glad there.

In this room with two navels
somebody wants to be born again.

So I unlock the pumpkin.
I carve out the lid
from which the stem raises
a dry handle on a damp world.
Lifting, I pull away
wet webs, vines on which hang
the flat tears of the pumpkin,

like fingernails or the currency
of bats. How the seeds shine,
as if water had put out
hundreds of lanterns.
Hundreds of eyes in the windless wood
gaze peacefully past me,
hacking the thickets,

and now a white dew beads the blade.
Has the saint surrendered
himself to his beard?
Has his beard taken root in his cell?

    Saint Pumpkin, pray for me,
    because when I looked for you, I found nothing,
    because unsealed and unkempt, your tomb rots,
    because I gave you a false face
    and a light of my own making.

The Feast of St. Tortoise

The day of her wedding, she crouches in the kitchen
and talks to the tortoise. He is older than she,
one of the family but celibate, reserved,

having taken holy orders in chapels of damp earth.
She admires his head, cobbled in ivory coins.

She touches his cowl, tender as chamois.
She praises his toadstool legs, his decisive beak,

and the raised ornament of his kindness
as he offers himself for a table

or a gameboard of fretted lacquer:
each hexagon fences a mound

into which a star has fallen so deeply
the whole field is on fire.

Let no guest go hungry.
She sets out a plate of lettuce chopped

into ruffles, the cool cheek
of an apple parceled and peeled.

This is for you, old friend.
He flippers forth. The bright worm of his tail
wags after him.

The Sleep of the Painted Ladies

This is my task: to move five cocoons
from an old jam jar to the butterfly cage.

Now they sway from the lid—
five corpses on a gallows

that drop their skins, shrunken to commas
and mark the leaf of their last meal.

I should knock before entering.
This is an ancient place

made for nothing but spinning
and falling asleep.

If I were smaller
or the room larger

I would see an old woman
draw from her outlawed wheel

my hundred years' sleep.
I would hear the snapping of threads,

their cry untuned
at the instant of breaking.

Here lies sleep, sheathed in five copper bullets
I can hold in my hand like aspirin,

five painted ladies who wanted
to travel, to forget everything.

NOTES

The Insects. Chartres, a city in Northern France, is famous for its cathedral. Maeterlinck (1862–1949) was a Belgian essayist, dramatist and poet. A burning glass is a lens for focusing the sun's rays.

Original Strawberry. A *mandala* is a Hindu or Buddhist symbol of the universe: a circle enclosing a square with a deity on each side.

How the Hen Sold Her Eggs to the Stingy Priest. The hen is speaking.

NANCY WILLARD

Books

Skin of Grace, 1967

The Lively Anatomy of God (stories), 1968

A New Herball, 1968

Testimony of the Invisible Man: William Carlos Williams, Francis Ponge, Rainer Maria Rilke, Pablo Neruda (criticism), 1970

19 Masks for the Naked Poet, 1971

Childhood of the Magician (prose), 1973

Carpenter of the Sun, 1974

A Visit to William Blake's Inn: Poems for Innocent and Experienced Travelers, 1981

Household Tales of Moon and Water, 1982

Angel in the Parlor: 5 Stories and 8 Essays, 1983

Things Invisible to See (novel), 1984

Criticism

Judith Baughman, "Nancy Willard," in *Dictionary of Literary Biography,* 1980.

Charles Wright
(b. 1935)

William Stafford

The poems of Charles Wright are filled with expressive language. Dense in detail, brimming with vitality, they strike us both as powerful representations of their subjects and as compelling verbal worlds in their own right. Certain stylistic features stand out right away. This poet loves proper names, for their weight and particularity—"It's hard freight / From Ducktown to Copper Hill, from Six / To Piled High"—and compound nouns for their way of fusing objects and movements, nouns and verbs, striking off small metaphors—"Spindrift and windfall: woodrot"— even as they enter the poem. Charles Wright is not afraid to use repetition and exaggeration, perhaps because he is a southerner, perhaps because his urge to write poetry was born while he was serving in the army and stationed in Italy, a country where the love of spoken language and high-flown expressiveness is both ancient and unabashed.

The music and energy of Wright's poems are always fitted to his subjects. The lush abundance of Dog Creek (near Hiwassee, North Carolina) is carefully re-created by the texture and emphasis of the verse in "Dog Creek Mainline," by the itemizing and elaborating, and by the figures of speech: turtles' heads as tomahawks, pike as knives in a drawer, the trees "in their jade death-suits." We feel that language and reality are being drawn closer together than is ordinarily possible. The poem begins to emerge as an exercise in memory, in which the obsessive ways of the imagination are matched to a landscape that reflects them. The poem closes with two parenthetical stanzas, as though the knowledge it moves toward, a kind of anatomy of our curious relation with the natural world, almost had to be whispered.

"Delta Traveller," on the other hand, uses a different kind of movement and a different atmosphere to explore the spiritual and psychological territory of grief and loss. An elegy for the poet's mother, it is a series of variations on the theme of loss and grief in which, once again, the extraordinary details and musical effects are entirely faithful to the subject. Some of the nine-line stanzas are one long sentence, but the moving tale of the empty dress is full of its own inevitable stops and starts: "The dress gets up, windbone and windskin, / To open the window. It is not there. / It goes to the door. It is not there. / The dress goes back and sits down. The dress gets up . . ." The pair of compound nouns here show how much compression Wright gets from his deft use of such words. "Windbone" and "windskin" are the shortest possible way of saying what is and isn't inside the dress, but they force the language into the foreground so that we sense the pressure of emotion, contorting its own expression. To read this poem aloud is to experience its cumulative force and superb control. The same can be said for "Virgo Descending," which might be called a family elegy for the way in which it imagines death as a gradual re-creation of the family home. Here, as in "Delta Traveller," there is an extraordinary mixture of dreaming and waking, real and surreal, cast in the form of a narrative that draws us forward powerfully, mixing humor and suspense, toward its thrilling, unparaphrasable ending.

"Dog Creek Mainline" is from Wright's 1973 volume, _Hard Freight,_ while "Delta Traveller" and "Virgo Descending" belong to _Bloodlines,_ published two years later. Each book is part of a carefully planned trilogy (dealing roughly with past, present, and future). From the third volume of that trilogy, _China Trace_ (1977) we have selected "Snow," "Stone Canyon Nocturne," "Spider Crystal Ascension," and "Sitting at Night on the Front Porch." As they indicate, the poems in this volume are relatively short, twelve lines or less. They take some of their inspiration from the journal-like meditations on landscape of Chinese poetry, but their distinctiveness comes from their metaphysical subject—they are poems about belief, about a spiritual quest or pilgrimage—and from the fact that they ask even more from language than Wright's previous poems, pushing expression to the limits of possibility. "Spider Crystal Ascension," a poem about looking at the night sky, particularly the Milky Way, illustrates this tendency. Its very title, as the poet has explained, consists of "three separate words that are supposed to give you the idea of what's coming in the whole poem." It represents an effort to "compress the language and the thought to such a point that they stop being small and start to enlarge." The short poems of *China Trace* do tend to expand enormously upon close consideration. They repay careful study.

Wright's trilogy was brought together, along with some earlier poems, in the 1982 volume *Country Music,* which won the American Book Award for Poetry. Meanwhile, the poet had embarked on a subsequent series of volumes that showed no slackening of inspiration or uncertainty of purpose. The three volumes published in the 1980s are distinguished by the same energy, experimentation, architectonic skill, and spiritual questing. From *The Southern Cross* (1981), we have included "Dog Day Vespers," "Dead Color," and "Hawaii Dantesca." From *The Other Side of the River* (1984) comes "Two Stories," and from *Zone Journals* (1988) our final selection, "March Journal." These three volumes are distinguished by, among other things, their use of the long line, a powerful command of narrative, surprising juxtapositions and arresting figurative language, and poems of impressive length and scope.

After a boyhood and education in Tennessee and North Carolina, some years in Italy, first with the Army and later through Fulbright Fellowships, Charles Wright studied at the Iowa Writers' Workshop. For some years he lived on the Southern California coast, teaching in the Writing Program at the University of California at Irvine. Since 1983 he has been a professor of English and a leading figure in the writing program at the University of Virginia.

DY

Dog Creek Mainline

Dog Creek: cat track and bird splay,
Spindrift and windfall; woodrot;
Odor of muscadine, the blue creep
Of kingsnake and copperhead;
Nightweed; frog spit and floating heart,
Backwash and snag pool: Dog Creek

Starts in the leaf reach and shoal run of the blood;
Starts in the falling light just back
Of the fingertips; starts
Forever in the black throat
You ask redemption of, in wants
You waken to, the odd door:

Its sky, old empty valise,
Stands open, departure in mind; its three streets,
Y-shaped and brown,
Go up the hills like a fever;
Its houses link and deploy
—This ointment, false flesh in another color.

                    *   *   *

Five cutouts, five silhouettes
Against the American twilight; the year
Is 1941; remembered names
—Rosendale, Perry and Smith—
Rise like dust in the deaf air;
The tops spin, the poison swells in the arm:

The trees in their jade death-suits,
The birds with their opal feet,
Shimmer and weave on the shoreline;
The moths, like forget-me-nots, blow
Up from the earth, their wet teeth
Breaking the dark, the raw grain;

The lake in its cradle hums
The old songs: out of its ooze, their heads
Like tomahawks, the turtles ascend
And settle back, leaving their chill breath
In blisters along the bank;
Locked in their wide drawer, the pike lie still as knives.

                              *   *   *

Hard freight. It's hard freight
From Ducktown to Copper Hill, from Six
To Piled High: Dog Creek is on this line,
Indigent spur; cross-tie by cross-tie it takes
You back, the red wind
Caught at your neck like a prize:

(The heart is a hieroglyph;
The fingers, like praying mantises, poise
Over what they have once loved;
The ear, cold cave, is an absence,
Tapping its own thin wires;
The eye turns in on itself.

The tongue is a white water.
In its slick ceremonies the light
Gathers, and is refracted, and moves
Outward, over the lips,
Over the dry skin of the world.
The tongue is a white water).

Delta Traveller
MWW, 1910–1964

Born in the quarter-night, brash
Tongue on the tongueless ward, the moon down,
The lake rising on schedule and Dr Hurt
Already across the water, and headed home—
And so I came sailing out, first child,
A stream with no bed to lie in,
A root with no branch to leaf,
The black balloon of promise tied to your wrist,
One inch of pain and an inch of light.

                              *   *   *

No wonder the children stand by those moist graves.
And produce is spread on the cobbled streets,
And portraits are carried out, and horns play.
And women, in single file, untangle
Corn from the storage bins, and soft cheese.
I shield my eyes against the sunlight,
Holding, in one hand, a death's-head,
Spun sugar and marzipan. I call it Love,
And shield my eyes against the sunlight.

       *   *   *

I lie down with you, I rise up with you.
If a grain turns in my eye,
I know it is you, entering, leaving,
Your name like a lozenge upon my tongue.
You drift through the antilife,
Scrim and snow-scud, fluff stem, hair
And tendril. You bloom in your own throat,
Frost flame in the frost dust,
One scratch on the slipstream, a closed mouth.

       *   *   *

High-necked and high-collared, slumped and creased,
A dress sits in a chair. Your dress,
Or your mother's dress, a dress
On a wooden chair, in a cold room, a room
With no windows and no doors, full of the east wind.
The dress gets up, windbone and windskin,
To open the window. It is not there.
It goes to the door. It is not there.
The dress goes back and sits down. The dress gets up . . .

       *   *   *

Three teeth and a thumbnail, white, white; four
Fingers that cradle a black chin;
Outline of eye-hole and nose-hole. This skull
And its one hand float up from the tar
And lime pit of dreams, night after slick night,
To lodge in the fork of the gum tree,
Its three teeth in the leaflight,
Its thumbnail in flash and foil,
Its mouth-hole a nothing I need to know.

       *   *   *

Cat's-eye and cloud, you survive.
The porcelain corridors
That glide forever beneath your feet,
The armed lawn chair you sit in,
Your bones like paint, your skin the wrong color—
All this you survive, and hold on,
A way of remembering, a pulse
That comes and goes in the night,
Match flare and wink, that comes and goes in the night.

         *   *   *

If the wafer of light offends me,
If the split tongue in the snake's mouth offends me,
I am not listening. They make the sound,
Which is the same sound, of the ant hill,
The hollow trunk, the fruit of the tree.
It is the Echo, the one transmitter of things:
Transcendent and inescapable,
It is the cloud, the mosquito's buzz,
The trickle of water across the leaf's vein.

         *   *   *

And so with the dead, the rock dead and the dust:
Worm and worm-fill, pearl, milk-eye
And light in the earth, the dead are brought
Back to us, piece by piece—
Under the sponged log, inside the stump,
They shine with their secret lives, and grow
Big with their messages, wings
Beginning to stir, paths fixed and hearts clocked,
Rising and falling back and rising.

Virgo Descending

Through the viridian (and black of the burnt match),
Through ox-blood and ochre, the ham-colored clay,
Through plate after plate, down
Where the worm and the mole will not go,
Through ore-seam and fire-seam,
My grandmother, senile and 89, crimpbacked, stands
Like a door ajar on her soft bed,
The open beams and bare studs of the hall
Pink as an infant's skin in the floating dark:
Shavings and curls swing down like snowflakes across her face.

My aunt and I walk past. As always, my father
Is planning rooms, dragging his lame leg.
Stroke-straightened and foreign, behind him,
An aberrant 2-by-4 he can't fit snug.
I lay my head on my aunt's shoulder, feeling
At home, and walk on.
Through arches and door jambs, the spidery wires
And coiled cables, the blueprint takes shape:
My mother's room to the left, the door closed;
My father's room to the left, the door closed—

Ahead, my brother's room, unfinished;
Behind, my sister's room, also unfinished.
Buttresses, winches, block-and-tackle: the scale of everything
Is enormous. We keep on walking. And pass
My aunt's room, almost complete, the curtains up,
The lamp and the medicine arranged
In their proper places, in arm's reach of where the bed will go . . .
The next one is mine, now more than half done,
Cloyed by the scent of jasmine,
White-gummed and anxious, their mouths sucking the air dry.

Home is what you lie in, or hang above, the house
Your father made, or keeps on making,
The dirt you moisten, the sap you push up and nourish . . .
I enter the living room, it, too, unfinished, its far wall
Not there, opening on to a radiance
I can't begin to imagine, a light
My father walks from, approaching me,
Dragging his right leg, rolling his plans into a perfect curl.
That light, he mutters, that damned light.
We can't keep it out. It keeps on filling your room.

Snow

If we, as we are, are dust, and dust, as it will, rises,
Then we will rise, and recongregate
In the wind, in the cloud, and be their issue,

Things in a fall in a world of fall, and slip
Through the spiked branches and snapped joints of the evergreens,
White ants, white ants and the little ribs.

Stone Canyon Nocturne

Ancient of Days, old friend, no one believes you'll come back.
No one believes in his own life anymore.

The moon, like a dead heart, cold and unstartable, hangs by a thread
At the earth's edge,
Unfaithful at last, splotching the ferns and the pink shrubs.

In the other world, children undo the knots in their tally strings.
They sing songs, and their fingers blear.

And here, where the swan hums in his socket, where bloodroot
And belladonna insist on our comforting,
Where the fox in the canyon wall empties our hands, ecstatic for more,

Like a bead of clear oil the Healer revolves through the night wind,
Part eye, part tear, unwilling to recognize us.

Spider Crystal Ascension

The spider, juiced crystal and Milky Way, drifts on his web through the
   night sky
And looks down, waiting for us to ascend . . .

At dawn he is still there, invisible, short of breath, mending his net.

All morning we look for the white face to rise from the lake like a tiny
   star.
And when it does, we lie back in our watery hair and rock.

Sitting at Night on the Front Porch

I'm here, on the dark porch, restyled in my mother's chair.
10:45 and no moon.
Below the house, car lights
Swing down, on the canyon floor, to the sea.

In this they resemble us,
Dropping like match flames through the great void
Under our feet.
In this they resemble her, burning and disappearing.

Everyone's gone
And I'm here, sizing the dark, saving my mother's seat.

Dog Day Vespers

Sun like an orange mousse through the trees,
A snowfall of trumpet bells on the oleander;
                           mantis paws
Craning out of the new wisteria; fruit smears in the west . . .
DeStael knifes a sail on the bay;
A mother's summons hangs like a towel on the dusk's hook . . .

Everything drips and spins
In the pepper trees, the pastel glide of the evening

Slowing to mother-of-pearl and the night sky.
Venus breaks clear in the third heaven.
Quickly the world is capped, and the seal turned.

I drag my chair to the deck's edge and the blue ferns.
I'm writing you now by flashlight,
The same news and the same story I've told you often before.
As the stag-stars begin to shine,
A wing brushes my left hand,
                              but it's not my wing.

Dead Color

I lie for a long time on my left side and my right side
And eat nothing,
                    but no voice comes on the wind
And no voice drops from the cloud.
Between the grey spiders and the orange spiders,
                              no voice comes on the wind . . .

Later, I sit for a long time by the waters of Har,
And no face appears on the face of the deep.

Meanwhile, the heavens assemble their dark map.
The traffic begins to thin.
Aphids munch on the sweet meat of the lemon trees.
The lawn sprinklers rise and fall . . .

And here's a line of brown ants cleaning a possum's skull.
And here's another, come from the opposite side.

Over my head, star-pieces dip in their yellow scarves toward their
                                        black desire.

Windows, rapturous windows!

Hawaii Dantesca

White-sided flowers are thrusting up on the hillside,
                    blank love letters from the dead.
It's autumn, and nobody seems to mind.

Or the broken shadows of those missing for hundreds of years
Moving over the sugar cane
                    like storks, which nobody marks or mends.

This is the story line.

And the viridescent shirtwaists of light the trees wear.
And the sutra-circles of cattle egrets wheeling out past the rain
    showers.

And the spiked marimbas of dawn rattling their amulets . . .

Soon it will be time for the long walk under the earth toward the sea.

And time to retrieve the yellow sunsuit and little shoes
                                        they took my picture in

In Knoxville, in 1938.

Time to gather the fire in its quartz bowl.

I hope the one with the white wings will come.
I hope the island of reeds is as far away as I think it is.

When I get there, I hope they forgive me if the knot I tie is the
                                        wrong knot.

Two Stories

Tonight, on the deck, the lights
Semaphore up at me through the atmosphere,
Town lights, familiar lights
                        pulsing and slacking off
The way they used to back on the ridge outside of Kingsport
35 years ago,
The moonlight sitting inside my head
Like knives,
            the cold like a drug I knew I'd settle down with.
I used to imagine them shore lights, as these are, then,
As something inside me listened with all its weight
For the sea-surge and the sea-change.

————————

There's a soft spot in everything
Our fingers touch,
                the one place where everything breaks
When we press it just right.
The past is like that with its arduous edges and blind sides,
The whorls of our fingerprints
                        embedded along its walls
Like fossils the sea has left behind.

————————

This is a story I swear is true.

I used to sleepwalk. But only
On camping trips,
            or whenever I slept outside.
One August, when I was 11, on Mount LeConte in Tennessee,

Campfire over, and ghost story over,
Everyone still asleep, apparently I arose
From my sleeping bag,
              opened the tent flap, and started out on the trail
That led to the drop-off, where the mountainside
Went straight down for almost a thousand feet.
Half-moon and cloud cover, so some light
As I went on up the path through the rhododendron,
The small pebbles and split roots
                    like nothing under my feet.
The cliffside was half a mile from the campsite.
As I got closer,
           moving blindly, unerringly,
Deeper in sleep than the shrubs,
I stepped out, it appears,
Onto the smooth lip of the rock cape of the cliff,
When my left hand, and then my right hand,
Stopped me as they were stopped
By the breathing side of a bear which woke me
And there we were,
           the child and the black bear and the cliff-drop,
And this is the way it went—
               I stepped back, and I turned around,
And I walked down through the rhododendron
And never looked back,
             truly awake in the throbbing world,
And I ducked through the low flap
Of the tent, so quietly, and I went to sleep
And never told anyone
Till years later when I thought I knew what it meant,
                which now I've forgot.

———————

And this one is questionable,
Though sworn to me by an old friend
Who'd killed a six-foot diamondback about seven o'clock in
   the morning
(He'd found it coiled in a sunny place),
And threw it into a croker sack with its head chopped off,
              and threw the sack in the back of a jeep,
Then left for his day's work
On the farm.
          That evening he started to show the snake
To someone, and put his hand in the sack to pull it out.
As he reached in, the snake's stump struck him.
His wrist was bruised for a week.

_____

It's not age,
            nor time with its gold eyelid and blink,
Nor dissolution in all its mimicry
That lifts us and sorts us out.
It's discontinuity
                and all its spangled coming between
That sends us apart and keeps us there in a dread.
It's what's in the rear-view mirror,
                                    smaller and out of sight.

_____

What do you do when the words don't come to you anymore,
And all the embolisms fade in the dirt?
And the ocean sings in its hammock,
                        rocking itself back and forth?
And you live at the end of the road where the sky starts its
    dark decline?

The barking goes on and on
                            from the far hill, constantly
Sticking its noise in my good ear.

Goodbye, Miss Sweeney, goodbye.
I'm starting to think about the psychotransference of all things.
It's small bones in the next life.
It's small bones,
            and heel and toe forever and ever.

March Journal

—After the Rapture comes, and everyone goes away
    Quicker than cream in a cat's mouth,
                                    all of them gone
    In an endless slip-knot down the sky
                                    and its pink tongue
    Into the black hole of Somewhere Else,

What will we do, left with the empty spaces of our lives
Intact,
        the radio frequencies still unchanged,
The same houses up for sale,
Same books unread,
                all comfort gone and its comforting . . .

For us, the earth is a turbulent rest,
                            a different bed

Altogether, and kinder than that—
After the first death is the second,
A little fire in the afterglow,
                    somewhere to warm your hands.
—The clean, clear line, incised, unbleeding,
  Sharp and declarative as a cut
               the instant before the blood wells out . . .
—*March Blues*

The insides were blue, the color of Power Putty,
When Luke dissected the dogfish,
                a plastic blue

In the whey
        sharkskin infenestrated:
Its severed tailfin bobbled like a wing-nut in another pan
As he explained the dye job
             and what connected with what,
Its pursed lips skewed and pointed straight-lined at the ceiling,
The insides so blue, so blue . . .

March gets its second wind,
                starlings high shine in the trees
As dread puts its left foot down and then the other.
Buds hold their breaths and sit tight.
The weeping cherries
        lower their languorous necks and nibble the grass
Sprout ends that jump head first from the ground,
Magnolia drums blue weight
           next door when the sun is right.
—Rhythm comes from the roots of the world,
            rehearsed and expandable.

—After the ice storm a shower of crystal down from the trees
  Shattering over the ground
               like cut glass twirling its rainbows,
  Sunlight in flushed layers under the clouds,
  Twirling and disappearing into the clenched March grass.

—Structure is binary, intent on a resolution,
  Its parts tight but the whole loose
           and endlessly repetitious.

—And here we stand, caught
  In the crucifixal noon
           with its bled, attendant bells,
  And nothing to answer back with.
  Forsythia purrs in its burning shell,
  Jonquils, like Dante's angels, appear from their blue shoots.

How can we think to know of another's desire for darkness,
That low coo like a dove's
                insistent outside the heart's window?
How can we think to think this?
How can we sit here, crossing out line after line,
Such 5-finger exercises
            up and down, learning our scales,

And say that all quartets are eschatological
Heuristically
       when the willows swim like medusas through the trees,
Their skins beginning to blister into a 1000 green welts?
How can we think to know these things,
Clouds like full suds in the sky
           keeping away, keeping away?

—Form is finite, an undestroyable hush over all things.

NOTES

Dead Color. Wright's own note quotes from A. Vollard: "When I saw Degas again, he happened to have a box of pastels in his hand, and was spreading them out on a board in front of the window. Seeing me watching him: 'I take all the color out of them that I can, by putting them in the sun.'

'But what do you use, then, to get colors of such brightness?'
'Dead color, Monsieur.' "

Hawaii Dantesca. The Dante reference is to the reed of humility in the first book of the *Purgatorio*.

CHARLES WRIGHT

Books

The Grave of the Right Hand, 1970
Hard Freight, 1973
Bloodlines, 1975
China Trace, 1977
Eugenio Montale, The Storm and
  Other Things (translations), 1978

The Southern Cross, 1981
Country Music, 1982
The Other Side of the River, 1984
Dino Campana, Orphic Songs
  (translations), 1984
Zone Journals, 1988

Interviews, Criticism

Wright: A Profile (Profile Editions, Grilled Flowers Press; with an interview, an essay, new poems by Charles Wright, and a select bibliography), 1979; "Charles Wright at Oberlin," in A FIELD Guide to Contemporary Poetry and Poetics, ed. Friebert and Young, 1980; Helen Vendler, Part of Nature, Part of Us: Modern American Poets, 1980; Sherod Santos, "An Interview with Charles Wright," in Quarterly West 12 (1981); Helen Vendler, The Music of What Happens, 1988.

part five

Ten Poets Born After 1940

Rita
Dove
(b. 1952)

Fred Viebahn

Rita Dove was born and raised in Akron, Ohio. She graduated from high school as a Presidential Scholar, went on to Miami University in Oxford, Ohio, then studied in Germany as a Fulbright Scholar before attending the Iowa Writers' Workshop. In the ten years that have followed her Iowa MFA, she has developed steadily and impressively as a poet, a development recognized by the award of the 1987 Pulitzer Prize for Poetry. The fourteenth woman to win the prize, and the second Afro-American, she was also, at 34, one of the youngest recipients.

Dove's poems operate by means of skillful combinations of narrative and metaphor. She explores the textures, sequences, and meanings of a variety of human lives. In the process, she tries to know what her characters know, through intimate engagement with their memories and imaginations, as well as to know beyond them, toward encompassing insights into their lives and deaths. Her poems are both acts of sympathy and efforts at transcendence, and they are characterized by a steadiness of vision and a discipline of style that make them all the more convincing.

The comparatively early "Banneker" shows her shaping this strategy by applying it to a curious historical figure, a brilliant and eccentric black from the early days of the American Republic. She enters Banneker's perspective from the real details of his life—the pear tree, the stew pot, the cloak and rifle—while working toward a larger understanding of him through exploratory metaphors—"a capacious bird / humming" and "a white-maned / figure stalking the darkened / breast of the Union"—until she is able to glimpse him as a visionary prophet, foreseeing in the stars and in the "rot of spring" both the good and bad that would grow from the "spiral of lights" taking shape as Washington, D.C., in an ironic echoing of an already questionable firmament.

Both men and women characters are subject to this searching and humane technique, as the Pulitzer Prize volume, *Thomas and Beulah,* demonstrates, and as the selection of poems following confirms. Poems like "Sunday Greens," "Dusting," "Daystar," and "Weathering Out" illustrate the assurance and delicacy with which Dove handles the inner and outer lives of women, while "The Satisfaction Coal Company" shows comparable achievement with a male protagonist and "Courtship" reflects her talent for exploring the intertwining of male and female perspectives. But the poems are never simply gender-oriented. Beulah's workday reverie in "Dusting," in which she eventually succeeds in remembering the name of an early suitor—an action persuasively mirrored in the image of the thawed and revived goldfish—is about human imagination, memory, and solace in the same way that these issues are handled, on a broader scale, in "The Satisfaction Coal Company." And the touching recollection of Beulah's pregnancy in "Weathering Out" makes room for Thomas's emotions too: If she is a lamp, he is one of the illuminated, and if she is the zeppelin, he is the man who "walked it out gingerly, like a poodle." The wit of that last comparison-within-a-comparison demonstrates the delicate skill of Rita Dove's art. And the larger context reminds us that her poems are inclusive: if they are about women, they are also about men; if about blacks, they are also about whites. They map and enrich our common humanity.

Rita Dove currently teaches at Arizona State University in Tempe. Both her achievement and her promise have placed her among the mostly highly regarded writers of her generation.

DY

Banneker

What did he do except lie
under a pear tree, wrapped in
a great cloak, and meditate
on the heavenly bodies?
Venerable, the good people of Baltimore
whispered, shocked and more than
a little afraid. After all it was said
he took to strong drink.
Why else would he stay out
under the stars all night
and why hadn't he married?

But who would want him! Neither
Ethiopian nor English, neither
lucky nor crazy, a capacious bird
humming as he penned in his mind
another enflamed letter
to President Jefferson—he imagined
the reply, polite and rhetorical.
Those who had been to Philadelphia
reported the statue
of Benjamin Franklin
before the library

his very size and likeness.
A wife? No, thank you.
At dawn he milked
the cows, then went inside
and put on a pot to stew
while he slept. The clock
he whittled as a boy
still ran. Neighbors
woke him up
with warm bread and quilts.
At nightfall he took out

his rifle—a white-maned
figure stalking the darkened
breast of the Union—and
shot at the stars, and by chance
one went out. Had he killed?
I assure thee, my dear Sir!
Lowering his eyes to fields
sweet with the rot of spring, he could see

a government's domed city
rising from the morass and spreading
in a spiral of lights . . . .

Dusting

Every day a wilderness—no
shade in sight. Beulah
patient among knicknacks,
the solarium a rage
of light, a grainstorm
as her gray cloth brings
dark wood to life.

Under her hand scrolls
and crests gleam
darker still. What
was his name, that
silly boy at the fair with
the rifle booth? And his kiss and
the clear bowl with one bright
fish, rippling
wound!

Not Michael—
something finer. Each dust
stroke a deep breath and
the canary in bloom.
Wavery memory: home
from a dance, the front door
blown open and the parlor
in snow, she rushed
the bowl to the stove, watched
as the locket of ice
dissolved and he
swam free.

That was years before
Father gave her up
with her name, years before
her name grew to mean
Promise, then
Desert-in-Peace.
Long before the shadow and
sun's accomplice, the tree.

Maurice.

Sunday Greens

She wants to hear
wine pouring.
She wants to taste
change. She wants
pride to roar through
the kitchen till it shines
like straw, she wants

lean to replace
tradition. Ham knocks
in the pot, nothing
but bones, each
with its bracelet
of flesh.

The house stinks
like a zoo in summer,
while upstairs
her man sleeps on.
Robe slung over
her arm and
the cradled hymnal,

she pauses, remembers
her mother in a slip
lost in blues,
and those collards,
wild-eared,
singing.

Daystar

She wanted a little room for thinking:
but she saw diapers steaming on the line,
a doll slumped behind the door.

So she lugged a chair behind the garage
to sit out the children's naps.

Sometimes there were things to watch—
the pinched armor of a vanished cricket,
a floating maple leaf. Other days
she stared until she was assured
when she closed her eyes
she'd see only her own vivid blood.

She had an hour, at best, before Liza appeared
pouting from the top of the stairs.
And just *what* was mother doing
out back with the field mice? Why,

building a palace. Later
that night when Thomas rolled over and
lurched into her, she would open her eyes
and think of the place that was hers
for an hour—where
she was nothing,
pure nothing, in the middle of the day.

Weathering Out

She liked mornings the best—Thomas gone
to look for work, her coffee flushed with milk,

outside autumn trees blowsy and dripping.
Past the seventh month she couldn't see her feet

so she floated from room to room, houseshoes flapping,
navigating corners in wonder. When she leaned

against a door jamb to yawn, she disappeared entirely.
Last week they had taken a bus at dawn
to the new airdock. The hangar slid open in segments

and the zeppelin nosed forward in its silver envelope.
The man walked it out gingerly, like a poodle,

then tied it to a mast and went back inside.
Beulah felt just that large and placid, a lake;

she glistened from cocoa butter smoothed in
when Thomas returned every evening nearly

in tears. He'd lean an ear on her belly
and say: *Little fellow's really talking,*

though to her it was more the *pok-pok-pok*
of a fingernail tapping a thick cream lampshade.

Sometimes during the night she woke and found him
asleep there and the child sleeping, too.

The coffee was good but too little. Outside
everything shivered in tinfoil—only the clover

between the cobblestones hung stubbornly on,
green as an afterthought. . . .

Courtship

1

Fine evening may I have
the pleasure . . .
up and down the block
waiting—for what? A
magnolia breeze, someone
to trot out the stars?

But she won't set a foot
in his turtledove Nash,
it wasn't proper.
Her pleated skirt fans
softly, a circlet of arrows.

King of the Crawfish
in his yellow scarf,
mandolin belly pressed tight
to his hounds-tooth vest—
his wrist flicks for the pleats
all in a row, sighing . . .

2

. . . so he wraps the yellow silk
still warm from his throat
around her shoulders. (He made
good money; he could buy another.)
A gnat flies
in his eye and she thinks
he's crying.

Then the parlor festooned
like a ship and Thomas
twirling his hat in his hands
wondering how did I get here.
China pugs guarding a fringed settee
where a father, half-Cherokee,
smokes and frowns.
I'll give her a good life—
what was he doing,
selling all for a song?
His heart fluttering shut
then slowly opening.

The Satisfaction Coal Company

1

What to do with a day.
Leaf through *Jet*. Watch T.V.
Freezing on the porch
but he goes anyhow, snow too high
for a walk, the ice treacherous.
Inside, the gas heater takes care of itself;
he doesn't even notice being warm.

Everyone says he looks great.
Across the street a drunk stands smiling
at something carved in a tree.
The new neighbor with the floating hips
scoots out to get the mail
and waves once, brightly,
storm door clipping her heel on the way in.

2

Twice a week he had taken the bus down Glendale hill
to the corner of Market. Slipped through
the alley by the canal and let himself in.
Started to sweep
with terrible care, like a woman
brushing shine into her hair,
same motion, same lullaby.
No curtains—the cop on the beat
stopped outside once in the hour
to swing his billy club and glare.

It was better on Saturdays
when the children came along:
he mopped while they emptied
ashtrays, clang of glass on metal
then a dry scutter. Next they counted
nailheads studding the leather cushions.
Thirty-four! they shouted,
that was the year and
they found it mighty amusing.

But during the week he noticed more—
lights when they gushed or dimmed
at the Portage Hotel, the 10:32
picking up speed past the B & O switchyard,
floorboards trembling and the explosive
kachook kachook kachook kachook
and the oiled rails ticking underneath.

3

They were poor then but everyone had been poor.
He hadn't minded the sweeping,
just the thought of it—like now
when people ask him what he's thinking
and he says *I'm listening.*

Those nights walking home alone,
the bucket of coal scraps banging his knee,
he'd hear a roaring furnace
with its dry, familiar heat. Now the nights
take care of themselves—as for the days,

there is the canary's sweet curdled song,
the wino smiling through his dribble.
Past the hill, past the gorge
choked with wild sumac in summer,
the corner has been upgraded.
Still, he'd like to go down there someday
to stand for a while, and get warm.

RITA DOVE

Books

The Yellow House on the Corner,
  1980
Museum, 1983

Fifth Sunday (short stories), 1985
Thomas and Beulah, 1986

Norman
Dubie
(b. 1945)

Jeannine Savard

I n his first major collection, *Alehouse Sonnets* (1971), Norman Dubie conducted highly inventive, spirited conversations with the nineteenth-century British essayist William Hazlitt, in which both men's lives seemed to merge. Dubie had hit on a method that, in one form or another, has served him ever since. Eschewing his own personality and voice more than any other contemporary poet, Dubie slips into a dazzling variety of historical figures: Queen Elizabeth I, Coleridge, Beethoven, Ibsen, Kafka, and the World War II saboteur-singer, Marie Triste, among others! He has taught himself to speak in character for all of them. Working with what might be called historical narratives, or dramatic fictions—some poems within this larger frame are purely dramatic monologues—Dubie goes about collecting and making up "facts" for the past and present as he takes up, in Marvin Bell's apt phrase, "the difficulties of personal histories, intimate and cultural, told or insinuated." The results are unlikely histories, which we enter as if through a seance, from an unlikely historian. One is reminded of similar efforts in contemporary fiction, where novelists like E. L. Doctorow and D. M. Thomas weave living and dead, real and fictional, personalities into vibrant tapestries. While it would be foolish to claim that Dubie's poetic constructions can be approached as historical documents, they make us feel, as does the best recorded history, the dynamic interplay among their unlikely protagonists. Dubie achieves this by carefully linking events, which are bathed in suggestive details that illuminate or illustrate rather than merely characterize, those moments in history that he takes to be formative. Without this linkage of events, history—or human activity—would amount to a series of random happenings.

Dubie mentions starting to write once by staring at his wall, on which hung "a narrow photograph of Dresden in a snowstorm, my only window." That is a useful way to think about his poems as well. All taught history is circumvented, and we are left with one slit into the past through these picture-poems, or, as he called an entire book of them, *The Illustrations* (1977). By staring at them, one enters a double consciousness in which the mass of history is blacked out so we can concentrate on a particular series of events that are projected before us. As we share in these images, and these images alone (see "The Ganges"), a new sense of history is born. As if to stress the importance of having but one window, or vantage point, Dubie moves his characters to where they can look out on a narrow scene and thus intensify their vision. In "The Fox Who Watched for the Midnight Sun," Henrik Ibsen "looks out / Into the March storm for an illustration," a sign of what to follow in his bafflement. Obsessed by these windows on the world, Dubie calls one book *The Window in the Field* (1982).

Both for Dubie and for his characters, caught in the frozen frames of their histories, events are clarified when seen through literal, or figurative, windows. The "funeral ghats" in "The Ganges" afford the same sort of passageway as Dubie's "narrow photograph" or the walk under the waterfall: They are a birth-chute through which we enter the next level and the next and the next—"It will be dark with a mist/ Where the stairs jump into the water." In "February: The Boy Breughel" something happens out past the trees as well, as "a boy in a red shirt who woke / A moment ago / Watches from the window" to see the fox eat its kill. It is something to do with lost innocence, with paying witness, something tiny at first that prefigures, or "inaugurates," as Dubie says of another poem, "something as huge as our Second World War."

But Dubie can also cast his visions on a much smaller scale as well, if the "story" merits lyricism and delicacy. The shorter pieces that close this section, "Thomas Hardy" and "Hummingbirds," both focus on birds as a way of helping us get past the larger presences—in the one instance, God's—that might stress our isolation and singularity, and they remind us that there is salvation in plurality, that creatures "feast in pairs," "two white birds are met by a third"; courage has eyes.

Norman Dubie was born in Vermont and grew up in the Northeast. He has degrees from Goddard College and the Iowa Writers' Workshop and currently teaches at Arizona State University in Tempe.

SF

February: The Boy Breughel

The birches stand in their beggar's row:
Each poor tree
Has had its wrists nearly
Torn from the clear sleeves of bone,
These icy trees
Are hanging by their thumbs
Under a sun
That will begin to heal them soon,
Each will climb out
Of its own blue, oval mouth;
The river groans,
Two birds call out from the woods

And a fox crosses through snow
Down a hill; then, he runs,
He has overcome something white
Beside a white bush, he shakes
It twice, and as he turns
For the woods, the blood on the snow

Looks like the red fox,
At a distance, running down the hill:
A white rabbit in his mouth killed
By the fox in snow
Is killed over and over as just
Two colors, now, on a winter hill:

Two colors! Red and white. A barber's bowl!
Two colors like the peppers
In the windows
Of the town below the hill. Smoke comes
From the chimneys. Everything is still.

Ice in the river begins to move,
And a boy in a red shirt who woke
A moment ago
Watches from his window
The street where an ox
Who's broken out of his hut
Stands in the fresh snow
Staring cross-eyed at the boy
Who smiles and looks out
Across the roof to the hill;
And the sun is reaching down
Into the woods

Where the smoky red fox still
Eats his kill. Two colors.
Just two colors!
A sunrise. The snow.

The Ganges

I'm sorry but we can't go to the immersions tonight
For the poor will not get down from the wheel, and
The musicians and the lorry won't budge
Without the money. We don't have it. But, we could

Walk to the cremations. It will be dark with a mist
Where the stairs jump into the water. These are
The funeral ghats. The corpses are brought in drapes
And that one will be dipped in the river and then
She will be anointed with clarified butter. To the
Left of us four men waist deep in the river sift
Through mud and ashes for gold rings.
With a straw torch
The dead mother's son starts the fire;
With a bone cudgel
He smashes her skull to release the images shared
By her with these

Postcards I am now passing to you:
Of the family pond entirely filled with limes,
White pigs rooting in coconut husks, and her six
Children watering their charges, the black lulled elephants.

Elizabeth's War with the Christmas Bear: 1601

For Paul Zimmer

The bears are kept by hundreds within fences, are fed cracked
Eggs; the weakest are
Slaughtered and fed to the others after being scented
With the blood of deer brought to the pastures by Elizabeth's
Men—the blood spills from deep pails with bottoms of slate.

The balding Queen had bear-gardens in London and in the country.
The bear is baited: the nostrils
Are blown full with pepper, the Irish wolf dogs
Are starved, then, emptied, made crazy with fermented barley:

And the bear's hind leg is chained to a stake, the bear
Is blinded and whipped, kneeling in his own blood and slaver, he is
Almost instantly worried by the dogs. At the very moment that
Elizabeth took Essex's head, a giant brown bear
Stood in the gardens with dogs hanging from his fur . . .
He took away the sun, took
A wolfhound in his mouth and tossed it into
The white lap of Elizabeth I—arrows and staves rained

On his chest, and standing, he, then, stood even taller, seeing
Into the Queen's private boxes—he grinned
Into her battered eggshell face.
Another volley of arrows and poles, and opening his mouth
He showered blood all over Elizabeth and her Privy Council.

The next evening, a cool evening, the Queen demanded
13 bears and the justice of 113 dogs: She slept

All that Sunday night and much of the next morning.
Some said she was guilty of *this* and *that.*
The Protestant Queen gave the defeated bear
A grave in a Catholic cemetery. The marker said:
Peter, a Solstice Bear, a gift of the Tsarevitch to Elizabeth.

After a long winter she had the grave opened. The bear's skeleton
Was cleared with lye, she placed it at her bedside,
Put a candle inside behind the sockets of the eyes, and, then
She spoke to it:

You were a Christmas bear—behind your eyes
I see the walls of a snow cave where you are a cub still smelling
Of your mother's blood which has dried in your hair; you have
Troubled a Queen who was afraid
When seated in *shade* which, standing,
You had created! A Queen who often wakes with a dream
Of you at night—
Now, you'll stand by my bed in your long white bones; alone, you
Will frighten away at night all visions of bear, and all day
You will be in this cold room—your constant grin,
You'll stand in the long, white prodigy of your bones, and you are,

Every inch of you, a terrible vision, not bear, but virgin!

The Fox Who Watched
for the Midnight Sun

Across the snowy pastures of the estate
Open snares drift like paw prints under rain, everywhere
There is the conjured rabbit being dragged
Up into blowing snow: it struggles
Upside down by a leg, its belly
Is the slaked white of cottages along the North Sea.

Inside the parlor Ibsen writes of a summer garden, of a
Butterfly sunken inside the blossoming tulip.
He describes the snapdragon with its little sconce of dew.
He moves from the desk to a window. Remembers his studies
In medicine, picturing the sticky
Overlapping eyelids of drowned children. On the corner
Of the sofa wrapped in Empress-silks there's a box
Of fresh chocolates. He mimics the deceptively distant,
Chittering birdsong within the cat's throat.
How it attracts finches to her open window.
He turns toward the fire, now thinking of late sessions in Storting.
Ibsen had written earlier of an emotional girl
With sunburnt shoulders,

Her surprise when the heavy dipper came up
From the well with frogs' eggs bobbing in her water.
He smiles.

Crosses the room like the fox walking away
From the woodpile.
He picks up his lamp and takes it
To the soft chair beneath the window. Brandy is poured.
Weary, he closes his eyes and dreams
Of his mother at a loom, how she would dip, dressing
The warp with a handful of coarse wool.

Henrik reaches for tobacco—tomorrow, he'll write
Of summer once more, he'll begin with a fragrance . . .
Now, though, he wonders about the long
Devotion of his muscles to his bones, he's worried by
The wind which hurries the pages in this drafty room.
He looks out
Into the March storm for an illustration: under a tree
A large frozen hare swings at the end of a snare-string.
The fox sits beneath it, his upturned head swinging with it,
The jaws are locked in concentration,

As if the dead hare were soon to awaken.

Thomas Hardy

The first morning after anyone's death, is it important
To know that fields are wet, that the governess is
Naked but with a scarf still covering her head, that
She's sitting on a gardener who's wearing
Just a blue shirt, or that he's sitting on a chair in the kitchen.
They look like they are rowing while instead outside in the mist
Two boats are passing on the river, the gardener's mouth
Is opening:

A white, screaming bird lifts off the river into the trees,
Flies a short distance and is joined
By a second bird, but then as if to destroy everything
The two white birds are met by a third. *The night
Always fails.* The cows are all now standing in the barns.
You can hear the milk as it drills into wooden pails.

Hummingbirds

They will be without arms like God.

By the millions their dried skins will be sought
In the new world.
Their young will be like wet slugs.
They will obsess the moon
Over a field of night-flowering phlox.
Their nests will be a delicate cup of moss.

In pairs
They will feast on a tarantula in thin air.

They have made a new statement
About our world—a clerk in Memphis
Has confessed to laying out feeders
Filled with sulphuric acid. She says

God asked for these deaths . . . like God
They are insignificant, and have visited us

Who are wretched.

NOTES

February: *The Boy Breughel*. Pieter Breughel (1525?–1569), the Flemish painter.

The Ganges. Ganges is a river flowing from the Himalayas in Northern India to the Bay of Bengal. It is sacred to the Hindus. A *ghat* is a passage or stairway descending to a river.

Elizabeth's War with the Christmas Bear: 1601. The Earl of Essex was a British soldier and a favorite of Queen Elizabeth I. Tsarevitch refers to the eldest son of the Emperor (Tsar) of Russia.

NORMAN DUBIE

Books

The Horsehair Sofa, 1968

Alehouse Sonnets, 1971

In the Dead of the Night, 1975

The Illustrations, 1977

The City of the Olesha Fruit, 1979

The Everlastings, 1980

The Window in the Field, 1982

Selected and New Poems, 1983

The Springhouse, 1986

Interviews

American Poetry Review 7, No. 4 (July/August 1978).

Laura
Jensen
(b. 1948)

Janet Ness

Laura Jensen writes a good deal about fear and distress, but her poems are also filled with surges of pleasure and delight. The voice that speaks of these emotional extremes is calm, and the poems have a lyrical lilt so that an interesting discrepancy sometimes arises between subject matter and tone. In addition, that quiet voice keeps turning unexpected corners; readers face new and sudden prospects without knowing how they got there. Altogether, the challenge of a Laura Jensen poem is not undertaken lightly, though the rewards for plucky readers are considerable.

Sometimes the speaker of a Jensen poem is in the presence of another person, and this "implied listener," whose position is more or less the same as the reader's, may find the relationship disquieting. In "The Red Dog," for instance, the speaker is moved to announce that the dog's lively vigor, his utter happiness on the beach, is a sign of his death, indeed that "this is the best time for it." The insistence, as though "you" were reluctant to accept this idea, suggests that the relation between speaker and listener constitutes the poem's real drama.

More often, however, the poetic voice in a Jensen poem is alone, reflecting. It may be remembering the pleasures of childhood, as in "The Ajax Samples" and "Kite," or re-exploring childhood dislocation, as in "An Age." It may move into considerations of the domestic, as in "Household," which grows fascinated with needles, or in "Kitchen," which maps a convincing psychological terrain. Other poems launch their meditations out of considerations of seasonal change, travel, and daily contacts of all kinds. Even the most familiar activities and objects take on a newness and a strangeness.

A closer look at one of Jensen's finest poems, "As the Window Darkens," should clarify some of her methods. In the series of clauses that opens the poem, "as" can mean both "while" and "in the same way that." This elaborate sentence, evoking dusk, turns out to be a reflexive statement about the poem. The reader–poem relationship is now equated with that of the protagonist, gazing out a darkening window that gradually becomes a mirror. The mirror tells us we aren't beautiful, and we remember how we have learned to live with our clumsiness. In the confusion of inner and outer that the window-mirror creates, the past seems manageable and friendly. But isn't that because we want it that way? "What the world likes," the poetic speaker says reflectively, "is a bootstrap and locket," comfortable tokens that stand for "work and sentiment ebbing with the light." But the poem goes on to give us another kind of token, the huge and unfathomable ocean that is "a dark vase / of flowers before a dark window" and "a dish of water carried by a woman, / where the worry of our lives lies down." The images translate it into a token, but it also remains the world beyond our ken, acting as it did when it was first made, and going on "forever." The deft and quiet progression of this poem, its beautiful comparisons, its steady tone and surprising reach, all show how expertly this unusual poet puts her poetic worlds together.

While some stress on the fears and difficulties in Jensen's poems is necessary to a good account of her work, it would be a serious oversight to neglect the elements of joy and celebration in her poetry, evident throughout this selection and epitomized by two poems: "The Cloud Parade," a wild and exuberant response to its subject; and "Kite," a tender, wry, and praising poem that calls forth Jensen's dual talents of close observation and imaginative comparison. The more melancholy side of her work has its redeeming moments too, as "Adoration of the Anchor" and "Pony Farm" demonstrate. In the first, the lonely old lady has a brief epiphany triggered by nothing more than a button. In "Pony Farm" the whole world seems to join in the speaker's despair as she moves toward the realization that we can never have what we want except perhaps in "little snatches."

Laura Jensen is a native of the Pacific Northwest, and except for a brief period of study at the Iowa Writers' Workshop, that is where she has always lived and worked. At present, she is living in Tacoma.

DY

The Red Dog

You know that he is going to die
as soon as I tell you
he is standing beside me
his hair in spikes and dripping
from his body. He turns his head.
Canadian geese
all of them floating along the shore.
The red dog is swimming for them
only his head shows now
they flap into a curve and move
farther along the bay.
You know that he is going to die
this is the time for it
this is the best time for it
while there is a way to vanish
while the geese are moving off
to be their hard sounds
as their bodies leave the water.

The Ajax Samples

They gave us the mysterious deep warehouse
filled with lavender and telephone books.
We emptied it.
I gave the last box to a beach house
on Brown's Point.
It was like running down into a stadium
crowds cheered in the blackberries on both sides
there was a wide blue field
with a sailboat anchored
the house with its shingles and screen door.

They gave us Alan Gentili.
He was our inspector.
Alan Gentili how beautiful your eyes are
your thin brown legs in your khaki shorts.

They released the pigeons over Melrose Street.
The pigeons turned together in the afternoon
again and again
and their shadow was a blessing.

It was like a sign to us.
It was like starting our lives in another way.
Saint Nicholas, the tooth fairy
they have nothing on us now.
We are so glorious that halos shine around us.
Jewels glint on Alan Gentili's panel truck.

We are the Magi traveling by moonlight.
We are Michael Anthony
giving million dollar checks to strangers.
We are the holy sunlit wanderers
and we leave gifts behind.

An Age

There is a growth that hurts the child
one was, the child who still knew
the ocean rock from a distance,
flocked like cloth, white like sugar,
a flower out of focus in the waves,

the waves, the thousands of horizons
seen again and again as blue Japan—
something that changes the freighters
twined with lights and evergreen
in the port of Seattle.

I remember being nowhere in the early light,
halfway over ocean to a northbound freighter
and walking back to my sister
where our white wood caught fire
in the white sand.

Household

Grudges mend and wear and turn in winter
but they turn again, astounded
if the wish has not been made,
not the stars considered,
nor time kept useful in absence.

These are the needles.
They are not thrown down
when they are stubborn.

But a fingertip is sleeping in a thimble.
There is a haystack of needles
leaving every farm with the country daughter,
needles spending their lives now
forgotten from raincoats in a rush,
shaking from cuffs and emptying from shoes.

It is not easy to sew with an ignorant needle.

Once building a needle, once building a weed
was a young time, once, that leaves itself be
a wheedling eye, a thread of light
between pins and the reputable grasses,
their brass teaching eyes to believe.

If there were no trouble, borrowing,
the troubles would be in the rivers
and the rivers would be rivers
that the troubled find.

The lake is rising like an argyle sock
on a darning egg grown wings.
And even with everything there would be
the fear, the warning, and the needles

looking down at my knees from my mind.
The needles close up in their packets
as they are remembered, what the feminine
should have kept in their lives,
so many eyes and only one authority of paper.

Kitchen

Flour is exhaustion.
There's always some
in the bag's bottom.

Butter is pain
and in the heat
it can only weep.

Salt is tears,
and cheap.

Onions are the same tunes
to their centers,
always singing to me.
It is their faith
that makes me cry—
they think I'll stop cutting.

Milk is a satisfied whisper.
Oranges
are harmony, one-two,
two-three,
and won't subdue
their shape to the bowl.
The child won't subdue
his shape to the shoe.

And the oven
is vast to the toast,
stingy to the turkey.

Broom is the purr
without the cat.

Candles are clever,
clever, clever—
like the cat stretching up
to the handle of the door.

Bones won't go,
bones won't turn
into a rib cage,
find the leg bones,
and go.

Sweetie pie, why
go out with the ashes?
Cookie, why?

The Cloud Parade

In deference to the cloud parade,
the horse has shed its winter red,
stamped its last horseshoe out of the shed,
has moved away, leaving no forwarding
address. The heavens turn furniture,
attics and beds, men with moustaches
heels over heads; they cover the sun
to a gloomy shade,
in deference to the cloud parade.

Scarves! Echoes! Pavillions!
The meat grain in bacon, the star-stun
in roast, the bone down the well, the moon
down the wane, the smoke from the fireplace,
beautifully made,
in deference to the cloud parade.

As the Window Darkens

As the window darkens, as the light yearns
over the couch, as the plants drift like swans,
this is a silent poem. It will not flower
in water like a party favor, nor
will it bleed like the universe. It will
be the knot of wood that looks like a rabbit.
A knot of wood tense and growing stiffer.

The window darkens to mirror. It chimes
the reflection and what it should have been.
Have the trees and antennas seen this
blot for years, pumping like a gauge?
No wonder the birds flew away, crying out.

It is not true that the beautiful
are always false and the ugly philosophical.
But the clumsy stand as surely as the deft
at dark windows, knowing they have been deceived.
This is unbearable because we know
we see a door closing and we wait to see
that door close in our dreams, shutting us out.

How many years can come as gently as lamplight
out of the wind, each year with its own place
and the circle it made around a friend?
What the world likes is a bootstrap and locket,
work and sentiment ebbing with the light.

The ocean is a sigh at night, a dark vase
of flowers before a dark window, salt water,
someone pouring it from an abalone shell
when it first was made. It goes on forever,
a fountain, a fortuneteller in the palm of sand.
The ocean is a dish of water carried by a woman,
where the worry of our lives lies down.

Kite

Dime store. The goldfish swam in the murky
back. I was a child there, where the helmeted
diver bubbled, where, in an enameled
white basin below, the turtles struggled.
They were a moist delight.
And, as I realize,
shaped as a child draws any animal:
round body, legs and head extending.

Kites are separate from toys, for they are
Seasonal. Toys are in the inner aisles
that follow age so faithfully a child
might guess what the next step might be.
Of skeins of baby yarn, of bibs and rattles
sings the hardwood floor—of mother. Then
of pencils, parties, powder, bobby pins, barrettes.
Suddenly, at the counter, a life has passed—
a history, an age, a generation.

But the kites, like the pleated paper bells,
are Seasonal. Making conversation,
the young father tells, "We're not looking
for some expensive kite now," as his son
and little daughters skip around grandly.

For months it was
Wouldn't your mother like a handkerchief
or perhaps a teapot for Christmas?
in the window display,
but now it is kites and flowers.

Not kites in trees or kites like heroines
in wires, but the kite that was a speck,
the opposite of fishing: to want nothing
caught in anything but the pretty sky,
to reel the color back down again
beside you, a celebrity who tells
what it is like in the altitude.

Adoration of the Anchor

She hopes to hear a word from her,
A short small word to make her be
Alone in a more deserving way.
Never to make the sun come up
The sky more rose, or fewer clouds
To turn to wisps in truer sky,
But after that—the summer day—
She hopes to hear a word on that.
She turns a box of buttons, white
And bone, green, yellow, red, and
Ivory, one like a blackberry,
One like a flower, and up comes
An anchor, raised blue on white ground.
It came from nowhere. A sea of faith
Rolls over her. She adores
The anchor where she sits, in a
Sewing corner, in her small chair.
A light at the window splashes
Where the lawn sprinkler washes.
A wave of real faith colored blue
Rolls over her where she adores
The anchor, then lowers it down
Back into the sea whence it came.
She looks around. Home is the same.

Pony Farm

The voices
are everywhere
circling
no money
I'm crying

The voices
I answer
I tell them
what I wanted

I wanted
to live at Pony Farm
and have the sun rise

every morning
and be mother
in a plaid skirt

Then the voices
are also crying
they wanted that too
they are crying

and the bus brakes
to a stop at the corner
and the squeal it makes
is crying
that it wanted that too

and we have it
little snatches
the ponies
in a circle
at the Pay & Save
the prettiest ponies
you ever saw

LAURA JENSEN

Books

Anxiety and Ashes, 1976   *Memory,* 1982
Bad Boats, 1977   *Shelter,* 1985

Larry
Levis
(b. 1946)

Randall Tosh

L arry Levis grew up on a farm near Fresno, California, with a reverence for nature and human labor. He is fond of saying, "the romance of poetry needs to be soiled by the human." In an essay, "Some Notes on the Gazer Within," he writes of the need to rediscover those landscapes where someone has actually lived and left a mark, places where "some delicate linkage is preserved between past and present"—the deserted streets of a small town, the closed warehouse, the steel mill. His first book, which won the U.S. Award of the International Poetry Forum, was called _Wrecking Crew;_ a recent poem is titled "To a Wall of Flame in a Steel Mill, Syracuse, New York, 1969." Given the sterility of so much modern landscape, Levis worries about "the eye's starvation" and subscribes to the poetic tradition, redefined by modern masters like Rilke and Montale, that the more we forget our personalities and let our subjects find us, the more we will have to say after "a neccessary immersion into voicelessness, the prophet's apprenticeship." If we write with no real subject in mind, it will lead to our superimposing values instead of discovering anything fresh about the world. This has led Levis, in an interesting extension, to cast his poems as "fables with no values." He turns things over and over to let their own meanings evolve, and the emphasis is on precision about things, rather than predisposed feelings.

Inside his "fables," on a line-by-line basis, Levis explores the conflict between the ways we experience things and the ways we think about our experiences. In rhythms that recite more than speak, that behave like arias in which elaborate melodies for a single voice work their way around a single repeated theme, Levis's poetry makes a case against prescribed meaning; repeated errors of mind, repeated lapses, are carefully tracked to suggest that nothing can be trusted. Going round and round feelings that are more complex than we imagine, Levis finds that more has gone wrong than we suppose. He takes these powers of observation farthest in "Linnets," in which he becomes a listener to those of our fears and worries that, as he notes, "assume a life more powerful than their sources."

Not only does "Linnets" rank as one of the most moving, sustained elegies of our time, it is a compendium of Levis's ways with his poems. Reminiscent of Coleridge's "The Rime of the Ancient Mariner" in its subject, and of Mark Strand's elegy for his father in its structure, "Linnets" begins plainly, almost bluntly, with the facts of an incident from the poet's childhood. Levis chose the subject because he thought it was the least likely subject for a poem, and he was interested in exploring the mood "of having nothing to say." By the final line of the first section, however, he has given himself up to the story and become aware of the possibilities in his subject: "He drove on the roads with a little hole in the air behind him." Now the poet relaxes and lets the connections come as they will; section 2 is "a fable of some kind of wild justice" meted out to his brother; and then he simply leaps from "bird to bestiary" in sections 3 to 5. Finally, writer, reader, and the brothers are whirled about so that we cannot be sure any longer who did the shooting or if there was a gun at all. What we do come to realize is that Levis has followed the poem, with appropriate gravity and a relieving sense of humor, to the secret places of our ghosts and guilts. Stanley Plumly has written of Levis's ability to "surrender completely to what he sees and suffers," which not only makes him vulnerable but renders what he says genuine. At the end of "Linnets," we ache with the tiredness of having survived some kind of long illness, ready for the backfiring car that drives off to put an end to all future sound.

Larry Levis studied with Philip Levine in Fresno, earned a Master's degree at Syracuse University, and has a Ph.D. from the University of Iowa, where he has taught in the Writers' Workshop. He is currently teaching at the University of Utah.

SF

Linnets

1

One morning with a 12-gauge my brother shot what he said was a linnet. He did this at close range where it sang on a flowering almond branch. Anyone could have done the same and shrugged it off, but my brother joked about it for days, describing how nothing remained of it, how he watched for feathers and counted only two gold ones which he slipped behind his ear. He grew uneasy and careless; nothing remained. He wore loud ties and two tone shoes. He sold shoes, he sold soap. Nothing remained. He drove on the roads with a little hole in the air behind him.

2

But in the high court of linnets he does not get off so easily. He is judged and sentenced to pull me on a rough cart through town. He is further punished since each feather of the dead bird falls around me, not him, and each falls as a separate linnet, and each feather lost from one of these becomes a linnet. While he is condemned to feel nothing ever settle on his shoulders, which are hunched over and still, linnets gather around me. In their singing, they cleanse my ears of all language but that of linnets. My gaze takes on the terrible gaze of song birds. And I find that I too am condemned, and must stitch together, out of glue, loose feathers, droppings, weeds and garbage I find along the street, the original linnet, or, if I fail, be condemned to be pulled in a cart by my brother forever. We are tired of each other, tired of being brothers like this. The backside of his head, close cropped, is what I notice when I look up from work. To fashion the eyes, the gaze, the tongue and trance of a linnet is impossible. The eyelids are impossibly delicate and thin. I am dragged through the striped zoo of the town. One day I throw down the first stillborn linnet, then another, then more. Then one of them begins singing.

3

As my brother walks through an intersection the noise from hundreds of thin wings, linnet wings, becomes his silence. He shouts in his loud clothes all day. God grows balder.

4

Whales dry up on beaches by themselves.
The large bones in their heads, their silence,
Is a way of turning inward.

Elephants die in exile.
Their tusks begin curling, begin growing
Into their skulls.

My father once stopped a stray dog
With a 12-gauge, a blast in the spine.
But you see them on the roads, trotting through rain.

Cattle are slaughtered routinely.
But pigs are intelligent and vicious to the end.
Their squeals burn circles.

Mice are running over the freezing snow.
Wolverines will destroy kitchens for pleasure.
Wolverines are so terrible you must give in.

The waist of a weasel is also lovely. It slips away.

The skies under the turtle's shell are birdless.

*   *   *

These shadows become carp rising slowly. The black
Trees are green again. The creeks are full
And the wooden bridge trembles.

The suicides slip beneath you, shining.
You think if you watched them long enough
You would become fluent in their ten foreign tongues

Of light and drummed fingers and inbreedings.

5

Snakes swallow birds, mice, anything warm.
Beaten to death with a length of pipe,
A snake will move for hours afterward, digesting.

In fact their death takes too long.
In their stillness it may be they outlast death.
They are like stones the moment after

A wind passes over.
The tough skin around a snake's eyes
Is ignorant and eternal.

They are made into belts and wallets.
Their delicate meat can be eaten.
But you can't be sure.

In the morning another snake lies curled
On the branch just over your head.

*   *   *

Under the saint's heel in the painting,
A gopher snake sleeps.
The saint's eyes are syphilitic with vision.

He looks the Lord in the face.
He is like the bridge the laborers shrug at
As they wade across the water at night.

When LaBonna Stivers brought a 4 foot bullsnake
To High Mass, she stroked its lifted throat;
She smiled: "Snakes don't have no minds."

6

You can't be sure. Your whole family
May be wiped out by cholera. As the plums
Blossom, you may hang yourself.

Or you may love a woman whose low laugh
Makes her belly shake softly.
She wants you to stay, and you should have.

*   *   *

Or like your brother, you may go
Into the almond orchard to kill
Whatever moves. You may want to go

Against the little psalms and clear gazings
Of birds, against yourself, a 12-gauge
Crooked negligently over your shoulder.

You're tired of summer.
You want to stop all the singing.
And everything is singing.

At close range you blow a linnet
Into nothing at all, into the silence
Of stumps, where everyone sits and whittles.

*   *   *

Your brother grows into a stranger.
He walks into town in the rain.
Two gold feathers behind his ear.

He is too indifferent to wave.
He buys all the rain ahead of him,
And sells all the silence behind him.

7. Linnet Taxidermy

I thought when finished
it would break into flight, its beak
a Chinese trumpet over the deepest lakes.
But with each feather it grows colder to the touch.
I attach the wings which wait for the glacier
to slide under them. The viewpoint of ice
is birdless. I close my eyes,
I give up.

                    *   *   *

I meet my brother in Los Angeles.
I offer him rain
but he clears his throat.
He offers me
the freeway and the sullen huts;
the ring fingers stiffening;
the bitten words.

There are no birds he remembers.
He does not remember owning a gun.
He remembers nothing of the past.

He is whistling "Kansas City"
on Hollywood Boulevard, a bird
with half its skull eaten away
in the shoebox tucked under his arm.

                    *   *   *

When the matinee ends, the lights come on
and we blink slowly
and walk out. It is the hour
when the bald usher
falls in love.

                    *   *   *

When we are the night and the rain,
the leper on his crutch will spit once,
and go on singing.

8. Matinee

Your family stands over your bed
like Auks of estrangement.
You ask them to look you in the eye,
in the flaming aviary.
But they float over in dirigibles:

in one of them
a girl is undressing; in another
you are waking your father.

Your wife lies hurt on the roadside
and you must find her.
You drive slowly, looking.

They lift higher and higher
over the snow on the Great Plains.
Goodbye, tender blimps.

9. 1973

At the end of winter
the hogs are eating abandoned cars.
We must choose between Jesus and seconal
as we walk under the big, casual spiders whitening
in ice, in tree tops. These great elms rooted in hell
hum so calmly.

My brother marching through Prussia
wears a chrome tie and sings.
Girls smoothing their dresses
become mothers. Trees grow more deeply
into the still farms.

The war ends.
A widow cradles her husband's
acetylene torch,
the flame turns blue,
a sparrow flies out of the bare elm
and it begins again.

I'm no one's father.
I whittle a linnet out of wood until
the bus goes completely dark around me.
The farms in their white patients' smocks join hands.
Only the blind can smell water,
the streams moving a little,
freezing and thawing.

*   *   *

In Illinois one bridge is made entirely
of dead linnets. When the river sings under them,
their ruffled feathers turn large and black.

10. At the High Meadow

In March the arthritic horses
stand in the same place
all day.
A piebald mare flicks her ears back.

Ants have already taken over
the eyes of the house finch
on the sill.

So you think someone
is coming,
someone already passing the burned mill,
someone with news of a city
built on snow.

But over the bare table
in the morning
a glass of water goes blind
from staring upward.

For you
it's not so easy.
You begin the long witnessing:
Table. Glass of water. Lone crow
circling.

You witness the rain for weeks
and there are only the two of you.
You divide yourself in two and witness yourself,
and it makes no difference.

*   *   *

You think of God dying of anthrax
in a little shed, of a matinee
in which three people sit
with their hands folded and a fourth
coughs. You come down the mountain.

11

Until one day in a diner in Oakland
you begin dying.
It is peace time.
You have no brother.
You never had a brother.
In the matinees no one sat next to you.
This brother for whom
you have been repairing linnets all your life,
unthankful stuffed little corpses,
hoping they'd perch behind glass in museums
that have been levelled, this brother
who slept under the fig tree
turning its dark glove inside out at noon, is no one;
the strong back you rode while
the quail sang perfect triangles, was no one's.
Your shy father extinct in a single footprint,
your mother a stone growing a cuticle.
It is being suggested that you were never born, that
it never happened in linnet feathers
clinging to the storm fence along the freeway;
in the Sierra Nevadas,
in the long azure of your wife's glance,

in the roads and the standing water,
in the trembling of a spider web gone suddenly still,
it never happened.

    12

This is a good page.
It is blank,
and getting blanker.
My mother and father
are falling asleep over it.
My brother is finishing a cigarette;
he looks at the blank moon.
My sisters walk gravely in circles.
My wife sees through it, through blankness.
My friends stop laughing, they listen
to the wind in a room in Fresno, to the wind
of this page, which is theirs,
which is blank.

They are all tired of reading,
they want to go home,
they won't be waving goodbye.

When they are gone,
the page will be crumpled,
thrown into the street.
Around it, sparrows will be feeding
on bits of garbage.
The linnet will be singing.
A man will awaken on his deathbed,
not yet cured.

I will not have written these words,
I will be that silence slipping around the bend
in the river, where it curves out of sight among weeds,
the silence in which a car backfires and drives away,
and the father of that silence.

LARRY LEVIS

Books

Wrecking Crew, 1972   *The Dollmaker's Ghost*, 1981
The Afterlife, 1977   *Winter Stars*, 1985

Essays

"Some Notes on the Gazer Within," in *A FIELD Guide to Contemporary Poetry & Poetics,* ed. Friebert & Young, 1980; "The Nature and Use of Place in Contemporary Poetry," *FIELD*, No. 26 (Spring 1982).

Thomas
Lux
(b. 1946)

Michael Lauchlin

Thomas Lux's poems are heady mixtures in which sorrow and laughter, real world and dream world, mingle wildly and unpredictably. The blaze in "Barn Fire" is both a terrible and wonderful thing, so that the horses' stupidity at the end is also a kind of wisdom. The wicked parody of pastoral sentiments in "Farmers" is informed by realistic knowledge of how deadening and exhausting farm labor can be, but it also manages some sly celebration of the "simple sweat mongers" who call down the rain and never forget that they have done that.

As "Farmers" suggests, Lux likes to play with clichés, casting his existential propositions into popular forms. The habit gives an edge of self-mockery to his poetry, and it complicates the traditional dialectic of reality and the imagination: the meaning of imagination is different when it includes all the silly and debased images that fill our lives. In one of the sections of "Flying Noises" the lovers in their rowboat drift past an older-style poet: "On the opposite shore Mallarme's / feeding some swans." Unlike Mallarme, who could exalt the imagination as an alternative to life, Lux sees the poet as unable to draw away from life; instead of purifying the dialect of the tribe and enshrining the artistic imagination, the poet is a poor clown like everybody else, soiled by the necessary entanglements of dreaming and waking, subject to pratfalls and ludicrous occupations: "Force-feeding swans—let me tell / you—was hard" ("Farmers").

Lux's wit is the element that gives his poems buoyancy and promise, a kind of implied counterweight to their pessimistic sense of human isolation and ignorance. The wit is verbal—"all the solunar tables / set with silver linen!" ("Solo Native")— but it is situational too: elements of parody lace through all of Lux's poems. He borrows from melodrama in writing about destruction ("Barn Fire"), and from science fiction in writing about isolation ("Solo Native"). Pastoral's traditional celebration of country life comes in for teasing, in "Farmers," in "There Were Some Summers," and in two sections of "Flying Noises," but the ribbing is not a dismissal; it's more like an acknowledgement of our dependence on nature as a source of wisdom and comfort, a dependence the poet shares. He is at one with a frightened and foolish humanity, laughing at our fears and misplaced hopes, but participating in them too.

Getting adjusted to the complex tone of Lux's poetry in shorter pieces will prepare the reader for one of his longer sequences, represented here by "Flying Noises." This kind of poem, journal-like and loose in subject, allows Lux to extend and deepen his poetic world by a technique that resembles the fugue: sections start but never fully stop, and new sections replace them. The resulting series of anecdotes, lists, meditations, parodies, and constantly shifting rhythms and moods creates a single poem that is rich and echoing, both in structure and subject. As an exploration of love and solitude it might be thought of simply as an expansion of the dreamlike characters and encounters of the shorter poems, tinged by self-consciousness and mordant wit. A good example is the "solo native," who sees that "the stars are pinholes, / slits in the hangman's mask," but who nevertheless, "after a few chiliads," begins to produce "an awkward first audible / called language."

Tom Lux grew up in the Boston area and was educated at Emerson College. He has taught at a number of schools, including Oberlin and the University of Houston, but for some years now has been part of the writing staff of Sarah Lawrence College.

DY

Barn Fire

It starts, somehow, in the hot damp
and soon the lit bales
throb in the hayloft. The tails

of mice quake in the dust,
the bins of grain, the mangers stuffed
with clover, the barrels of oats
shivering individually in their pale

husks—animate and inanimate: they know
with the first whiff in the dark.
And we knew, or should have: that day
the calendar refused its nail

on the wall and the crab apples hurling
themselves to the ground . . . Only moments
and the flames like a blue fist curl

all around the black. There is some
small blaring from the calves and the cows'
nostrils flare only once
more, or twice, above the dead dry

metal troughs. . . . No more fat tongues worrying
the salt licks, no more heady smells
of deep green from silos rising now

like huge twin chimneys above all this.
With the lofts full there is no stopping
nor even getting close: it will rage

until dawn and beyond,—and the horses,
because they know they are safe there,
the horses run back into the barn.

Farmers

Force-feeding swans—let me tell
you—was hard. And up
every morning 4:30 counting

the lambs out to pasture,
each one tapped on the forehead with a stick
to be sure it's there.

Uncle Reaper half the time so drunk
he'd pull his milkstool
under the horse: more work

explaining the difference. Gramma
and Cousin Shroud putting up
8000 jars of beets, Auntie Bones

rapping her wooden spoon
against my ear: "More bushels, bumbler!"

I'll tell you—I understand
how come the dancing bear tore off his skirt
and headed back to the Yukon,
how come all of a sudden jewels in avalanche
down the spine of my sleep. . . .

But still, still when it rains
I remember all of us: farmers, simple sweat mongers
of the dirt whose turnips depend on it,

I remember how we called it down, how down
we desired it to fall: the rain.

Solo Native

Suppose you're a solo native here
on one planet rolling, the lily
of the pad and valley.

You're alone and you know
a few things: the stars are pinholes,
slits in the hangman's mask.
And the crabs walk sideways
as they were taught by the waves.

You're the one thing upright
on hind legs, an imaginer,
an interested transient.
Look—all the solunar tables
set with silver linen!

This is where you'll live, exactly
here in a hut on the green and gray belly
of the veldt. You'll be

a metaphor, a meatpacker,
a tree dropping or gaining
its credentials. You'll be

a dancer with two feet dancing
in the dirt-colored dirt. All this,
and after a few chiliads,

from your throat a noise,
an awkward first audible
called language.

Flying Noises

*   *   *

The horses out of their brains bored all
winter gnawing on stalls
Outside the snow several fetlocks deep
Pounding our noses
against the ice everywhere
you could say
we had our souls in backwards
we were dumb from trudging away from noon
we were lame like the bread that lies on the table
One child's dream sledding down a slag heap
every day going at it with the cold

*   *   *

So he deposits the moth in a matchbox
and flails with a flashlight
into the forest a mile or two fox-
like crosses a few gullies streams
stopping finally before a final ravine
where he slides open removes the moth
lays down the light on the perfect
theater of moss
as backdrop a few slim branches
and on that greenly illuminated stage it dances
to an audience of darkness plus one

                    *   *   *

He was absolved prematurely they forgot
what he might do from the point
of absolution to the next point what's it called
So he filled in he could do anything
He disregarded the live hearts
of live humans he did misconduct before
his mother and father he coveted
his neighbor's wife and speedboat
he propped open a baby's eyes with matches
He did it like a good thief
having already been absolved

                    *   *   *

The mattress always acts as a raft
He's aware of that that's why he hopes
to bob in the wakes there
He never takes a path nonchalantly solo
knowing that's of course where
beasts do their dreaming also
He joins nothing He joins the other peasants
waving pitchforks not getting
dung for our wheat we've had it
up to our haircuts thinking we're salved
until we're mistaken is obvious

                    *   *   *

Approximately dawn some people exercise Take X
He goes out to a dirt road
with a club and bashes small stones
like in a ballgame Sending
a shot deep into the east slows down dawn
The first peeps of light In India
they have a word for it it's a child's name
you can't make a close paraphrase
The very beginning light
when roof and bush and animal
become apart from air

                    *   *   *

As if hands undoing our clothes from the inside
we fumble around in a rowboat
One oar floats downriver What a day
On the opposite shore Mallarmé's
feeding some swans How will we row

Which port our oars arriving
days ahead of us With you
voyaging you also voyaging
There's the lovely sword of moon
There's the cricket warming up his cello
There's the various positions in which we exult

                    *   *   *

Once gone like gloss in a flashflood
Once an animal loving another of another species
Once one joyful crumb of the fully individual
Once a convict dreaming of mowing a hayfield
Once an avenue upon a bench sits one moment of present
Once under deep enough to ring the literal sleep-bells
Once the dead changing shirts in their small booths
Once farmers merely bored by drought
Once all the birds invented as toys
Once the heart-angles the trillion u-turns of blood
Once the flying noise

                    *   *   *

Slow tarantula slow blink by blink
the afternoon unspools a wind primping
the fir tree's common hair
A blue calf bleats in the far pasture
Reduced by bucolia
it always hauls him back
gaping like a lump of gold shocked
in the sludge-sifter's hand
One water moccasin rolls over a few times
A hill hunches somewhat
while memorizing the earth's sore fictions

                    *   *   *

His mouth connecting lines the puzzle
from nape to the slope beneath
her ankles the dunes He takes
pleasure there and giving it it's simply the hearts
simply the lungs simply two
to swerve beneath the fell cleavers of day to day
Their nerves on overdrive together
two odd ones warbling around an oasis
alert to the blue thuds in the wrist
And that other pulse the pulse of top lip
to bottom lip and bottom lip to top

*   *   *

Loving the incunabula the beginnings
like one obsessed by desert
loving its freeze at night
because it reminds him more of water
than the heat of afternoon Lined
up and loaded like something on wheels
small wafers of anger off his bureau
spinning A window is open
On the table there is sky
And behind the curtain one marvelous belly
or else the wind is bringing the usual

There Were Some Summers

There were some summers
like this: The blue barn steaming,
some cow-birds dozing with their heads
on each other's shoulders, the electric fences
humming low in the mid-August heat . . .
So calm the slow sweat existing
in half-fictive memory: a boy
wandering from house, to hayloft, to coop,
past a dump where a saddle rots
on a sawhorse, through the still forest
of a cornfield, to a pasture talking to himself
or the bored, baleful Holsteins nodding
beneath the round shade of catalpa, the boy
walking his trail towards the brook
in a deep but mediocre gully,
through skunk cabbage and pop-weed,
down sandbanks (a descending
quarter-acre Sahara), the boy wandering,
thinking nothing, thinking: *Sweatbox,*
sweatbox, the boy on his way
toward a minnow whose slight beard
tells the subtleties of the current, holding there,
in water cold enough to break your ankles.

Tarantulas on the Lifebuoy

For some semitropical reason
when the rains fall
relentlessly they fall

into swimming pools, these otherwise
bright and scary
arachnids. They can swim
a little, but not for long

and they can't climb the ladder out.
They usually drown—but
if you want their favor,
if you believe there is justice,
a reward for not loving

the death of ugly
and even dangerous (the eel, hog snake,
rats) creatures, if

you believe these things, then
you would leave a lifebuoy
or two in your swimming pool at night.

And in the morning
you would haul ashore
the huddled, hairy survivors

and escort them
back to the bush, and know,
be assured that at least these saved,
as individuals, would not turn up

again someday
in your hat, drawer,
or the tangled underworld

of your socks, and that even—
when your belief in justice
merges with your belief in dreams—
they may tell the others

in a sign language
four times as subtle
and complicated as man's

that you are good,
that you love them,
that you would save them again.

The Milkman and His Son

for my father

For a year he'd collect
the milk bottles—those cracked,
chipped, or with the label's blue
scene of a farm

fading. In winter
they'd load the boxes on a sled
and drag them to the dump

which was lovely then: a white sheet
drawn up, like a joke, over
the face of a sleeper.
As they lob the bottles in

the son begs a trick
and the milkman obliges: tossing
one bottle in a high arc,
he shatters it in midair

with another. One thousand astonished
splints of glass
falling . . . Again
and again, and damned
if that milkman,
that easy slinger
on the dump's edge (as the drifted
junk tips its hats
of snow), damned if he didn't
hit almost half! Not bad.
Along with gentleness,

and the sane bewilderment
of understanding nothing cruel,
it was a thing he did best.

THOMAS LUX

Books

Memory's Handgrenade, 1972
The Glassblower's Breath, 1976

Sunday, 1979
Half Promised Land, 1986

Sandra
McPherson
(b. 1943)

Coni Mariels

To take a common subject—a children's story, a coconut, a microscope—or an uncommon subject—a mummy, a collapsar, a bittern—and do more with it, take it further than we could have foreseen, is the specialty of Sandra McPherson. The thoughtfulness of her poems is striking: they are the products of a complex mind as well as a vivid imagination. The intricate design and emotional configuration of "Gnawing the Breast" demonstrate this capacity; the little zoo (we're not told precisely where we are until stanza four) affords a consideration of life stretching all the way from birth to death. The cool detachment the speaker brings to watching the prairie dogs, a naturalist's unsentimental observation, is trained on the children as well: "Pretty things, when will you have earned // your beauty sleep? And when have eaten enough love to live on love / though you throw so much away?" This poem ends with a snatch of mystic speculation that gives it a fuller tone and ampler meaning. The little hill, a new grave, is climbed in imagination, with the discovery that it provides cooler and fresher air and that "the hill might even move a little, feeling the kick of a child."

The engagement-detachment polarity that provides the structure and the drama of "Gnawing the Breast" is fascinating to trace through Sandra McPherson's work. In "Games," for example, which involves a mother and daughter, we get not the warmth we might expect but a coolness in the mother toward the child's innocent cruelty—"She forgets it easily. / Who never speaks of losing"—that is almost scornful. Contrarily, when alienation might seem the most natural state of affairs, as in the imaginary possession of a mummy, we get closeness and sympathy: "My room-temperature friend and I / I with my hands like peaches // And my friend all / Shortbread and roots." The poem about the natural historians—dioramicist, skinner, taxidermist, stringer, egg-gatherer, even janitor—who collaborate to create the natural history museum ("The Museum of the Second Creation") is, similarly, more involved and passionate than we might expect.

These reversals of expectation about how close or distant the speaker is going to be have the rhetorical advantage of keeping us off balance, pleasantly surprised; but they go deeper as well, to reveal an essential soundness and sanity in the poet. She knows how to redress imbalances and correct one-sided impressions, and she brings a clear-eyed fairness to her account of things. "Resigning from a Job in a Defense Industry" might easily have become a condemnation of both the industry and its workers; instead it finds magic in the technical vocabulary and sympathy for the awkard creative urges expressed in the company art show. "A Coconut for Katerina," about a friend's miscarriage, has good reason to lose itself in anger or sorrow, but it finds hope and wonder instead by taking the coconut, "This baby's head, this dog's head, this dangerous acorn," as a microcosm, a world in which life can begin again, a token of human resiliency and imaginative strength.

Perhaps the need to strike balance and assert sanity stems from the strong influence of Sylvia Plath on McPherson's early poems, as if she had to define the ways in which she was different from an obsessed and self-destructive model. Perhaps it is just a leading characteristic of her personality. Whatever its origin, it makes her a poet whom readers can trust and return to. Whether she is mainly exercising her great powers of observation and association or undertaking a complex meditation, Sandra McPherson shows herself as a poet who is never content with easy judgments or haphazard effects. Before reading "Peter Rabbit," try imagining what you might have to say about that familiar story: then compare the imagery, diction, and tonal complexity of McPherson's treatment. You'll soon recognize that you are in the presence of an extraordinary poet.

Born in San Jose, California, where she grew up and went to San Jose State College, Sandra McPherson continued her education at the University of Washington and worked for a short time as a technical writer for Honeywell. With the exception of two stints of teaching at Iowa, she lived many years in Portland, Oregon, before moving to the University of California at Davis to direct the Writing Program.

DY

Resigning from a Job in a Defense Industry

The names of things—sparks!
I ran on them like a component:
henries, microhenries, blue
beavers, wee wee ductors:
biographer of small lives,
of a plug and his girl named Jack,
of Utopian colonies which worked—
steel, germanium, brass, aluminum,
replaceables.
              Outside, afloat, my words
swung an arm charting the woman
who was the river bottom.

We tried, beyond work, at work,
to keep what we loved. Near
Christmas I remember the office
women trimming their desperately
glittering holy day trees. And,
just as I left, the company
talent show, the oils and sentiment
thick on still lifes and seacoasts,
the brush strokes tortured as a child's
first script. Someone
had studied driftwood; another man,
the spray of a wave, the mania
of waters above torpedoes.

Wanting a Mummy

I've always wanted one,
A connection,

Leaning against the bureau, an in
To atrocious kingships,

To stone passages,
Those nights carrying the planets of the dead.

I'd like being able to ask it,
How do you like the rain?

Are you 3000 years old or still 25?
And to hear it replying,

Voluble with symbols
And medallions.

There we would debate, faced off
Across the room,

My room-temperature friend and I,
I with my hands like peaches

And my friend all
Shortbread and roots.

Peter Rabbit

Mushrooms grew near the tree
Nearly black with foliage.
Each footfall was a special touch.
Mother Rabbit wore a carrot-
Colored jacket and a broad purple skirt,
She was beyond hopping.
Over her paw a basket; her forearm, umbrella.
No no no! we're waiting for her to demand.
She looks that way though kind.

Father father's in the pie.
It was an accident.
It was a stupid way to die.
Peter knows how to be very naughty.
There is a shimmer
About the lettuce, French beans,
Radishes, and parsley—
Of evil or of humanity.
Peter is a thief.

Peter my hero I am a thief.
Peter I am a child.

Peter was most dreadfully frightened
And shed big tears.
Mr. McGregor was upon him
With his size huge shoe.
Of course we are going to win.

Lippity-lippity we wander
With puzzled Peter
But I don't want the story to be over.
They will make us wash the green
From our hands and our knees.

Gnawing the Breast

of a fallen sparrow, the prairie dog first softens
it with his teeth then frees and finishes the piece,
      his head high.
   The she-dog eats stems of grass.
Meat-eater tries to make love to grass-eater.
But no, she'd rather lie almost flat as water,
   contracting and rolling while she sleeps.

Young girls keep running up and asking me if she
      is dying.
She sleeps, smaller and darker of the two.
They attribute despair inside her to her shade and size.
   She might also be old-fashioned,
      a baby could kill her.
And then, inclusive kids, they nose about what I am

doing; why I am doing it; what I do when I'm not
      doing this;
till one squeals that she hates what I do because
   it puts her to sleep.
When they run off kicking, the prairie dog wakes
and otters through the grass: while I think,
   Pretty things, when will you have earned

your beauty sleep? And when have eaten enough love
   to live on love
though you throw so much away? Well, it's just a tiny
guilty zoo. The keeper wishes he could feed
   the animals more blossoms.
I ask him, "Where did you get that hill that wasn't
      there before?"

   "A new grave," he says.
Maybe it was Aesop, diving, doing research as a
universal bird and ending up in the mouth of this dog.
   The hill will give it a viewpoint.
I think if I could climb that hill,
the air would be cooler, fresher, as it always used to be
   on ones I didn't know the source of.

And the hill might even move a little, feeling the kick
      of a child.

A Coconut for Katerina

Inside the coconut is Katerina's baby. The coconut's hair, like
    Katerina's brown hair.
Like an auctioneer Katerina holds the coconut, Katerina in her dark fur
    coat
covering winter's baby, feet in the snow. Katerina's baby is the milk
and will not be drinking it.

Ropes hanging down from the trees—are they well ropes? Ropes on a
    moss
wall. Not to ring bells but used for climbing up and down
or pulling, I mean bringing. Anchor ropes on which succulent ropy
    seaplants grow.

And floating like a bucket of oak or like a light wooden dory, the
    coconut bobs,
creaking slowly, like a piling or a telephone pole with wet wires
downed by a thunderstorm over its face.

This baby's head, this dog's head, this dangerous acorn is the grocer
of a sky-borne grocery store where the white-aproned grocer or doctor
    imprints it
with three shady fingerprints, three flat abysses the ropes will not cross.

What of it? There is enough business for tightrope walkers in this
    jungle.
The colonizers make a clearing
for a three-cornered complex of gas-stations, lit with a milky spotlight
at night.

            And here we dedicate this coconut to Katerina. We put our
    hand
on the round stomach of Katerina. We put our five short ropes of
    fingers on the lost
baby of Katerina and haul it in to the light of day and wash it with
    sand.

Coconut, you reverse of the eye, the brown iris in white, the white
    center
in brown sees so differently. The exposed fibrous iris,
the sphere on which memory or recognizing must have latitude and
    longitude
to be moored
or preserved in the big sky, the sea's tug of war. The tugging of water
held in and not clear. Lappings and gurglings of living hollows half
    filled,
half with room
for more empty and hopeful boats and their sails.

The Bittern

Because I have turned my head for years
in order to see the bittern
I won't mind not finding
what I am looking for
as long as I know it could be there,
the cover is right,
it would be natural.

I loved you for what you had seen
and because you took me to see things,

alpine flowers
and your heart under your shirt.

The birds that mate for life
we supposed to be happiest,

my green-eyed,
bitter evergreen.

The bough flies back into the night.

I might be driving by a marsh
and suddenly turn my head—
That's not exactly the way you see them, you say.
So I look from the corners of my eyes
as if cheating in school
or overcoming a shyness.

In the end I see
                   nothing
but how I go blindly on loving
a life from which something is missing.

Clouds rushing across the sun,
gold blowing down on the reeds—

nothings like these . . .

Games

I play pool. I aim toward the faces
          Across the room. My daughter
Takes these quarters for the pinball
          She plays with a dying

Butterfly on her left hand. It
          Will not leave, it is tired,
And all its strength is in its legs.
          I set it on my arm

Then give it back. I'll take her hand
      That way when dying, stick
Out my tongue, like its curled black one,
      Green crutch of a Kentucky

Wonder Bean, and *Look,* she cries
      Its body fell away.
It's all wings and head. Short life
      Has culled mistaken

Parts and dropped the mite-sized heart and
      Killed the steering place.
Or else she did this, quickened its
      Death among the games

And flunked it too soon. And even so
      The golden-mica'd wings
Are best. She forgets it easily,
      Who never speaks of losing.

The Museum of the Second Creation

The dioramacist does not know
How the Creator shows emotion.
So he flings the passenger pigeon across the sunset
As a guess. And the pigeons look joyous.
In fact, he says, I could call it a sunrise,
No one will ever know.

If there is a whole
Table of feet, and one
Of skulls, and a rugful of antlers, a bench of pelts,
A skinner has loved to give samples to touch,
A collector has strewn away the danger
By pooling big and little teeth.

And the taxidermist must be happy each time
He's given a weasel to stuff, maybe that's
His favorite animal, and best if it's a Least
Weasel, once full of night courage, at the neck
Of a cat or the heel
Of a cow.

Who fills museums
Loves to recreate little horses.
I have seen them in most big cities, little horses
In a rodeo through swamps, little horses
That could companion us
Like dogs.

Joining the fruit-bat's bones,
The stringer loves to reveal its outgrown fingers,
Strokes of fossil longer than our own. Flying on a wire
At dusk, its mouseflesh gone, its tarp wings rotted,
Big starlight hands.
The visitor says: Lost love, your body is so

Recreated in me
That I can look in the glass
Polished round the animal we loved the most
And see how nearly real you are.
What reincarnation is there? What can I learn
From the egg-gatherer

Sitting on his license to clean a new lilac shell,
Turning its most ecstatic face upward?
What can I glean from the late-late janitor
Sweeping up moths that fall
Through seal ribs strung near the light?
Their wings are now his—

Their sparkle's on his broomstraws.

Helen Todd: My Birthname

They did not come to claim you back,
To make me Helen again. Mother
Watched the dry, hot streets in case they came.
This is how she found a tortoise
Crossing between cars and saved it.
It's how she knew roof-rats raised families
In the palmtree heads. But they didn't come—
It's almost forty years.

I went to them. And now I know
Our name, quiet one. I believe you
Would have stayed in trigonometry and taken up
The harp. Math soothed you; music
Made you bold; and science, completely
Understanding. Wouldn't you have collected,
Curated, in your adolescence, Mother Lode
Pyrites out of pity for their semblance
To gold? And three-leaf clovers to search
For some shy differences between them?

Knowing you myself at last—it seems you'd cut
Death in half and double everlasting life,
Quiet person named as a formality
At birth. I was not born. Only you were.

The Microscope in Winter

Caught in my mittens' mohair barbs—
goosedown like thrown boas of a chorus line,
evergreen needles with pitch stitches,
some wavy unshaven seeds of virgin's bower.
My eye looks down the funnel: under the light
the crooked finger of a pervert in a car;
dew in the golf-tee goblet of a lichen—
a lone crystal of glamour in a darkened theatre.
Such quiet bodies, gathered in the dusk,
thalluses and plumose fruits, silvery everything.

I bought this for my mother in crisis
so her outlook could rise
to the height of a bur
and leap the distance through a quill.
But she says, *Not yet,* feet the size
of catkin stamens. For she will study
her sleep, she says, she'll diet her curiosity,
blink to this charming mouse-food, blind
except to nightmares. She focuses on children
and we are terror. We are all too big.

Yet precisely because of your monster, dearest,
we require technology for you.
A good spider must have more eyes
than two: she needs a camera,
telescope for undomesticated space,
binoculars to hoop the faster birds.
Through these prescription lenses, face
beings who do not care you're there.
Then, to your relief, neither will you.

Boodee—dew in its eye—reflects the light,
a flashbulb in a mirror; green tastebuds
bulge all over, nappy as a rug and knotted.
Or see this red oak leaf like our mother-flesh.
Shiny. Like jerky. Or potato-chip skins
where insects chewed us for another hour of life.

It is chilly when I wrest the sweater from the tree.
Dial it in clear: there is your monster
saying to all the larger world that scares it

I grow kinked but not mad,
so rest on me, liverwort-haired maenad,
scientific muddy shepherdess. Look into this,
how, scintillating under battery light,
I am a greater power of moss.
My microscopic cushion shows its claws.

SANDRA McPHERSON

Books

Elegies for the Hot Season, 1970   Patron Happiness, 1983
Radiation, 1973   Streamers, 1988
The Year of Our Birth, 1978

David
St. John
(b. 1949)

James Lightner

In the poems of David St. John, "there's only one story, but it's told many times" ("Portrait, 1949") to expose the painful and frightening, but also the joyous, aspects of experience in order that the process of healing can begin. The poems focus primarily on love and friendship, with their corollaries of jealousy and desire. He tells them slowly, in deliberate, muted tones, but is not afraid to resort to pulsing rhythms that evoke Eliot and Yeats at times. St. John works with exquisite pastels—lavender boats, orange and yellow smoke, lemon derbies, and reddened walls—that soften his landscapes so we can bear the harsh events. These stories need time to unfold. They are studded with qualifying detail, questions of who said what, memories that pile up and must be sorted out. Frequently, the people in the poems seek solace in sleep, using their dreams to try to order their lives. However, "When you are asleep, dreaming of another country, / This is the country" ("Dolls"): one longs for elsewhere, but has perhaps been in the right place all the while. In spite of feeling dislocated, confronting paradoxes they cannot resolve, no one gives up in these poems—"those who give up finally give up too much" ("Four O'Clock in Summer: Hope"). In honest fights, in meditative asides, the characters salvage something from their sometimes wicked, sometimes loving encounters with each other. We admire them as we watch, in Anthony Hecht's phrase, "the grime and sadness turn to melody and grace." Grace follows, because St. John does not foreshorten the "grime and sadness." The poems, the people in them, take the long way around, as in "Slow Dance" they sail back into the past and move out again toward the future.

This distance we must travel to flesh out the full story of our lives is emphasized in poem after poem. "The Boathouse" puts it this way: "Homer had it right. A man sails / The long way home." Anything less would not do justice to what people have been through together.

Things are not what they seem in these poems, but they reveal themselves in private moments if we are as patient as the poet with his material: "the young / Acolyte. . . / . . . twirling his gold & white satin / Skirts so that everyone can see his woolen socks & rough shoes" ("Slow Dance"). Catching sight of the primitive footwear under the acolyte's sacred robes, we are struck with the full meaning of revelation: "an act of grace & disgust." Staged comically here—as other incidents are tragically staged—the moment celebrates the secular in the liturgical and thus avoids a false romanticism. In a spirit of art for life's sake, "Slow Dance" keeps going from image to Fellini-like image and makes it possible for us to accept the rhythms of the human dance, from the kicking of Anna Karenina's heels to the "nervous goose-step" of puppet-soldiers to today's dance between parents and children who are beginning to learn the right steps. The mood invokes Eliot's "lifting heavy feet in clumsy shoes, / Earth feet, loam feet, lifted in country mirth / Mirth of those long since under earth / . . . Keeping time / Keeping the rhythm in their dancing" ("East Coker": *Four Quartets*) as the poem takes its place in a long tradition that continues to find new forms.

Two somber but delicate family poems, "Hush" and "Iris," would seem to be in sharp contrast to St. John's large concerns for what has been happening in the world, concerns he not only mentions in many another poem but also addresses. In effect, however, as they "let go a whole cadenza of beliefs," "Hush" and "Iris" are of the same cloth we have been looking at in the other texts: loss and absence. In "Hush," father and son are far apart and getting farther: "Sometimes, you ask / About the world; sometimes, I answer back." Only a nightmare can console the father, "as sleep returns sleep / To a landscape ravaged / & familiar. The dark watermark of your absence, a hush." As in "Dolls," the doll the father makes of his son is a deformed gesture. In "Iris," mesmerized by the double image of train and flower (over which the eye's iris passes), there is only the long good-bye to savor, detail by pitifully beautiful detail. For grandmother and grandson are dead; "you remain" to respect the intimacy of their private grief, but your (our) memory is fading fast.

David St. John grew up in California and, like Larry Levis, studied with Philip Levine in Fresno. He did graduate work at the Writers' Workshop at the University of Iowa. He has taught in the Writing Seminars at Johns Hopkins University and currently teaches at the University of Southern California.

SF

Iris

Vivian St. John (1891–1974)

There is a train inside this iris:

You think I'm crazy, & like to say boyish
& outrageous things. No, there is

A train inside this iris.

It's a child's finger bearded in black banners.
A single window like a child's nail,

A darkened porthole lit by the white, angular face

Of an old woman, or perhaps the boy beside her in the stuffy,
Hot compartment. Her hair is silver, & sweeps

Back off her forehead, onto her cold & bruised shoulders.

The prairies fail along Chicago. Past the five
Lakes. Into the black woods of her New York; & as I bend

Close above the iris, I see the train

Drive deep into the damp heart of its stem, & the gravel
Of the garden path

Cracks under my feet as I walk this long corridor

Of elms, arched
Like the ceiling of a French railway pier where a boy

With pale curls holding

A fresh iris is waving goodbye to a grandmother, gazing
A long time

Into the flower, as if he were looking some great

Distance, or down an empty garden path & he believes a man
Is walking toward him, working

Dull shears in one hand; & now believe me: The train

Is gone. The old woman is dead, & the boy. The iris curls,
On its stalk, in the shade

Of those elms: Where something like the icy & bitter fragrance

In the wake of a woman who's just swept past you on her way
Home

& you remain.

Hush

For My Son

The way a tired Chippewa woman
Who's lost a child gathers up black feathers,
Black quills & leaves
That she wraps & swaddles in a little bale, a shag
Cocoon she carries with her & speaks to always
As if it were the child,
Until she knows the soul has grown fat & clever,
That the child can find its own way at last;
Well, I go everywhere
Picking the dust out of the dust, scraping the breezes
Up off the floor, & gather them into a doll
Of you, to touch at the nape of the neck, to slip
Under my shirt like a rag—the way
Another man's wallet rides above his heart. As you
Cry out, as if calling to a father you conjure
In the paling light, the voice rises, instead, in me.
Nothing stops it, the crying. Not the clove of moon,
Not the woman raking my back with her words. Our letters
Close. Sometimes, you ask
About the world; sometimes, I answer back. Nights
Return you to me for a while, as sleep returns sleep
To a landscape ravaged
& familiar. The dark watermark of your absence, a hush.

Wedding Preparations in the Country

This is a poem like a suitcase
Packed with flour. The baker eloping
With his lover insists on making his own wedding
Cake. Or, the mime in whiteface penciling his brows.
The white marble tombstone that Jude
Left blank, save
For the star more like a man's hand with the fingers
Spread than any star. In other words,
What is bleak is a table covered with snow, & the man
Beside it sipping coffee on his terrace
With a woman who is pale with anger pointing a pistol out
Across the blank, white lawn. Now the boy in whiteface

Delivers his bouquet: Cold lilies perhaps,
But more likely he tosses the limbs of a drama onto the terrace,
Or a few Chinese roses, & the promise of despair
Is as reliable as winter. As a suitcase spilling on the stairs.
The cake! Those squibs of icing,
Those stars squeezed from the nozzle of a paper cone
Onto these broad fields of cake.
The sorry stone admits that something's gone. Or someone.
Someone like you. Like the little man & woman riding
The cake. Close the suitcase. Go back down the snowy stairs.

Slow Dance

It's like the riddle Tolstoy
Put to his son, pacing off the long fields
Deepening in ice. Or the little song
Of Anna's heels, knocking
Through the cold ballroom. It's the relief
A rain enters in a diary, left open under the sky.
The night releases
Its stars, & the birds the new morning. It is an act of grace
& disgust. A gesture of light:
The lamp turned low in the window, the harvest
Fire across the far warp of the land. The somber
Cadence of boots returns. A village
Pocked with soldiers, the dishes rattling in the cupboard
As an old serving woman carries a huge, silver spoon
Into the room & as she polishes she holds it just
So in the light, & the fat
Of her jowls
Goes taut in the reflection. It's what shapes
The sag of those cheeks, & has
Nothing to do with death though it is as simple, & insistent.
Like a coat too tight at the shoulders, or a bedroom
Weary of its single guest. At last, a body
Is spent by sleep: A dream stealing the arms, the legs.
A lover who has left you
Walking constantly away, beyond that stand
Of bare, autumnal trees: Vague, & loose. Yet, it's only
The dirt that consoles the root. You must begin
Again to move, towards the icy sill. A small
Girl behind a hedge of snow
Working a stick puppet so furiously the passers-by bump
Into one another, watching the stiff arms

Fling out to either side, & the nervous goose-step, the dances
Going on, & on
Though the girl is growing cold in her thin coat & silver
Leotard. She lays her cheek to the frozen bank
& lets the puppet sprawl upon her,
Across her face, & a single man is left twirling very
Slowly, until the street
Is empty of everything but snow. The snow
Falling, & the puppet. *That girl.* You close the window,
& for the night's affair slip on the gloves
Sewn of the delicate
Hides of mice. They are like the redemption
Of a drastic weather: Your boat
Put out too soon to sea,
Come back. Like the last testimony, & trace of desire. Or,
How your blouse considers your breasts,
How your lips preface your tongue, & how a man
Assigns a silence to his words. We know lovers who quarrel
At a party stay in the cool trajectory
Of the other's glance,
Spinning through pockets of conversation, sliding in & out
Of the little gaps between us all until they brush or stand at last
Back to back, & the one hooks
An ankle around the other's foot. Even the woman
Undressing to music on a stage & the man going home the longest
Way after a night of drinking remember
The brave lyric of a heel-&-toe. As we remember the young
Acolyte tipping
The flame to the farthest candle & turning
To the congregation, twirling his gold & white satin
Skirts so that everyone can see his woolen socks & rough shoes
Thick as the hunter's boots that disappear & rise
Again in the tall rice
Of the marsh. The dogs, the heavy musk of duck. How the leaves
Introduce us to the tree. How the tree signals
The season, & we begin
Once more to move: Place to place. Hand
To smoother & more lovely hand. A slow dance. To get along.
You toss your corsage onto the waters turning
Under the fountain, & walk back
To the haze of men & women, the lazy amber & pink lanterns
Where you will wait for nothing more than the slight gesture
Of a hand, asking
For this slow dance, & another thick & breathless night.
Yet, you want none of it. Only, to return
To the countryside. The fields & long grasses:

The scent of your son's hair, & his face
Against your side,
As the cattle knock against the walls of the barn
Like the awkward dancers in this room
You must leave, knowing the leaving as the casual
& careful betrayal of what comes
Too easily, but not without its cost, like an old white
Wine out of its bottle, or the pages
Sliding from a worn hymnal. At home, you walk
With your son under your arm, asking of his day, & how
It went, & he begins the story
How he balanced on the sheer hem of a rock, to pick that shock
Of aster nodding in the vase, in the hall. You pull him closer,
& turn your back to any other life. You want
Only the peace of walking in the first light of morning,
As the petals of ice bunch one
Upon another at the lip of the iron pump & soon a whole blossom
Hangs above the trough, a crowd of children teasing it
With sticks until the pale neck snaps, & flakes spray everyone,
& everyone simply dances away.

Dolls

They are so like
Us, frozen in a bald passion
Or absent
Gaze, like the cows whose lashes
Sag beneath their frail sacks of ice.
Your eyes are white with fever, a long
Sickness. When you are asleep,
Dreaming of another country, the wheat's
Pale surface sliding
In the wind, you are walking in every breath
Away from me. I gave you a stone doll,
Its face a dry apple, wizened, yet untroubled.
It taught us the arrogance of silence,
How stone and God reward us, how dolls give us
Nothing. Look at your cane,
Look how even the touch that wears it away
Draws up a shine, as the handle
Gives to the hand. As a girl, you boiled
Your dolls, to keep them clean, presentable;
You'd stir them in enormous pots,

As the arms and legs bent to those incredible
Postures you preferred, not that ordinary, human
Pose. How would you like me?—
Leaning back, reading aloud from a delirious
Book. Or sprawled across your bed,
As if I'd been tossed off a high building
Into the street,
A lesson from a young government to its people.
When you are asleep, walking the fields of another
Country, a series of shadows slowly falling
Away, marking a way,
The sky leaning like a curious girl above a new
Sister, your face a doll's deliberate
Ache of white, you walk along that grove of madness,
Where your mother waits. Hungry, very still.
When you are asleep, dreaming of another country,
This is the country.

DAVID ST. JOHN

Books

Hush, 1976   No Heaven, 1986
The Shore, 1980

James
Tate
(b. 1943)

GiGi Kayser

James Tate was born in Kansas City in 1943. By 1967, when he received his MFA from the Iowa Writers' Workshop, he had won the Yale Younger Poets competition and published his first collection, *The Lost Pilot*. It was a fast start to what has been a prolific career. Tate found his voice and manner early and has been faithful to them, in poems, prose poems, and short stories, ever since.

Tate's appearance in the late Sixties coincided with the embrace of surrealism by many American poets. It was also the time when postmodernism, especially as manifested in pop art, arrived on the scene to stay. Ideas about what constituted serious art and about the difference between high and low culture were being challenged everywhere. Andy Warhol was painting soup cans and making Brillo boxes. A popular music group called the Beatles were being taken seriously as creative artists. The high seriousness of modern art was being teased and parodied on many fronts. It was a perfect climate for a young poet with a strong sense of the absurd, a wildy inventive imagination, a sardonic view of culture and history, and an urge to release language from its normal confines. Other poets were experimenting with unusual subjects and bizarre metaphors. Tate would do that and go further, letting language itself be both creative and decreative, opening up new possibilities of eloquence, music, and form.

While his work has interesting links with that of other poets in this anthology—most notably John Ashbery, Charles Simic, Russell Edson, and Thomas Lux—Tate has always been out on the leading edge of determined experimentation associated with the avant-garde tradition. One result is an elusiveness that defies both interpretation of individual poems and confident discussion of the poet's development. It may well be that personal experience and private emotions provide raw material for Tate's poems; indeed, it is likely. But these origins are not laid open to us as they are with poets who cultivate a different kind of subjectivity. Tate's poems insist that we acknowledge, more fully and consistently than usual, the *difference* between art and experience, or the inadequacy of seeing art as reportage of, and commentary upon, personal experience. We must learn to see these poems as objects, not reflections of other things but things in themselves. Language is, of course, always referential, but Tate drives us back from our normal assumptions about referentiality. When we hear, for example, of a "sleepy city of reeling wheelchairs" ("The Wheelchair Butterfly"), we understand that it is a city we will never travel to. The "orange garage of daydreams" that appears later in the same poem has referential meaning, of course, but not of the kind found in a phrase like "The garage next door to James Tate's house." Forced into this new relationship with language, wherein it floats free and becomes an event and set of objects in itself rather than simply reflection of specific events and objects, we may experience first frustration, then exhilaration, imaginative release, and amusement. What is happening resembles something that often happens with poetry—excitement about language, release from "sensible" discourse—but in a purer and somehow more concentrated form. It's like inhaling oxygen instead of normal air; it may tend to make us a little giddy.

The shift in assumptions about language leads to other shifts as well. Take a poem like "Breathing." As we watch this poem unfold, or listen to it, we begin to realize that it fabricates itself before our eyes, shimmers for a moment like a soap bubble, and then vanishes. Again, the process replicates other experiences of reading, but more self-consciously. This poem *knows* that it is creating and then erasing itself. It teases the idea of significance—of the poet as sensitive reporter and potential prophet, of the poem as expert comment on "reality." And yet before we dismiss it as having no value, we need to consider how much the reality of language (perhaps the only one most of us really possess) has drawn us into a world where a comparison ("the sound of a snowball / hitting a snowman") is as valid as the event that produced it ("the muted thump / of the ball kissing the racket"), and where the comparison itself produces poetic form by governing the direction of the sequence ("a snowman's head rolling / into a river, a snowman with / an alarm clock for a heart"). Poetic diction, figurative language, and literary form are all being questioned. There are many challenges inherent in the extravagant wit and daring invention of James Tate's postmodern and surrealist poetics.

Since 1970, James Tate has been teaching at the University of Massachusetts at Amherst, where he has acquired a deserved reputation as a teacher. Like most good teachers, he produces students who do not imitate him. They write in many different styles. But ponderousness, literalism, and a tendency to take themselves too seriously would seem to be qualities they can all avoid, having as their mentor this particular poet.

DY

The Wheelchair Butterfly

O sleepy city of reeling wheelchairs
where a mouse can commit suicide if he can

concentrate long enough
on the history book of rodents
in this underground town

of electrical wheelchairs!
The girl who is always pregnant and bruised
like a pear

rides her many-stickered bicycle
backward up the staircase
of the abandoned trolleybarn.

Yesterday was warm. Today a butterfly froze
in midair; and was plucked like a grape
by a child who swore he could take care

of it. O confident city where
the seeds of poppies pass for carfare,

where the ordinary hornets in a human's heart
may slumber and snore, where bifocals bulge

in an orange garage of daydreams,
we wait in our loose attics for a new season

as if for an ice-cream truck.
An Indian pony crosses the plains

whispering Sanskrit prayers to a crater of fleas.
Honeysuckle says: I thought I could swim.

The Mayor is urinating on the wrong side
of the street! A dandelion sends off sparks:
beware your hair is locked!

Beware the trumpet wants a glass of water!
Beware a velvet tabernacle!

Beware the Warden of Light has married
an old piece of string!

Breathing

I hear something coming,
something like a motorcycle,
something horrible with pistons awry,
with camshafts about to fill the air
with redhot razor-y shrapnel.
At the window, I see nothing.
Correction: I see two girls

playing tennis, they have no
voices, only the muted thump
of the ball kissing the racket,
the sound of a snowball
hitting a snowman, the sound

of a snowman's head rolling
into a river, a snowman with
an alarm clock for a heart
deep inside him. Listen:
someone is breathing.

Someone has a problem
breathing. Someone is blowing
smoke through a straw.
Someone has stopped breathing.
Amazing. Someone broke
his wrist this morning,
broke it into powder.
He did it intentionally.
He had an accident

while breathing.
He was exhaling
when his wrist broke.
Actually

it's a woman breathing.
She's not even thinking
about it. She's thinking
about something else.

Deaf Girl Playing

This is where I once saw a deaf girl playing in a field.
Because I did not know how to approach her without startling
her, or how I would explain my presence, I hid. I felt
so disgusting, I might as well have raped the child, a grown
man on his belly in a field watching a deaf girl play.
My suit was stained by the grass and I was an hour late
for dinner. I was forced to discard my suit for lack of a
reasonable explanation to my wife, a hundred dollar suit!
We're not rich people, not at all. So there I was, left
to my wool suit in the heat of summer, soaked through by
noon each day. I was an embarrassment to the entire firm:
it is not good for the morale of the fellow worker to flaunt
one's poverty. After several weeks of crippling tension,
my superior finally called me into his office. Rather than
humiliate myself by telling him the truth, I told him I
would wear whatever damned suit I pleased, a suit of armor
if I fancied. It was the first time I had challenged his
authority. And it was the last. I was dismissed. Given
my pay. On the way home I thought, I'll tell her the truth,
yes, why not! Tell her the simple truth, she'll love me
for it. What a touching story. Well, I didn't. I don't
know what happened, a loss of courage, I suppose. I told
her a mistake I had made had cost the company several
thousand dollars, and that, not only was I dismissed, I
would also somehow have to find the money to repay them
the sum of my error. She wept, she beat me, she accused
me of everything from malice to impotency. I helped her
pack and drove her to the bus station. It was too late to
explain. She would never believe me now. How cold the
house was without her. How silent. Each plate I dropped
was like tearing the very flesh from a living animal. When
all were shattered, I knelt in a corner and tried to imagine
what I would say to her, the girl in the field. What could
I say? No utterance could ever reach her. Like a thief
I move through the velvet darkness, nailing my sign on
tree and fence and billboard. DEAF GIRL PLAYING. It is
having its effect. Listen. In slippers and housecoats
more and more men will leave their sleeping wives' sides:
tac tac tac: DEAF GIRL PLAYING: tac tac tac: another
DEAF GIRL PLAYING. No one speaks of anything but nails
and her amazing linen.

Teaching the Ape to Write Poems

They didn't have much trouble
teaching the ape to write poems:
first they strapped him into the chair,
then tied the pencil around his hand
(the paper had already been nailed down).
Then Dr. Bluespire leaned over his shoulder
and whispered into his ear:
"You look like a god sitting there.
Why don't you try writing something?"

"Dreamy Cars Graze on the Dewy Boulevard"

Dreamy cars graze on the dewy boulevard.
Darkness is more of a feeling inside the drivers.
The city is welded together
out of hope and despair.
The seasons pass imperceptibly,
more of a feeling inside the streetcleaners:

"Come quick, Hans,
a leaf is falling inside of me!"

In a Motel on Lake Erie

Tequila & chicken
causing lunar distress.
Nothing promising
on the tb—one symphony
of skeletons, two
black dots, one mountebank
of incurable disease,
one rainbow ground into
dog-ticks. Oh, it is dark here.

I can hear squeaks, probably
elephants. I try to call
the cops but they're
at the ballgame, a benefit
for those who can see.
I turn the lights on in my skull—
what a beautiful evening!
It is like a tombstone
full of vital information.
The highway eagles now
living out this dream.

Rooster

Tomorrow, since I have so few,
and Tomorrow, less dramatically,
and Tomorrow any number of times.
As for renouncing, isn't that
the oldest?

Rooster crowing: dark blue velvet
that knows itself too well—
empty wallet, busted heart—
Oh yes, my very good friend,
a voice searching for orchids,
that dances alone.

And then for that one hour
there are no familiar faces:
this lovely, misbegotten animal
created from odd bits of refuse
from minute to minute
splits us down the middle.

Goodtime Jesus

Jesus got up one day a little later than usual. He had been dreaming so
deep there was nothing left in his head. What was it? A nightmare, dead
bodies walking all around him, eyes rolled back, skin falling off. But he
wasn't afraid of that. It was a beautiful day. How 'bout some coffee? Don't
mind if I do. Take a little ride on my donkey, I love that donkey. Hell, I
love everybody.

Land of Little Sticks, 1945

Where the wife is scouring the frying pan
and the husband is leaning up against the barn.
Where the boychild is pumping water into a bucket
and the girl is chasing a spotted dog.

And the sky churns on the horizon.
A town by the name of Pleasantville has disappeared.
And now the horses begin to shift and whinny,
and the chickens roost, keep looking this way and that.
At this moment something is not quite right.

The boy trundles through the kitchen, spilling water.
His mother removes several pies from the oven, shouts at him.
The girlchild sits down by the fence to stare at the horses.
And the man is just as he was, eyes closed, forehead
against his forearm, leaning up against the barn.

Neighbors

Will they have children? Will they have more children?
Exactly what is their position on dogs? Large or small?
Chained or running free? Is the wife smarter than the man?
Is she older? Will this cause problems down the line?
Will he be promoted? If not, will this cause marital stress?
Does his family approve of her, and vice versa? How do
they handle the whole inlaw situation? Is it causing some
discord already? If she goes back to work, can he fix
his own dinner? Is his endless working about the yard
and puttering with rain gutters really just a pretext
for avoiding the problems inside the house? Do they still
have sex? Do they satisfy one another? Would he like to
have more, would she? Can they talk about their problems?
In their most private fantasies, how would each of them
change their lives? And what do they think of us, as neighbors,
as people? They are certainly cordial to us, painfully
polite when we chance-encounter one another at the roadside
mailboxes—but then, like opposite magnets, we lunge backward,
back into our own deep root systems, darkness and lust
strangling any living thing to quench our thirst and nourish
our helplessly solitary lives. And we love our neighborhood
for giving us this precious opportunity, and we love our dogs,
our children, our husbands and wives. It's just all so damned
difficult!

JAMES TATE

Books

The Lost Pilot, 1967

The Oblivion Ha-Ha, 1970

Hints to Pilgrims, 1971

Absences, 1972

Hottentot Ossuary, 1974

Viper Jazz, 1976

Riven Doggeries, 1979

Constant Defender, 1983

Reckoner, 1986

Interviews, Criticism

Comments on "A Box for Tom," in *Fifty Contemporary Poets*, ed. Alberta Turner, 1977; James Crenner, "Introducing Night and Wind: An Approach to James Tate," *The Seneca Review*, 1980; Mark Rudman, "Private But No Less Ghostly Worlds," *American Poetry Review*, 1981; Richard Jackson, "The Heart of the Periphery: An Interview With James Tate," *The Poetry Miscellany*, No. 12, 1982; Helena Minton and others, interview for *American Poetry Observed: Poets on Their Work*, 1984; Thomas Gardner, "A Lifetime of Witnessing," *The CEA Critic*, 1985.

C. D. Wright
(b. 1949)

Kay Duvernet

C D. Wright was born and raised in the Ozark Mountains of Arkansas. While her life has taken her to many different locations—San Francisco, Mexico, Rhode Island—she has kept her deep roots in her native region, both literally—she is the Poet Laureate of Boone County, Arkansas—and figuratively, drawing on the rich sensibility and lively, diverse vocabulary that enliven the artistic traditions of our southern states. Reading her poems, one thinks of the pleasures of storytelling that inform folk culture and become a basis for literature, and of the enjoyment of human eccentricity that seems to be one sure feature of Southern writing, though by no means exclusive to it. One also thinks of jazz, and of flamboyant eating, drinking, and dancing. The poems are neither melodramatic nor romantic in the way some Southern poetry is; they are fast, tough, funny and unpredictable. Their streetwise ways might swing an arc of recognition from our east coast cities to their west coast counterparts, but the center of that arc, its pendulum point of rest, would have to be somewhere just above New Orleans.

If the Arkansas heritage gives us one frame through which to see Wright's poems, their populism and political cast provide another. Most poets do not manage to avoid sounding simplistic and pompous when they address political questions or articulate social concerns. Wright succeeds because she avoids doctrine and simply plunges into the reality of being an ordinary citizen in this time and place. *O tempora, o mores*! What she finds often horrifies her, both in the grim realities of ordinary lives and in the large historical disasters that seem to loom ahead, but she is determined to document her perceptions and to keep her spirits up by making music, as blues singers and jazz musicians do, out of what would otherwise be too painful to think about.

The aesthetic heritage and artistic agenda described above are founded on an impressive command of technique. C. D. Wright knows how to establish and maintain an intensity of effect that makes her poems both difficult and rewarding. Her music ranges from caterwaul to lullaby. Her sense of detail is both rich and precise; conjoined with her willingness to take risks with diction, it gives rise, again and again, to unforgettable images. Thus, stories are told and lives characterized through a tumbling kaleidoscope of brilliant, unsettling, familiar details, both real and dreamy, a jazzy set of sliding and popping variations on familiar themes. The way "Spread Rhythm," for example, careens through its reverie of gritty, common-place images—the panel van, the roadhouse, the "slum of cardboard boxes," the movie-set desert, the overpasses on the Interstate where the dogs of hell are barking—makes the speaker's summary of her future and her needs in the last two stanzas wholly believable, especially the "chicken in the basket / four days a week" that is scarcely one step up from the roadhouse coffee of her reality. The poem is sharply witty, expertly paced, touching, and full of little recognitions: we didn't think these kinds of lives and dreams could be put into poems until we saw it happening before our delighted eyes.

C. D. Wright currently teaches at Brown University. For a poet of such wide sympathies and distinctive accomplishments, she is still relatively unknown. Her circle of devoted readers, however, seems to be growing steadily.

DY

Obedience of the Corpse

The midwife puts a rag in the dead woman's hand,
takes the hairpins out.

She smells apples,
wonders where she keeps them in the house.
Nothing is under the sink
but a broken sack of potatoes
growing eyes in the dark.

She hopes the mother's milk is good a while longer,
and the woman up the road is still nursing.
But she remembers the neighbor
and the dead woman never got along.

A limb breaks,
she knows it's not the wind.
Somebody needs to set out some poison.

She looks to see if the woman wrote down any names,
finds a white shirt to wrap the baby in.
It's beautiful she thinks
like snow nobody has walked on.

Woman Looking Through a Viewmaster

She was going on the bus he could see
between the buttons her breast quiver like the light
on the wedding knife she said she and the wandering jew
needed water and sun he never said Stay
The room in midtown cost ninety it was near the zoo
late at night she heard the big cats complain
If she played her horn before breakfast the brakeman
threw dirty books at her door she tied her kimono
and cut her bangs crooked watching von Nowak
pick the leaves off his hood he scrubbed the tires
with a toothbrush she hung in a hammock
Her toe dragged the dirt
The man who could see the light would be going
to work he wore summer khakis
a mechanical pencil on his ear he drank
V-8 his hair was the kind you didn't have to comb
it felt like a woman's so did his back
The waitress wants him if those days weren't over
she'd get a motion picture contract

Then if the woman hadn't got off the bus
she could be in TerreBonne Parish
playing a squeezebox eating red peppers living
in a stilt house learning to make gumbo praying
to Saint Anne to get rid of her sty one night
she'd go home with a trapper named Clothilde
a fleet of children would pass in pirogues singing
nous sommes tout seul and the song sends the girl
mending mosquito net to the Holiday Magazine
that leaves her where she can cut a star into the ice

Spread Rhythm

I drift off in a panel van waiting for Isolda
to come back with coffee
so we can drive through the night.

In the roadhouse they are shoulder to shoulder.
The jukebox surrenders to the steady tread of boots,
sloshing pitchers, bright balls breaking
over the felt expanse of green.

My life an endless slum of cardboard boxes
tearing off behind us.
If we do not make the ocean
the desert can claim us
slumped over the wheel with blistered lips.

If we come to a river we'll throw our bones in.
If not we will surely drown
or, like a diamondback
curled up under the saguaro's spiky arms
doze until the cool comes.

The van yaws back onto the Interstate—
dogs barking on the overpass
of their transcendental forays
in and out of hell.

Myself, I'll wind up a crazy woman on a boat
or wake alone in the Mojave dreaming
of the Rogers boys who wore white shirts to high school
because they were going to be in finance.

I don't want so much:
a house of native rock, fruit trees
raised from seedlings, chicken in the basket
four days a week.

Provinces

Where the old trees reign with their forward dark
light stares through a hole in the body's long
house. The bed rolls away from the body,
and the body is forced to find a chair. At some hour
the body sequesters itself in a shuttered room
with no clock. When a clean sheet of paper floats by,
the head inclines on its axis. It is one of those
common bodies that felt it could not exist without loving,
but has in fact gone on and on without love.
Like a cave that has stopped growing, we don't call it dead,
but dormant. Now the body is on all fours, one arm
engaged in pulling hair from a trap, an activity
the body loathes. When the time comes, the body
feeds on marinated meats and fruits trained to be luscious.
Once the body had ambitions—to be tall and remain
soft. No more, but it enjoys rappelling to the water.
Because the body's dwelling is stone, perched over water,
we say the body is privileged. Akin to characters
in Lawrence books, its livelihood is obscured. It owns
a horse named Campaign it mounts on foggy morns.
That was the body's first lie. It has no horse
and wouldn't climb on one. Because the body lives
so far from others, it likes reading about checkered lives
in the metropoli. It likes moving around at night under its dress.
When it travels, bottles of lotion open in its bags.
Early in March the big rains came—washing all good thoughts
from the body's cracks and chinks. By now the body admits
it is getting on, and yet, continues to be tormented
by things being the way they are. Recently the body took
one of the old trees for a wife, but the union has broken down.
The light has bored out of the body's long house.
Fog envelops its stone flanks. Still the body
enjoys rappelling to the water. And it likes the twenty-four-hour stores,
walking up and down the aisles, not putting a thing in its basket.

The Complete Birth of the Cool

Under this sun voices on the radio run down,
ponds warp like a record.
In the millyard men soak; roses hang from the neck.
Everyone is thankful for dusk

and the theater's blue tubes of light.
But evenings are a non-church matter.
On the cement step—damp from my swimming suit
I sort out my life or not,
an illustrated dictionary on my lap.
If I want hamburger I make it myself.
Behind the wrapped pipes
Sister expels a new litter
in the crawlspace. Even she can see
the moon poling across the water
to guard the giant melon in my patch.
Awe provides for us.

The Legend of Hell

A few hours ago a woman went on a walk.
Her phone rang and rang.
What a pleasure, she said to herself,
To walk in the fields and pick walnuts.

A moment ago a white dog
whose chain snared a shopping cart,
barked and barked.
Someone sauntered through an orchard
with murdering the whole family on his mind.

At the Black Pearl dancing was nightly.
That Sonnyman showed up again,
too tall for his clothes.
The pretentious copper beech threw its final shadow
on the D.A.'s house. Where we were living,
you wouldn't dream of going unaccompanied.

A few hours ago you could be at the movies,
borrow a comb from a stranger.
In the cities you had your braille libraries;
couples dining on crustacean
with precious instruments. In the provinces
you had your jug bands, anabaptists sharing their yield.

Then comes the wolf:
in a room of a house on a plain
lie the remains of Great Aunt Gladys
the quintessential Bell operator
sent many a rose by many a party in pain.

(By remains, we mean depression
left by her big body on her high bed);
over here we have an early evening scene without figures,
the soft parts of children blown into trees.
Our neighbors are putting on their prettiest things.
Their clocks have stopped but all hearts calibrated.

They say they are ready now
to make their ascension into light.
And you Edward Teller we know you're out there
shelling nuts; saying to yourself alone,
Now this is a pleasure.

                    homage to Barbara McClintock

Further Adventures With You

We are on a primeval river in a reptilian den.

There are birds you don't want to tangle with, trees
        you cannot identify . . .

    Somehow we spend the evening with Mingus
in a White Castle. Or somewhere. Nearly drunk. He says
        he would like to play for the gang.

    All of us ride to Grandmother Wright's house
in a van. It's her old neighborhood. I think we look
like a carton of colas sitting up stiffly
        behind the glass.

    She is recently dead. Some of her belongings
are gone. Her feather mattress has been rolled back
from the springs. It turns out Mingus has forgotten
his cello. We lay on our sides in jackets and jeans
        as if it were a beach in fall.

    Then it is Other Mama's house. She is
recently dead. We stretch out on Other Mama's carpet
        pulling at its nap.

You and I have stomped into A-Mart to buy papers
and Schnapps. Two boys, one pimply, the other clear-skinned
        blow in like snow with blue handkerchiefs
and a gun. Blue is the one color I notice tonight.
    They tell us, Take off.

We're gone. We're on the back of the bus with the liquor.
    The silly boys have shot the package store clerk.
We're the only suspects. You have a record so you're in a sweat.
You're flashing black, white. Around the nose and mouth
    you remind me a little of Sam Cooke. I think
he was shot in a motel. A case of sexual madness. We get off
    at an old bar that shares a wall with a school for girls.

The police collar us there. They separate us for questioning.
    You show a work card that swears you're a male dancer.
You pull out a gun. Where did you get that. And you blast them.
    It's their hearts, I think My god.

    You yell out a non-word and hit the doors. I run
through the back. It's the girls school. They seem to be
    getting ready
for a revue. I try to blend in—hoist a mattress, somebody's music
up a staircase. There are racks of costumes on wheels,
    flats of moving scenery . . .

There is the river, the horrible featherless bird. The tree,
    not a true palm but of the palm family.

On the Eve of Our Mutually Assured Destruction

we were not even moving. No one was moving.
We had the windows rolled
so we could hear. No one was hurt. They
were working on the bridge. A woman
held the sign: men working. The radio was beat.
Somebody must have ripped off the aerial
in the lot. Wednesday, March 6: wind shovelling fog.
We were talking about going to another place . . .
until the worst was over . . . where insects nest
in the ears of convolvuli, clear soups are imbibed.
We didn't have change. Not a bill.
After the bridge came the tunnel, then
the toll. We felt so lonesome we wanted to cry.
The couple ahead of us lit up.
Their baby thrashed in its carrier.
We talked about following
the migration of protected beings.

We wanted to leap or turn around. There
could be no turning around. We would get rid
of the chairs and the stoneware. Find a home
for the black mollies. We would rent
bicycles in an old town under a machicolated wall.
Clatter over cobbles in public health specs
arguing about Trotsky. Like thirties' poets.
Yes there would be the dense canopy,
the floor of mosses, liverworts and ferns.
I would open my legs like a book
letting the soft pencils of light
fall on our pages, like doors
into a hothouse, cereus blooming there.
I would open up like a wine list, a mussel, wings
to be mounted without tearing.
I would part my legs in the forest
and let the fronds impress themselves in the resin
of my limbs; smooth your rump
like a horse's. To wit the whole world would not be lost.

C. D. WRIGHT

Books

Alla Breve Loving, 1976

Room Rented By a Single Woman,
  1977

Terrorism, 1979

*Translations of the Gospel Back into
  Tongues*, 1982

Further Adventures With You, 1986

Franz
Wright
(b. 1953)

Franz Wright was born in 1953 in Vienna, Austria, where his father, the poet James Wright (see p. 375), was studying German literature on a Fulbright Fellowship. The family subsequently lived in Seattle and Minneapolis. Following their parents' divorce, Franz and his brother moved with their mother to California, where Franz graduated from high school in Walnut Creek in 1971. After a period of travel and study in Europe he attended Oberlin College, graduating in 1977. Postgraduate fellowships have taken him to Berkeley and Irvine in California, the University of Virginia, and the Provincetown Fine Arts Work Center in Massachusetts.

Franz Wright has a long-standing interest in translation. He and his father worked together on the poems of Hermann Hesse, and he has since translated Rainer Maria Rilke, René Char, and the contemporary Swiss prose poet, Erica Pedretti. One result is that he is steeped in the traditions of post-Romantic French and German poetry, from Rimbaud to the present, from Symbolism to Hermeticism and Minimalism. His own poetry might be characterized as a cross between American Gothic and European existentialism. It discloses a dusky and haunted world, where ghosts and other spiritual presences cohabit uneasily with a refractory physical reality. Fragile communications occur in this world, not only between past and present, old and young, parent and child, but between dreaming and waking, living and dead. These exchanges may lead to illumination and insight, but they can also be oppressive and frightening, opening into vistas of failure and routines of compulsive self-destructiveness. The poet often finds both joy and humor in this darkened and mysterious reality, but the dominant notes are nonetheless of melancholy, bitterness, and loss, and this young poet sees himself accurately as a "strange, elderly child." Being the son of a famous poet who was by turns a dazzling mentor and an absent, alcoholic, and eventually fatally ill father cannot have been easy or conducive to a poetry of simple affirmation. Still, Franz Wright does not indulge his sorrows or dwell on bitter episodes; like Kafka, after whom he is named, he works with all the resources available to him to metamorphose pain into a strange and unforgettable beauty.

These artistic resources are considerable. They include a dedication to the art that is almost priestly and just a touch old-fashioned. They bespeak a deeply considered relation to literary tradition and a careful study of poetic form. Each poem feels hard-won, pared-down, resilient. The haunting ideas and images are housed in a deliberately limited vocabulary. Each word is weighed and measured. Phrases seem bitten off or compressed to essential meanings. Superfluous gestures have been banished. Line breaks are firm and sometimes startling. The overall impression is of pressure from strong emotions held in check by a rigorous discipline. The recurring images—sleep, somnambulism, and insomnia; twilight turning to darkness; empty or sparsely occupied houses; muteness, literal or metaphoric, as an emblem of essential human separateness—help familiarize us with this world without reducing its profound mystery and fundamental strangeness. No wonder that a cemetery, for example, should turn out to be a quintessential Franz Wright setting. It is not selected as a stage for horrific goings-on; its combining of physical and spiritual, communal and solitary, past and present, life and death, provides a powerful distillation of this poet's troubling and encompassing vision. What we finally take away from Franz Wright's poems is not a sense of his personal concerns or preoccupations so much as a melancholy and oddly solacing knowledge of the risks and mysteries that go with being human, having memories, experiencing isolation even among friends and family, and loving the world despite its indifference to us.

Franz Wright currently lives and works in Boston, teaching writing and literature at Emerson College.

DY

Mosquitoes

Playing your trumpets
thin as a needle
in my ear,
standing on my finger

or on the back of my neck
like the best arguments
against pity I know.
You insignificant vampires

that sip my life
through a straw;
you drops of blood
with wings;

carriers
of insomnia
I search for
with a lit match . . .

I had a job once
driving around in a truck
to look for your eggs.
They can be found

in ditches, near
train tracks, outside
of a barn
in an upright piano filled with rainwater.

It is impossible to kill
all of you,
invisible in the uncut grass
at the edges of the cemetery:

when the dogs go down there it
looks like they've gotten into birds.

Drinking Back

From where I am
I can hear the rain in the telephone
And the voices of nuns singing
In a green church in Brugge three years ago.

I can still see the hill,
The limestone fragment of an angel,
Its mouth which has healed with
The illegible names in the cemetery,

With the braillelike names of dead people.
The names of children, suicides, and the rest—
The names of people
Buried with their watches running . . .

They are not sleeping, don't lie.

But it's true that once
Every year of their death
It is spring.

Blood

My blood sits upright in a chair
its only thought, breath.

Though I walk around empty,
disconsolate,
somebody's still breathing in me.

Mute, deaf and blind
yes,—but someone
is still breathing
in me: the blood

which rustles and sleeps.
The suicide in me
(I mean the murderer.)
The dreamer, the unborn.

But when I cut myself
I have to say:
this is my blood shed
for no one in particular.

If I get a nosebleed
I lie down on the cot, lie
there still, suspended
between the ceiling and floor

as though the bleeding
had nothing to do with me,
as though I'd been in an accident
but died one second before the collision . . .

In a hospital room
I have to turn my face
from the bright needle;
I see it, nevertheless,

and I see the blood,

and I see the test tube
in which my nurse carries it
obliviously, like the candle
in a sleepwalker's hand.

The Old

Their fingernails and hair continue to grow.
The bandaged eggs of their skulls
are frequently combed by the attendants
and friends no one has told them are dead.

A few of them wander around in the hallway,
waiting to be led off to the bathroom.
And these move as if underwater, as if
they were children in big people's shoes,

exploring each thing in their own rooms
for the first time:
mirror, glasses, a vial of morphine
with a name typed microscopically on it,

impossible to make out.

Their memories tear
beside places recently stitched . . .

When I get up in the morning I'm like them
for four or five minutes: I'm anyone
frightened, hungry, somnambulistic, alone.

Wind rustles the black trees.

Then I grow young.

The Journey

9 o'clock. The bells come floating in
from town a mile or so off,
the sky is getting dark now:
not far from my fingers
your photograph is developing
a new expression somehow, more secret, august . . .
Why is it so frightening to look at the blind
eyes in a picture;
and how did it happen
that I came to live in a room
with someone who's not there?
Once, I had to get to
the part of the city
where I knew you were living then,
600 miles away—
and now I will have to relive this forever,
and hear my footsteps in empty side streets again
and again, the distant, electrical
rustling of late afternoon
foreshadowing rain
as I make my way down your block,
as I ring the door of your dark apartment.
I find out you live by the river: I walk there
and sit down on a bench. It's getting cold. I wait
and know nothing, feel nothing, see nothing
but this black river flowing blindly to the sea,
the pale hand on my leg.
A ship appears with all its lights out.
Now I can remember something
like it from my childhood: a large house
gliding slowly through town on a platform
a foot off the ground
in the summer dusk, the silence before trains. Sleep
casts its clear and healing shadow over me,
because I have never been this by myself yet
and still have a long way to go.

1973–1980

I Did Not Notice

I did not notice
it had grown dark as I sat there.

Needless to say,
speech no longer came
to your lips even soundlessly now.

You had been out for some time

when, in one slow unwilled motion,
your arm began to rise from the bed,

fingers spread, in a gesture resembling
the one you used to interrupt me,
that we might not miss
a particular passage of music.

Untitled

Will I always be eleven,
lonely in this house,
reading books
that are too hard for me,
in the long fatherless hours.
The terrible hours of the window,
the rain-light
on the page,
awaiting the letter,
the phone call,
still your strange elderly child.

Joseph Come Back as the Dusk

(1950–1982)

The house is cold. It's raining,
getting dark. That's Joseph

for you: it's that time
of the day again . . .

We had been drinking, strangely enough.
He left.

I thought, a walk—
It's lovely to walk.

His book and glasses on the kitchen table.

Alcohol

You do look a little ill.

But we can do something about that, now.

Can't we.

The fact is you're a shocking wreck.

Do you hear me.

You aren't all alone.

And you could use some help today, packing in the
dark, boarding buses north, putting the seat back and
grinning with terror flowing over your legs through
your fingers and hair . . .

I was always waiting, always here.

Know anyone else who can say that.

My advice to you is think of her for what she is: one
more name cut in the scar of your tongue.

What was it you said, "To rather be harmed than harm, is
not abject."

Please.

Can we be leaving now.

We like bus trips, remember. Together

we could watch these winter fields slip past, and
never care again,

think of it.

I don't have to be anywhere.

FRANZ WRIGHT

Books

The Earth Without You, 1980

The One Whose Eyes Open When
    You Close Your Eyes, 1982

The Unknown Rilke (translations),
    1983

No Siege Is Absolute (translations of
    René Char), 1984

Going North in Winter, 1986

Winter Entries, 1989

Acknowledgments (Continued)

"Tale of Time": "I. What Happened"; "II. The Mad Druggist"; "III. Answer Yes or No"; "IV. The Interim"; "V. What Were You Thinking, Dear Mother?"; "VI. Insomnia" copyright © 1966, 1985 by Robert Penn Warren. Reprinted from *New and Selected Poems, 1923–1985* by Robert Penn Warren, by permission of Random House, Inc., and the William Morris Agency, Inc., in behalf of the author.

"Glazunoviana" by John Ashbery is from *Some Trees,* published by Yale University Press, 1956. "Civilisation and Its Discontents" is from *Rivers and Mountains,* published by Holt, Rinehart, and Winston, 1967. Copyright © 1956, 1962, 1963, 1964, 1966, 1985 by John Ashbery. Reprinted by permission of Georges Borchardt, Inc., the author, and Carcanet Press Limited.

"Märchenbilder," "Friends," "Whatever Is Poetry," and "My Erotic Double" from *Selected Poems* by John Ashbery. Copyright © 1985 by John Ashbery. "Shadow Train" and "But Not That One" from *Shadow Train* by John Ashbery. Copyright © 1980, 1981 by John Ashbery. "On Autumn Lake" from *Self-Portrait In a Convex Mirror* by John Ashbery. Copyright © 1972, 1973, 1974, 1975 by John Ashbery. All rights reserved. Reprinted by permission of Viking Penguin Inc., Georges Borchardt, Inc., and Carcanet Press Limited.

"Driving Toward the Lac Qui Parle River" from *Silence in the Snowy Fields* © 1962 by Robert Bly, published 1962 by Wesleyan University Press. "August Rain" from *Morning Glory* © 1973 by Robert Bly. Reprinted by permission of the author.

"Snowbanks North of the House," © 1980 by Harper & Row Publishers, Inc., "Mourning Pablo Neruda" © 1975 by World Poetry, Inc., and "Visiting Emily Dickinson's Grave with Robert Francis" © 1981 by Robert Bly are all from *The Man in the Black Coat Turns.* Reprinted by permission of Doubleday, a division of Bantam, Doubleday, Dell Publishing Group, Inc.

"Three Presidents" and "Turning Away from Lies" from *The Light Around the Body,* copyright © 1966, 1962 by Robert Bly. "Six Winter Privacy Poems" from *Selected Poems,* copyright © 1970 by Robert Bly. Reprinted by permission of Harper & Row Publishers, Inc.

"Damon & Pythias," "After Lorca," "A Gift of Great Value," "And," "The City," "The Statue," "The Turn," "Time," "For W.C.W," "Somebody Died," and "Place" by Robert Creeley from *Collected Poems of Robert Creeley,* copyright © 1982 by The Regents of the University of California. Reprinted by permission of the University of California Press.

"Falling," "Hedge Life," and "Bread" by James Dickey from *Falling, May Day Sermon, and Other Poems,* copyright 1981 by James Dickey. Reprinted by permission of Wesleyan University Press. "Falling" and "Hedge Life" first appeared in *The New Yorker.*

"Howl" by Allen Ginsberg from *Howl,* copyright © 1956, 1986 by Allen Ginsberg, reprinted by permission of Harper & Row Publishers, Inc.; and from *Collected Poems 1947 to 1980,* copyright © 1984 by Allen Ginsberg, reproduced by permission of Penguin Books Ltd.

"Ox Cart Man" by Donald Hall from *Kicking the Leaves* (Harper & Row). Reprinted by permission; copyright © 1977 The New Yorker Magazine, Inc.

"The Black Faced Sheep" from *Kicking the Leaves* by Donald Hall. Copyright © 1976 by Donald Hall. Reprinted by permission of Harper & Row, Publishers, Inc., and the author.

"Wedding Party," "The Long River," "An Airstrip in Essex," "The Old Pilot," "New Hampshire," "Apples," and " 'Reclining Figure,' " by Donald Hall. Reprinted by permission of the author.

"1614 Boren," "Napoli Again," "The Lady in the Kicking Horse Reservoir," "A Map of Montana in Italy," "The Freaks at Spurgin Road Field," "In Your Bad Dream," and "Open Country" by Richard Hugo from *Selected Poems* of Richard Hugo, reprinted by permission of W.W. Norton & Co., Inc. Copyright © 1979, 1977, 1975, 1973 by W.W. Norton & Co., Inc.

"Landscape with Little Figures" and "On The Death of Friends in Childhood" by Donald Justice from *Summer Anniversaries,* copyright © 1953, 1959 by Donald Justice. "Bus Stop" and "Dreams of Water" by Donald Justice from *Night Light,* copyright 1966, 1965 by Donald Justice. Reprinted by permission of Wesleyan University Press. "Landscape with Little Figures" first appeared in *Poetry*; "Dreams of Water" first appeared in *The New Yorker*.

"Nostalgia and Complaint of the Grandparents" from *The Sunset Maker*, copyright © 1987 by Donald Justice. "A Dancer's Life," "White Notes," "Sonatina in Yellow," and "Childhood' from *Selected Poems*, copyright © 1979 by Donald Justice. Reprinted by permission of Atheneum Publishers, an imprint of Macmillan Publishing Co.

"His Wife" reprinted from *The Floor Keeps Turning* by Shirley Kaufman by permission of the University of Pittsburgh Press. Copyright © 1970 by the University of Pittsburgh Press. "Looking at Henry Moore's Elephant Skull Etchings in Jerusalem During the War" reprinted from *From One Life to Another* by Shirley Kaufman by permission of the University of Pittsburgh Press. Copyright © 1979 by Shirley Kaufman. "Nechama" reprinted from *Gold Country* by Shirley Kaufman by permission of the University of Pittsburgh Press. Copyright © 1973 by Shirley Kaufman.

"The Dream of Completion" from *Claims*, copyright © 1985 by Shirley Kaufman. Reprinted by permission of Sheep Meadow Press.

"The Angel" and "The Shroud" from *The Past* by Galway Kinnell, copyright © 1985 by Galway Kinnell. "Little Sleep's-Head Sprouting Hair in the Moonlight" from *The Book of Nightmares* by Galway Kinnell, copyright © 1971 by Galway Kinnell. "Ruins Under the Stars" and "Flower Herding on Mount Monadnock" from *Flower Herding on Mount Monadnock* by Galway Kinnell, copyright © 1963 by Galway Kinnell. "Freedom, New Hampshire" from *What a Kingdom It Was* by Galway Kinnell, copyright © 1960 by Galway Kinnell. Reprinted by permission of Houghton Mifflin Co. and Andre Deutsch Ltd.

"Olga Poems" by Denise Levertov from *Poems, 1968–1972*, copyright © 1965 by Denise Levertov. "Six Variations" by Denise Levertov from *Poems, 1960–1967*, copyright © 1960 by Denise Levertov Goodman. "Earliest Spring" by Denise Levertov from *Life in the Forest*, copyright © 1978 by Denise Levertov. "Window-Blind" by Denise Levertov from *Breathing the Water*, copyright © 1987 by Denise Levertov. "Olga Poems" and "Six Variations" first published in *Poetry*. All reprinted by permission of New Directions Publishing Corporation.

"Milkweed" from *Seven Years from Somewhere* by Philip Levine, copyright © 1979 by Philip Levine; "They Feed They Lion" from *They Feed They Lion* by Philip Levine, copyright © 1972 by Philip Levine; "Sweet Will" from *Sweet Will* by Philip Levine, copyright © 1985 by Philip Levine; "1933" from *1933* by Philip Levine, copyright © 1974 by Philip Levine. Reprinted by permission of Atheneum Publishers, an imprint of Macmillan Publishing Co.

"Heaven" from *Not This Pig* by Philip Levine, copyright © 1966 by Philip Levine. Reprinted by permission of Wesleyan University Press.

"Clouds" from *Red Dust* (Kayak Books) by Philip Levine, copyright © 1971 by Philip Levine. Reprinted by permission of the author.

"In the Dark" and "The Pier: Under Pisces" from *Late Settings* by James Merrill, copyright © 1985 by James Merrill. Reprinted by permission of Atheneum Publishers, an imprint of Macmillan Publishing Co. "Lost In Translation" from *Divine Comedies* by James Merrill, copyright © 1976, 1977 by James Merrill. Reprinted by permission of Atheneum Publishers, an imprint of Macmillan Publishing Co., and Oxford University Press.

"Witnesses" from *Moving Target* by W.S. Merwin. "The Last One," "Caesar," "The River of Bees," and "When You Go Away" from *The Lice* by W.S. Merwin. "The Broken" from *Houses and Travellers* by W.S. Merwin. "A Door" from *Writings to an Unfinished Accompaniment* by W.S. Merwin. "The Black Jewel" and "Yesterday" from *Opening the Hand* by W.S. Merwin. "Low Fields and Light" from *Selected Poems* by W.S. Merwin. Copyright © 1963, 1967, 1977, 1973, 1983, 1988 by W.S. Merwin. Reprinted by permission of Atheneum Publishers, an imprint of Macmillan Publishing Co., and Georges Borchardt Inc.

"An Image of Leda," "Interior" (With Jane), "Poem" (I don't know as I get what D.H. Lawrence is driving at), "In Hospital," "Homosexuality," "Answer to Voznesensky & Evtushenko," and "1951" from *The Collected Poems of Frank O'Hara* by Frank O'Hara, edited by Donald Allen. Copyright © 1971 by Maureen Granville-Smith, Administratrix of the Estate of Frank O'Hara; reprinted by permission of Alfred A. Knopf, Inc.

''The Day Lady Died'' from *Lunch Poems* by Frank O'Hara, copyright © 1964 by Frank O'Hara. Reprinted by permission of City Lights Books Inc.

''Blocks'' from *Meditations in an Emergency* by Frank O'Hara, copyright © 1957 by Frank O'Hara. Reprinted by permission of Grove Press, a division of Wheatland Corp.

''In the Wake of Home,'' ''The Burning of Paper Instead of Children,'' and ''After Dark'' reprinted from *The Fact of a Doorframe, Poems Selected and New, 1950–1984*, by Adrienne Rich, by permission of W.W. Norton & Co., Inc. Copyright © 1984 by Adrienne Rich. Copyright © 1975, 1978 by W.W. Norton & Co., Inc. Copyright © 1981 by Adrienne Rich.

''Children Playing Checkers at the Edge of the Forest'' by Adrienne Rich, first appeared in *FIELD*. Reprinted by permission.

''The Fury of Overshoes'' and ''Sixth Psalm'' from *The Death Notebooks* by Anne Sexton. ''What's That'' from *To Bedlam and Part Way Back* by Anne Sexton. ''The Abortion'' and ''The Truth the Dead Know'' from *All My Pretty Ones* by Anne Sexton. Copyright © 1974, 1960, 1962 by Anne Sexton. ''Rowing'' from *The Awful Rowing Toward God* by Anne Sexton, copyright © 1975 by Loring Conant, Jr., Executor of the Estate of Anne Sexton. ''Sylvia's Death'' from *Live or Die*, copyright © 1966 by Anne Sexton. Reprinted by permission of Houghton Mifflin Co. and Sterling Lord Literistic, Inc.

''The Expulsion,'' ''Kissing Stieglitz Goodbye,'' ''The Dancing,'' and ''Romania, Romania'' from *Paradise Poems* by Gerald Stern. Copyright © 1982, 1983, 1984 by Gerald Stern. Reprinted by permission of Random House, Inc.

''There Is Wind, There Are Matches'' from *The Red Coal* by Gerald Stern (Houghton Mifflin Co.), copyright © 1981 by Gerald Stern. ''Morning Harvest'' from *Lucky Life* by Gerald Stern (Houghton Mifflin Co.), copyright © 1977 by Gerald Stern. Reprinted by permission of the author.

''The Mind-Reader'' from *The Mind-Reader* by Richard Wilbur, copyright © 1972 by Richard Wilbur; first published in *The New Yorker*. ''A Black November Turkey'' and ''Beasts'' from *Things of This World* and *Poems 1943–56* by Richard Wilbur, copyright © 1953, 1981, 1956, 1984 by Richard Wilbur. ''Stop'' from *Advice to a Prophet and Other Poems* by Richard Wilbur, copyright © 1961 by Richard Wilbur; first published in *The New Yorker*. ''Thyme Flowering among Rocks'' from *Walking to Sleep* by Richard Wilbur, copyright © 1968 by Richard Wilbur. All reprinted by permission of Harcourt Brace Jovanovich, Inc., and Faber and Faber Ltd.

''Transit'' by Richard Wilbur first appeared in *The New Yorker*, 1979. Reprinted by permission of the author.

''Ohioan Pastoral'' and ''A Winter Daybreak above Vence'' from *This Journey* by James Wright, copyright © 1981 by Anne Wright, Executrix of the Estate of James Wright. Reprinted by permission of Random House, Inc.

''Mutterings over the Crib of a Deaf Child'' from *Collected Poems* by James Wright, copyright © 1971 by James Wright; first published in *The Green Wall*, published by Yale University Press. ''Saint Judas'' from *Saint Judas*, copyright © 1959 by James Wright. From *The Branch Will Not Break* by James Wright: ''Stages on a Journey Westward'' copyright © 1963 by James Wright; ''Twilights'' copyright © 1962 by James Wright, first appeared in *The Sixties*; ''Two Hangovers,'' copyright © 1961 by James Wright, first appeared in *The Hudson Review* and *The New York Times*; ''Milkweed,'' copyright © 1962 by James Wright, first appeared in *The Minnesota Review*. ''Outside Fargo, North Dakota'' and ''The Life'' from *Shall We Gather at the River*, copyright © 1968 by James Wright; both first appeared in *Poetry*. All reprinted by permission of Wesleyan University Press.

''Game After Supper,'' ''Trainride, Vienna–Bonn,'' ''Last Poem,'' ''Vultures,'' ''Landcrab,'' ''The Robber Bridegroom,'' ''The Woman Who Could Not Live With Her Faulty Heart,'' and ''Damside'' by Margaret Atwood. Reprinted by permission of the author.

''The Fall'' from *What a Man Can See* by Russell Edson. ''A Journey Through the Moonlight,'' ''The Automobile,'' and ''The Death of an Angel'' from *The Intuitive Journey and Other Works*, copyright © 1973 by Russell Edson. ''The Long Picnic'' and ''A Cottage in the Wood'' from *The Reason Why the Closet-Man Is Never Sad*, copyright © 1977 by Russell Edson. ''In the Forest,'' ''The Wheelbarrow,'' ''The Pilot,'' ''An Old Man's Son,'' ''The Wounded Breakfast,'' ''Counting Sheep,'' ''The Amateur,'' and ''Darwin Descending'' by Russell Edson. Reprinted by permission of the author.

"The Dance of the Elephants," "Homage to the New World," "Kin," "Grandfather," "Nightmare Begins Responsibility," "We Assume: On the Death of Our Son, Reuben Masai Harper," "Landfill," and "Last Affair: Bessie's Blues Song" by Michael Harper. Reprinted by permission of the author.

"The Manor Garden" and "Watercolor of Grantchester Meadows" from *The Colossus and Other Poems* by Sylvia Plath, copyright © 1960 by Sylvia Plath. Reprinted by permission of Alfred A. Knopf, Inc., and Olwyn Hughes Literary Agency.
From *Collected Poems* by Sylvia Plath, edited by Ted Hughes, published by Faber and Faber Ltd., copyright © 1981 by Ted Hughes: "Morning Song" copyright © 1961 by Ted Hughes; "Poppies in October," "The Couriers," "Death & Co.," and "Winter Trees" copyright © 1963 by Ted Hughes; "Poppies in July," "Ariel," "The Night Dances," "Sheep in Fog," and "Words" copyright © 1965 by Ted Hughes; "Nick and the Candlestick" copyright © 1966 by Ted Hughes. All reprinted by permission of Harper and Row Publishers, Inc., and Olwyn Hughes Literary Agency.

"Out-of-the-Body-Travel," "The Iron Lung," "Peppergrass," and "For Esther" from *Out-of-the-Body-Travel*, copyright © 1974, 1975, 1976 by Stanley Plumly. "Wildflower" and "After Whistler" by Stanley Plumly. Reprinted by permission of the author.

"String," "Making a Door," "Making Chicago," and "Mile Hill" copyright © 1976, 1977, 1978, 1979, 1980 by Dennis Schmitz, from *String* by Dennis Schmitz, published by The Ecco Press in 1980. "A Letter to Ron Silliman on the Back of a Map of the Solar System" and "A Picture of Okinawa" copyright © 1985 by Dennis Schmitz, from *Singing* by Dennis Schmitz, published by The Ecco Press in 1985. "Star & Garter Theater" and "Queen of Heaven Mausoleum" copyright © 1968, 1969, 1970, 1971, 1972, 1973, 1974, 1975, 1976 by Dennis Schmitz from *Goodwill Inc.* by Dennis Schmitz, published by The Ecco Press in 1976. All reprinted by permission of the publisher.
"Bird-Watching" by Dennis Schmitz first appeared in *FIELD*, No. 36, Spring 1987. Reprinted by permission.

"The Marvels of the City," "Dark Farmhouses," and "Promises of Leniency and Forgiveness" from *Unending Blues*, copyright © 1986 by Charles Simic. Reprinted by permission of Harcourt Brace Jovanovich, Inc.
"Butcher Shop," "Tapestry," "Psalm," "Bestiary for the Fingers of My Right Hand," and "Fork" from *Dismantling the Silence* copyright © 1971 by Charles Simic; "Ballad" from *Return to a Place Lit by a Glass of Milk* copyright © 1974 by Charles Simic; "Animal Acts" from *Charon's Cosmology* copyright © 1977 by Charles Simic; "Empire of Dreams," "Begotten of the Spleen," "Classic Ballroom Dances," and "Harsh Climate" from *Classic Ballroom Dances* copyright © 1980 by Charles Simic. All reprinted by permission of George Braziller, Inc., Publishers.

"Hitch Haiku" and "Hop, Skip, and Jump" from *The Back Country* by Gary Snyder, copyright © 1965, 1968 by Gary Snyder. "Mother Earth: Her Whales" from *Turtle Island* by Gary Snyder, copyright © 1972 by Gary Snyder. "It" and "Song of the Taste" from *Regarding Wave* by Gary Snyder, copyright © 1968, 1970 by Gary Snyder; "Song of the Taste" was first published in *Poetry*. All reprinted by permission of New Directions Publishing Corporation.
"Above Pate Valley" and "Water" from *Riprap* by Gary Snyder. Reprinted by permission of the author.

"Keeping Things Whole" (1964), "The Prediction" and "The Dance" (1970), "Elegy for My Father" (1973), and "Where Are the Waters of Childhood?" (1978) from *Selected Poems* by Mark Strand, copyright © 1980 by Mark Strand. Reprinted by permission of Atheneum Publishers, an imprint of Macmillan Publishing Co.

"Orpheus and Eurydice" and "Pilgrims" from *Pilgrims* by Jean Valentine, copyright © 1965, 1966, 1967, 1968, 1969 by Jean Valentine. "After Elegies" from *Ordinary Things* by Jean Valentine, copyright © 1972, 1973, 1974 by Jean Valentine. "Living Together," "The Forgiveness Dream: Man from the Warsaw Ghetto," "The Field," "Silences: A Dream of Governments," and "December 21st" from *The Messenger* by Jean Valentine, copyright © 1974, 1975, 1976, 1977, 1978 by Jean Valentine. Reprinted by permission of Farrar, Straus and Giroux, Inc.
"The Second Dream" from *The Dream Barker* copyright © 1965 by Jean Valentine. Reprinted by permission of Yale University Press.

"The Insects," "Original Strawberry," "Angels in Winter," "How the Hen Sold Her Eggs to the Stingy Priest," "Questions My Son Asked Me, Answers I Never Gave Him," "Night Light," "Saint Pumpkin," "The Feast of St. Tortoise," and "The Sleep of the Painted Ladies" by Nancy Willard. Reprinted by permission of the author.

"Dog Creek Mainline" from *Hard Freight*, copyright © 1972 by Charles Wright, first appeared in *Poetry*. From *Bloodlines* by Charles Wright: "Virgo Descending" copyright © 1975 by Charles Wright, first appeared in *The Ohio Review*; "Delta Traveller" copyright © 1974 by Charles Wright, first appeared in *Lillabulero*. From *China Trace* by Charles Wright: "Snow" copyright © 1975 by Charles Wright, first appeared in *FIELD*; "Stone Canyon Nocturne" copyright © 1976 by Charles Wright, first appeared in *The New Yorker*; "Spider Crystal Ascension" copyright © 1977 by Charles Wright, and "Sitting at Night on the Front Porch" copyright © 1977 by Charles Wright, first appeared in *Vanderbilt Review*. All reprinted by permission of Wesleyan University Press.
    "March Journal," "Dog Day Vespers," "Dead Color," and "Hawaii Dantesca" by Charles Wright. Reprinted by permission of the author.
    "Two Stories" from *The Other Side of the River* by Charles Wright. Copyright © 1984 by Charles Wright. Reprinted by permission of Random House, Inc.

"Sunday Greens," "Daystar," "Banneker," "Dusting," "Courtship," "The Satisfaction Coal Company," and "Weathering Out" by Rita Dove. Reprinted by permission of the author.

"February: The Boy Breughel," "The Ganges," "Elizabeth's War with the Christmas Bear: 1601," "The Fox Who Watched for the Midnight Sun," and "Thomas Hardy" reprinted from *Selected and New Poems* by Norman Dubie, by permission of W.W. Norton & Co., Inc. Copyright © 1983 by Norman Dubie. "Hummingbirds" reprinted from *The Springhouse* by Norman Dubie, by permission of W.W. Norton & Co., Inc. Copyright © 1986 by Norman Dubie.

"The Red Dog" and "The Ajax Samples" by Laura Jensen. "Kite" by Laura Jensen first appeared in *The New Yorker*. "An Age," "Household," "Kitchen," "The Cloud Parade," "As the Window Darkens," "Adoration of the Anchor," and "Pony Farm" by Laura Jensen. All reprinted by permission of the author.

"Linnets" from *Afterlife* copyright © 1977 by Larry Levis. Reprinted by permission of the author.

"There Were Some Summers," "Tarantulas on the Lifebuoy," and "The Milkman and His Son" from *Half Promised Land* by Thomas Lux. Copyright © 1986 by Thomas Lux. Reprinted by permission of Houghton Mifflin Co.
    "Barn Fire," "Farmers," "Solo Native," and "Flying Noises" from *Sunday*, copyright © 1979 by Thomas Lux. Reprinted by permission of the author.

"Gnawing the Breast," "A Coconut for Katerina," and "The Bittern" copyright © 1973, 1974, 1975, 1976, 1977, 1978 by Sandra McPherson. From *The Year of Our Birth* by Sandra McPherson, published by The Ecco Press in 1978. "Games," "The Museum of the Second Creation," and "Helen Todd: My Birthname" copyright © 1979, 1980, 1981, 1982 by Sandra McPherson. From *Patron Happiness* by Sandra McPherson, published by The Ecco Press in 1983. "Resigning from a Job in a Defense Industry" copyright © 1970 by Sandra McPherson. From *Elegies for the Hot Season* by Sandra McPherson, published by The Ecco Press in 1982. "Wanting a Mummy" and "Peter Rabbit" copyright © 1970, 1971, 1972, 1973 by Sandra McPherson. From *Radiation* by Sandra McPherson, published by The Ecco Press in 1973. Reprinted by permission of the publisher.
    "The Microscope in Winter" by Sandra McPherson, first appeared in *FIELD*, No. 36, Spring 1987. Reprinted by permission.

"Iris," "Hush," Slow Dance," and "Dolls" from *Hush* copyright © 1975, 1976 by David St. John. "Wedding Preparations in the Country" by David St. John. Reprinted by permission of The Johns Hopkins University Press.

"The Wheelchair Butterfly," "Breathing," "Deaf Girl Playing," "Teaching the Ape to Write Poems," " 'Dreamy Cars Graze on the Dewy Boulevard,' " "In a Motel on Lake Erie," "Rooster," "Goodtime

Jesus," "Neighbors," and "Land of Little Sticks, 1945" by James Tate. Reprinted by permission of the author.

"Obedience of the Corpse," "Woman Looking Through a Viewmaster," "Spread Rhythm," "Provinces," "The Complete Birth of the Cool," "The Legend of Hell," "Further Adventures With You," and "On the Eve of Our Mutually Assured Destruction" by C.D. Wright. Reprinted by permission of the author.

"Untitled," "Joseph Come Back as the Dusk," "Drinking Back," "The Old," "Mosquitoes," "Blood," "I Did Not Notice," "Alcohol," and "The Journey" by Franz Wright. Reprinted by permission of the author.